Church, Faith and Culture in the Medieval West

General Editors
Brenda Bolton, Anne J. Duggan and
Damian J. Smith

About the series

The series *Church, Faith and Culture in the Medieval West* reflects the central concerns necessary for any in-depth study of the medieval Church – greater cultural awareness and interdisciplinarity. Including both monographs and edited collections, this series draws on the most innovative work from established and younger scholars alike, offering a balance of interests, vertically through the period from *c.* 400 to *c.* 1500 or horizontally across Latin Christendom. Topics covered range from cultural history, the monastic life, relations between Church and State to law and ritual, palaeography and textual transmission. All authors, from a wide range of disciplinary backgrounds, share a commitment to innovation, analysis and historical accuracy.

About the volume

Bishops were central figures in medieval society and the circumstances of their appointments are of great historical importance. This book considers the theory and practice of free canonical election in its heyday under Henry III and Edward I, and the nature of and reasons for the subsequent transition to papal provision. An analysis of the theoretical evidence for this subject (including canon law, royal pronouncements and Lawrence of Somercote's remarkable 1254 tract on episcopal elections) is combined with a consideration of the means by which bishops were created during the reigns of Henry III and the three Edwards.

About the author

Katherine Harvey is Associate Lecturer in Medieval History at Birkbeck University of London.

EPISCOPAL APPOINTMENTS IN ENGLAND, c. 1214-1344

Church, Faith and Culture in the Medieval West

General Editors
Brenda Bolton, Anne J. Duggan
and Damian J. Smith

Other titles in the series:

Joachim of Fiore and the Influence of Inspiration
Essays in Memory of Marjorie E. Reeves (1905-2003)
Edited by Julia Eva Wannenmacher

Entering a Clerical Career at the Roman Curia, 1458-1471
Kirsi Salonen and Jussi Hanska

Pope Alexander III (1159-81)
The Art of Survival
Edited by Peter D. Clarke and Anne J. Duggan

Motherhood, Religion, and Society in Medieval Europe, 400-1400
Essays Presented to Henrietta Leyser
Edited by Conrad Leyser and Lesley Smith

Hugh of Amiens and the Twelfth-Century Renaissance
Ryan P. Freeburn

Commemorating the Dead in Late Medieval Strasbourg
The Cathedral's Book of Donors and Its Use (1320-1521)
Charlotte A. Stanford

Ansgar, Rimbert and the Forged Foundations of Hamburg-Bremen
Eric Knibbs

Saving the Souls of Medieval London
Perpetual Chantries at St Paul's Cathedral, c.1200-1548
Marie-Hélène Rousseau

Readers, Texts and Compilers in the Earlier Middle Ages
Studies in Medieval Canon Law in Honour of Linda Fowler-Magerl
Edited by Martin Brett and Kathleen G. Cushing

Shaping Church Law Around the Year 1000
The *Decretum* of Burchard of Worms
Greta Austin

Episcopal Appointments in England, c. 1214-1344

From Episcopal Election to Papal Provision

KATHERINE HARVEY

Routledge
Taylor & Francis Group
LONDON AND NEW YORK

First published 2014 by Ashgate Publishing

Published 2016 by Routledge
2 Park Square, Milton Park, Abingdon, Oxfordshire OX14 4RN
711 Third Avenue, New York, NY 10017, USA

First issued in paperback 2016

Routledge is an imprint of the Taylor & Francis Group, an informa business

British Library Cataloguing in Publication Data
A catalogue record for this book is available from the British Library

The Library of Congress has cataloged the printed edition as follows:
Harvey, Katherine.
Episcopal appointments in England, c. 1214-1344 : from episcopal election to papal provison / by Katherine Harvey.
pages cm.—(Church, faith, and culture in the medieval west)
Includes bibliographical references and index.
ISBN 978-1-4094-5615-5 (hardcover)
1. Bishops—Appointment, call, and election—History.
2. Clergy—Appointment, call, and election—History. 3. Election law (Canon law) 4. Great Britain—Church history—1066-1485. I. Title.
BV664.H38 2014
262'.1224209022—dc23

2013014529

ISBN 13: 978-1-138-25009-3 (pbk)
ISBN 13: 978-1-4094-5615-5 (hbk)

Contents

Figures and Tables

Figures

Tables

Acknowledgements

I would like to thank the Arts and Humanities Research Council for funding this research. The Department of History and Graduate School at King's College London and the Royal Historical Society made valuable contributions to travel expenses.

The History Department at King's College London (where I began this book) and the Department of History, Classics and Archaeology at Birbeck University of London (where I finished it) have both provided a congenial working environment throughout my time there. I am also indebted to numerous libraries and their staff, including the Maughan Library (especially the Inter-Library Loans department), the Institute of Historical Research, Worcester Cathedral Library, the British Library and the National Archives.

The advice and support of several individuals have been invaluable throughout the course of this project. I am especially grateful for the patience, guidance and enthusiasm of David Carpenter and Anne Duggan; this book could not have been completed without them. I would also like to thank David D'Avray and Philippa Hoskin, who read an earlier draft in full, for their feedback and encouragement.

Many people have answered my questions, discussed episcopal appointments with me or sent me copies of their papers, amongst them Julia Barrow, Lesley Boatwright, Barbara Bombi, Melanie Brunner, Joseph Creamer, Alain Marchandisse, Joel Rosenthal and Alice Taylor. Audiences at the International Medieval Congress, the Early Middle Ages and Late Medieval Seminars at the Institute of Historical Research, the History Department Seminar at King's College and at seminars at the universities of Manchester and Oxford have provided valuable feedback on various aspects of my research.

I am greatly indebted to numerous people at Ashgate for helping me to turn my manuscript into a book, and especially to Emily Yates, Sarah Charters, Lindsey Brake, the series editors and the anonymous reader.

I am above all grateful to my family for their continued interest and support.

Abbreviations

Works not included in the abbreviations are referred to in full upon first citation; subsequent references are given in shortened form. Full details of all works cited are given in the bibliography. Multi-volume works are identified by volume number, with the exception of chancery rolls volumes; these are referred to by chronological range (e.g. *CPR 1232-47*).

AM	*Annales Monastici*, ed. H. R. Luard (5 vols, RS, 1864-69)
Anglia Sacra	*Anglia Sacra*, ed. H. Wharton (2 vols, London, 1691)
Bath Chartularies	*Two Chartularies of the Priory of St. Peter at Bath*, ed. W. Hunt (London, 1893)
CCR	*Calendar of the Close Rolls Preserved in the Public Record Office. Edward I* (5 vols, London, 1900-1908) *Calendar of the Close Rolls Preserved in the Public Record Office. Edward II* (4 vols, London, 1892) *Calendar of the Close Rolls Preserved in the Public Record Office. Edward III* (14 vols, London, 1896-1913) *Calendar of the Close Rolls Preserved in the Public Record Office. Henry IV* (5 vols, London, 1927-38)
Chron. E1&E2	*Chronicles of the Reigns of Edward I and Edward II*, ed. W. Stubbs (2 vols, RS, 1882-83)
CIC	*Corpus Iuris Canonici*, ed. E. Friedberg (2 vols, Leipzig, 1879-81)

CLI	*The Letters of Pope Innocent III (1198-1216) Concerning England and Wales: A Calendar*, ed. C. R. Cheney and M. G. Cheney (Oxford, 1967)
CLR	*Calendar of the Liberate Rolls Preserved in the Public Record Office. Henry III* (6 vols, London, 1916-64)
CM	*Matthæi Parisiensis, Monachi Sancti Albani, Chronica Majora*, ed. H. R. Luard (7 vols, RS, 1872-83)
CPL	*Calendar of Entries in the Papal Registers relating to Great Britain and Ireland*, ed. W. Bliss *et al.* (16 vols, London, 1893-1989)
CPR	*Patent Rolls of the Reign of Henry III* (6 vols, London, 1901-13), vols 3-6 *Calendar of the Patent Rolls Preserved in the Public Record Office. Edward I* (4 vols, London, 1893-98) *Calendar of the Patent Rolls Preserved in the Public Record Office. Edward II* (5 vols, London, 1893-1901) *Calendar of the Patent Rolls Preserved in the Public Record Office. Edward III* (6 vols, London, 1891-1916)
CR	*Close Rolls of the Reign of Henry III Preserved in the Public Record Office* (14 vols, London, 1902-38)
C&S	*Councils and Synods, with Other Documents Relating to the English Church*, II: *A.D. 1205-1313*, ed. F. M. Powicke and C. R. Cheney (2 vols, Oxford, 1964)
Douie, *Pecham*	D. L. Douie, *Archbishop Pecham* (Oxford, 1952)
Ecumenical Councils	*Decrees of the Ecumenical Councils*, ed. N. P. Tanner (2 vols, London, 1990)

EEA	*English Episcopal Acta*, ed. D. M. Smith, P. M. Hoskin *et al.* (39 vols, Oxford, 1980-)
EHR	*English Historical Review*
Fasti 1066-1300	John le Neve *et al.*, *Fasti Ecclesiae Anglicanae 1066-1300* (10 vols, London, 1968-)
Fasti 1300-1541	John le Neve *et al.*, *Fasti Ecclesiae Anglicanae 1300-1541* (11 vols, London, 1962-67)
FES	D. E. R. Watt and A. L. Murray (eds), *Fasti Ecclesiae Scoticanae Medii Aevi Ad Annum 1638*, rev. edn (Edinburgh, 2003)
Flores Hist.	*Flores Historiarum*, ed. H. R. Luard (3 vols, RS, 1890)
Gervase	*The Historical Works of Gervase of Canterbury*, ed. W. Stubbs (2 vols, RS, 1870-80)
Gibbs and Lang, *Bishops*	M. Gibbs and J. Lang, *Bishops and Reform, 1215-1272* (London, 1936)
Graham, *Winchelsey*	R. Graham, 'Archbishop Winchelsey: From his Election to his Enthronement', *Church Quarterly Review*, 148 (1949), pp. 161-75
Grosseteste	*The Letters of Robert Grosseteste, Bishop of Lincoln*, ed. F. A. C. Mantello and J. Goering (Toronto, 2010)
Guala	*The Letters and Charters of Cardinal Guala Bicchieri, Papal Legate in England 1216-1218*, ed. N. Vincent (Woodbridge, 1996)
Haines, *Ecclesia*	R. M. Haines, *Ecclesia Anglicana: Studies in the English Church of the Later Middle Ages* (Toronto, 1989)

Hist. Angl.	*Matthæi Parisiensis, Monachi Sancti Albani: Historia Anglorum, sive, ut Vulgo Dicitur, Historia Minor*, ed. F. Madden (3 vols, RS, 1866-69)
Howell, *Regalian Right*	M. Howell, *Regalian Right in Medieval England* (London, 1962)
JEH	*Journal of Ecclesiastical History*
Life of St Edmund	*The Life of St Edmund by Matthew Paris*, ed. C. H. Lawrence (Stroud, 1996)
Magna Vita	*Magna Vita Sancti Hugonis*, ed. D. L. Douie and H. Farmer (2 vols, London, 1961)
Mandagot	*Tractatus universi iuris, duce, et auspice Gregorio XIII pontifice maximo in unum congesti* (25 vols, Venice, 1584-86), vol. 15.1
Melrose	*A Medieval Chronicle of Scotland: The Chronicle of Melrose*, ed. J. Stevenson (Lampeter, 1991)
Menache, *Clement*	S. Menache, *Clement V* (Cambridge, 1998)
Murimuth	*Adae Murimuth Continuatio Chronicarum*, ed. E. M. Thompson (RS, 1889)
ODNB	H. C. G. Matthew and B. Harrison (eds), *Oxford Dictionary of National Biography*, 61 vols (Oxford, 2004), accessed via www.oxforddnb.com
Peltzer, *Elections*	J. Peltzer, *Canon Law, Careers and Conquest: Episcopal Elections in Normandy and Greater Anjou, c. 1140-1230* (Cambridge, 2008)
PL	*Patrologia Latina*, ed. J.-P. Migne (221 vols, Paris, 1844-65)

PR	*Patent Rolls of the Reign of Henry III* (6 vols, London, 1901-13), vol. 1 (1216-1225) and vol. 2 (1225-1232)
Reg. Alex. IV	*Les Registres d'Alexandre IV*, ed. B. de la Ronciére, J. de Loye, P. de Cerival and A. Coulon (3 vols, Paris, 1895-1959)
Reg. Ant. Linc.	*The Registrum Antiquissimum of the Cathedral Church of Lincoln*, ed. C. Foster and K. Major (10 vols, Hereford, 1931-75)
Reg. Clem. IV	*Les Régistres de Clement IV*, ed. E. Jordan (6 vols, Paris, 1893-1945)
Reg. Greg. IX	*Les Registres de Grégoire IX*, ed. L. Auvrey (4 vols, Paris, 1896-1955)
Reg. Inn. IV	*Les Registres d'Innocent IV*, ed. E. Berger (4 vols, Paris, 1884-1920)
Reg. Melton	*The Register of William Melton, Archbishop of York, 1317-40*, ed. R. Hill *et al.* (6 vols, Woodbridge, 1955-2011)
Reg. Nic. III	*Les Registres de Nicholas III (1277-1280)*, ed. J. Gay (Paris, 1938)
Reg. Pecham	*The Register of John Pecham, Archbishop of Canterbury 1279-92*, ed. D. Douie (2 vols, Woodbridge, 1968-69)
Reg. Romeyn	*The Register of John Le Romeyn, Lord Archbishop of York, 1286-1296*, ed. W. Brown (2 vols, Durham, 1913-17)
Reg. St Osmund	*Vetus Registrum Sarisberiense Alias Dictum Registrum S. Osmundi Episcopi: The Register of S. Osmund*, ed. W. Jones (2 vols, RS, 1883-84)

Reg. Sede Vacante	*The Register of the Diocese of Worcester during the vacancy of the see, usually called 'Registrum sede vacante'*, ed. J. Willis Blund (Oxford, 1897)
Reg. Winchelsey	*Registrum Roberti Winchelsey Cantuariensis Archiepiscopi, 1294-1313*, ed. R. Graham (2 vols, Oxford, 1952-56)
RLC	*Rotuli Litterarum Clausarum in Turri Londinensi Asservati*, ed. T. D. Hardy (2 vols, London, 1833-44)
RLP	*Rotuli Litterarum Patentium in Turri Londinensi Asservati*, ed. T. D. Hardy (London, 1835)
RS	Rolls Series
Script. Tres	*Historiae Dunelmensis Scriptores Tres: Gaufridus de Coldingham, Robertus de Graystanes et Willielmus de Chambres*, ed. J. Raine (London, 1839)
SHR	*Scottish Historical Review*
SLI	*Selected Letters of Pope Innocent III concerning England (1198-1216)*, ed. C. R. Cheney and W. H. Semple (London, 1953)
Somercote	*Der Traktat des Laurentius de Somercote, Kanonikus von Chichester,* über *die Vornahme von Bischofswahlen entstanden im Jahre 1254*, ed. A. von Wretschko (Weimar, 1907)
TRHS	*Transactions of the Royal Historical Society*
Vita Edwardi	*Vita Edwardi Secundi*, ed. W. Childs (Oxford, 2005)
Wells MSS.	*Calendar of the Manuscripts of the Dean and Chapter of Wells*, ed. W. H. Bird and W. P. Baildon (2 vols, London, 1907-14)

Introduction

The bishop was a figure of great importance in medieval English society. As a spiritual leader, he was the most senior clergyman in his diocese, with responsibility for the welfare of many thousands of souls and for the conduct of hundreds of priests, monks and nuns. He was also the highest source of ecclesiastical jurisdiction within the diocese; only the pope (or a papal legate) could overturn his judgements. England's bishops were also secular lords, enjoying control of extensive landholdings and considerable wealth. They played an important role in local government, but also in national politics, acting as royal advisors, as diplomats and even, in a handful of cases, as military commanders.[1] This combination of secular and ecclesiastical authority meant that the bishops were amongst the most powerful individuals in the realm; together, they were an extremely formidable force.

Consequently, when a bishop died, interest in the identity of his replacement was widespread. By the early thirteenth century, only the members of the relevant cathedral chapter had the right to participate in an episcopal election, but concern about the outcome of this process was certainly not confined to the chapter house. External influences on the electors were numerous. Three other parties had formal rights and responsibilities, which they often exploited to ensure that suitable candidates (in their eyes) were appointed: the king, the archbishop of the province and the pope. Ambitious men sought appointment to a bishopric; others, more reluctant to take on the burden of episcopal office, did their best to avoid it. Other individuals and groups, with no formal role to play but a strong interest in the outcome of the election, proposed, supported or opposed candidates. Amongst this final group were queens, aristocrats, royal ministers, foreign monarchs, members of the local ruling classes and high-ranking churchmen.

For the historian of medieval England (or, indeed, of anywhere else in Europe), episcopal appointments are of interest because they were the focus of interactions between so many elements of society. From the most powerful figures

---

[1] The body of historiography on the role of the medieval bishop is sizeable, but little of it relates solely to England. For contrasting but complementary studies of the role of the bishop, see Robert Benson, *The Bishop-Elect* (Princeton, 1960); Constance Bouchard, *Spirituality and Administration: The Role of the Bishop in Twelfth-Century Auxerre* (Cambridge, Mass., 1979); Jean Gaudemet, *Le Gouvernement de l'Église à l'Époque Classique*, vol. II: *Le Gouvernement Local* (Paris, 1979), pp. 7-215; Jane Sayers, 'Jocelin of Wells and the Role of a Bishop in the Thirteenth Century' in Robert Dunning (ed.), *Jocelin of Wells: Bishop, Builder, Courtier* (Woodbridge, 2010), pp. 34-52.

in society, exercising rights of confirmation and veto over capitular choices, to the humblest city-dweller, witnessing the formal entry of the new bishop into his cathedral city, any individual could participate in the bishop-making process. Episcopal appointments are particularly significant as touchstones of church–state relations, and thus the study of this topic goes some way towards answering important questions such as how far secular and ecclesiastical authorities were able to work together to ensure that the candidate appointed was acceptable to both, and able to fulfil both his spiritual and his temporal duties. What happened when the two sectors were unable to agree on a single candidate? Was the English crown able to influence the English Church or the papacy more effectively?

The thirteenth and early fourteenth centuries are of particular interest to the historian of episcopal appointments because of the major transition that took place during this period. During the course of the eleventh and twelfth centuries, churchmen (from the pope down) had become increasingly vocal about the need for secular control of episcopal appointments to be reduced, in order that the long-cherished ideal of free canonical election might become a reality. By the mid-1210s, this ideal was well on the way to becoming a reality; it was enshrined for the whole of Latin Christendom in the canons of the Fourth Lateran Council, and in England in the Freedom of Election charter issued by King John in 1214. For the rest of the thirteenth century, capitular election became the normal means by which an English bishop was appointed, and for some time it must have seemed that a golden age of electoral freedom had arrived. The heyday of free canonical election was, however, relatively short-lived, for the electoral rights of the cathedral chapter, so recently wrested from the hands of the king, were soon usurped by another, even greater, power. The first papal provision to an English bishopric was made in 1224 and the numbers of such appointments increased slowly but steadily over the next few decades. Initially, papal provision was used to resolve electoral disputes, but by the early 1300s provisions were being made almost immediately upon the death of a bishop. The last English bishop to have his election confirmed was Thomas Bek of Lincoln, in 1341; after this date, every bishop was appointed by papal provision.

***

Whilst the methods by which the English bishops of this period were selected were subject to a good deal of change, the structures of the church into which they were appointed were considerably more stable. In the thirteenth century, as today, the English Church was divided into two provinces: Canterbury and York. These provinces were already centuries old, having been established at the time of the Augustinian conversion mission. Gregory the Great had envisaged the creation of two archbishoprics, at London and York; each archbishop would be directly subject to papal authority, and each would exercise metropolitan jurisdiction over a further twelve bishoprics.[2] However, whilst the English Church did, in broad terms, develop along these lines, Gregory's plans were not fully realized. Augustine established the first English bishopric at Canterbury and metropolitan jurisdiction was never transferred to London. By 1200, the archbishop of Canterbury served as metropolitan of seventeen dioceses, thirteen of them in England and four (Bangor, Llandaff, St Asaph and St David's) in Wales.[3] In the north, York did become the archiepiscopal see, but its incumbent never achieved mastery of anything like a dozen bishoprics; in this period only three bishops (Carlisle, Durham and Whithorn) were subordinate to this archbishop.[4]

Each bishopric was focused around a cathedral, which served as a base for the spiritual and administrative functions of the prelate. Each cathedral was staffed by a large number of clergy, men who (at least in theory) lived a communal life and carried out the spiritual, pastoral, educational and administrative functions of such a church. Amongst the duties of these men, who collectively made up the cathedral chapter, was the election of the bishop of their diocese. Across most of Western Christendom, cathedral chapters consisted solely of secular canons, headed by a dean, but the English situation was somewhat anomalous. Approximately half of the English cathedral chapters were made up of secular canons: Chichester, Exeter, Hereford, Lichfield, Lincoln, London, Salisbury, Wells and York. The rest had cathedral convents, headed by a prior. The majority of these cathedral priories (Bath, Canterbury, Coventry, Durham, Ely, Norwich, Rochester, Winchester and Worcester) belonged to the Benedictine order; one, at Carlisle, was composed of Augustinian canons.[5]

Another complication of the English system was the existence of two bi-cephalous bishoprics, at Coventry and Lichfield and at Bath and Wells. From the seventh to eleventh centuries the former see had been based at Lichfield alone, but was moved to Chester in 1074, and then to Coventry in 1102. Nevertheless, the bishop continued to emphasize his links to Lichfield Cathedral, the chapter

[2] *The Ecclesiastical History of the English People*, ed. B. Colgrave, R. Collins and J. McClure (Oxford, 1994), pp. 55-6.

[3] Since Wales was not under the rule of the English crown for much of the thirteenth century, the Welsh dioceses have not been included in this study.

[4] Although subordinate to an English archbishop, Whithorn was located within the Scottish kingdom and is therefore considered in Chapter 6. On the relationship between Whithorn and York, see Richard Oram, 'In Obedience and Reverence: Whithorn and York, c.1128-c.1250', *Innes Review*, 42 (1991), pp. 83-100.

[5] For the origins and functions of the secular cathedrals, see Kathleen Edwards, *The English Secular Cathedrals in the Middle Ages* (Manchester, 1967) and David Lepine, *A Brotherhood of Canons Serving God: English Secular Cathedrals in the Later Middle Ages* (Woodbridge, 1995). The monastic cathedrals are covered in Joan Greatrex, *The English Benedictine Cathedral Priories: Rule and Practice, c.1270-c.1420* (Oxford, 2011).

of which continued to assert its right to elect the bishop. The dual nature of the see received papal recognition in the late 1220s, after which time the incumbent was usually referred to as bishop of Coventry and Lichfield. The pope also ruled that the two chapters should hold joint elections; the venue should alternate between the two cathedrals, but the prior of Coventry should always have the first voice in announcing the election. A further agreement was made in 1255, when Bishop Roger Weseham confirmed that the representatives of the two chapters should be reckoned as if they were equal in number.[6]

The bishopric of Bath and Wells began life as the bishopric of Wells in the year 909, before being moved to Bath (home to an extremely wealthy abbey, which became the bishop's seat) in 1090. The church of Wells nevertheless remained under episcopal patronage and throughout the twelfth century its canons made repeated attempts to assert their claim to participate in episcopal elections. Not until 1245 was Bath formally reinstated as one of the episcopal seats; henceforth the incumbent was to be styled 'bishop of Bath and Wells'.[7] In such double sees, the two chapters were supposed to jointly elect their shared bishop. Unsurprisingly, such electoral collaborations rarely passed off smoothly.

The final English anomaly was the peculiar constitutional position of the bishopric of Rochester in relation to the archbishopric of Canterbury. The see of Rochester was one of the oldest in England, founded in 604. Despite its geographical proximity to Canterbury, it appears to have functioned as an independent bishopric throughout the Anglo-Saxon period, with the incumbent doing homage to the king and receiving the episcopal ring and staff from his hands. The relationship between the two prelates began to change in 1075, when Bishop Arnost was appointed and invested by Archbishop Lanfranc in the chapter house at Canterbury. During the episcopate of Bishop Gundulf (1077-1108), the position and functions of his diocese were completely redefined.[8] Henceforth, the bishop of Rochester was 'the special and personal chaplain of the church of Canterbury',[9] fulfilling many of the functions of the recently abolished *chorepiscopus* of St Martin's.[10] Subsequent archbishops used this precedent to justify their claims to be patron of the church of Rochester and to control both the spiritualities and the temporalities of the see during a vacancy; their right to do so was confirmed by Alexander III in 1174.[11] Gregory IX granted the right of election to the prior and chapter of Rochester

---

6 *Fasti 1066-1300*, XI, pp. xxvii-xxxi, xl-xli, 6.

7 *Fasti 1066-1300*, VII, pp. 21-9.

8 Reginald Smith, 'The Place of Gundulf in the Anglo-Norman Church', *EHR*, 231 (1943), pp. 257-72, at pp. 261-4.

9 *Gervase*, I, p. 133.

10 Smith, 'Place of Gundulf', p. 261.

11 Irene Churchill, *Canterbury Administration: The Administrative Machinery of the Archbishopric of Canterbury* (2 vols, London, 1933), I, pp. 279-87.

in 1238,[12] but the ties between Canterbury and Rochester remained unusually close. Nearly a century later, the monks of Rochester continued to refer to the archbishop as 'our patron'[13] and their bishop could still be described as 'the archbishop's chaplain'.[14]

***

Unsurprisingly, a number of historians have studied the episcopal appointments that took place in thirteenth- and early fourteenth-century England. During the first half of the twentieth century, several historians published journal articles and book chapters that considered appointments over a shorter chronological span, typically focusing on a single reign;[15] two significant theses on this topic were completed at around the same time.[16] More recent work has been almost entirely limited[17] to examinations of individual elections,[18] material included in biographies of prominent members of the episcopate[19] and the outlines provided by three works of inestimable value to the historian of medieval England, and of the medieval English Church in particular: the *Fasti Ecclesiae Anglicanae*, the *English Episcopal Acta* series and the *Oxford Dictionary of National Biography*.

---

12 *Registrum Roffense*, ed. J. Thorpe (London, 1769), pp. 95-8.

13 Ibid., p. 112.

14 Smith, 'Place of Gundulf', p. 264.

15 Alfred Sweet, 'The Control of English Episcopal Elections in the Thirteenth Century', *Catholic Historical Review*, 12 (1927), pp. 573-82; Gibbs and Lang, *Bishops*, pp. 53-93; Waldo Smith, *Episcopal Appointments and Patronage in the Reign of Edward II: A Study in the Relations of Church and State* (Chicago, 1938), pp. 1-49; Maurice Powicke, *King Henry III and the Lord Edward* (2 vols, Oxford, 1947), I, pp. 259-89.

16 Phyllis Scotney, 'An Examination of the Theory and Practice of Appointments to Bishoprics during the Reigns of Henry III and Edward I ... and of their Historical Significance' (University of London, MA thesis, 1925); William Evers, 'Disputes about Episcopal Elections in the Reign of Henry III, with Special Reference to Some Unpublished Durham Documents' (University of Oxford, B.Litt. thesis, 1934).

17 For an important exception, see Roy Haines, "The Episcopate during the Reign of Edward II and the Regency of Mortimer and Isabella', *Journal of Ecclesiastical History* 56 (2005), pp. 657-709.

18 See, for example, Graham, *Winchelsey*, pp. 161-75; Walter Ullmann, 'The Disputed Election of Hugh Balsham, Bishop of Ely', *Cambridge Historical Journal*, 9 (1949), pp. 259-68; John Grassi, 'William Airmyn and the Bishopric of Norwich', *EHR*, 60 (1955), pp. 550-61; Art Cosgrove, 'The Elections to the Bishopric of Winchester, 1280-2', *Studies in Church History*, 3 (1966), pp. 169-78; Jeffrey Denton, 'Canterbury Archiepiscopal Appointments: The Case of Walter Reynolds', *Journal of Medieval History*, 1 (1975), pp. 317-27; Nicholas Vincent, 'The Election of *Pandulph* Verracclo as Bishop of *Norwich* (1215)', *Historical Research*, 68 (1995), pp. 143-63; Nicholas Vincent, 'Jocelin of Wells: The Making of a Bishop in the Reign of King John' in Dunning, *Jocelin of Wells*, pp. 9-33.

19 Including Douie, *Pecham*, pp. 47-53; Constance Fraser, *A History of Anthony Bek, Bishop of Durham 1283-1311* (Oxford, 1957), pp. 28-49; Roy Haines, *Archbishop John Stratford: Political Revolutionary and Champion of the Liberties of the English Church* (Toronto, 1986), pp. 136-50.

Yet, despite the scale of the shift to provision, which transformed the manner in which English bishops were appointed, there has yet to be a full-length study of English episcopal appointments that covers the whole of the transitional period. Furthermore, many of the works listed above focus on single elements of the appointment process, most usually the role of the king and the electoral disputes that arose as a result of royal intervention. Building on the work of previous historians, this study presents an examination of episcopal appointments in England covering the whole of the period between c.1214 and c.1334, and looks at these processes from the bottom up, as well as from the top down.

Part I focuses on 'The Age of Election', which is defined as the period during which capitular election was the dominant form of appointment; this is broadly equivalent to the thirteenth century (c.1214-c.1307). It begins by examining the proper process of episcopal elections in the thirteenth century, as set out in the canon law, in tracts on the conduct of election and in other miscellaneous texts such as the Freedom of Election charter of 1214. Combining these sources enables us to build up a detailed picture of how elections were supposed to be conducted, and of the rights and responsibilities of the core quintet of participants in an electoral process: the cathedral chapter, the king, the archbishop, the pope and the candidate.

The focus then shifts from the rules of election to the realities: how did the experience of election compare to the ideal? Chapter 2 considers the ritual and finance of election, focusing on practices that were customary within the context of thirteenth-century England, but developed outside the constraints of canon law. These customs were not required to make an election valid, and whilst some could bolster the electoral process, others appear to sit rather uncomfortably alongside the legal developments of the period and could potentially undermine capitular choices. Nevertheless, they were a key component of the bishop-making process as experienced in England at this time.

The final chapter in this section considers the practice of election during the reigns of Henry III and Edward I. Based on in-depth case studies of approximately 125 elections,[20] from straightforward capitular elections to major disputes, this chapter provides a detailed analysis of this material. The roles of each of the core quintet of participants are examined in turn, with an additional section considering the involvement of other parties, both lay and clerical. The chapter demonstrates the ways in which real elections conformed to, and differed from, the model provided in Chapter 1; it also discusses the responses to, and results of, these elections. It thus illuminates the complex electoral realities of the period.

Part II examines the transition to provision, focusing on the years c.1307 to c.1344. Chapter 4 focuses on the theoretical aspects of this transition, outlining the changes to the canon law which lay behind the rise of provision, and detailing

---

20 All of these elections are listed and outlined in the Appendix.

the impact these changes had on the rights and responsibilities of the key quintet of participants. The final portion of this chapter considers how far these changes altered the customs and costs of the appointment process. In Chapter 5, the focus shifts to the practical dimensions of the rise of provision. A further batch of case studies (approximately 50)[21] forms the basis of an evaluation of English responses to provision. Both hostile reactions and the ways in which those involved became accustomed to (and even accepting of) the new methods of appointment are considered. The impact of the transition on the composition of the English episcopate is also examined.

Part III places the English experience, as discussed in the two previous sections, within a European context. My findings, as detailed in the previous five chapters, are combined with existing works on episcopal appointments elsewhere in Europe to produce a comparison between England and three other countries: Scotland, France and Italy. This comparative approach highlights the peculiarities of the history of bishop-making in England, but also demonstrates the extent to which the English narrative was also a European one.

***

Given the importance of the bishop in medieval society, and the wide range of participants in the bishop-making process, it is unsurprising that references to episcopal appointments can be found in a wide range of sources. These can be divided into five broad categories. The first of these is those sources that are wholly or primarily of a prescriptive nature, such as canon law, royal decrees and tracts on the conduct of elections.

The second category consists of the records of royal and papal administration. These have yielded a great deal of material, including many of the formal documents (such as licences to elect and bulls of provision), but also less formulaic texts which illuminate not only the roles played by those authorities, but also their interactions with other participants. The third category, local sources produced within the diocese, includes *sede vacante* registers, as well as registers kept by cathedral priories and bishops. In some sees, the formal documentation relating to individual vacancies has been preserved, providing detailed information about the election itself from the perspective of the cathedral chapter.

The English chroniclers of the thirteenth and fourteenth centuries produced a great deal of high quality material;[22] their output, amongst which can be found numerous references to bishops and their appointments, forms the fourth category of source material. The level of detail provided varies considerably in

---

21 These are also outlined in Appendix A.

22 For a survey, see Antonia Gransden, *Historical Writing in England* (2 vols, London, 1974-82).

accordance with the writer's level of interest. Many records simply name the new bishop, his see and the year of his appointment, but others are far more substantial, giving lengthy narratives peppered with asides about the elect and his election. Matthew Paris was a particularly enthusiastic commentator and wrote at length about many of the more contentious appointments of the early thirteenth century, but he was far from alone in his fascination with such matters. The final category is miscellanea, those sources that do not fit within any of the previous three categories, but have provided crucial information for this project. Examples include letter collections, ecclesiastical schedules of complaint, records of proctors at the papal curia, saints' lives and poetic works. Once all of these primary sources are combined with the existing secondary literature, the historian of episcopal appointments in late medieval England has a relative wealth of material on which to draw.

***

Two decades ago, Bernhard Schimmelpfennig complained that there were no studies of medieval (specifically twelfth- and thirteenth-century) episcopal elections that gave equal consideration to legal, theoretical, political and local dimensions of the process.[23] This study cannot hope, and does not claim, to achieve the comprehensiveness to which he suggested historians of this topic should aspire. Nevertheless, by piecing together a range of texts produced over a century and a half, by dozens of authors, it is possible to produce a synthesis of the history of episcopal appointments in England between c.1214 and c.1344. In doing so, it is at least possible to shed some light on the experiences of each of the participants in the appointment process during this crucial transitional period.

---

[23] Bernard Schimmelpfenning, 'Papst-und Bischofswahlen seit dem 12. Jahrhundert' in Reinhard Schneider and Harald Zimmermann (eds), *Wahlen und Wählen in Mittelalter* (Sigmaringen, 1990), p. 174, cited by Peltzer, *Elections*, p. 3, which is itself a major step towards the filling of this historiographical gap.

PART I
The Age of Election

Chapter 1
The Theory of Election

For the whole of the thirteenth century, the usual means of appointment to an English bishopric was by capitular election, followed by acceptance by the elect, assent by the king and examination and confirmation by the archbishop. The pope became involved only if there was a dispute which needed settlement, and an appeal was made to Rome. Once all of the parties involved had acknowledged that both the new bishop and his election were suitable and sound, the spiritualities and temporalities of the see were restored, and the ceremonies of consecration and enthronement celebrated.[1]

This chapter begins with a consideration of how this situation came about, paying particular attention to the notion of free capitular election as the sole acceptable form of appointing a bishop. This was an ideal with a centuries-old history, which crystallized in England in the early thirteenth century with the appearance of two key texts: the Freedom of Elections charter issued by King John in 1214 and the legislation of the Fourth Lateran Council (1215). The significance of these texts is considered at length. The second part of the chapter looks at the electoral process as it was supposed to function during the reigns of Henry III and Edward I; that is, during the years before papal provision became commonplace and the decline of episcopal election began in earnest. This examination takes a sequential approach to the process, beginning with the death of the old bishop and ending with the enthronement of his successor. It pays particular attention to the role each of the key participants in a conventional episcopal election (the chapter, the king, the elect and the archbishop) was expected to play. The final section covers variations to the standard election

---

1 The processes of episcopal elections, whilst never a popular subject for historical research, are the subject of several works in English and French. Two early twentieth-century historians considered this topic as it was manifested in thirteenth-century England: Phyllis Scotney, in an MA thesis (1925) which covered the theory and practice of elections during the reigns of Henry III and Edward I (Scotney, 'Theory and Practice of Appointments') and Marion Gibbs, whose *Bishops and Reform* (1936), included a survey of the canonical procedure for elections during the reign of Henry III (Gibbs and Lang, *Bishops*, pp. 55-68). In the 1970s, Jean Gaudemet produced a further survey, broader in its chronological and geographical scope; see Gaudemet, *Gouvernement*, pp. 55-73. More recently, Jörg Peltzer has written on the development of electoral theory in the late twelfth and early thirteenth centuries, with reference to Normandy and Greater Anjou (Peltzer, *Elections*, pp. 20-56). Several historians have focused their attention on the role of a particular party; the most notable works of this kind are Geoffrey Barraclough, 'The Making of the Bishop in the Middle Ages: The Part of the Pope in Law and Fact', *Catholic Historical Review*, 19 (1933/34), pp. 275-319 and Irene Churchill, *Administration*, I, pp. 241-54.

process, focusing on the three occasions when papal involvement was required: when an archbishop was elected, when a candidate was postulated[2] and when an appeal was made against an election.

The source material relating to the conduct of a canonical election is rich and diverse. Much of our knowledge stems from the substantial body of canon law related to this topic; by 1200 this had been nearly a millennium in the making, and it continued to grow throughout the thirteenth century. This can be supplemented by a number of tracts on the conduct of episcopal elections, in particular those produced at Canterbury and Chichester during the reign of Henry III. The surviving records of the Plantagenet government are also a valuable source, providing various statements of the rights of the crown.

The Ideal of Electoral Freedom

The requirement that a bishop should be elected was established early in the history of the Catholic Church, being recorded as Canon four of the First Council of Nicaea (325).[3] The principle of free election was confirmed by the *responsa* of Popes Celestine I and Leo I in the fifth century.[4] In reality, however, the appointment of bishops was dominated by secular rulers throughout the early Middle Ages, with the election being little more than a formal signification of assent to the ruler's choice.[5] This situation began to change only with the advent of the so-called Gregorian reform movement in the eleventh century: the reformers' concern to prevent simony and free the church from subjection to secular authorities led them to oppose practices that gave secular rulers a role in ecclesiastical appointments. Lay investiture (the formal conferment of the symbols of ecclesiastical office on a new bishop by the secular ruler) and the performance of homage to the king by ecclesiastics were particular concerns.[6]

---

[2] A postulation was an appeal to the papacy to sanction the appointment of an individual who was somehow disqualified from holding episcopal office, or to translate a bishop from one see to another.

[3] *Ecumenical Councils*, I, p. 7. On the theory of episcopal elections in late antiquity, see Peter Norton, *Episcopal Elections 250-600: Hierarchy and Popular Will in Late Antiquity* (Oxford, 2007), pp. 18-51.

[4] Celestine I, *PL*, l, 436-7, no. 5; Leo I, *PL*, liv, 633-4, no. 10, 665-6, no. 13; Norton, *Elections*, pp. 43-4.

[5] See, for examples, Henry Beck, 'Canonical Election to Suffragan Bishoprics According to Hincmar of Rheims', *Catholic Historical Review*, 43 (1957), pp. 137-59; Catherine Cubitt, 'Wilfred's "Usurping Bishops": Episcopal Elections in Anglo-Saxon England, c.600-c.800', *Northern History*, 25 (1989), pp. 18-38.

[6] For recent summaries of the Investiture Controversy in England, see Ute-Renate Blumenthal, *The Investiture Controversy: Church and Monarchy from the Ninth to the Twelfth Century* (Philadelphia, 1991), pp. 142-59; David Carpenter, *The Struggle for Mastery: Britain 1066-1284* (London, 2003), pp. 135-40.

Reviving the ancient principle of election by the clergy and people, the reformers decided that a bishop should be chosen by the former and acclaimed by the latter; the whole process must be confirmed by the metropolitan or by the pope.[7] During the course of the twelfth century, the exact composition of the electoral body remained the subject of debate. The Second Lateran Council (1139) ruled that cathedral chapters must seek the counsel and consent of *religiosi viri*; the exclusion of this latter group rendered the election invalid and the electors should be excommunicated.[8] Yet elections were increasingly made by cathedral chapters alone,[9] and certain canonists disputed the validity of the 1139 decree, on the grounds that it contradicted the older (and therefore weightier) ruling of the Council of Nicaea.[10] The dispute was settled by Innocent III in 1200 with the issue of the decretal *Dilecti filii clerici* (= *Cum ecclesia Sutrina*); this stated that the right to elect the bishop lay with the cathedral chapter, unless local custom dictated the inclusion of a third party.[11]

Whilst the ideal of free election by the cathedral chapter was thus well established by the dawn of the thirteenth century, its existence in practice was greatly strengthened in England by two developments which took place in 1214-15: the granting of the Freedom of Election charter to the English Church in 1214[12] and the holding of the Fourth Lateran Council in the following year.[13]

King John's Freedom of Election Charter (1214)

King John's decision to grant the Freedom of Election charter can only be understood in the context of England's electoral history during the years 1066-1214. From the Norman Conquest of England until the early thirteenth

7 Peltzer, *Elections*, pp. 20-21.

8 *Ecumenical Councils*, I, p. 203 (c. 28). Exactly who these *religiosi viri* were was the subject of some debate during the twelfth century; it was agreed that the group should consist of local clerics, but the level of seniority required, and the exact area from which they should be drawn, was less certain. Peltzer, *Elections*, pp. 28-9.

9 Em Roland, *Les Chanoines et les Élections Épiscopales du XIe au XIVe siècle* (Aurillac, 1909), pp. 36-43.

10 It was subsequently omitted from the *Liber Extra* of 1234. Peltzer, *Elections*, pp. 27-9; Gaudemet, *Gouvernement*, pp. 59-61.

11 *Die Register Innocenz' III*, ed. Othmar Hageneder *et al.* (Rome, 1968-), II, no. 271 (283); Peltzer, *Elections*, p. 29. In order to be upheld by the papacy, the local custom needed to be exceptionally strong. This ruling was issued in 1200 in response to a dispute at Sutri, where the clergy of various collegiate churches in the city claimed the right to participate in the election of the bishop. They lost their appeal, on the grounds that participation in the previous three elections did not constitute a custom.

12 For the text, see *C&S*, I, pp. 40-41.

13 cc. 23-6 relate to episcopal elections: *Ecumenical Councils*, I, pp. 246-8.

century, English episcopal (and many abbatial[14]) elections were dominated by the crown.[15] Although it was acknowledged that bishops should be canonically elected, the idea was relatively ill-defined, and it was widely accepted that secular rulers would be heavily involved. Norman and Angevin kings took their powers over such appointments for granted; their voice in such matters was decisive, and they were rarely disappointed in their attempts to create a loyal episcopate made up primarily of king's men. Elections were typically conducted in a manner that echoed the Concordat of Worms (1122), a text that was circulated widely in England and demanded election in the royal presence, with any disputes to be settled 'by the judgement or counsel of the archbishop and the bishops of the province'.[16] Until at least the 1130s, sees that fell vacant when the king was overseas were not filled until he returned to England.[17] Consequently, long vacancies were common and there was no real expectation of electoral freedom, the royal wishes typically being made very clear. For example, when Anselm became archbishop of Canterbury in 1093, almost four years after the death of Lanfranc,

> [William II] declared that Anselm was the man most fitted for this work. There was universal acclamation, and both clergy and people commended the king's judgement without a single voice being raised in contradiction.[18]

Neither Henry I's Coronation Charter (1100)[19] nor the charter of ecclesiastical liberties granted by King Stephen in 1136[20] made any reference to episcopal

---

14 For abbatial elections in thirteenth-century England, see Susan Wood, *English Monasteries and their Patrons in the Thirteenth Century* (Oxford, 1955), pp. 40-74.

15 For what follows, see Donald Bethell, 'English Black Monks and Episcopal Elections in the 1120s', *EHR*, 84 (1969), pp. 673-98; Martin Brett, *The English Church Under Henry I* (Oxford, 1975), pp. 104-12; Frank Barlow, *The English Church, 1066-1154* (London, 1979), pp. 118, 277, 302; Stephanie Christelow, 'Chancellors and Curial Bishops: Ecclesiastical Promotions and Power in Anglo-Norman England', *Anglo-Norman Studies*, 22 (1999), pp. 49-69; Robert Bartlett, *England Under the Norman and Angevin Kings, 1075-1225* (Oxford, 2000), p. 406; Judith Green, *Henry I: King of England and Duke of Normandy* (Cambridge, 2009), pp. 261-8.

16 Karl Leyser, 'England and the Empire in the Early Twelfth Century', *TRHS*, 5th series, 10 (1960), pp. 61-83.

17 Lauren Jared, 'English Ecclesiastical Vacancies during the Reigns of William II and Henry I', *JEH*, 42 (1991), pp. 362-89.

18 *The Life of St Anselm, Archbishop of Canterbury, by Eadmer*, ed. R. W. Southern (Oxford, 1962), pp. 64-5. For fuller accounts of his appointment, see *Eadmeri Historia Novorum in Anglia*, ed. M. Rule (London, 1884), pp. 32-7; Frank Barlow, *William Rufus* (London, 1983), pp. 300-8; Richard Southern, *Saint Anselm: A Portrait in a Landscape* (Cambridge, 1990), pp. 186-94.

19 *English Historical Documents*, vol. 2: *1042-1189*, ed. D. C. Douglas and G. W. Greenaway (London, 1953), pp. 400-402.

20 Ibid., pp. 403-4.

elections amongst their pledges to redress the wrongs of previous reigns. Some slight movements towards canonical election were made during the reign of Stephen (1135-54) – most notably the 'fully canonical' election of Archbishop Theobald to Canterbury in 1138[21] – but the crown remained the dominant force.

The clearest statement of the king's rights over ecclesiastical appointments prior to 1214 dates from the reign of Henry II, when the Constitutions of Clarendon (1164) stated that:

> And when they come to provide for the church, the lord king must cite the chief persons of the church, and the election must take place in the chapel of the lord king himself, with the assent of the lord king, and the advice of the persons of the realm whom he shall have summoned to do this. And the person elected shall there do homage and fealty to the lord the king as to his liege lord for his life and limbs and earthly honour, saving his order, before he can be consecrated.[22]

This clause stopped short of asserting a direct right of appointment; indeed, as Anne Duggan has noted, it is 'broadly in conformity with canonical tradition'. The language of the canon law, is, however, noticeably absent, with no reference to 'free' or 'canonical' election, and royal authority is predominant throughout the electoral process as here described.[23] The reality of the situation is nicely encapsulated in the writ Henry II allegedly sent to the monks of Winchester in 1173: 'I order you to hold a free election, but nevertheless I do not wish you to accept anyone except Richard, my clerk, the archdeacon of Poitiers.'[24]

Nevertheless, the tide was beginning to turn, and during the fifty years between 1164 and 1214, electoral freedom became an increasingly significant issue in church–state relations. In 1168, Pope Alexander ordered Henry II to allow free elections to be held and to desist from making his own nominations.[25] Four years later, the cardinal legates Albert and Theodwin secured an informal

---

21 Marjorie Chibnall, 'Innocent II and the Canterbury Election of 1138' in Coloman Viola (ed.), *Mediaevalia Christiana (XIe-XIIIe siècles), Hommage à Raymonde Foreville* (Brussels, 1989), pp. 237-45; Anne Duggan, 'Law and Practice in Episcopal and Abbatial Election before 1215: With Special Reference to England' in Corinne Péneau (ed.), Élections et Pouvoirs Politiques du VIIe au XVIIe siècle (Bordeaux, 2008), pp. 43-62, at pp. 48-51. For the argument that the crown retained greater control over elections during the Anarchy than has previously been acknowledged, see Stephen Marritt, 'The Bishops of King Stephen's Reign' (University of Glasgow, PhD thesis, 2002), pp. 230-34.

22 *English Historical Documents*, 2, p. 721.

23 Duggan, 'Law and Practice', pp. 51-2.

24 *Recueil des historiens des Gaules et de la France*, ed. M. Bouquet *et al.*, new edn directed by L. Delisle (19 vols, Paris, 1869-80), XVI, p. 645. The writ itself does not survive; the allegation that it was sent was made in writing by the Young King at the time of his rebellion against his father.

25 *Materials for the History of Thomas Becket, Archbishop of Canterbury*, ed. J. C. Robertson and J. B. Sheppard (7 vols, RS, 1875-85), VI, pp. 503-5.

agreement from Henry II that he would permit free elections to take place,[26] although this was soon broken by the king.[27] Consequently, he was rebuked by St Hugh of Lincoln, who accused Henry of 'abusing the powers which his predecessors had usurped in connection with the appointments of bishops and abbots', and argued that he should 'permit freedom of election in accordance with the rules of canon law'.[28] The king was not the only one to be subject to criticism over his approach to elections; Archbishop Richard of Dover was the recipient of the decretal *Qua fronte*, in which he was reproached by Alexander III for confirming elections made in the king's chamber.[29]

Ecclesiastical censure meant that the formal processes of election were usually observed, but Richard I retained a level of control over episcopal appointments that mirrored that enjoyed by his father.[30] At the beginning of his reign, in September 1189, he convened an ecclesiastical council at Pipewell Abbey, during the course of which he nominated a set of *curiales* to the vacant sees of Winchester, Ely, Salisbury and York; in each case, the electors ratified the royal choices.[31] Even imprisonment in Germany did not hinder Richard's ability to control elections, as his surviving correspondence about the appointment of Hubert Walter to Canterbury (1193) demonstrates.[32]

Essentially, then, and despite the changing position of the church, both Henry II and Richard I managed to maintain strong personal control of English elections. At the time of John's accession, therefore, the idea of the king offering pledges of electoral freedom would have been almost unthinkable, but the events of the next fifteen years changed that. During the early years of John's reign the crown continued to control elections, but was increasingly subject to papal censure for doing so.[33] In February 1203, Innocent III complained to John

---

26 *Radulfi de Diceto Decani Lundoniensis Opera Historica*, ed. W. Stubbs (2 vols, RS, 1876), I, p. 367.

27 Duggan, 'Law and Practice', pp. 53-5. For the 1184 Rochester election, for which the prior and twelve of his monks were summoned to Westminster, see Colin Flight, *The Bishops and Monks of Rochester, 1076-1214* (Maidstone, 1997), p. 290.

28 *Magna Vita*, I, pp. 71-2.

29 *X*, 2. 28. 25 (*CIC*, II, pp. 417-18); Christopher Cheney, *From Becket to Langton: English Church Government 1170-1213* (Manchester, 1956), p. 23.

30 Ralph Turner, 'Richard Lionheart and English Episcopal Elections', *Albion*, 29 (1997), pp. 1-13; Duggan, 'Law and Practice', pp. 55-6. For detailed examples of the manner in which elections were conducted under the Angevin kings, see *Magna Vita*, I, pp. 92-103, and *Jocelin of Brakelond: Chronicle of the Abbey of Bury St Edmunds*, ed. D. Greenway and J. Sayers (Oxford, 1989), pp. 7-24.

31 *Chronica Magistri Rogeri de Houedene*, ed. W. Stubbs (4 vols, RS, 1868-71), II, p. 85; Duggan, 'Law and Practice', p. 55.

32 *Chronicles and Memorials of the Reign of Richard I*, ed. W. Stubbs (2 vols, RS, 1865), II, pp. 363-6.

33 For a detailed analysis of elections in England during the reign of King John, see Christopher Cheney, *Pope Innocent III and England* (Stuttgart, 1976), pp. 121-78.

that 'You are claiming for yourself power beyond your rights, you are applying the revenues of the churches to your own uses, you are attempting to prevent elections, and in the end by your unlawful persecution you are forcing the rightful electors to choose in accordance with your arbitrary decision.' Innocent was particularly critical of John's approach to the see of Lincoln, which had been vacant since November 1200, and accused him of delaying the election in order to maintain control of the revenues.[34]

It was not until the archbishopric of Canterbury fell vacant, by the death of Hubert Walter in July 1205,[35] that the simmering tensions between crown and papacy finally exploded into the open. The election held at Canterbury produced a split result, with some of the monks electing their sub-prior and others favouring John's candidate, John de Gray, bishop of Norwich. Consequently two monastic delegations went to Rome, both seeking confirmation of their choice. Both elections were eventually quashed, and a new election was held in Rome. The resultant archbishop-elect was Cardinal Stephen Langton, a choice warmly endorsed by the pope.[36]

John, however, was decidedly less enamoured of the new archbishop, and refused to assent to his election, claiming that his assent to the holding of an election had not been sought and that Langton was unknown to him. Indeed, he replied to Innocent's request that he consent so 'insolently and impudently as though threatening and expostulating'; he would not defer to Rome 'even as far as the law requires', but instead attacked the papal honour in an unprecedented fashion. If John was now prepared to 'humbly agree with us', Innocent pledged, no prejudice would attach itself to John or his successors as a consequence of this business. To continue in opposition would, conversely, engage John in 'a difficulty from which he could not easily be freed'.[37]

John could not prevent the consecration of Archbishop Stephen, which took place at Viterbo on 17 June 1207,[38] but he could and did prevent him from entering the country, declaring Langton's supporters to be public enemies and seizing the estates of the see.[39] Deadlock had now been reached, and in November Innocent III began to threaten an interdict.[40] At this stage many in

---

34 *SLI*, pp. 50-51 (no. 17). John's role in the Sées election of 1201-1203 (he had threatened the canons and was preventing the new bishop from holding the see) was also criticized; see Peltzer, *Elections*, pp. 123-32.

35 *Fasti 1066-1300*, II, p. 5.

36 For a fuller account of the election, see David Knowles, 'The Canterbury Election of 1205-6', *EHR*, 53 (1938), pp. 211-20.

37 *SLI*, pp. 86-90 (no. 29).

38 *Fasti 1066-1300*, II, p. 6.

39 *Memoriale Walteri de Coventria*, ed. W. Stubbs (2 vols, RS, 1872-73), II, p. 199; *RLP*, I, p. 74.

40 *SLI*, pp. 97-9 (no. 32).

England were on John's side,[41] but tensions continued to build and in early May 1208, England learned that it was under interdict.[42] If John was meant to be cowed by this measure, then it failed spectacularly, since he merely exploited the new financial opportunities it offered to him.[43] He also continued to add 'transgression to transgression', by delaying and hindering free elections.[44] Consequently, in November 1209 he was excommunicated.

Only in July 1214, after England had become a papal fief, was the interdict formally lifted.[45] Despite this settlement, the conduct of episcopal elections continued to be a troublesome issue, largely due to the role played by Nicholas, cardinal-bishop of Tusculum, the papal legate in England during the period 1213-14. The legatine mission was aimed at reconciling John to the Roman Church; in the matter of elections, he did this so successfully that he provoked the ire of Langton and the episcopate. When, in July 1213, John tried to summon various electors into his presence, he met with resistance.[46] But his control of elections was not seriously threatened by the legate's presence. Nicholas' policy was rooted in the orders he received from Rome, which not only required him to respect the king's right to grant licence to elect as well as to give assent to the outcome, but also allowed him to pay considerable respect to the royal wishes. Suitable men were to be elected or postulated according to Nicholas' recommendation, and a suitable man was defined as one who was 'not only distinguished in life and learning, but also loyal to the king, profitable to the kingdom, and capable of giving counsel and help'.[47] It was even suggested that 'any honourable request of his which preserves the liberty of the church' should be granted[48] – a suggestion that says a lot about Innocent III's desire to resolve the dispute with John, as well as undermining the traditional view that Innocent was aiming at 'world dominion'. Given that cathedral chapters were obliged to accept such legatine recommendations,[49] it is perhaps unsurprising that Nicholas' respect for the king's wishes soon prompted complaints to the papal curia. It was alleged that the legate was showing too much complaisance

[41] *AM*, I, p. 28; Wilfred L. Warren, *King John*, 2nd edn (London, 1978), pp. 164-6.

[42] *SLI*, pp. 102-3 (no. 34).

[43] For a summary of these opportunities, which included the confiscation of the assets of all ecclesiastical corporations and individuals who observed the interdict, see Warren, *John*, pp. 166-9; Christopher Harper-Bill, 'John and the Church of Rome' in Stephen Church (ed.), *King John: New Interpretations* (Woodbridge, 1999), pp. 289-315, at pp. 306-7.

[44] *SLI*, pp. 115-16 (no. 38).

[45] Warren, *John*, pp. 206-11.

[46] *C&S*, I, p. 22.

[47] *SLI*, pp. 166-7 (no. 62).

[48] *CLI*, no. 939.

[49] *CLI*, nos. 938, 939.

to the crown, even allowing royal proctors to attend elections, to the detriment of ecclesiastical liberties.[50]

Unsurprisingly, John was happy to comply with this form of bishop-making,[51] but Archbishop Stephen was rather less pleased, complaining that Nicholas was appointing unworthy men, recommended by the king, to vacant churches.[52] By January 1214, some form of agreement over the conduct of elections had been reached, probably with papal involvement; we know this because John wrote to Langton that 'the form notified to us for the making of elections is acceptable to us saving in all things our right'. But, despite royal assertions that 'there is no controversy between us',[53] the archbishop remained sufficiently concerned to summon a meeting of his suffragans at Dunstable at the end of the month. He then sent two proctors to the legate, forbidding him to appoint to vacant churches, since this was an infringement of archiepiscopal rights. The legate ignored this order, and both sides sent proctors to Rome.[54] Nicholas remained in England until November 1214, when he was recalled to Rome.[55] But the conduct of episcopal elections remained the subject of considerable dispute between the king and the church. It was at this point, on 21 November, that John granted the Freedom of Election charter.

It is clear, then, that the Freedom of Election charter was the product of a point in time when the ever-present gulf between royal and ecclesiastical approaches to the filling of episcopal vacancies had become untenably wide. What exactly did John concede in November 1214? Superficially, the answer is straightforward: he pledged that, henceforth, 'the elections of all prelates whatsoever ... be free forever'. The simple fact that John had acknowledged this right was a major triumph for both the English Church and the papacy. Whereas the Constitutions of Clarendon provided a vigorous statement of the crown's rights over the electoral process, John's charter renounced 'the custom in our times and of our predecessors' and emphasizes the limits of royal power. The chapter should ask for licence to elect from the crown, but the king would not 'deny or defer' its issue; if he did so, the election might go ahead regardless, and thus it was no longer possible for the crown to prevent elections by withholding the licence. This licence having been granted, the king 'will neither hinder not suffer nor procure to be hindered by our ministers that ... the electors should, whenever they will, freely set a pastor over them'. Although the chapter must seek royal assent to the outcome of their election, this could only be refused if

50 *CLI*, no. 968; *Memoriale Walteri de Coventria*, II, p. 216; *CM*, II, p. 571.

51 *RLC*, I, pp. 160a, 162a.

52 *CM*, II, p. 571; Maurice Powicke, *Stephen Langton* (Oxford, 1928), p. 105.

53 *RLC*, I, p. 160a.

54 *Roger Wendover's Flowers of History*, ed. J. A. Giles (2 vols, London, 1849), II, pp. 292-30.

55 *RLC*, I, pp. 177b, 181b; *C&S*, I, p. 21.

the king can 'put forth some reasonable excuse and lawfully prove it'. Edward II would later recall, somewhat wistfully, that 'before the time of King John, all his ancestors, kings of England ... freely conferred bishoprics without any contradiction';[56] henceforth, because of this charter, it would never again be so. Through the concessions made in 1214, John ceded the direct personal control over ecclesiastical elections his predecessors had enjoyed.

And yet, these concessions were perhaps not as extensive as they initially appear when one reads the charter for the first time. In a typically controversial passage, Richardson and Sayles argued that the charter was essentially worthless to the church, being little more than 'an empty concession'.[57] This is clearly an overstatement, yet there is some truth in their assertion, for John retained considerable powers over the electoral process – both official and unofficial. The right to grant the *congé d'élire* was, in many ways, a symbolic one, since it could no longer be denied – but the symbolism of the king allowing the chapter to hold an election was nevertheless important. It would henceforth be impossible for a king to prolong vacancies deliberately for financial gain by refusing licence – a practice for which the Angevins had become notorious. But even so, the reassertion of the custom of regalian right[58] – the holding of the episcopal temporalities by the crown during a vacancy – was not without value, partly because even a relatively brief vacancy could bring the king substantial amounts of extra revenue, but also because the threat of damage to these properties could prove a powerful incentive to elect the king's candidate. Similarly, the statement that royal assent could only be withheld if 'reasonable excuse' could be found was open to considerable exploitation, given the complexities of the canon law relating to elections. It was almost always possible to find a flaw in the conduct of an election or the quality of an elect if one were inclined to do so – in which case the king would continue to receive the revenues of the see until the dispute was settled.

If what the charter said is significant, what it did not say may be even more important. Although it was no longer possible for the king to impose his wishes on the chapter, there was nothing to stop him indicating his wishes to the electors. There was no explicit renunciation of the traditional practice of holding elections in the royal presence – although this was clearly at odds with the spirit of the charter, and does seem to have stopped – or of the practice that replaced it, the sending of royal proctors to the electors. Indeed, based on the contents of this document, there was no reason why elections should not continue to take

[56] *Reg. Sede Vacante*, p. 105.

[57] Henry Richardson and George Sayles, *The Governance of Mediaeval England from the Conquest to Magna Carta* (Edinburgh, 1963), p. 381.

[58] 'Saving to us and our heirs custody of vacant churches and monasteries which belong to us'.

place as they had throughout Nicholas' time as legate; that is, not directly under royal control, but nevertheless heavily influenced by royal wishes.

If the charter did little to change the status quo, then why did it need to be issued at all? Answers to this question have traditionally focused on the political difficulties John faced during the last years of his reign. His position, it is argued, had already been weakened by the protracted dispute with the church, and by the manner in which this dispute was ended. When John returned to England from the continent in October 1214, his kingship had been further undermined by defeat at the Battle of Bouvines. Domestic opposition to his rule was rapidly growing.[59] Thus, in a desperate attempt to contain dissent, John granted the Freedom of Election charter, hoping to detach the English Church from the rebellious barons.[60]

This interpretation makes a great deal of sense, for John undoubtedly was faced with great political difficulties in late 1214. The bishops, and in particular Archbishop Stephen, were known to be dissatisfied with various aspects of his rule, including his perceived lack of respect for electoral liberties.[61] Granting a charter that pledged electoral freedom was a major concession on the part of the king, which was certain to please the clergy, serving as a form of compensation for the difficulties of the past decade.[62] Furthermore, John was clearly engaged in settling his differences with the church at this time, as a series of grants made to senior churchmen on or around 21 November indicates; amongst these was the confirmation of the archiepiscopal rights over the diocese of Rochester[63] and the remission of certain debts owed to the crown by the bishops of Lincoln and Ely.[64] It is therefore hard to escape the conclusion that the Freedom of Election charter was granted as part of a campaign to conciliate the episcopate.

Nevertheless, to explain the charter solely in such terms is overly simplistic. To do so is to imply that John came to an agreement with the English Church only when he was backed into a corner; that it was a document granted with the sole aim of pleasing the church; that John had nothing to gain from such an agreement. The reality is rather more complex, for electoral disputes were not merely an English problem. Whilst Stephen Langton was undoubtedly much concerned by the question of electoral freedom, his interest was matched by that of Innocent III, whose pontificate was characterized by his insistence on the

---

59 Warren, *John*, pp. 224-6.

60 For Wendover's allegations that Langton was active in encouraging the barons to recover their lost liberties, see *CM*, II, pp. 552-4; Powicke, *Langton*, pp. 115-16.

61 *CM*, II, p. 571.

62 For the prominence of the idea of compensation in the charter, see Cheney, *Innocent III and England*, p. 363.

63 *RLC*, I, p. 179; *RLP*, I, p. 124; *Rotuli Chartarum in Turri Londinensi Asservati*, ed. T. D. Hardy (London, 1837), p. 202b.

64 *Reg. Ant. Linc.*, I, p. 143.

importance of ecclesiastical liberties. Significantly, John was far from being the only European ruler to grant electoral freedom to the local church during the years 1199-1216; similar concessions were made in Sicily, the Romano-German Empire, Austria and Aragon. The details of these pledges varied somewhat. In 1198, Constance of Sicily negotiated a settlement with Innocent III, by which the crown would be notified of the vacancy and entitled to give assent to the election;[65] this agreement was reconfirmed by the emperor Frederick II in 1212.[66] Given the connections between Sicily and the empire, it was perhaps inevitable that pledges of electoral freedom played a role in the imperial election dispute; in 1201, as a candidate for this office, Otto of Brunswick pledged to respect the electoral freedom of the church, and eight years later this pledge was formally restated. In 1211, the accord made between Duke Leopold VI of Austria and the archbishop of Salzburg contained a ducal pledge of free elections.[67] In his statute of 1207, Pedro II went further, giving up even his right to give assent to elections held within his kingdom and asking only that new bishops be presented to him in order to demonstrate their loyalty to the crown.[68]

Royal pledges to allow ecclesiastical elections to be held freely were a European-wide phenomenon during the first few years of the thirteenth century. Such parallels reaffirm the notion that such grants were seen as a source of political capital for rulers who were in some way vulnerable, but they also indicate that debates about electoral procedure were not limited to England, and that this charter was more than a result of the tensions between John and Langton. Instead, it was about the nature of the relationship between *regnum* and *sacerdotium* as it was being defined and developed in the early thirteenth century.

A common theme in all of these agreements was papal involvement; such promises pleased not only the English Church, but also the pope. This charter was issued in the wake of England's conversion into a papal fief, and John is known to have skilfully exploited his position as a papal vassal; Cheney described his decision to take the cross in March 1215 as 'a shrewd move'.[69] The charter might be described in the same way, for it was sure to enhance John's standing in papal eyes. There is certainly strong evidence of papal influence over the contents of the charter; a comparison of its contents with a letter sent by Innocent III to Legate Nicholas in late 1213 or very early 1214 is extremely suggestive. In it, the pope sets out a procedure for the holding of an election which Nicholas is ordered to enforce:

---

65 Donald Matthews, *The Norman Kingdom of Sicily* (Cambridge, 1992), p. 297.

66 Ibid., p. 309.

67 Gaudemet, *Gouvernement*, pp. 78-9.

68 Damian Smith, *Innocent III and the Crown of Aragon* (Aldershot, 2004), p. 63.

69 Cheney, *Innocent III and England*, p. 262.

> When a bishop or abbot is to be elected, messengers from the chapter should be sent to the king, who they should ask for licence to elect in this manner: 'Lord, we wish, if it pleases you, to elect our pastor'. And he, without prejudice to his rights, should reply: 'Elect in the name of the Lord'. The proctors having returned, the whole chapter should assemble and, using your counsel, elect for themselves a suitable person for their prelate, who they should solemnly and publicly announce to the king and humbly ask that he give assent to the election which has been made; he will not delay the giving of royal favour.[70]

The similarities with the Freedom of Election charter are striking: the seeking of licence to elect; the holding of the election, by implication, away from court; the need for royal assent, which will not be delayed. It seems impossible that those involved in drafting the charter did not have this papal letter in mind. Amongst their number must surely have been its recipient, the Legate Nicholas who, like John, would have been aware of the impact this grant would have in Rome. Indeed, it is plausible (although this is entirely speculation) that Nicholas had been tasked with securing such an agreement during his mission to England.

To date, historians have almost unanimously assumed that, whilst the charter was pleasing to both the English Church and to Rome, it was utterly distasteful to John. Undoubtedly he would have preferred to enjoy the same control over elections that his predecessors had exercised. And yet, he must also have been able to see the charter's potential value, for it brought long-term benefits to the crown, as well as serving as a ploy to stave off trouble in the short term. In a climate in which royal control of elections appeared to be under threat – and this was certainly the case during John's reign – having one's rights outlined in a charter confirmed by the pope was no bad thing. Innocent III had made some extremely provocative statements about the role of the prince in episcopal elections, notably in relation to the Armagh archiepiscopal election of 1202, when he announced that the exclusion of King John from the election did not violate the royal dignity.[71] Royal objections to Langton's election had been based on the allegation that the new archbishop was unknown to the king, but also on the circumstances of his election at Rome – neither licence to elect nor assent to the election had been sought.[72] It is surely significant that John had tried to secure an explicit confirmation of his own rights in elections during his doomed negotiations with the pope in 1207-1208.[73] Unless he could secure such a confirmation, John could cite only custom in defence of his rights, and thus he was reliant on claims that 'all my predecessors conferred archbishoprics,

70 *CLI*, no. 939.

71 *Quod Sicut, Reg. Innocenz' III*, v. 82 (83).

72 *SLI*, p. 29 (no. 10).

73 Warren, *John*, p. 166.

bishoprics and abbeys in their chamber', and on tales about previous bishops. At a conference held in 1211, for example, John reminded the Legates Pandulph and Durand of the story of St Wulfstan's staff, conferred on him by St Edward the Confessor, which miraculously adhered itself to the dead king's tomb when William the Conqueror attempted to take it away. According to John, the story demonstrated not only the royal right to confer episcopal office, but also the irrevocability of appointments made in this way. He also pointed out that 'my father conferred the archbishopric of Canterbury on St. Thomas'. In theory, John had a strong case, for he could cite plenty of precedents. But the legates had morality, canon law and papal authority on their side, and could easily demolish such arguments, in this case by pointing out that Becket had later repudiated his own election, and by claiming that John was not the heir of the Confessor, as he claimed to be, but of the Conqueror.[74] It would prove much harder for ecclesiastics to challenge royal rights contained in a charter confirmed by their own head.

The date of the charter also suggests that it was issued at least in part in response to John's fears that his control over episcopal appointments was at risk. Legate Nicholas' sojourn in England had served to bolster royal influence, and if this situation could have continued, there is no reason to suppose that John would have done anything to alter it. But, at some time in late October or early November 1214, Nicholas was recalled to Rome, apparently at very short notice.[75] From John's perspective, this changed everything. With the legate's departure, the archbishop once again became the most powerful churchman in England, and his stance on elections was well known. It was surely not a coincidence that John decided to issue this charter only weeks before his ally left England.

The Freedom of Election charter was the product of a short-term crisis, but it had a long afterlife. It was almost immediately reissued, on 15 January 1215, shortly after the Epiphany great council. The reasons for this reissue are obscure, since the text and witness list of the two versions are identical. It may have been thought necessary to consult with the barons over the pledges made regarding abbatial elections, since many of them were monastic patrons with rights over such matters;[76] alternatively, the reissue may simply have been made in preparation for the dispatch of the charter to Rome. The party responsible for its dispatch to Rome is also unknown. Cheney argued that it must have

---

[74] *AM*, I, p. 211.

[75] In late October, he was summoned to attend a great council on ecclesiastical affairs, which was to be held at Reading shortly after Christmas (*RLC*, I, p. 176), but by 16 November he had been recalled (*RLC*, I, pp. 177b, 181b; *C&S*, I, p. 21).

[76] During the course of the thirteenth century, many English barons made similar pledges of electoral freedom to the religious houses over which they held rights of patronage. Wood, *Monasteries*, pp. 45-7.

been carried by archiepiscopal proctors; he could not credit the possibility that John was responsible. Indeed, Cheney went so far as to suggest that the king appealed against the charter, on the grounds that he told the monks of Bury St Edmunds that he had 'consulted the pope, by my envoys, about all elections in England, which are now in derogation of my liberties'. But, as Cheney himself acknowledged, making such an appeal would have been a rather impolitic move.[77] Furthermore, the possibility that John sent the charter to Rome, or that he cooperated with its sending, cannot be discounted. At some point in March 1215, an English delegation, which had been preparing for departure since mid-November, arrived in Rome. The party carried with them letters of credence to the pope and cardinals, given to them by John; were they also carrying the charter?[78] The timing is plausible, since the charter received papal confirmation on 30 March.[79] Matthew Paris certainly thought that John had a hand in its dispatch to the papal curia, stating both that the king entreated the pope to confirm it and that the confirmation was sought by the king, magnates and prelates.[80] John himself claimed that 'we ... obtained confirmation of this from the Lord Pope Innocent III'.[81]

Whoever sent the charter to Rome, it arrived before the end of March 1215, when it was confirmed by a papal letter of grace. Innocent praised God for allowing the dispute between the English king and the English priesthood over the election of prelates to be settled by means of this charter. 'Regarding this as acceptable and valid', he confirmed the concession, including the text of the charter in his bull 'for the greater security and perpetual record of the business'. Any man who infringed or opposed the charter would 'incur the anger of Almighty God and of SS Peter and Paul His apostles'.[82] The charter's value was greatly strengthened by this papal confirmation; it was to be bolstered still further in June, when it was summarized in the first clause of Magna Carta, in which John pledged that 'the English church shall be free, and shall have its rights undiminished and its liberties unimpaired'.[83] Its inclusion is usually attributed to Langton, and there is no reason to doubt this – although, again, it may not have been as repugnant to John as has often been supposed. Its association with Magna Carta was, however, to be short-lived, for this section of the clause was removed from all subsequent issues. Its deletion in 1216 should be understood

---

77 *Memorials of St Edmund's Abbey*, ed. T. Arnold (3 vols, RS, 1890-96), II, p. 125; Cheney, *Innocent III and England*, pp. 364-5.

78 *RLP*, p. 123b; *Rotuli Chartarum*, 202b, 204b; Cheney, *Innocent III and England*, p. 365 n. 45. The delegation included the abbot of Beaulieu, Alan Martel, Thomas of Erdington and Peter Saracenus.

79 *SLI*, pp. 198-201 (no. 76).

80 *CM*, II, pp. 606-7.

81 James Holt, *Magna Carta*, 2nd edn (Cambridge, 1992), pp. 448-51 (c. 1).

82 *SLI*, pp. 198-201 (no. 76).

83 Holt, *Magna Carta*, pp. 448-51.

as a response to political circumstances, since at this time it might confer not freedom from royal intervention, but freedom to elect supporters of Prince Louis.[84]

Less easily explained is the fact that although Magna Carta and the Forest Charter[85] were both regularly confirmed during the course of the thirteenth century, the reference to elections in the former was never restored, and the Election Charter itself was never reconfirmed by an English king. The most obvious explanation for this is that it was not in the interests of the crown to do so. In addition, it had in some ways been superseded by the canons of the Fourth Lateran Council, issued in 1215, which included the ruling that any election that came about as a result of the abuse of secular power was automatically rendered invalid.[86] Furthermore, the charter was very much a product of its age – an age in which a trio of extremely forceful men had clashed over a debate which began to change once they were removed from the scene. Both Innocent III and King John died in 1216. Stephen Langton outlived them by over a decade, dying in 1228, and it is unlikely to be a coincidence that the charter received papal reconfirmation in January of that year;[87] the elderly archbishop may well have requested that this be done, in a last attempt to protect the ecclesiastical liberties for which he had fought so hard.[88] But by this stage, on many levels, the crisis had passed; electoral disputes continued, but elections were, for the most part, no longer the political minefield they had been fifteen years earlier.

More specifically, disputes over electoral practice increasingly focused on detailed disagreements over specific elections and the relative rights of the various parties involved, rather than centring on the abstract ideal of electoral freedom. Partly as a result of John's charter, the dispute over exactly how the right of the English Church to free election should be implemented came to an end during the course of the thirteenth century; this rapidly became an established principle accepted by the laity as well as by the clergy. Following John's example, a significant number of monastic patrons, both clerical and lay,

---

84 David Carpenter, *The Minority of Henry III* (London, 1990), p. 23.

85 The Forest Charter, issued alongside the 1217 reissue of Magna Carta, regulated the bounds and administration of the royal forest.

86 *Ecumenical Councils*, I, pp. 246-8 (cc. 23-6).

87 *Concilia Magnae Brittanniae et Hiberniae*, ed. D. Wilkins (4 vols, London, 1737), I, p. 621.

88 The literature on Langton's contribution to Magna Carta is too extensive to cite in full here, but for recent discussions, see John Baldwin, 'Master Stephen Langton, Future Archbishop of Canterbury: The Paris Schools and Magna Carta', *EHR*, 123 (2008), pp. 811-46; Nicholas Vincent, 'Stephen Langton, Archbishop of Canterbury' in Louis-Jacques Bataillon, Nicole Bériou, Gilbert Dahan and Riccardo Quinto (eds), Étienne Langton: Prédicateur, Bibliste, Théologien (Turnhout, 2010), pp. 51-123; David Carpenter, 'Archbishop Langton and Magna Carta: His Contribution, His Doubts and His Hypocrisy', *EHR*, 126 (2011), pp. 1041-65.

made pledges to allow free capitular election.[89] Furthermore, two documents from the early years of Edward I's reign reflect the fact that such practices had become part of English custom. In 1272, a protest against papal intervention in elections was made in the chapel royal at Westminster, in the king's name; it was pointed out that cathedral churches were traditionally filled by 'canonical election', with royal assent.[90] Then, in 1275, the First Statute of Westminster included a clause that threatened 'great men' with forfeiture if they attempted to disrupt an election 'because elections ought to be free'.[91] A hundred years earlier, it would have been unthinkable for a king to talk in such terms, but it had since become unremarkable.

Perhaps as a consequence of this shift in attitudes, some of the worst abuses of royal power – the things that had so enraged the church in the twelfth and very early thirteenth centuries – were no longer practised. Chapters were no longer denied licence to elect, with the consequence that the lengthy vacancies that had occurred under the Angevins – most outrageously at Carlisle, which lacked a bishop for almost fifty years[92] – were a thing of the past. Furthermore, elections were no longer held in the king's chapel, instead taking place away from court in the cathedral chapter of the vacant see.

Of, course, John, Henry III and indeed all subsequent medieval kings of England enjoyed a great deal of influence over episcopal appointments, but this does not mean that the charter was an empty concession with no subsequent importance. Because the king's behaviour was rarely entirely satisfactory to the church, the clergy continued to complain about the conduct of elections. Intriguingly, they never seem to have pressured Henry to reconfirm the charter, but it was intermittently mentioned within the context of such disputes. The fact that it was cited at all indicates that it continued to be valued by the English clergy, as a standard against which royal failings could be measured and condemned. For example, when the bishopric of Hereford fell vacant in 1240, Robert Grosseteste feared that the election would be characterized by 'the oppressive malady of terror, threats, violent intimidation and bribery'. Part of the cure that he suggested to the archbishop of Canterbury was the clear and public exposition of John's charter, and its papal confirmation.[93] Matthew Paris suggests that in 1256, the clergy discussed the charter, but concluded that it was

---

89 Wood, *Monasteries*, pp. 43-9.

90 *CCR 1272-1279*, p. 39.

91 'First Statute of Westminster', c. 5 in *The Statutes of the Realm* (11 vols in 12, London, 1810-28), I, p. 28.

92 1156/7-1203. Paulinus of Leeds was elected in 1186, at the request of Henry II, but refused. Bernard of Ragusa's appointment was probably the result of papal intervention. See *EEA 30: Carlisle, 1133-1192*, ed. D. M. Smith (Oxford, 2005), pp. xxxv-xxxviii, for the exceptional circumstances behind this uniquely long vacancy.

93 *Grosseteste*, pp. 283-5 (letter 83).

of limited value because even the pope took the line that it was not expedient to oppose princes. His negative assessment of its value should probably be balanced against his extremely negative opinion of both popes and princes; he himself copied the papal confirmation into this portion of his chronicle 'on account of the advantages to be derived from an inviolate observance of it',[94] and other English churchmen continued to make use of it. John of Wallingford states that the charter was produced in 1253, during the negotiations leading up to the reconfirmation of Magna Carta.[95] It was mentioned again at the 1257 council of the Canterbury province, which complained that Henry was seeking to control elections in a manner 'contrary to the charter on elections which his father granted',[96] whilst a list of grievances that oppressed the land of England, dating from January 1264, complains that the king frequently deprived the clergy of 'the right of free election which by law they ought to have'.[97]

Even during the fourteenth centuries, as episcopal election was supplanted by papal provision as the dominant, and eventually only, form of episcopal appointment, the charter retained some importance. Copies continued to be made, amongst them a notarial copy of 1305 which survives in the National Archives at Kew, and a copy in the register of Walter Stapeldon, bishop of Exeter under Edward II.[98] Edward II used the charter to defend his rights against the threat of papal provision,[99] and in the reign of Henry IV it was copied onto the close rolls.[100] Even if the charter was initially a declaration of ecclesiastical liberties, in less than a century it had been completely subverted into a prop for royal rights over the English Church.

The Fourth Lateran Council

Promises of electoral freedom such as the one given by John in 1214 were the product of an age in which the papacy was increasingly determined to promote ecclesiastical liberties. This agenda was vigorously pursued by Innocent III, a strongly political pope who was not afraid to address the question of just how

[94] *CM*, V, p. 541.

[95] *Cronica Johannis de Oxenedes*, ed. H. Ellis (RS, 1859), pp. 196-7. The *Chronica Majora*, on which Wallingford's chronicle was based, omits this detail; see *CM*, V, p. 377. For the relationship between the two chronicles, see R. Vaughan, 'The Chronicle of John of Wallingford', *EHR*, 73 (1958), pp. 66-70.

[96] *C&S*, I, pp. 539-40.

[97] *Documents of the Baronial Movement of Reform and Rebellion, 1258-67*, ed. R. F. Treharne and I. J. Sanders (Oxford, 1973), p. 271.

[98] *CLI*, no. 1004.

[99] *Reg. Sede Vacante*, pp. 104-7.

[100] *CCR 1405-1409*, p. 410.

far secular rulers should interfere in the affairs of the Latin Church.[101] His vision for the conduct of episcopal elections was given its clearest and most formal expression in the canons of the Fourth Lateran Council (1215), four of which related to this issue. Innocent attacked lengthy vacancies (which were usually caused by secular rulers); cathedral churches and monasteries were not to remain prelate-less for more than three months, because prolonged vacancies damaged both the church and the souls for which it was responsible. If an election was not held with this limit, the right to appoint devolved upon the 'immediate superior' (in most cases the archbishop of the province), who must do his duty within three months or face canonical penalties.[102] The manner in which an election should be held was set out, with three forms of election being recognized. A chapter might choose their bishop by way of scrutiny (all full members of the chapter vote), by way of compromise (the election is delegated to a small number of electors, and accepted by all) or by way of inspiration (the divinely inspired choice of one candidate is unanimously acclaimed by the chapter). All other forms were prohibited, as were clandestine elections; the outcome should be published as soon as it was known.[103] The council also legislated against the 'abuse of secular power, against canonical freedom'. Elections made through the intervention of a secular power were invalid, and all who participated in such a process were suspended from their benefices and deprived of the right to elect for three years.[104] The last of this group of canons set out the penalties for improperly confirming an election. No election should receive archiepiscopal confirmation before it had been properly examined, in order that no man 'of insufficient learning or dishonest life or unlawful age' be promoted to the episcopate. Those directly subject to the pontiff must obtain their confirmation from him, unless they obtained a papal dispensation not to do so.[105]

The Fourth Lateran Council was not the first time that the conduct of elections had been the subject of formal definition: it had been addressed at the earliest church councils,[106] and the First (1123), Second (1139) and Third (1179) Lateran Councils had all included canons on this subject, which had established key principles such as the supremacy of the greater and wiser part, the need for an election to be held within three months and the qualities

---

101 Jane Sayers, *Innocent III: Leader of Europe, 1198-1216* (London, 1994); John Moore, *Pope Innocent III (1160/61-1216): To Root Up and to Plant* (Turnhout, 2003).

102 *Ecumenical Councils*, I, p. 246 (c. 23).

103 Ibid., I, pp. 246-7 (c. 24).

104 Ibid., I, p. 247 (c. 25). No English cathedral chapter was punished in this manner during the period in question.

105 Ibid., I, pp. 247-8 (c. 26).

106 See above, p. 12.

required to be a bishop.[107] Elections had also been the focus of a great deal of canonical writing.[108] This pattern continued throughout the thirteenth century; new papal rulings on the conduct of elections continued to be made until the process was itself replaced by provision. Nevertheless, the canons of the Fourth Lateran Council were of great importance for the conduct of episcopal elections in England, particularly since they were issued within a year of the Freedom of Election charter. Electors were extremely familiar with both texts; the Lateran clause 24 (*Quia propter*) was routinely read out on the day of an election.[109]

Tracts on the Conduct of Elections

Cathedral chapters derived much of their knowledge of electoral procedure directly from the Fourth Lateran's decrees, which were absorbed into English synodal statutes as well as into the *Liber Extra*.[110] During the thirteenth century, a new source of information emerged: the tract on the conduct of elections. Such tracts were distinguished from earlier works on the subject by their focus on the practical applications of the theory; previous writers had been more concerned by theoretical discussions than by real elections.[111] Three such texts are of particular relevance to the study of English episcopal elections, being produced and/or widely circulated in England.

The earliest English example of such a tract was written by an anonymous Canterbury chronicler, probably in the late 1220s; it is appended to a lengthy account of the disputed Canterbury election of 1228. Entitled *De modo electionis celebrandae*, it discusses how to obtain the licence to elect, how to prepare for the election, the manner in which the three permitted forms of election should be conducted, the possibility of postulation, the proclamation of the election and the production of the decree of election (a statement of election to which all the electors had to subscribe). There is also a list of the qualities that make a candidate unsuitable for promotion to the episcopate.[112] The Canterbury text is relatively brief and there is little evidence for its circulation beyond the cathedral priory in which it seems to have been produced. It is, nevertheless, significant

---

107 *Ecumenical Councils*, I, pp. 190 (Lateran I, c. 3), 203 (Lateran II, c. 28), 212 (Lateran III, c. 3) and 219 (Lateran III, c. 16).

108 Peltzer, *Elections*, pp. 26-56, provides a detailed overview of the evolution of the canon law on elections between c.1130 and c.1230.

109 *Somercote*, p. 31.

110 On the implementation of the Lateran reforms in England, see Gibbs and Lang, *Bishops*, pp. 94-173.

111 *Somercote*, p. 27.

112 *Gervase*, II, pp. 124-6. See below, p. 43.

as the earliest surviving text (in England, if not in Europe) to engage with the complex realities of holding an episcopal election.

The second of the English tracts, written at Chichester by Lawrence of Somercote, is considerably longer, and rather more polished, than its Canterbury counterpart. Somercote was a canon of Chichester and papal subdeacon, and had been in turn a member of the *familia* of Bishops Walter Suffield and Richard Wyche.[113] His tract was completed in June 1254,[114] two months after he had participated in the election of John Climping as bishop of Chichester.[115] Whilst this election had passed without serious difficulty, the previous vacancy in this see had provoked one of the major electoral disputes of Henry III's reign.[116] It is therefore unsurprising that Somercote was awake to the need for a volume that explained 'the method and form of proceeding to an election in reality ... the drawing-up of the decree, and other matters which are called for in affairs of this sort'.

He was greatly concerned to ensure that his text was clear and easy to use, colour-coding the various sections of the treatise (instructions in vermillion, documents in black) and emphasizing that he had composed it for 'the simple convenience' of his readers.[117] The text not only contained detailed instructions for the conduct of elections, from the death of the bishop to the publication of the new election, but also included numerous exemplars of the texts that should be produced, amongst them the petition to the king for licence to elect, the letters sent to absent canons, the decree of election and the letters sent to king, archbishop and (if appropriate) pope to request confirmation of the election. Where necessary, various forms of each letter were included to indicate how they should be modified depending on which form of election is used.[118] That the tract was widely circulated is demonstrated by the fact that there are at least eighteen manuscript copies still in existence, found not only in England, but also across Europe.[119]

Another significant electoral tract was composed by William de Mandagot, archdeacon of Nîmes, and later one of the compilers of the *Liber Sextus*. Writing around three decades after Somercote completed his tract (probably in 1284-85),[120] Mandagot produced a treatise that is longer and rather less user-friendly than the Englishman's tract, for it is far more concerned with abstract problems

---

113 Christopher Lawrence, 'Laurence of Somercotes', *ODNB*.

114 *Somercote*, p. 50.

115 *Fasti 1066-1300, V*, p. 5.

116 *Saint Richard of Chichester: The Sources for His Life*, ed. D. Jones (Lewes, 1995), pp. 95-101.

117 *Somercote*, p. 28.

118 Ibid., pp. 27-50.

119 Ibid., pp. 1-8.

120 Paul Viollet, 'Guillaume de Mandagout, Canoniste' in *Histoire Littéraire de la France* (43 vols, 1733-), XXXIV, p. 25. Viollet provides a detailed summary of the tract at pp. 25-53.

and contains a good deal of glossing of technical terms. Nevertheless, whilst it did not relate directly to the practicalities of holding an election in England, it was also widely circulated, and several English cathedrals possessed a copy.[121]

The Electoral Process

The texts discussed in the previous section (that is, the canon law, royal documents and electoral tracts) can be combined to produce a detailed picture of how a canonical episcopal election should be celebrated during the thirteenth century.

When a bishop died, the first duty of his chapter was to bury him in a suitable manner; there must be no discussion of the election before this was done.[122] After this, however, speed was of the essence, for the chapter had only three months (from the day after the bishop's death) to complete their part in the electoral process; if they failed to elect by this deadline, their right of appointment devolved to the immediate superior (the archbishop or pope).[123] This time limit could only be expanded, stated Mandagot, in a handful of exceptional circumstances. If the chapter wished to elect a candidate who was in some way disqualified, they might need extra time in which to seek the approval of the superior. Alternatively, the chapter's right to elect might be in some way impaired, for example by excommunication or interdict; in such circumstances they might take more than three months to secure the requisite dispensation, in which case they should be allowed extra time. In addition, if an election was quashed due to the unsuitability of the elect, the chapter should be allowed to elect again, even if the three months had passed, providing the faults of the elect had previously been unknown to them.[124]

Before an election could be held, permission must first be obtained from the crown. Messengers chosen from within the chapter should be dispatched to the court, in order to obtain the *congé d'élire* from the king; they should carry with them letters in which the king was formally informed of the bishop's death (in many cases he would already be aware and have taken the temporalities into royal custody)[125] and petitioned for permission to choose his successor. King John, in his charter of 1214, had pledged that he and his successors would not

[121] Copies survive at Lincoln, Hereford, Worcester and Lambeth; there are also several manuscript copies (as well as several early printed versions) in the British Library.

[122] *Somercote*, p. 28; *Mandagot*, c. 1; *Bonae memoriae* (Dec. Greg. IX, *X*, 1.6.36, *CIC*, II, pp. 82-3).

[123] *Ecumenical Councils*, I, p. 246 (Lateran IV, c. 23); *Mandagot*, cc. 1, 3.

[124] *Mandagot*, c. 2.

[125] Howell, *Regalian Right*, p. 62. On at least two occasions mandates for the seizure of the temporalities had to be cancelled because the incumbent, although dying, was not yet dead.

'deny or defer' the licence, but acknowledged that a canonical election might still be held if the licence was refused.[126] The terms of the charter were echoed by the Canterbury chronicler who stated that petition for a licence should be made on up to three consecutive days. If it was still withheld, then the election might proceed regardless.[127]

The licence having been obtained, the monks/canons should assemble to set a time and day for the election to be held,[128] and set about the task of summoning any absent electors. By the early thirteenth century, it was generally assumed that the cathedral chapter was the sole electoral body,[129] and the participation of the *religiosi viri* was extremely atypical, if not yet unheard of. In thirteenth-century England, the right to elect the archbishops of Canterbury and York, and the fifteen bishops who were their immediate subordinates, belonged to the cathedral chapter of their respective sees. Almost uniquely in medieval Europe, the electors included regular clergy as well as secular canons, for over half of these chapters consisted of monks, primarily members of the Benedictine order.[130] In two dioceses, Coventry and Lichfield and Bath and Wells, the right of election was shared by two chapters, one secular and one monastic; the arrangement of an election in these dioceses was thus complicated by the need to arrange the presence of two chapters in one place. At Bath and Wells, elections were held in the former city,[131] but at Coventry and Lichfield elections were supposed to alternate between the two cathedrals.[132]

Even once the right to elect had been firmly confined to the members of the cathedral chapter, there was still some debate over the exact composition of the electoral body. Consequently, each of the tracts considers in detail who should be allowed to participate in the election, and the methods by which they should be summoned. All fully professed members of the chapter had the right to participate in the election,[133] and indeed must do so unless they were prevented

126 *C&S*, I, pp. 40-41.

127 *Somercote*, p. 28; *Gervase*, II, p. 124. Mandagot makes no mention of the need for royal licence, probably because the process was not universal in late thirteenth-century France and appears to have been uncommon in Nîmes. Viollet, 'Mandagout', p. 51.

128 *Somercote*, p. 29; *Mandagot*, c. 4.

129 *Ecumenical Councils*, I, pp. 246-7 (c. 24).

130 The monastic convents were Bath, Canterbury, Carlisle, Coventry, Durham, Ely, Norwich, Rochester, Winchester and Worcester; all were Benedictine houses, with the exception of Carlisle, which belonged to the order of the Augustinian canons. The chapters at Chichester, Exeter, Hereford, Lichfield, Lincoln, London, Salisbury, Wells and York consisted of secular canons.

131 *CPL*, I, p. 208; *Wells MSS.*, I, pp. 110-11.

132 *Fasti 1066-1300*, XI, pp. xxxviii-xxxix.

133 *Ex eo* (*Sext.* 1.6.32, *CIC*, II, p. 964). Benedictines were supposed to serve a novitiate of at least a year before they could be professed as monks; after this they were referred to as novices, or juniors, until they received priestly orders. Given that profession made a brother eligible for active participation in the daily chapter meetings, it seems likely that he would also be allowed to participate in elections,

from being present by reasonable grounds (such as serious illness or overseas travel).[134] It was not necessary to cite those who were excommunicate, under interdict or suspended to participate, since they were automatically excluded from participation in elections.[135] Boy canons (*impuberes canonici*)[136] and novice monks[137] should usually be excluded,[138] whilst those of unsound mind should participate only if they were enjoying a lucid period at the time of the election.[139] It seems to have been generally accepted that those monks/canons that were overseas should not be summoned;[140] the infirm might be excluded,[141] although Mandagot considers the possibility that, in certain circumstances, proctors might be sent to the sick beds of electors resident in the city in order to obtain their votes.[142] Both Somercote and Mandagot insist on the need for the summons of the absent canons to be done publicly, and recorded in writing, in order that the absentees could not subsequently claim that they had been excluded from the

even before he took orders. See Joan Greatrex, *English Benedictine Cathedral Priories*, pp. 83-8; the inference is mine.

134 *Bonae memoriae* (*X*, 1.6.36, *CIC*, II, pp. 82-3); *In Genesi* (*X*, 1.6.55, *CIC*, II, pp. 94-5).

135 *Mandagot*, c. 6.

136 Boy canons (that is, canons who had not reached the canonical age for holy orders; it was usually necessary for a man to reach 21, the age at which he could be ordained a subdeacon, before being instituted to a cathedral prebend) were a relatively rare phenomenon in England. The best-known example is George Neville (b.1432), who received the prebend of Chardstock (Salisbury) in 1442 and the extremely wealthy prebend of Masham (York) four years later. His appointment was regularized by a papal dispensation of 1447, which allowed him to hold both benefices 'notwithstanding his defect of age'. He did not become a subdeacon until 1453, and was ordained priest the following year; in 1456, still aged only 24, he was provided to the bishopric of Exeter. Neville's was an exceptional case, but the statutes of both Salisbury and Wells made provision for the seating of the boy canons in the cathedral stalls. For Neville, see Michael Hicks, 'George Neville', *ODNB*; for his dispensation see *CPL*, X, pp. 2, 110. For the seating of boy canons, see *Statutes and Customs of the Cathedral Church of the Blessed Virgin Mary of Salisbury*, ed. C. Wordsworth and D. Macleane (London, 1915), p. 64, and *Wells Cathedral: Its Foundation, Constitutional History, and Statutes*, ed. H. Reynolds (Leeds, 1881), p. 1. On boy canons and the requirements for institution to a cathedral prebend, see Lepine, *Brotherhood of Canons*, pp. 66-72; Edwards, *Secular Cathedrals*, pp. 34-5, 307; Julia Barrow, 'Grades of Ordination and Clerical Careers, c.900-c.1200', *Anglo-Norman Studies*, 30 (2008), pp. 41-61, especially p. 49.

137 Three thirteenth-century chapters of the English Black Monks (in 1219, 1221 and 1278) ruled that the minimum age for entry to a Benedictine house should be fixed at 18; although a few monks are known to have entered one of the cathedral priories at the age of 16 or 17, it seems that this rule was widely adhered to. A year's novitiate followed before the prospective monk made his profession (see Greatrex, *English Benedictine Cathedral Priories*, p. 53). Theoretically, then, in the monastic chapters participation in the electoral process was limited to those who had passed their nineteenth birthday.

138 *Mandagot*, cc. 7-8.

139 Ibid., c. 7.

140 *Gervase*, II, p. 124; *Somercote*, p. 29.

141 *Gervase*, II, p. 124.

142 *Mandagot*, c. 25.

election, which was consequently invalid.[143] If a canon proved difficult to find, Mandagot also allowed for the summons to be made by *edictum publicum* (that is, by crier), either in the church or in his usual place of residence.[144]

Any elector who received a summons but could not be present due to a 'lawful impediment' on the day set for the election was obliged to inform his superior (the abbot or dean) of his absence, and appoint a proctor to vote in his place.[145] This proctor must be a member of the chapter and beyond reproach (*persona talis quae de jure alias non valeat reprobari*).[146] Unless the chapter saw fit to dispense with the formality, the proctor would be required to swear an oath, truthfully and in good faith, that the absentee was too far away to return and engaged on important business (giving details of both), and that this explanation remained true at the time of the election.[147] Typically, the proctor would be endowed with the power to assent to whichever form of election was chosen, and to make another choice if the absentee's favoured candidate was found to be ineligible.[148]

In the interim between the initial meeting and the day of election, the electors must prepare themselves by observing a solemn fast.[149] The day named for the election dawning, the electoral process must begin, providing a majority of the electors were present. Election by a minority of the chapter would be considered invalid, unless it took place at the very end of the three-month time limit.[150] If sufficient electors were present, they should assemble in the church where, before the celebration of the election could begin, the mass should be celebrated. This should be followed by the singing of the hymn *Veni creator spiritus*, invoking the Holy Spirit; the prayer *Deus qui corda fidelium* should also be recited.[151] Afterwards, the electors should withdraw (usually to the chapter house), with all other parties being excluded.[152] However, if possible, a scribe should be present to keep a record of the process of the election; he must be a *clericus*, for the laity should not concern themselves with ecclesiastical business,

---

143 *Somercote*, pp. 29-30; *Mandagot*, c. 4, f. 1-2, 4.

144 *Mandagot*, c. 5.

145 *Ecumenical Councils*, I, pp. 246-7 (c. 24); *Somercote*, p. 30.

146 *Mandagot*, c. 10.

147 Ibid., cc. 11-12.

148 Ibid., cc. 14-15.

149 *Gervase*, II, p. 125.

150 *Auditis et* (*X*, 1.6.29, *CIC*, II, p. 74); *Mandagot*, cc. 16-17.

151 *Somercote*, p. 30.

152 Ibid.; *Mandagot*, c. 20, discusses the possibility that it may be impossible to exclude the intruders, in which case the electors must protest (secretly, if necessary). The intruders should be prevented from voting, or their votes must be discounted.

and should ideally be learned in the law. If such a man could not be found, he might be replaced by two 'suitable men who can write everything down'.[153]

Once the appropriate parties were assembled, even more preliminaries had to be observed: a sermon was preached, the letters of the absent canons read aloud and the constitution *Quia propter* recited.[154] The electors then had to decide which form of election they wished to observe.[155] *Quia propter* (clause 24 of the Fourth Lateran Council) allowed three forms of election: by divine inspiration, by way of compromise and by way of scrutiny. Elections held by any other method would be judged invalid,[156] and each of the authors discussed the correct procedure for each form at considerable length in their respective tracts.

There was some dispute regarding whether election by way of inspiration was actually a form at all; Somercote thought that it was 'an exception to the forms', but since the Holy Spirit was the agent of the process, the way of inspiration had 'the first place in elections'.[157] Whilst the Fourth Lateran Council referred to election *quasi per inspirationem divinam*,[158] commentators typically dropped the 'quasi' and instead referred to 'inspiration', endowing such elections with a supernatural quality.[159] William de Mandagot described election by way of inspiration as follows:

> An election is said to be celebrated by inspiration when everyone, all at once, suddenly, unexpectedly and unanimously elects someone, with one voice, with no previous discussion, and no human incitement having preceded this.[160]

Election by divine inspiration required one of the electors, usually the most senior member of the chapter, to announce, in words similar to the following: 'Dearly beloved, we are assembled here in the name of Jesus to elect a bishop. It seems to me that our canon N. may be deservedly chosen as bishop.' Every member of the chapter must then acclaim the election as one, calling out their consent together. Individual consent was not sought, and indeed should not be given, or else the election was rendered invalid. For this form of election to be judged canonically sound, it was essential that the whole chapter agreed on the choice; an election by divine inspiration was invalidated by the dissent of a

153 *Quoniam* (*X*, 2.19.2, *CIC*, II, pp. 306-7); *Mandagot*, c. 19.

154 *Somercote*, pp. 30-31.

155 *Gervase*, II, p. 125.

156 *Ecumenical Councils*, I, p. 246.

157 *Somercote*, p. 31.

158 *Ecumenical Councils*, I, p. 246 (c. 24).

159 *Mandagot*, c. 52; Viollet, 'Mandagout', p. 47.

160 *Mandagot*, c. 52.

single elector.[161] It was also deemed invalid if it had been preceded by any form of discussion.[162]

Alternatively, the electors could choose to proceed by way of scrutiny – a form riddled with dangers, since any small flaw in the process would render it invalid.[163] In this form of election, three trustworthy members of the chapter were chosen; it was their job to 'diligently find out, in confidence and individually, the opinions of everybody'.[164] The three scrutineers should withdraw from the main assembly, either to a corner of the chapter house or into another room altogether.[165] According to Somercote, they should cast their own votes first; this was not required by canon law, but removed suspicion that their choice might by influenced by the votes of their fellow electors.[166] Each member of the chapter should then be summoned in turn, according to his rank within the chapter, and asked, in the name of the Trinity and with consideration for his soul, to name his choice for the bishopric; he should put aside 'all hate and worldly love and human influence' and name the man whom he considered most useful to the church and most fit for episcopal office.[167] Each vote must be firm and unconditional,[168] and could not be withdrawn, unless the candidate was subsequently found to be disqualified.[169] Anyone who knowingly voted for an unsuitable candidate would be deprived of all benefices for three years.[170] As soon as the elector had made his choice, one of the scrutineers (or the scribe who was assisting them) was to record both the namer and the named on a roll.[171] The votes having been cast and counted, the next stage of the process must begin without delay.[172] The electors should immediately reassemble and the votes be read out: this was the *publicatio*.[173] Opinions varied as to what should happen in the unlikely event that only a single candidate had been named. Somercote through that his election should be proclaimed, without any further examination of the votes.[174]

---

161 *Somercote*, pp. 31-2; *Gervase*, II, p. 125.

162 *Mandagot*, c. 52.

163 *Mandagot*, c. 22; *Somercote*, p. 40.

164 *Ecumenical Councils*, I, p. 246 (c. 24).

165 *Somercote*, p. 41; *Gervase*, II, p. 125; *Mandagot*, c. 23.

166 *Somercote*, p. 41.

167 *Somercote*, p. 42; *Mandagot*, c. 23.

168 *Ecumenical Councils*, I, p. 285 (c. 5); *Mandagot*, c. 26.

169 *Nulli licere* (*Sext.* 1.6.8, *CIC*, II, pp. 950-51).

170 *Mandagot*, c. 27. This penalty could clearly not be applied to monastic electors but Mandagot, writing with a secular audience in mind, did not specify the punishment for errant monks.

171 *Mandagot*, c. 28; *Somercote*, p. 41.

172 *Quum post* (*X*, 1.6.46, *CIC*, II, p. 90).

173 *Mandagot*, c. 30.

174 *Somercote*, p. 43.

Bernard of Compostella[175] agreed with the Chichester tract, whereas Mandagot, along with Hostiensis,[176] thought that there should be a *collatio* even if the vote was unanimous.[177] If the vote was divided, the need for a comparison was unquestioned. This process involved the further examination of the votes, which must be collated according to number, zeal (of electors, linked to age, office and wisdom) and merit (of candidates).[178] Number was crucial since the validity of the election depended on the elect being the choice of the majority.[179] Johannes Andreae (c.1270/5-1348), whose tract on elections drew heavily on Mandagot's work, suggested that this tally should be done by sending the supporters of each candidate to a different corner of the room. If their numbers matched the numbers on the election roll, the first part of the *collatio* could be considered complete.[180]

Counting the number of votes was a relatively straightforward process; measuring the zeal (*zelus*) and merits of the electors and the elect was far more complex. The zeal (or fervour) of the electors was dependent on their age, wisdom and rank,[181] whilst the merit of the candidates was determined by a comparison of their strengths and weaknesses.[182] Such a comparison was inevitably subjective and, since the canon law allowed for the choice of the *maior vel sanior pars* to be upheld,[183] the majority often found themselves being

---

175 Bernard of Compostella the younger was a canonist and papal chaplain active between 1245 and 1267. See Geoffrey Barraclough, 'Bernard of Compostella', *EHR*, 49 (1934), pp. 487-94.

176 Hostiensis (c.1200-71), otherwise known as Henry de Susa, was one of the most prominent canonists of the thirteenth century. Having taught canon law in Paris, he ascended through the ranks of the church and ended his career as cardinal-bishop of Ostia. His involvement in the Winchester electoral dispute of the early 1240s will be discussed below. For an overview of his career, see Kenneth Pennington, 'Henricus de Segusio (Hostiensis)' in his *Popes, Canonists and Texts, 1150-1550* (Aldershot, 1993), XVI.

177 *Mandagot*, c. 32; Viollet, 'Mandagout', p. 37.

178 *Somercote*, pp. 41-4; *Gervase*, II, pp. 125-6; *Ecclesia vestra* (*X*, 1.6.48, *CIC*, II, p. 91); Gaudemet, *Gouvernement*, p. 65.

179 *Ecumenical Councils*, I, p. 246 (c. 24).

180 Viollet, 'Mandagout', pp. 35-6.

181 Gaudemet, *Gouvernement*, p. 65.

182 *Somercote*, p. 44.

183 *Ecumenical Councils*, I, p. 246 (c. 24). Given that unanimity in elections is rare, it is unsurprising that the acceptability of the majority choice was established very early, at the Council of Nicea (325): *Ecumenical Councils*, I, p. 9 (c. 6). *Sanioritas* (moral superiority) was also mentioned in connection with episcopal elections throughout the early Middle Ages, and in clause 64 of the Rule of St Benedict, on the election of the abbot: *The Rule of Saint Benedict in Latin and in English*, ed. J. McCann (Tunbridge Wells, 1952), pp. 144-7. However, it was only with the advent of the Gregorian reform movement that the idea of combining the two qualities to determine the outcome of elections was seriously explored in canonical writings, and only at the Third Lateran Council (1179) that the phrase 'maiori et seniori parte' entered canon law: *Ecumenical Councils*, I, p. 219 (c. 16). See Peltzer, *Elections*, pp. 41-8; Robert Helmholz, *The Spirit of Classical Canon Law* (Athens, Ga., 1996), pp. 52-5.

challenged by a self-identified *sanior pars*. Many elections conducted by way of scrutiny were subsequently quashed because there was no clear outcome to the process.[184] If, however, the *collatio* was satisfactorily completed, the result of the election should be proclaimed to the electors by one of their number, as follows:

> I, N., on my own behalf and on the behalf and on the instructions of all who have agreed upon Master N. of such a place, and have named him in the scrutiny, elect the same Master N. as bishop of Chichester.

If this communal election was not completed, then the election was deemed to be invalid.[185]

The third form of election permitted by the Fourth Lateran Council was election by way of compromise, in which 'the power of electing shall be committed to some suitable persons who, acting on behalf of everybody, shall provide the bereaved church with a pastor'.[186] This form could be chosen only with the unanimous assent of the whole chapter.[187] The compromisers (the members of the chapter to whom the power to elect was delegated) must also be picked unanimously;[188] once appointed, these men could not delegate their task any further.[189] An odd number of delegates must be appointed, and their names immediately recorded in a letter to which was attached the seal of the chapter.[190] Mandagot noted that, unless a time limit was placed on the delegates' powers, their authority remained in force until the three-month deadline was complete; he therefore recommended that a shorter time limit should be set, so that the election could proceed by a different method if the compromisers failed to make a choice.[191]

The compromisers should withdraw to a private place in order to discuss the election,[192] whilst the rest of the chapter remained together and prayed. It was not permissible for the compromisers to be instructed to elect a particular individual.[193] Instead, every member of the chapter must be discussed, including each member of the committee;[194] it was presumably also permissible to consider

184 *Gervase*, II, p. 126.

185 *Somercote*, p. 44; *Mandagot*, c. 34; *Gervase*, II, p. 125.

186 *Ecumenical Councils*, I, p. 246.

187 *Mandagot*, c. 39.

188 Ibid.

189 Ibid., c. 44.

190 *Somercote*, pp. 36-7.

191 *Mandagot*, c. 43.

192 *In causis* (*X*, 1.6.30, *CIC*, II, pp. 74-6).

193 *Mandagot*, c. 45.

194 *Somercote*, p. 37; *Mandagot*, c. 48.

external candidates at this stage. Once discussions began, they must not be stopped.[195] The content of these discussions must not be disclosed, under penalty of anathema, for fear of causing offence or damage to the reputation of another chapter member.[196] The delegates were required to elect by an absolute majority (that is, two-thirds or more);[197] the only exception to this rule was made if three of a committee of seven elected a fourth member, in which case their minority vote was allowed to stand.[198] Once made, their choice must be committed to writing and announced to the assembled electors.[199] Although Mandagot's tract considers whether a compromise could be revoked, and decides that that this might occasionally be done, the canon law stated quite clearly that the electors were bound to accept the choice made by the compromisers.[200]

Whichever of these three forms was chosen, the election should then proceed in the following fashion. The process must be recorded in writing; the resultant text, the decree of the election, had to be couched in very specific terms and signed by each of the electors. The consent of the bishop-elect should be sought, assuming he was present. The chant *Te deum laudamus* would then be sung. If the elect was present, he would be led to the altar, before which he should prostrate himself. This having been done, the doors were opened and the election was announced to the clergy and people of the diocese.[201]

The bishop-elect's new flock were not the only people to whom his election must be announced. If the elect was not a member of the cathedral chapter, it was possible that he did not yet know of his election. It was forbidden for his assent to be sought before the election was made, since this would lead to claims of ambition and unworthiness, and render the choice invalid,[202] but once the election was complete, the elect must be notified within eight days. Failure to comply with this rule could lead to the electors being deprived of their benefices.[203] The elect then had a month to decide whether to accept the promotion offered to him.[204] He was obliged to refuse if the election had been brought about by secular interference, if he was ineligible[205] or if he had already

195 *In causis* (*X*, 1.6.30, *CIC*, II, pp. 74-6).

196 *Somercote*, p. 37.

197 *Mandagot*, c. 46.

198 *Quum dilectus* (*X*, 1.6.32, *CIC*, II, pp. 77-9).

199 *Somercote*, pp. 37-8.

200 *Quum dilectus* (*X*, 1.6.32, *CIC*, II, pp. 77-9).

201 *Somercote*, pp. 32-3, 38-9, 44; *Mandagot*, cc. 35, 51; *Ecumenical Councils*, I, p. 247 (c. 24).

202 *Somercote*, p. 33; *Mandagot*, c. 36.

203 *Cupientes ecclesiarum* (*Sext.* 1.6.16, *CIC*, II, pp. 954-5); *Mandagot*, c. 36. Such a punishment could only be applied in the case of secular canons; it is unclear whether there was an equivalent punishment for monastic electors.

204 *Mandagot*, c. 37.

205 *Quisquis electionum* (*X*, 1.6.43, *CIC*, II, p. 89).

consented to another election.[206] Even if the bishop-elect intended to accept, it was customary for him to protest his unworthiness (*nolo episcopari*), although such protestations must not be too extreme, for this was in itself 'a kind of folly'.[207]

It was also necessary to obtain the assent of both the king (as stated in the Freedom of Election charter)[208] and the elect's immediate superior (the archbishop of the province or, in the case of an archbishop, the pope) to the election. Much of Somercote's tract is taken up with examples of the letters that should be sent to these authorities. These letters would be carried to the king and the archbishop by proctors of the cathedral chapter, usually drawn from amongst their number. These proctors would also carry with them copies of the decree of election, signed by every member of the chapter, in which the process of the election was outlined.[209]

Most episcopal elections went unchallenged and were examined and confirmed by the relevant archbishop.[210] (Archiepiscopal elections were the only exception to this rule; they were routinely confirmed by the pope, since he was the immediate superior.)[211] The bishop-elect was obliged to seek confirmation from his metropolitan within three months of consenting to his election.[212] In England it was usual for the king, having given his assent to the election, to send immediately a writ to the archbishop notifying him of this, and requiring him to 'do his part'[213] – that is, to proceed to examination and confirmation. The archbishop should be presented with this letter, along with the documentation of the election, including the decree.[214] By the early fourteenth century, if not before, the archbishop would summon all those who opposed an election into his presence to explain their objections as part of the examination process.[215] The examination was usually conducted by the archbishop in person although, if he

---

206 *Ut quis duas electiones* (*Sext.* 1.6.25, *CIC*, II, p. 962).

207 *Life of St Edmund*, pp. 47-8, 130.

208 *C&S*, I, pp. 40-41.

209 *Somercote*, pp. 33-6.

210 For the development of the confirmation process throughout the Middle Ages, see Véronique Julerot, 'La Confirmation des Élections Épiscopales à la Fin du Moyen Âge: Origine et Enjeux', *Revue Historique de Droit Français et Étranger*, 81 (2003), pp. 173-94.

211 *Reg. St Osmund*, II, pp. 110-16, describes the examination and confirmation of an election at Rome.

212 *Quam sit ecclesiis* (*X*, 1.6.6, *CIC*, II, p. 950).

213 *CPR 1247-1258*, p. 559.

214 Churchill, *Administration*, I, p. 245.

215 For an example of such a summons, relating to the 1305 Chichester election, see *Reg. Winchelsey*, II, p. 801.

was detained on other business, he might delegate this duty to a small group of senior churchmen.[216]

The confirmation typically took place in a church and opened with the proctor of the chapter presenting the elect and his election to the archbishop. A public exposition of the form of the election and the reading of the decree of election would follow, before the proctor requested the archbishop to examine and confirm the election.[217] The examination covered both the process of the election and the suitability of the elect. No detailed narrative of an archiepiscopal examination survives, but it is possible to reconstruct the process from other sources. Robert Bingham was elected as bishop of Salisbury in 1228, following the translation of Richard Poore from Salisbury to Durham. Since the archbishopric of Canterbury was then vacant, Bingham's election was examined at Rome, and an account of the examination has survived. The cardinals (wrote the capitular proctors):

> Examined us on the process and form of the election, and very keenly and searchingly of the place, the time and of all the other circumstances; what time had passed, namely between the time of the translation and the election ... how many canons were in the church, and what number took part in person, and of those who had been sought, whether they had excused themselves, whether their wishes had been entrusted to others of the chapter, and whether we had letters of excuse as of commission. Thus it went on so that we almost despaired, because it seemed to us that we pressed on to no other end than that they might overturn it. [218]

That such searching questioning was not unusual is suggested by the lists of the questions to be asked during the examination of an abbatial election, which survive in the records of St Albans Abbey and Ramsey Abbey.[219]

The investigation into the suitability of the bishop-elect was equally probing. It was necessary for the archbishop to examine in detail the candidate's life prior to his election,[220] and he could seek information about him in his former place of residence if this was considered necessary.[221] Canon 26 of the Fourth Lateran Council (1215), which set out the penalty for improperly confirming an election, stated that anyone who confirmed the election of 'a man of insufficient learning

[216] Churchill, *Administration*, I, p. 245; *The Register of Walter Bronescombe*, ed. O. F. Robinson (3 vols, Woodbridge, 1995-2003), I, p. 3.

[217] *Reg. Winchelsey*, II, p. 702; Scotney, 'Theory and Practice of Appointments', p. 67.

[218] *Reg. St Osmund*, II, p. 115.

[219] *Cartularium Monasterii de Rameseia*, ed. W. Hart and P. Lyons (3 vols, RS, 1884-93), II, pp. 39-40; *Gesta Abbatum Monasterii Sancti Albani*, ed. H. T. Riley (3 vols, RS, 1867-69), II, pp. 9-12.

[220] *C&S*, II, p. 779 (Constutions of the Legate Otto, c. 31).

[221] *Postquam* (*X*, 1.6.3, *CIC*, II, p. 49).

or dishonest life or unlawful age' should be punished.[222] In practice, the range of qualities that made a man unfit for episcopal office was much wider than this ruling suggests. The Canterbury chronicler's tract on the conduct of elections included a passage on the characteristics that made a candidate unsuitable:

> We should take care not to elect anyone reprehensible, that is he should not be guilty of any crime, or even of any infamous fault, either before entry nor afterwards, nor be illegitimate nor of low birth, because this provokes the king and so perhaps the court, nor should he be of servile condition, nor by trustworthy accounts can he be alleged to be an enemy of or even suspected by the king, nor can he be noted for avarice, nor in the same manner simple.[223]

An elect who was illegitimate or pluralist would be required to produce a valid dispensation to prove his suitability for office,[224] whilst any elect might find himself being asked detailed theological questions; if his answers were unsatisfactory, his election would be quashed, as Robert Passelewe discovered to his cost.[225] Inquiries were also made about the conduct of the elect during the period between the election and the examination, since canon law forbade him to interfere in the administration of his diocese.[226] The law on this issue was tightened even further in 1274, when the elect was forbidden to assume the title of administrator or procurator of his diocese in order to meddle in its business.[227]

If the archbishop was satisfied that both the elect and the election were sound, he should then proceed to the confirmation of the election. This was done publicly, almost always on the same day as the examination (which might suggest that the process was not always as rigorous as in Robert Bingham's case), and triggered another flurry of document production. Notification of the confirmation was sent to the newly confirmed bishop, and mandates to obey him were dispatched to his chapter, and to the clergy and people of his diocese. Letters were also sent to the keeper of the spiritualities,[228] ordering that they be released to the bishop, and also to the king, requesting that he issue a similar mandate to the keeper of the temporalities.[229] Medieval commentators often

---

222 *Ecumenical Councils*, I, pp. 247-8 (c. 26).

223 *Gervase*, II, p. 127. Mandagot's tract includes a similar list, c. xxviii.

224 *C&S*, II, p. 779.

225 *CM*, IV, p. 401; *Saint Richard*, p. 172.

226 *Qualiter post* (*X*, 1.6.17, *CIC*, II, p. 58); *Cartularium*, II, p. 40; *Gesta Abbatum*, II, p. 12; Robert Benson, *The Bishop-Elect* (Princeton, 1960), pp. 108-15.

227 *Avaritiae caecitas* (*Sext.* 1.6.5, *CIC*, II, pp. 949-50).

228 The archiepiscopal official who during an episcopal vacancy controlled revenues (such as tithes and offerings) that could only be received by a clergyman.

229 *Reg. Winchelsey*, pp. 803-4.

talked of the election process as a form of marriage;[230] according to Bernard of Compostella the elder (writing in the first decade of the thirteenth century) the examination of a bishop was equivalent to the consummation of a marriage. Consequently, from this point forwards the election was considered irreversible except by papal mandate.[231]

However, the bishop-making process was not yet complete. The temporalities would be restored only when the new bishop had received archiepiscopal confirmation and taken an oath of fealty to the crown. Preparations should then begin for the consecration ceremony, a very public occasion at which the archbishop officiated, unless unable to do so due to illness or another substantial reason.[232] The suffragan bishops also had the right to participate.[233] In the southern province, the ceremony usually took place at Canterbury, since licence had to be obtained from the prior and chapter of the cathedral priory for an episcopal consecration to take place elsewhere.[234] In the northern province, on the other hand, a substantial number of consecrations were held away from York: at least two of the thirteenth-century bishops of Carlisle were consecrated at Easby Abbey, near Richmond,[235] whilst Anthony Bek, bishop of Durham (1283-1311), was consecrated in his own cathedral.[236] In exceptional circumstances, a northern bishop might even be consecrated in the southern province: in 1258, Robert de Chaury of Carlisle was consecrated at Bermondsey, with the bishops of Salisbury and Bath officiating.[237] If an election was confirmed at Rome, the consecration ceremony might be performed there. Throughout the thirteenth century, the new bishop would make a profession of obedience to the archbishop at the time of the consecration; initially this simply consisted of a promise to obey the metropolitan, but Boniface of Savoy added a pledge to defend the rights of Canterbury.[238]

---

230 For a recent examination of the development of this theory, see Megan McLaughlin, *Sex, Gender and Episcopal Authority in an Age of Reform, 1000-1122* (Cambridge, 2010), pp. 16-91.

231 Julerot, 'Confirmation', pp. 174-5.

232 Gaudemet, *Gouvernement*, p. 67; R. Brentano, *York Metropolitan Jurisdiction and Papal Judges Delegate (1279-1296)* (Berkeley, 1959), pp. 4-8.

233 Scotney, 'Theory and Practice of Appointments', p. 75; see *Reg. Winchelsey*, II, pp. 1113-14, for letters summoning the suffragans to the consecrations of the bishops of Bangor and Bath and Wells.

234 Churchill, *Administration*, I, pp. 273-5.

235 Silvester Everdon (in 1247) and Thomas Vipont (in 1255); see *Chronicon de Lanercost, 1201-46*, ed. J. Stevenson (Edinburgh, 1839), pp. 53, 62.

236 *AM*, IV, p. 295.

237 *CM*, V, p. 588. Chaury's election had been opposed by Sewal de Boville, archbishop of York, but received papal confirmation. Given that Boville died less than a month later (*AM*, IV, p. 18), he may well have been ill at the time of the consecration, which would explain why there was apparently no protest from York at such an affront to the archiepiscopal rights.

238 Scotney, 'Theory and Practice of Appointments', pp. 77-8.

The final stage of the appointment process was the formal entry of the bishop into his cathedral city and his enthronement in the cathedral. In the southern province, the enthronement was almost always performed by the archdeacon of Canterbury, whose right to do so was based on centuries-old custom.[239] The bishop displayed his humility by performing the *adventus* barefoot,[240] but the day also included feasting and other displays of wealth and power. Thus the creation of the new bishop was completed.

Variations in the Electoral Process

A large number of English episcopal elections during this period passed off without difficulty, following the procedures outlined above. Yet despite, or perhaps because of, the fact that knowledge of how to hold a canonically sound election was widespread, the electoral process was subject to frequent complications; these were usually resolved by the involvement of a higher authority: the papacy. During the thirteenth century, there were three standard reasons for papal intervention in English episcopal appointments: the election of an archbishop, the postulation of a bishop and the making of an appeal. In contrast to the fourteenth century, when papal management of appointments became strongly proactive, each of these sets of circumstances required the pope to act in a primarily reactive fashion, and he would not intervene in the bishop-making process unless circumstances demanded that he do so.

As noted above, episcopal elections were examined and confirmed by the metropolitan of the relevant diocese, since he was the immediate superior of the newly elected bishop. However, the immediate superior of the English archbishops was the pope, and consequently archbishops-elect were expected to appear before the pontiff in person. Only if he judged the elect fit for office, and there was no canonical impediment to his promotion, might the new archbishop 'finally enter into the fullness of his office'. If the elect was unable to attend in person, he might send proctors, who would be interrogated about the process of the election and about the elect. Specific provision was also made for those 'who are in very distant parts, namely outside Italy', a criterion which would clearly apply to English candidates for the episcopate; they might seek a special dispensation, 'on account of the need and benefit of the churches', to administer both the spiritualities and temporalities, and to receive consecration,

239 Churchill, *Administration*, I, p. 276.

240 J. Maciejewski, '*Nudo Pede Intrat Urbem*: Research on the *Adventus* of a Medieval Bishop through the First Half of the Twelfth Century', *Viator*, 41 (2010), pp. 89-100.

without travelling to Rome.[241] If such a dispensation were obtained, the new archbishop would be consecrated by one or more of his suffragan bishops.

Archiepiscopal elections were not the only appointments that required papal involvement as a matter of course. Each of the three standard forms of election might also be used in order to make a postulation, which was necessary if the chapter wished to appoint an individual who was in some way ineligible and whose appointment thus required papal approval. Lawrence of Somercote listed five cases in which a postulation must be made: if a consecrated bishop was requested by another see, if a confirmed (but as yet unconsecrated) bishop was requested by another see, if the candidate was in minor orders, if he was underage or if he was illegitimate.[242] The translation of bishops between sees could be performed only by the papacy.[243] Election was considered preferable to postulation. Consequently, if both an election and a postulation were made, the latter was to be preferred only if the number of postulators was double the number of electors and the postulate was considered suitable.[244] In the case of a postulation, proctors might also carry letters to Rome, in order to seek papal confirmation of their choice.[245]

Another reason for deviations from the standard electoral process described above was the possibility of an appeal being made against the election. Neither of the English tract-writers discussed the potential for such difficulties, although they are alluded to in frequent references to certain procedures being 'dangerous', whilst Mandagot covered it only briefly. Appeals were usually made by one of two parties. Objections to an election might be made by a member or members of the electoral body, particularly by those who believed that their electoral rights had been slighted. The Freedom of Election charter allowed the king to withhold his consent (and thus, implicitly, to launch an appeal), if he could find grounds to 'propose reasonably, and prove legitimately, on account of which we ought not to consent'.[246] Such appeals must be based on reasonable objections either to the manner in which the election had been held or to the candidate elected. Throughout the thirteenth century, the majority of appeals were handled in Rome, where they would be examined by the pope (or by his representatives, either in Rome or in England). In 1257, Alexander IV ruled that any disputed episcopal election was a *causa major* and was thus automatically

241 *Ecumenical Councils*, I, pp. 247-8 (Lateran IV, c. 26).

242 *Somercote*, p. 46; *Mandagot*, cc. 53-4.

243 This rule was included in the *Dictatus papae* of Pope Gregory VII: *Das Register Gregors VII*, ed. E. Caspar, 2 vols in 1 (Berlin: Weidmannsche Buchhandlung, 1920-23), pp. 202-8 (c. 13). On the development of translation, see Kenneth Pennington, *Pope and Bishops: A Study of Papal Monarchy in the Twelfth and Thirteenth Centuries* (Philadelphia, 1984), pp. 85-100.

244 *Scriptum est* (*X*, 1.6.40, *CIC*, II, pp. 84-8); *Gervase*, II, p. 126.

245 *Somercote*, pp. 47-8.

246 *C&S*, II, pp. 40-41.

subject to papal jurisdiction. The decree was short-lived; it produced such a flood of appeals that it was modified by clause nine of the Second Council of Lyons in 1274, which ruled that only formal written appeals based on legitimate reasons should be considered.[247] Nevertheless, Mandagot's discussion of appeals assumed that objections would be dealt with in Rome.[248] In such circumstances, the elect must depart for Rome within a month of giving his assent to the election, taking with him all the relevant documentation (including the decree of election) to seek papal confirmation. If he arrived at the curia more than twenty days after he could reasonably be expected, he was deemed to have forfeited his rights. Moreover, the electors and their opponents (or the proctors of each) must also go to Rome.[249] The circumstances of the election and the suitability of the elect would be examined and the election either confirmed or quashed. In the first half of the century the papal quashing of an election would usually be accompanied by a mandate to re-elect; from the 1260s onwards, it became increasingly common for a provision to be made in such circumstances.

***

By the time of Henry III's accession to the throne in 1216, the principle of free episcopal election by cathedral chapters was well established in both canon and secular law, and widely acknowledged by those who were entitled to participate in elections. As a consequence, for perhaps the first time in the history of the English Church, the monks and canons who made up its cathedral chapters could realistically expect to choose their own bishops, without outside interference. Nevertheless, whilst the position of the electors was greatly strengthened by the theoretical and legal developments of the twelfth and thirteenth centuries, they continued to share their right to participate in the electoral process with other parties – secular rulers, archbishops, would-be bishops and the pope. Given that all of these groups were equally enthusiastic to defend, and where possible extend, the exercise of their electoral rights and responsibilities, it was inevitable that straightforward canonical elections conducted in accordance with the procedure described above were relatively rare.

Despite the fact that real-life electoral processes were generally far more complicated than the theoretical models might suggest, the study of these ideals nevertheless provides a valuable starting point for the historian of episcopal elections. This was the template on which each of the elections that took place

---

247 *Reg. Alex. IV*, no. 2230; Hugh Lawrence, 'The Thirteenth Century' in Hugh Lawrence, *The English Church and the Papacy in the Middle Ages*, rev. edn (Stroud, 1999), pp. 117-56, at pp. 145-6; Ullmann, 'Hugh Balsham', p. 267; *Ecumenical Councils*, I, pp. 320-21.

248 *Mandagot*, cc. 56-8, 60.

249 Ibid., c. 57.

in thirteenth-century England was based. Deviations from this unrealistic norm illuminate the attitudes of those involved and reveal the underlying tensions, as well as the open disagreements, between them. Furthermore, each group of participants was adept not only at using these laws and customs to insist that their rights should be upheld, but also at manipulating them in order to attack the rights of rival parties. Therefore, it is only with an appreciation of how episcopal elections were meant to work that it becomes possible to understand the complexities of how they actually happened.

Chapter 2
The Custom of Election: Ritual and Finance

The manner in which elections were conducted was largely determined by legal requirements, but this was not the only force shaping such procedures: the details of the electoral process were also influenced by custom. Consequently, the majority of the elections conducted during this period were characterized by features that were not required by canon law, but were expected in the English tradition. These customs can be divided into two main categories: rituals and financial practices.

The sources for these aspects of electoral history are less well defined than those for the study of the canon law of election. For the study of ritual elements, the major sources are narrative accounts of the bishop-making process written by those who were closely associated with the cathedral chapter. Such accounts are found in chronicles (notably the account of the 1228 Canterbury election included in the continuation of Gervase of Canterbury's chronicle) or, more frequently, amongst the records of the chapter and diocese (especially those of Canterbury and Worcester). Local records are also of great value for the study of electoral finances, with much of the information being derived from episcopal registers, the Worcester *sede vacante* registers and memoranda of electoral expenditure. Incidental references to both forms of custom are scattered throughout a range of other sources, including (but not limited to) the chancery rolls and calendars of papal letters.

Ritual[1]

In order for an election to be held, it was first necessary for a vacancy to occur. A small number of English bishops resigned their see, either on the grounds of

---

1 The problems associated with the study of ritual in a medieval context have been the subject of considerable debate in recent years, especially since the publication of Philippe Buc, *The Dangers of Ritual: Between Medieval Texts and Social Scientific Theory* (Princeton, 2001). In what follows I use the term in a broad sense, to refer to public (or quasi-public) displays of formulaic behaviours which conveyed symbolic meanings to contemporary observers.

incapacity[2] or to enter a religious order,[3] but in both cases permission to do so had to be obtained from the pope, and was only rarely granted. Vacancies due to the translation of the incumbent to a different see were rare before the late fourteenth century. Almost all vacancies occurred because of the death of the bishop; it was at the point that he breathed his last that the process by which he was replaced began.[4]

Immediately after the bishop's death, a notary drew up a public instrument recording his death.[5] His body would then be publicly transferred to his cathedral, where it would lie in state until his funeral; when Stephen Langton died in 1228, his corpse was displayed before the high altar at Canterbury.[6] According to canon law, no formal steps towards the election of the new bishop should be taken until the deceased bishop had been buried.[7] Episcopal funerals were great public ceremonies,[8] however, and were attended by many members of the secular and clerical elites. When St Hugh died in 1200, his body was carried in procession from London to Lincoln, attracting great crowds all along the route. On the sixth day after his death, the cortege arrived 'at the foot of the hill almost a mile outside the city', where it was met by 'the kings of England and Scotland, the archbishops, bishops, magnates, abbots and nobles and an immense crowd of clergy and people, such as had scarcely ever been seen in England before this gathering'. Many of these 'men of high rank and position' sought the privilege of bearing the coffin on its final journey up the hill to Lincoln Cathedral, amongst them King John and numerous prelates; the Scottish king, however, 'was so overcome that he could not approach the coffin, but remained behind weeping bitterly'.[9] The bishops of London and Rochester were amongst the mourners at Archbishop Pecham's funeral,[10] whilst the burial of Archbishop Winchelsey (1313) was conducted in the presence of the bishops of Llandaff, Winchester, Worcester, Exeter, Bath and Wells, and Ely, the heads of several major religious houses and laymen including Gilbert de Clare, earl of Gloucester.[11] It seems

[2] For example, Nicholas Farnham resigned the bishopric of Durham in 1249 because of ill health. *EEA 29: Durham, 1241-1283*, ed. P. Hoskin (Oxford, 2005), p. xxvi.

[3] In 1239, Ralph of Maidstone resigned the bishopric of Hereford in order to become a Franciscan friar. *EEA 35: Hereford, 1234-1275*, ed. J. Barrow (Oxford, 2009), pp. xxxvi-xxxvii.

[4] For an evocative account of the events that followed the death of St Hugh of Lincoln, see *Magna Vita*, II, pp. 217-32.

[5] Haines, *Ecclesia*, p. 26.

[6] *Gervase*, II, p. 115.

[7] *Bonae memoriae* (Dec. Greg. IX, X, 1.6.36, *CIC*, II, pp. 82-3).

[8] David Lepine, 'High Solemn Ceremonies: The Funeral Practice of the Late Medieval English Higher Clergy', *EHR*, 61 (2010), pp. 18-39.

[9] *Magna Vita*, II, pp. 225-8.

[10] Graham, *Winchelsey*, p. 161.

[11] Haines, *Ecclesia*, p. 26.

highly implausible that various members of such an assembly would not have discussed the election at hand, and perhaps even have suggested potential candidates to the chapter.

Once the bishop had been buried, preparations for the election could begin in earnest. Firstly, licence to elect had to be obtained from the king; a small delegation from the chapter would be sent to court to request this vital document. The Canterbury chronicle provides a unique account of the experiences of the delegation sent to seek *congé d'élire* in 1228, following Langton's death.[12] Arriving at court, the monks' representatives (their prior, along with several senior members of the convent) were honourably received by Henry III, to whom they presented their petition. Henry explained that he wished to think the matter over for at least one night, and to take counsel from the bishops and barons. The following morning, 'the bishops and the leading men and other countless persons' assembled in the royal presence; the prior and his entourage approached the king and handed over the letters patent of Canterbury Cathedral Priory, in which the monks begged the king to concede to them the right to freely elect a new pontiff. Having taken counsel, Henry, 'displaying a cheerful and kind countenance to them', announced his decision to grant licence to elect, saying:

> Lord Prior, I have heard your petition; I have heard and fully understood what you have proposed in my presence on behalf of your chapter. And since it does not befit a Catholic prince to knowingly obstruct the rules of canon law, of my pure and unadulterated will, I grant most willingly my royal consent to you and your chapter for electing a pontiff for yourself; you should know without doubt that I love and will love your church, with the most tender love, depending on you to stand firm. I ask also that you should try to unanimously agree on a single individual, by whose promotion God, the Church, I and my kingdom will be most enhanced; for it is very necessary and useful for me and for you that you will incline neither to the right nor the left, on account of influence, hatred or favour.[13]

The simple entry of the licence to elect on the patent rolls conceals the ceremony surrounding the issue of the *congé d'élire*, reducing it to a straightforward administrative procedure. This account suggests that it was instead a piece of political theatre,[14] with strong echoes of the electoral model set out in King

[12] Briefer mentions of this aspect of the electoral process, referring to the repeated attempts of a Durham delegation to secure *congé d'élire* in 1226, are to be found in Durham Miscellanea 5520, transcribed in the appendix to Evers, 'Disputes', pp. 5, 9, 11-15.

[13] *Gervase*, II, pp. 115-17.

[14] On the deployment of ritual and ceremony by secular rulers in a secular context, see Paul Hyams, 'What did Henry III of England Think in Bed and in French about Kingship and Anger?' in Barbara Rosenwein (ed.), *Anger's Past: The Social Uses of an Emotion in the Middle Ages* (Ithaca,

John's charter. The public issue of the licence reinforced the idea of the king generously allowing the chapter to hold an election, and thus underlined his place at the heart of the electoral process. It also enabled the king to present himself as a defender of ecclesiastical freedom; not only must the chapter avoid making choices for secular reasons, but they should aspire to elect unanimously, presumably by divine inspiration.

The audience to this performance is also of interest. On one level, of course, the assembled bishops, barons and other persons were present simply as witnesses to the royal magnanimity, and the gratitude of the monks. It seems likely, though, that this was a remnant of the ancient tradition that a bishop should be chosen not simply by his cathedral chapter, but by the local elites and the people.[15] Although the practice of communal election had become strictly non-canonical by the thirteenth century, it is likely that the involvement of the wider community in the ceremonial aspects of the electoral process was intended as a symbol of popular inclusion and assent.

This notion is reinforced by the devotions performed in the cathedral city in the run up to the election. Some of these were limited to the members of the chapter: the acclamation of God when the licence to elect was presented in the chapter house, for example,[16] and the observance of a solemn fast lasting three days.[17] Many others included the wider community. During the three days of fasting that preceded the 1228 Canterbury election, the monks processed barefoot through their cemetery, whilst 'the clergy and people of the city made their own procession between one church and another with many showers of tears'.[18] In 1292, the date of the election was announced to the clergy and people in the cathedral; once again, processions and devotions were encouraged.[19] At the next Canterbury vacancy, the clergy and people of the same diocese were encouraged to take part in barefoot processions and to carry out other religious observances, both night and day, in the run up to the 1313 archiepiscopal election.[20]

1998), pp. 92-124; Malcolm Vale, *The Princely Court: Medieval Courts and Culture in North-West Europe* (Oxford, 2001), pp. 200-46; Bjorn Weiler, 'Symbolism and Politics in the Reign of Henry III' in Michael Prestwich, Richard Britnell and Robin Frame (eds), *Thirteenth Century England IX* (Woodbridge, 2003), pp. 15-41; Timothy Reuter, *Velle sibi fieri in forma hac*: Symbolic Acts in the Becket Dispute' in Timothy Reuter and Janet Nelson (eds.), *Medieval Polities and Modern Mentalities* (Cambridge, 2006), pp. 167-90.

15 Norton, *Elections*, pp. 42-3.

16 *Gervase*, II, p. 117.

17 *Gervase*, II, pp. 117, 125. For the significance of fasting, see Caroline Bynum, *Holy Feast and Holy Fast: The Religious Significance of Food to Medieval Women* (Berkeley, 1989), pp. 31-47.

18 *Gervase*, II, p. 117.

19 Graham, *Winchelsey*, p. 163.

20 Haines, *Ecclesia*, p. 27.

The election itself was, in accordance with canon law, a private affair, and those who were not members of the chapter were locked out of the chapter house during this stage of the proceedings. Even so, it included many ritual elements. Having performed the customary observances for the day, the monks or canons were summoned to the chapter house by the ringing of a bell. Before the election could begin, further devotions were performed, beginning with readings from the rule (presumably omitted in secular chapters) and the Gospel,[21] followed by a blessing given by the prior.[22] Relics might be brought into the chapter house: in 1228 'the wood of the cross of Christ, the veil of the Blessed Mary, and the crown of the Blessed Martyr Thomas were brought in to terrify those in the chapter',[23] and in 1292 and 1313 a small reliquary containing the consecrated host and the corona of St Thomas (Becket) was set up in the centre of the room and surrounded by candles.[24] The prior would then deliver an address, exhorting the monks to unity: in 1228, John of Sittingbourne took Psalm 133 as his text,[25] whilst Henry of Eastry preached on Psalm 79.[26]

From here, the later assembly proceeded to the business of the election.[27] In 1228, however, further displays of piety followed. The prior led the monks in prayer; he then rose from his seat, extended his hand to heaven and began the chant *Veni, Creator Spiritus*. The monks joined in one by one, on the signal of the prior. Then they began to weep:

> What weeping, what sighs came forth from their hearts, whilst that heavenly chant was sung in the heart and on the lips of all, I do not believe that by speech or even by pen it can be easily explained! Then having chanted the same chant with great devotion and immense sobbing, each one returned to his proper place in the chapter house.[28]

These emotional outbursts continued throughout the day. It was decided to elect by way of compromise, and five men were selected to choose a bishop on behalf of their brethren; the five tearfully prostrated themselves at the feet of the convent and prayed for divine aid.[29] They were then led away to a separate room to make their choice; when the door was bolted, 'with moaning and weeping

---

21 *Gervase*, II, p. 117; Graham, *Winchelsey*, pp. 163-4; Haines, *Ecclesia*, p. 27.

22 *Gervase*, II, p. 117.

23 *Gervase*, II, p. 120.

24 Graham, *Winchesley*, p. 164; Haines, *Ecclesia*, p. 27.

25 *Gervase*, II, p. 118. 'Ecce quam bonum et quam jocundum ...'.

26 Haines, *Ecclesia*, p. 27. 'Elegit David ...'.

27 Haines, *Ecclesia*, pp. 27-8.

28 *Gervase*, II, p. 118.

29 *Gervase*, II, p. 120.

... they began to pray' and to chant *Veni Creator Spiritus*. Outside, the prior and convent sang the seven penitential psalms and the great litany, 'with great devotion and unrestrained showers of tears'.[30] After some time, the sub-prior tearfully read out the result: Walter de Eynsham was elected as archbishop. His election being proclaimed, he 'dissolved completely into tears' and prostrated himself, declaring his unworthiness for the task. When brought before the altar he again began to weep.[31]

Once the electors had made their decision, the result of the election had to be published. The canon law focused on the need to record the electoral process in writing and for the entire chapter to subscribe to the decree of election, but again these technical proceedings were surrounded by ceremonial features. The election was firstly proclaimed to the assembled monks (or canons), who were required to give thanks to God, and the *Te Deum laudamus* was sung.[32] In 1228, the elect being present, the prior led him to the high altar during this chant. Further prayers were said, the relics and the gospels kissed, and the new bishop led to his seat. Once seated, he received the kiss of peace from each member of the convent, in order of seniority. At this point, the clergy and people were readmitted, and acclaimed the election, shouting 'Blessed is the Lord who chose you for our pastor'. The prior then formally proclaimed the election from the pulpit. Finally the monks returned to their chapter house, where they sat on a carpet at the feet of their seated bishop and prepared the decree of election.[33]

One of the most striking features of these narratives of election is the emphasis on ritual elements; from the perspective of the electoral body, an election was not just a legal process, but also a spiritual experience. Even when a unanimous choice by means of divine inspiration could not be made, there was great concern to ensure that the will of God was done, with the aid of the Holy Spirit and through the use of prayers and chants. The outcome of the election was interpreted as the will of God. Descriptions of the pious practices in which the electors engaged during the course of election were intended to reinforce the impression that they had been motivated by pious considerations rather than worldly ones; hence the emphasis on prayers, relics and tears.

The 1228 Canterbury election is the only occasion on which such prolific weeping is described and it is impossible to know whether such behaviour was replicated elsewhere. Nevertheless, the emphasis placed on the monks' tears, and the author's obvious concern to demonstrate that the election was canonically

[30] *Gervase*, II, p. 121. Exactly the same recitations were performed whilst the compromisers carried out their discussions in 1292 (Graham, *Winchelsey*, p. 165), raising the possibility that there was an informal time limit within which the electors were expected to make their choice.

[31] *Gervase*, II, pp. 121-2.

[32] *Gervase*, II, p. 122; Graham, *Winchelsey*, p. 165; Haines, *Ecclesia*, p. 28.

[33] *Gervase*, II, pp. 122-3. In 1292, the announcement of the election was followed by the retirement of the monks to the refectory, where they ate their dinner. Graham, *Winchelsey*, p. 166.

sound, suggests that such displays of emotion within an electoral context could be perceived in a positive manner. For medieval Christians, tears contained a wealth of religious significance, demonstrating the weeper's connection to God. Monks were encouraged to shed tears when praying and seeking penance, for weeping, granted by God, could wash sins away.[34] Suggesting that the monks had been blessed with the gift of tears during the election was therefore a powerful claim, implying that their choice was made whilst they were in a purified state; the tears shed during the chanting of the penitential psalms were perhaps particularly significant in this respect. The monks (and the chronicler who described their weeping) may also have considered the significance of tears within the system of the four humours. Tears are hot and moist, but rational thought is cold and dry; weeping therefore removes some of the barriers to rational thought, including boredom and indifference.[35] The electors' tears could therefore be taken as an indication of the rationality of their choice. There was, however, some risk associated with such behaviour, for excessive displays of pious emotion could be greeted with scepticism. In the mid-twelfth century, John of Salisbury was a particularly fierce critic of those hypocrites who 'are suddenly flooded with artificial and obsequious tears'.[36]

The meaning of Walter de Eynsham's tears is less mysterious, and at least one other bishop-elect responded to his election in the same manner: John de Sancto Germano, elected to Worcester in 1302, also assented tearfully.[37] Such reluctance was expected of a bishop-elect; custom demanded that he protest his unworthiness of the office he was offered: *nolo episcopari*.[38] When St Hugh of Lincoln was informed that he had been nominated as bishop of Lincoln, he immediately declared that 'I am quite unfit for so great an honour, and unequal to such heavy responsibilities'.[39] Edmund of Abingdon would not consent to his election for two days; only 'under pressure of prayer and persuasion from many people and in bitterness of spirit' did he 'at last, but with reluctance' give his

---

34 Piroska Nagy, 'Religious Weeping as Ritual in the Medieval West' in Don Handelman and Galina Lindquist (eds), *Ritual in its Own Right: Exploring the Dynamics of Transformation* (Oxford, 2005), pp. 119-37; Piroska Nagy, *Le don des larmes au Moyen Âge* (Paris, 2000).

35 Mary Carruthers, 'On Affliction and Reading, Weeping and Argument: Chaucer's Lachrymose Troilus in Context', *Representations*, 93 (2006), pp. 1-21, esp. p. 7.

36 Giles Constable, 'Moderation and Restraint in Ascetic Practices' in his *Culture and Spirituality in Medieval Europe* (Aldershot, 1996), X, quote at p. 324 (original pagination).

37 *AM*, IV, p. 554: 'cum lacrymis consensu'. For a detailed examination of episcopal weeping in the later middle ages, see Katherine Harvey, 'Episcopal Emotions: Tears in the Life of the Medieval Bishop', *Historical Research* (Forthcoming).

38 *Life of St Edmund*, p. 47. Such displays of reluctance were also thought seemly in newly elected popes; Innocent III responded to his election by 'weeping, lamenting and resisting'. *Gervase*, I, 550; Maria Taylor, 'The Election of Innocent III' in Diana Wood (ed.), *The Church and Sovereignty, c.590-1918* (Oxford, 1991), pp. 97-112, at p. 109.

39 *Magna Vita*, I, pp. 95-6.

assent.[40] Robert Winchelsey was equally reluctant to consent to his election, and made excuses as to why he should not do so; after much persuasion by Prior Eastry, he tearfully assented. His words were copied down by the notary who recorded his election:

> I, Robert of Winchelsey, being unwilling to resist the will of God, for the honour of the Trinity, of the Blessed Virgin Mary and of the blessed Thomas the Martyr consent to my election as archbishop of Canterbury.[41]

As with the preparation stage of the process, the election itself involved the community as well as the cathedral chapter. These accounts suggest that outside the closed doors of the chapter house there was an atmosphere of anticipation, with the clergy and people waiting to discover the identity of their next bishop. In a significant gesture of inclusion, the proclamation of the election was made in the vernacular, at least by the early fourteenth century.[42] The publication of the election, and the acclamation of the new bishop by the populace, again indicates that whilst clergy and people no longer had a formal role in the electoral process, they still expected – and were expected to – play a part in the making of a bishop.[43]

Once the election had been made, it was necessary to secure royal and archiepiscopal assent. Unsurprisingly, both were obtained publicly and included an element of public acclamation. After Robert Winchelsey had assented to his election as archbishop of Canterbury, he set out to find the king, accompanied by Prior Eastry and others. Finding the king near Nottingham, they presented a letter from the convent in which royal assent was requested; Edward I replied that he would give his answer on the following day. The following day, the court (including the king and his councillors) assembled after mass and Anthony Bek, bishop of Durham, read out the king's statement of assent and pledge of support. Those present responded by applauding the archbishop-elect and his election.[44]

As an archbishop-elect, Winchelsey then embarked for Rome, in order to seek papal confirmation of his election.[45] A bishop, however, would have sought

40 *Life of St Edmund*, pp. 130-31.

41 Graham, *Winchelsey*, p. 166.

42 Haines, *Ecclesia*, p. 28.

43 The role of the populace in thirteenth-century English elections is similar to that outlined by Gratian, who stated that, whilst laymen must not elect, they should not be excluded from the election, and should be able to give their humble assent to the clerical choice by way of popular acclamation of the candidate (D.63 c. 25 (*CIC*, I, pp. 242-3)).

44 Graham, *Winchelsey*, pp. 166-7.

45 Ibid., pp. 167-73.

out the archbishop, in order to have his election examined and confirmed.[46] He then had to return to the royal presence to request the restoration of the temporalities, which would be granted once the bishop had sworn an oath of fealty.[47]

Even once a bishop had received confirmation of his election from his ecclesiastical superior, and the king's assent to his appointment, the bishop-making process was far from complete. This is not the place for a full consideration of episcopal consecration and enthronement; nevertheless, aspects of these ceremonies are of interest to the student of episcopal election. Of particular significance is the role played by the wider community in both ceremonies; such broad participation was a powerful means of maintaining the fiction of assent even after the right to elect was limited to the cathedral chapter.

The archbishop of the province had the right to officiate at episcopal consecrations, but canon law and ecclesiastical tradition demanded that at least three other bishops should be in attendance.[48] It was thus customary for the suffragan bishops to be summoned in order that they might assist the archbishop.[49] For example, when Thomas Cantilupe was consecrated at Canterbury on 8 September 1275, Archbishop Kilwardby officiated, assisted by all the bishops of the southern province save those of London and Rochester.[50] In the northern province, the paucity of suffragans meant that the archbishop of York was often assisted by bishops from other provinces. In either province, if the archbishop was unable to officiate (because he was overseas, because the archiepiscopal see was vacant or because he was himself being consecrated) then the suffragans could act alone. Henry Newark, archbishop of York, was consecrated in 1298 by Anthony Bek, bishop of Durham, assisted by the bishops of Coventry, St Asaph and Cork.[51]

---

[46] Since the archiepiscopal examination and confirmation was part of the canonical procedure of episcopal election, and its form and content were heavily influenced by canon law, it is discussed above, at pp. 41-4.

[47] Graham, *Winchelsey*, p. 174, gives the text of the oath sworn by Archbishop Robert Winchelsey.

[48] Gratian D.65 c. 5§1 (*CIC*, I, p. 251). See also *Ecclesiastical History*, pp. 45-6, for Gregory I's *Responsiones* to Augustine (601), in which he states that 'no consecration of a bishop should take place ... except in the presence of three or four bishops'; an exception could only be made if there were fewer than three or four consecrated bishops in the relevant region, for example in early seventh-century England. *The Pontifical of Egbert, Archbishop of York, A. D. 732-766*, ed. W. Greenwell, Surtees Society, 27 (Durham: G. Andrews, 1853), p. 1, also requires the presence of three bishops in addition to the officiating archbishop.

[49] *Reg. Winchelsey*, II, p. 799.

[50] *AM*, IV, p. 265; *Gervase*, II, p. 280.

[51] *Reg. Romeyn*, II, 307-8; *The Historians of the Church of York and its Archbishops*, ed. J. Raine (3 vols, RS, 1879-94), II, p. 410.

The participation of the bishops in the consecration ceremony was surely also a remnant of the ancient tradition of the participation of the *religiosi viri*.[52] The bishops could no longer participate in elections, but they could still demonstrate their assent to the capitular choice by participating in his consecration. They did so as members of an intangible chapter, which had previously claimed the right to elect the archbishop of Canterbury. Although the right of election had been lost, their relative positions within this chapter retained some significance[53] and occasionally became the cause of much dissent, usually when the archbishop was absent and another prelate was required to deputize for him. When Eustace of Fauconberg sought consecration as bishop of London in 1221, Archbishop Langton was overseas, meaning that the duty would usually fall to the bishop of Winchester or London. Since Peter des Roches was also abroad, and Fauconberg could hardly consecrate himself, the dean and chapter of St Paul's had applied to the Legate Pandulph for permission to allow another bishop to preside at the consecration and this was granted. However, when the bishops gathered for the consecration, an unseemly squabble broke out. The bishop of Bath, Jocelin of Wells, claimed that, as the longest-standing bishop, he should preside. The bishop of Salisbury, Richard Poore, asserted that he was precentor in the province of Canterbury, and that he therefore had the right to consecrate Fauconberg. Furthermore, Benedict Sawston of Rochester claimed that, as bishop co-adjutor (substitute bishop) for the Canterbury province, he was entitled to act as Langton's proxy.[54] The dean and chapter of St Paul's eventually agreed that Sawston should preside, but without detriment to the claims of the other bishops.[55] The dispute made for a tense ceremony: Henry of Avranches

---

[52] For the inclusion of the local bishops in this group in the early twelfth century, and on the decline of this tradition, see Peltzer, *Elections*, pp. 26-31.

[53] Adrian Morey and Christopher Brooke, *Gilbert Foliot and his Letters* (Cambridge, 1965), pp. 226-9; David Johnson, 'Bishops and deans: London and the province of Canterbury in the twelfth century', *Historical Research* (Forthcoming).

[54] For the unique relationship between Rochester and Canterbury, on which Sawston's claims were presumably based, see above, pp. 4-5.

[55] British Library Add. Ch. 36449, a charter of the Bishop of Rochester, outlines the consecration dispute; it is summarized in *The Shorter Latin Poems of Henry of Avranches relating to England*, ed. J. C. Russell and J. P. Heironimus (Cambridge, Mass., 1935), p. 62, and *EEA 26: London, 1189-1228*, ed. D. P. Johnson (Oxford, 2003), pp. 180-81; the latter also has Fauconberg's profession of obedience, dated 25 April. For chronicle accounts of the consecration, in which there appears to be some confusion over the date of the ceremony, and most of which say nothing of the dispute, see *CM*, II, p. 66, and *Hist. Angl.*, II, p. 248, which have 27 April; Waverley annals (*AM*, II, p. 294) and Worcester annals (*AM*, IV, p. 414); *Annales Londonienses* (*Chron. E1&E2*, I, p. 23) has 28 April. *Walteri de Coventria*, II, p. 249, says that the bishops of Bath, Salisbury and Rochester all participated in the consecration, but does not indicate which of them presided over the ceremony. That the dispute continued even after the ceremony was completed is reflected in a charter of the bishop of Rochester, in which he disclaims any injury to the rights of Salisbury by his consecration of Fauconberg. *Charters and Documents Illustrating the History of the Cathedral,*

contrasts the beauty of the spring outside with the unease of the assembly inside the chapel.[56]

Also present at the majority of consecration ceremonies were members of the secular elites, whose attendance should also be understood as a form of approval. Archiepiscopal consecrations may have been especially well attended: Edmund of Abingdon was consecrated as archbishop of Canterbury 'in the presence of King Henry, thirteen bishops and a great multitude of magnates'.[57] But the consecration of even a relatively minor bishop could attract a substantial audience: those present at Richard of Wendene's consecration as bishop of Rochester (1238) included Archbishop Edmund (who presumably performed the anointment), four bishops (to assist the archbishop), the archdeacon of Canterbury and 'many noble persons'.[58]

Even once a bishop had been consecrated, he still had to participate in one more ceremony in order to complete his transformation: his entry into his cathedral city, and his enthronement in the cathedral. These rituals had a dual function: they celebrated both his *adventus* (arrival) and his *possessio* (taking of legitimate possession of his city and see).[59] Uniquely amongst the various stages of the bishop-making process, this final ceremony was not governed by canon law, but instead developed from and in parallel to biblical precedent (notably Christ's entry into Jerusalem on Palm Sunday), secular ceremonies and papal rituals.[60] Consequently, many local variations of the ceremony developed, each based around similar models and ideals, but simultaneously reflecting local concerns.[61]

City and Diocese of Salisbury in the Twelfth and Thirteenth Centuries, ed. W. R. Jones and W. D. Macray (RS, 1891), pp. 109-10.

56 *Avranches*, pp. 85-7.

57 *Life of St Edmund*, p. 131.

58 *Flores Hist.*, II, p. 230.

59 For recent discussions of episcopal *adventus* in late medieval Europe, see Jeffrey Tyler, *Lord of the Sacred City: The 'Episcopus Exclusus' in Late Medieval and Early Modern Germany* (Leiden, 1999), pp. 123-50; Maureen Miller, 'The Florentine Bishop's Ritual Entry and the Origins of Medieval Episcopal *Adventus*', *Revue d'Histoire Ecclésiastique*, 96 (2002), pp. 5-28; Véronique Julerot, 'La Première Entrée de l'Évêque: Reflexions sur son Origine', *Revue Historique*, 308 (2006), pp. 635-75; Jacek Maciejewski, 'Research on the *Adventus*', pp. 89-100; Katherine Harvey, 'The First Entry of the Bishop: Episcopal *Adventus* in Fourteenth-Century England' in Jeffrey Hamilton (ed.), *Fourteenth Century England VIII* (Woodbridge, forthcoming).

60 Miller, 'Florentine Bishop's Ritual Entry', pp. 9-10; Tyler, *Lord of the Sacred City*, pp. 148-50; Julerot, 'Entrée', pp. 667-73; Susan Twyman, 'Papal *Adventus* at Rome in the Twelfth Century', *Historical Research*, 69 (1996), pp. 233-53; Gordon Kipling, *Enter the King: Theatre, Liturgy and Ritual in the Medieval Civic Triumph* (Oxford, 1998).

61 For a particularly unusual development of the *adventus* ritual, see Sharon Strocchia, 'When the Bishop Married the Abbess: Masculinity and Power in Florentine Episcopal Entry Rites, 1300-1600', *Gender and History*, 19 (2007), pp. 346-68.

English accounts of episcopal (and archiepiscopal) enthronement for the period under consideration are rare, particularly before the late thirteenth century. The *Magna Vita* of St Hugh of Lincoln includes a brief account of his arrival in Lincoln, but pays more attention to Hugh's unusual relationship with a swan than to the ritual dimension of this occasion.[62] Many enthronements went completely unmentioned in the chronicles, or were mentioned only in passing. Nevertheless, by combining the fragments of information from early references with more detailed accounts of slightly later ceremonies at Canterbury, Worcester and York, it is possible to uncover at least some of the significance of such events.

Mass participation was one of the key features of the enthronement ritual; unlike the consecration, where the emphasis appears to have been on the presence of the members of the ecclesiastical and secular elites, this final celebration included all social ranks.[63] When he reached the outskirts of the city, the new bishop was met by a large delegation. When William Gainsborough entered Worcester in June 1303, the prior, accompanied by a number of monks and servants, went to Kempsey to welcome their prelate. The narrative continues:

> Forthwith, he was met by the Abbots of Evesham, Pershore, and Tewkesbury, and other officials, and by the bishops of Hereford and Llandaff and various Archdeacons, and by Sir Thomas de Berkeley and Sir Hugo de Vere ... it was estimated that more than 70 horsemen met the bishop. The first procession met the bishop at Red Hill. The second procession of Friars Minors met the bishop at the hospital of St. Wulfstan.[64]

The bishops and monks, along with the representative of the archdeacon of Canterbury (who claimed the right to enthrone every bishop in the southern province[65]), played the most prominent role in the ceremony, escorting the bishop and performing the actual ceremony of enthronement. Nevertheless, the people of the city were clearly present in large numbers: Gainsborough was concerned that the ceremony be performed early in the day 'on account of the heat of the day and the crowd of people', and later in the day there was a 'press of people'. On the following day, the people were again present for the bishop's first sermon.[66]

Gainsborough's enthronement seems to have been an event with a strong local flavour, attended almost entirely by people from within his own diocese or neighbouring dioceses. The enthronement of a favoured *curialis* might, on the other hand, attract national figures, including the king and queen; Henry III

62 *Magna Vita*, I, pp. 103-6.

63 Julerot, 'Entrée', p. 652.

64 *Reg. Sede Vacante*, pp. 52-3.

65 Churchill, *Administration*, I, p. 276.

66 *Reg. Sede Vacante*, pp. 52-4.

and Eleanor of Provence went to Worcester for the enthronement of Walter de Cantilupe in 1237.[67] The presence of the king and barons was customary at Canterbury;[68] John Pecham's enthronement (1279), for example, was attended by Edward I, both Queen Eleanors and a large number of bishops, abbots and magnates.[69] When Robert Winchelsey became archbishop, his *adventus* and enthronement were separated by several months in order that the king might attend the latter event. When it was finally held, the attendees included Edward I, his brother Edmund of Lancaster, the future Edward II, seven bishops, five earls and many other nobles and prelates.[70]

The contrast between the extremely limited numbers involved in the election itself and the masses of people who participated in the surrounding ceremonies is striking, but far from being the only interesting feature of the enthronement ceremony. The bishop's entry into his see could be combined with opportunities for him to display his suitability for the position, and thus to demonstrate the justice of his appointment. Immediately after his enthronement, William Gainsborough celebrated the Mass of St Wulfstan (an important acknowledgement of the cathedral's resident saint) and granted a six days' indulgence to all who heard it. On the following day, he preached a sermon, before conducting a business meeting with his clerks and those of the convent. On the following Monday he confirmed boys at the Franciscan friary.[71] Thus the enthronement process allowed him to demonstrate both administrative and pastoral skills.

The demonstration of such skills could be especially important if the bishop had not been chosen by the cathedral chapter or if his election had been the subject of a dispute. Many of the rituals of enthronement were clearly designed to display, or at least to encourage, unity between the bishop and his flock, as well as harmonious relations with the wider political and ecclesiastical communities. The theme of Bishop Gainsborough's enthronement sermon, 'We are one body in Christ' was a highly appropriate one for such an occasion.[72] Another important symbol of unity was evoked near the end of the process, just before the bishop was led to his palace, when 'he kissed all the convent in the chapter in turn, as is the custom'.[73] In addition, an enthronement was an occasion for much conviviality; in 1316, the celebrations that followed the

67 *AM*, III, p. 146.

68 Haines, *Ecclesia*, p. 31.

69 *AM*, II, p. 391; Douie, *Pecham*, p. 66.

70 Graham, *Winchelsey*, pp. 174-5.

71 *Reg. Sede Vacante*, p. 54.

72 Ibid.

73 Ibid. For a detailed discussion of the significance of the kiss of peace, see Kiril Petkov, *The Kiss of Peace: Ritual, Self and Society in the High and Late Medieval West* (Turnhout, 2003).

enthronement of William Melton as archbishop of York lasted for three days.[74] Hospitality and feasting were at the heart of the festivities. Important guests had to be accommodated and fed, and thus lavish banquets were provided.[75] At Worcester, the prior lodged at the episcopal palace for two days and the monks also received meals at the bishop's expense.[76]

Inevitably, however, such efforts to promote good will towards the new bishop were not always entirely successful. Peter Aigueblanche was enthroned at Hereford shortly after Christmas 1240,[77] but his tenants seem to have withheld the aid customarily made to a new bishop in this diocese; a royal mandate to the free tenants of the diocese 'to make an aid to P. bishop of Hereford in his entry into the see such as they have been accustomed to make to his predecessors when they entered therein' was issued on 18 March 1241.[78] John Kirkby of Carlisle was consecrated in 1332, but within a year of this ceremony Archbishop Melton was ordering the excommunication of 'all those who had attacked John de Kirkby bishop of Carlisle and his followers with blasphemous words, arrows and stones, for which reason the city of Carlisle had already been put under an interdict'.[79] It is just possible that this violence took place on the day of Kirkby's enthronement, but even if this was not the case, it is clear that the goodwill that surrounded the bishop's arrival was not always durable.

The significance of enthronement is most clearly illustrated by the experiences of William Raleigh. Postulated as bishop of Winchester in 1240, in the face of strong royal opposition, he faced a four-year struggle to gain possession of his see.[80] Like many bishops who received papal confirmation against the wishes of the king, Raleigh was subject to economic sanctions, most notably the withholding of the temporalities.[81] Henry III's determination to stop the new bishop entering Winchester may also have been motivated by a desire to prevent Raleigh staging his *adventus* and enthronement, and thus receiving popular acclaim for his election. The bishop's barefooted approach to the city echoed one of the customary features of this ritual;[82] given that he had already been consecrated (after his election to Norwich) and had received papal confirmation,

---

74 *Historians of the Church of York*, II, pp. 415-16.

75 Graham, *Winchelsey*, p. 175; Nicholas Vincent, 'The Politics of Church and State as Reflected in the Winchester Pipe Rolls, 1208-80' in Richard Britnell (ed.), *The Winchester Pipe Rolls and Medieval English Society* (Woodbridge, 2002), pp. 157-81, at p. 167.

76 *Reg. Sede Vacante*, p. 54.

77 *AM*, I, p. 117.

78 *CPR 1232-1247*, p. 248.

79 *Reg. Melton*, I, p. 95.

80 See below, pp. 73-4.

81 The temporalities were finally restored on 10 September 1244 (*CPR 1232-1247*, p. 435), a year after his election received papal confirmation on 17 September 1243 (*Reg. Inn. IV*, no. 113).

82 *CM*, IV, p. 266; *AM*, II, pp. 89, 331-2.

any enthronement would presumably have been valid. If this was Raleigh's intention, he was thwarted: when he arrived at Winchester in late December 1243, he was barred from entering the city, and the mayor, prior and some of the monks cooperated in this resistance.[83] Even though the ritual of enthronement could take place only once an election had received confirmation, it could still, on occasion, be used as a weapon in electoral disputes.

Finance

Elections were extremely costly affairs. One substantial expense was travel and subsistence, for seeking the requisite permissions from higher authorities meant that capitular delegations and the bishop-elect were obliged to undertake a minimum of three journeys to the royal court, one to the archbishop's residence and another to the place of consecration. Even if the king was overseas, electoral business still had to be transacted in person.[84] In exceptional circumstances, foreign travel might be necessary in order to find the archbishop. In 1251, Archbishop Boniface received a papal licence 'to examine and confirm or annul elections of bishops ... when not in his province';[85] as a consequence, William of Kilkenny, bishop of Ely, was consecrated at Belley, Savoy in 1255.[86] Archbishops seeking confirmation, and chapters and candidates embroiled in electoral disputes, would have to undertake the long journey to the papal curia;[87] if they were unfortunate enough to arrive during a papal vacancy, they might have to remain there for months, or even years.

There were also many customary dues to be paid. Upon the death of a bishop, the king was entitled to receive certain goods, including his best palfrey (with saddle and bridle), a cup with a gold cover, a basin and ewer, a gold ring and a kennel of hounds. The deceased bishop's second best ring was given, along with his seals, to the archbishop of the province.[88] Even if an election was uncontested,

83 *AM*, IV, p. 89; *CM*, IV, pp. 263-4. It seems certain that this was done in accordance with Henry's wishes, but there is no actual record of such an order on the rolls.

84 Only once was an exception to this rule made, at the start of Edward II's reign, when the new king went to France for his wedding and delegated the relevant powers to Piers Gaveston. *CPR 1307-1313*, p. 43.

85 *CPL*, I, p. 267.

86 *Gervase*, II, p. 205.

87 The journey from England to Rome took approximately fifty days. Lawrence, 'Thirteenth Century', p. 129. For an account of the difficulties of this journey, focusing on the mid-fourteenth century (when the papacy was based in Avignon), see Karsten Plöger, *England and the Avignon Popes: The Practice of Diplomacy in Late Medieval Europe* (Oxford, 2005), pp. 144-60. The journey to Rome, which necessitated the crossing of the Alps, was even more arduous.

88 The earliest authority for the king's entitlement dates from the seventeenth century, but there is contemporary evidence to indicate that Edward I exercised his right to the ring; in 1299-

and handled entirely in England, the sums owed to various officials in return for services provided could be substantial, as a Lincoln memorandum relating to the election of Oliver Sutton (1280) demonstrates. When the elect arrived at the king's court to seek confirmation of his election, he was expected to pay 100 shillings to the chamberlain; his palfrey should be given to the marshal (one of whose duties was the management of the king's horses[89]) and twenty-two shillings were owed to the chancellor for two pairs of letters patent. Similar payments were owed to officials within the archiepiscopal household, where the elect had to pay twenty shillings each to the chamberlain, marshal and steward of the court.[90]

If a visit to the papal curia was required, then the costs of election were much greater. In 1232, just before he embarked for Rome, John Blund, the archbishop-elect of Canterbury, received 2,000 marks from Peter des Roches 'to help him in obtaining his promotion'.[91] Although several chronicles insinuated that there was something morally dubious about this transaction, it is quite possible that the money was simply intended to cover his costs at the curia, including the customary gifts.[92] Those without a wealthy benefactor would be forced to contract loans to cover their expenses. The canons of Wells, for example, owed 2,600 marks by the time the election of Roger of Salisbury was confirmed in 1244.[93] Hugh Balsham and the monks of Ely took ten years to pay off the debt of almost £7,000 that they owed to a single company of Florentine merchants, which was possibly connected to his election as bishop.[94]

The costs facing those who sought confirmation at the curia increased towards the end of the thirteenth century, with the formalization of the payment of the services (*servitia*), which were owed by all bishops (and abbots) confirmed or appointed at Rome. Although they originated as gifts, by the late thirteenth century the payment of these *servitia* had become compulsory; by 1330 they had been fixed at one-third of the prelate's annual income and the greater part

1300 the royal treasury held the rings of three archbishops, five bishops and three abbots (*Liber Quotidianus Contra Rotularis*, ed. J. Topham (London, 1787), pp. 343-8). That the archbishop claimed his dues is indicated by a dispute over the pontifical ring of Robert Orford of Ely (*Reg. Winchelsey*, II, pp. 1071-2). See John Cherry, 'The Medieval Episcopal Ring' in Janet Backhouse (ed.), *The Medieval English Cathedral* (Donington, 2003), pp. 208-17, at pp. 210-11.

89 John Round, *The King's Serjeants and Officers of State* (London, 1911), pp. 84-5.

90 *Reg. Ant. Linc*, III, pp. 305-6.

91 *CM*, III, p. 243.

92 *CM*, III, p. 243; *AM*, IV, pp. 73-4; *Hist. Angl.*, II, p. 355; Nicholas Vincent, *Peter des Roches: An Alien in English Politics, 1205-1238* (Cambridge, 1996), pp. 367-71.

93 Charles M. Church, *Chapters in the Early History of the Church of Wells* (London, 1894), p. 249.

94 See Nicholas Vincent, 'The Thirteenth Century' in Peter Meadows (ed.), *Ely: Bishops and Diocese, 1109-2009* (Woodbridge, 2010), pp. 26-69, at p. 40, where he also suggests other origins of the debt, including the payment of papal taxation.

went directly to the pope, with a small amount going to the cardinals and other officials involved in the case.[95] Several new bishops contracted huge loans, almost certainly in order that they might pay this tax. In 1299, John Salmon (who had just been provided to Norwich) was granted a papal licence to contract a loan of 13,000 florins to meet his expenses at Rome,[96] and in 1302 Robert of Orford borrowed the same sum from the Florentine firm of Spini.[97]

Even after the election was confirmed, the costs continued to build, for consecration and enthronement were costly affairs, involving expensive ceremonies and celebrations. Thus the *Magna Vita* referred to 'the immense cost of the consecration ceremony' for St Hugh,[98] whilst John Pecham borrowed 2,000 marks to pay for his enthronement.[99] Some of these costs were related to the lavish installation feast the bishop was expected to provide. Ideally this would be provided from the resources of the episcopal estates; for William Raleigh's enthronement at Winchester (1244), provisions were sourced from virtually every one of the episcopal manors.[100] However, Pecham incurred further debts to feed the guests at his enthronement, making a contract with Henry le Waleys for the supply of wine, oxen and other meat.[101]

The need to pay customary dues was an added burden on the finances of the new bishop. A set of gifts was due to the archdeacon to whom the right of enthronement belonged. He received the palfrey on which the bishop rode into his city, along with its harnesses, the bishop's boots, spurs, chapel goods, gloves, a gold chalice and ten marks for his expenses.[102] At Canterbury, the chief vassals of the see, who enjoyed a hereditary right to perform certain ceremonial functions at the archbishop's installation feast, also expected to receive certain perquisites. When Archbishop John Pecham was consecrated, the earl of Gloucester received a cup, seven scarlet robes, thirty gallons of wine, thirty pounds of wax, provision for eighty horses and three days hospitality at one of the archiepiscopal manors in return for his services; three other chief tenants were similarly well rewarded.[103]

So far, all of the expenditure considered can be clearly identified as customary and obligatory; any would-be bishop would be required to make such payments. However, in many cases the expenses of election would be greatly increased

---

95 William Lunt, *Papal Revenues of the Middle Ages* (2 vols, New York, 1934), I, pp. 81-91.

96 *CPL*, I, p. 582.

97 *CPL*, I, pp. 603-4.

98 *Magna Vita*, I, p. 103.

99 *Reg. Pecham*, I, p. 27; Douie, *Pecham*, p. 66.

100 Vincent, 'Pipe Rolls', p. 167.

101 *Reg. Pecham*, I, pp. 12-13.

102 *Reg. Ant. Linc.*, III, pp. 305-6; *Reg. Sede Vacante*, p. 53.

103 Douie, *Pecham*, p. 66.

by the need to engage in gift-giving; whilst both canon law[104] and models of courtly behaviour demanded that a façade of voluntariness surrounded this practice, in reality it was usually necessary to make substantial offerings in order to gain the favour (or even the attention) of powerful individuals.[105] Throughout the thirteenth century, the English seem to have held a strong belief that considerable expenditure was necessary in order to secure a favourable judgement at the papal curia. Thus in 1243, the canons of Wells instructed their dean (who was representing them at Rome in the cause of the election of Roger of Salisbury) to 'make friends of the mammon of unrighteousness'[106] and to spend as much money as necessary, for 'we love our honour more than our money'.[107] In 1293, whilst Robert Winchelsey was at the papal curia attempting to secure confirmation of his election to Canterbury, he was advised (by who is unclear) that it would be necessary to give liberally if the desired outcome was to be achieved.[108] In 1302, Richard of Bromwich informed the prior of Worcester that John de Sancto Germano had resigned his election and a new bishop had been provided in his place:

> This news was most unpleasant. But now is come to pass what is said in the Book of Proverbs: 'A man's gift makes room for him, and brings him before great men'.[109]

By the late thirteenth century (and probably throughout the century), it was relatively common for pensions to be offered to those who assisted a candidate to obtain confirmation of his election. One of Henry of Newark's first acts as archbishop of York was to establish pensions for various cardinals who had taken the trouble to promote his election; he also offered his services in return.[110]

Offering gifts and payments to potential supporters was clearly, for many would-be bishops, a good way of securing office. However, the strategy was not without its dangers, for there was a very fine line between gratitude and simony (the purchase of spiritual office); the difference was often one of perspective.[111] Simony had been denounced since biblical times, and was consistently

---

104 See, for example Gratian, c. 2 D Causae I, Q. ii (*CIC*, I, p. 407), where in was stated that 'it is one thing to make a voluntary offering; it is another thing to pay an exaction'.

105 Georges Duby, *The Early Growth of the European Economy* (London, 1975), pp. 60-69; Marcel Mauss, *The Gift: The Form and Reason for Exchange in Archaic Societies*, trans. Wilfred Halls (London, 1990).

106 *Wells MSS.*, I, p. 117.

107 Church, *Chapters*, p. 251.

108 *Reg. Winchelsey*, II, pp. 1279-80.

109 *Reg. Sede Vacante*, p. vii. The verse quoted is Proverbs 18: 16.

110 *Reg. Romeyn*, II, pp. 296-9.

111 Timothy Reuter, 'Gifts and Simony' in Esther Cohen and Mayke de Jong (eds), *Medieval Transformations: Texts, Power and Gifts in Context* (Turnhout, 2001), pp. 157-68.

condemned in councils from the Council of Chalcedon (451) to the Fourth Lateran Council.[112] Despite, or perhaps because of this, several putative bishops were accused of this offence during the course of the thirteenth century. Some were said to have offered bribes in order to secure their election. Adam of Kendal spent huge sums in a doomed attempt to ensure his election as bishop of Carlisle.[113] Thomas Melsonby of Durham was reported to have paid members of the English nobility to support his election; the king also claimed that he had granted Odo of Kilkenny, a royal clerk, a benefice to the same end.[114] Simon Walton was the subject of a jingle that suggested he had paid 300 marks to the monks of Norwich to secure his election,[115] and Boniface of Savoy alleged that Hugh Balsham had promised favours to the monks of Ely if they would chose him as their bishop.[116]

Others were accused of making morally dubious payments in order to secure papal confirmation. Matthew Paris thought that William Raleigh had spent 8,000 marks to this end.[117] In the 1260s, securing provision to Winchester was rumoured to have cost John Gervase the considerably more substantial sum of 12,000 silver marks.[118] In 1281, Archbishop Pecham ordered an investigation into claims that a proctor of Richard de la More, elect of Winchester, had offered bribes at the papal curia[119] – claims that were widely repeated in the chronicles, although it was also suggested that his election was quashed because he refused to commit simony.[120]

Such stories of simony are virtually impossible to prove or disprove. Formal accusations of simony relating to episcopal elections were rare during the thirteenth century, being included in only two formal appeals;[121] such allegations were almost always made by chroniclers. It is therefore extremely likely that,

---

112 Simon Magus, after whom the offence was named, was condemned for simony in Acts 8: 9-24. For Chalcedon, see *Ecumenical Councils*, I, pp. 87-8 (c. 2) and for the Fourth Lateran Council, ibid., I, p. 264 (c. 63).

113 *Register and Records of Holm Cultram*, ed. F. Grainger and W. Collingwood (Kendal, 1929), pp. 133-4.

114 *Script. Tres*, p. lxxiii.

115 *Chron. E1&E2*, I, p. 50.

116 Roger Lovatt, 'Hugh Balsham, Bishop of Ely 1256/7-1286' in Rosemary Horrox and Sarah Rees-Jones (eds), *Pragmatic Utopias: Ideals and Communities, 1200-1360* (Cambridge, 2001), pp. 60-83, at p. 64.

117 *CM*, IV, p. 346.

118 *Gervase*, II, pp. 218-19.

119 *Reg. Pecham*, II, p. 147.

120 *AM*, II, p. 399; III, p. 284; IV, pp. 293-4; *Bartholomæi de Cotton, Monachi Norwicensis, Historia Anglicana*, ed. H. Luard (RS, 1859), p. 163; Douie, *Pecham*, p. 107.

121 Henry III's appeal against Thomas Melsonby and Boniface of Savoy's appeal against Hugh Balsham. Melsonby was also accused of accepting money and lands from postulants to Durham Cathedral Priory (*Script. Tres*, p. lxxiii), and Simon Elmham (of Norwich) was said to

in some cases, there was genuine confusion over, or resentment of, legitimate payments, especially early examples of *servitia*.[122] Given the focus on payments made at the curia, it is likely that xenophobia conditioned at least some of these stories. On the other hand, given that a good deal of money and many gifts changed hands during the course of the electoral process, it is not impossible that illicit, or semi-licit, payments were made.

Even if bribes were not required, the making of a bishop was an extremely expensive business and this must have shaped the choices and behaviour of all those involved in the process. The expenses of the election were traditionally borne by the cathedral chapter, but might, by papal authority, be transferred to the new bishop. John Blund's election left the prior and convent of Canterbury in debt to a total of 612 silver marks, but they were granted a mandate to add this sum to the debts of the (already heavily indebted) archbishopric.[123] At Ely, Hugh Balsham bound himself to pay the expenses of his election and confirmation from the episcopal rents; his successors were to be bound in the same manner.[124] Particularly when combined with royal exploitation of the episcopal temporalities, the costs of election could leave bishops and their cathedral chapters in dire financial straits. Matthew Paris claimed that the Winchester dispute of 1238-44 left the see so depleted that William Raleigh was obliged to spend his final months in exile at Tours with a small household, for reasons of economy.[125] When William Gainsborough, the newly provided bishop of Worcester, returned from Rome in 1303, his finances were so depleted that he was unable to pay for his enthronement and was forced to ask the prior and convent for financial assistance.[126] Unfortunately, the cathedral convent was also in debt; they had borrowed £60 from the king's almoner, which they were unable to repay, and therefore could only give the bishop £20.[127] By the time of the bishop's enthronement, a tangled web of loans existed between the

have purchased the patronage of several churches (*CPL*, I, 163; *EEA 21: Norwich 1215-1243*, ed. C. Harper-Bill (Oxford, 2000), p. xxix).

122 The language of the Canterbury chronicler's accusation against John Gervase may be particularly relevant here: 'Ipse enim servierat M. Jordano vicecancellario in VI Milibus marcarum sterlingorum, et postea domino pape in VI Milibus marcarum sterlingorum; et sic recessit a curia confusus tanquam Symoniacus' (*Gervase*, II, pp. 218-19). The verb *servio* was used from the mid-thirteenth century to refer to the payment of papal *servitia*. Ronald Latham, *Revised Medieval Latin Word-List, from British and Irish Sources* (Oxford, 1980), p. 436.

123 *CPL*, I, pp. 146-7.

124 *CPL*, I, p. 365.

125 *CM*, V, pp. 178-9. Paris may well have somewhat overstated Raleigh's poverty; for a survey of the episcopal finances during his episcopate, see Vincent, 'Pipe Rolls', pp. 161-70.

126 *Reg. Sede Vacante*, pp. 37, 46.

127 Ibid., pp. 38, 40.

bishop, the convent and the almoner, who was threatening to 'take other means' to recoup his money if repayment was not forthcoming.[128]

Against this background, it would be unsurprising if financial considerations were amongst the factors determining the electoral choices made by cathedral chapters. Major electoral disputes occurred most frequently in the wealthiest sees, a trend that has usually been attributed to greater royal concern with these bishoprics, but might also be related to the greater ability of such sees to bear the financial burden of a dispute, enabling them to make more daring choices, at least intermittently. Poor sees, on the other hand, must often have been unable to afford to engage in electoral disputes and therefore more likely to favour safe choices. Chapters may also have taken into consideration the ability of the candidate (or his supporters) to pay some of the costs of election. Although candidates could not pay all of the relevant expenses (witness Ralph Neville's refusal to pay the expenses of the Canterbury monks who carried his name to Rome lest he be charged with simony[129]), a curial or aristocratic bishop would be better placed to shoulder part of the burden, and to replenish the diocesan finances once confirmed.

Electing a candidate who was acceptable to the king also increased the likelihood that royal gifts would be made at the time of the consecration and enthronement, thus offsetting some of the costs of these ceremonies. When Boniface of Savoy was elected as archbishop of Canterbury, Henry III gave him two substantial presents: a mitre with precious stones (worth 300 marks)[130] and 60 tuns of wine, to be placed in the cellar at Canterbury for Boniface's arrival.[131] The king also purchased a mitre worth fourteen marks for Peter Aigueblanche[132] and 'a complete set of episcopal vestments with a becoming mitre' for William of York, bishop of Salisbury.[133] Less substantial gifts of foodstuffs for the consecration feast might also be made; for example, two bishops of Exeter received six deer for their consecration feasts.[134]

It was also possible to supplement royal gifts by asking one's guests to supply some of the provisions for the enthronement feast. When John Pecham became archbishop of Canterbury in 1279, he invited a large number of important guests to his enthronement, including several bishops, the abbots of a number of important religious houses, a selection of earls, the king, the queen and the

128 Ibid., pp. 52, 55.

129 *CM*, III, p. 207.

130 *CLR 1240-1245*, p. 277.

131 Ibid., p. 212.

132 *CLR 1226-1240*, p. 502.

133 *CLR 1245-1251*, p. 152. The outfit cost the king 32*l.* 9*s.* 10*d.*

134 William Brewer, in 1224 (*RLC*, I, p. 593b), and Richard Blund, in 1245 (*CR 1242-47*, p. 342).

queen mother. The letter of invitation sent to the suffragans of the province requested that they send the traditional presents of venison and game for the feast.[135] Electing a bishop was a costly business and the weight of the burden was borne largely by the new bishop and his electors; nevertheless, it is important to recognize that customary gifts could, and did, move in both directions.

***

Although the canon law of election has been studied in considerable detail by a range of historians, the custom of election has received considerably less attention, especially within the English context. Nevertheless, the study of the latter is of great importance, for just as the law shaped elections, so too did the requirements of custom: chapters must have considered the opinions given to them at the bishop's funeral and at court, just as they must have pondered the financial implications of disregarding these opinions and provoking an appeal to Rome. Rituals allowed the participants to display their adherence to the canon law; thus the granting of the licence to elect was accompanied by a declaration of royal respect for the chapter's right of free election, and the electors might make their choice with floods of tears, in order to demonstrate their purity and sincerity, and the validity of their choice.

On the other hand, some of the customs that developed around episcopal elections ran counter to the prevailing trends as indicated by the canon law. Most significant in this respect is the emphasis on the ritual participation of great masses of people, at a time when popes and canonists were increasingly insistent that only the members of the cathedral chapter had the right to elect. Whilst the English were obliged to conform to legal requirements, and thus the election itself became a private affair, public involvement in the bishop-making process and widespread approval of the chapter's choice clearly remained significant.

Episcopal election was a legal process, for the simple reason that failure to adhere to legal requirements invalidated the process. However, this was only one aspect of the bishop-making process, which also had ritual, spiritual and financial dimensions. The combination of these elements ensured that an episcopal election was always a major event for the diocese concerned, but also for the country as a whole. Once the conflicting interests and agendas of the various participants were added to the mixture, the process became even more complex.

---

135 *Reg. Pecham*, I, pp. 37-8; Douie, *Pecham*, p. 66.

Chapter 3
The Practice and Problems of Episcopal Election, c.1214-c.1307

As the preceding chapters have outlined, by the thirteenth century there existed a clearly defined model for the correct conduct of elections; this model was widely disseminated and all of those who typically participated in elections would have been extremely familiar with it. Nevertheless, as many historians have pointed out, elections were rarely conducted in exact accordance with this ideal. According to Stubbs, 'the [electoral] history of the thirteenth century is a long record of disputes ... appointments to the bishoprics were a constant matter of dispute. The freedom of election promised by John had resulted in a freedom to litigate and little more.'[1] His view has been echoed by many subsequent historians, and there are numerous works on the subject of church–state relations during this period emphasizing the role of episcopal elections as a cause of conflict between the two estates.[2] This focus on electoral disputes in which the king reacted violently to the outcome of an election is understandable, but it is also unrepresentative on two counts. Contrary to the impression one gains from most of the historiography on this subject, such disagreements were rare and a clear majority of vacant dioceses were filled without serious upset, although this is not to say that they were straightforwardly canonical affairs. Furthermore, a significant proportion of appeals to Rome resulted not from royal displeasure, but from discord between or within electoral bodies, or from archiepiscopal decisions. This chapter therefore considers the wide range of potential deviations from the ideal of free canonical election, incorporating both subtle but commonplace differences and the upheaval of major disputes. Elections are considered from the perspective of the core quintet of participants (cathedral chapter, king, archbishop, papacy and candidate) and the roles played by a range of other non-official participants are also discussed.

---

[1] William Stubbs, *The Constitutional History of England: In its Origin and Development* (3 vols, Oxford, 1891-98), III, pp. 313-15.

[2] See, amongst others, Sweet, 'Control of Episcopal Elections', pp. 573-82; Gibbs and Lang, *Bishops*, pp. 53-93; John Moorman, *Church Life in England in the Thirteenth Century* (Cambridge, 1946), pp. 158-68; Powicke, *Henry III*, I, pp. 259-89; Carpenter, *Struggle*, p. 349; Michael Prestwich, *Plantagenet England, 1225-1360* (Oxford, 2005), p. 90.

The Role of the Cathedral Chapter

Although Stubbs argued that the elections held in the century after the Freedom of Election charter was issued remained essentially unfree, there were in fact a number of elections in which it is difficult or impossible to detect any undue royal influence, with the king's role being confined to the fulfilment of his responsibilities. Such elections usually took place in sees that were low in financial and political value, such as Exeter, where the chapter seems to have been allowed to hold elections that were not only canonical but genuinely free from royal intervention on three occasions during the course of the thirteenth century. Richard Blund (1245-57) appears to have owed his election solely to local connections (he was a member of a prominent Exeter family) and long-term membership of the cathedral chapter, of which he was the chancellor.[3] Similarly, the elections of Peter Quinel (1280-91) and Thomas Bitton (1291-1307) were apparently motivated by local dynamics rather than national politics.[4] The extent of the seeming lack of royal interest in Exeter is particularly striking, but just as most sees faced the royal displeasure at one time or another, so most also enjoyed at least one opportunity to elect their own choice. This trend became especially marked during the reign of Edward I, when even the wealthy, politically significant and dispute-prone sees of Durham and Winchester managed to promote one of their brethren to the episcopate.[5]

Such textbook elections were somewhat anomalous, but the canonical election was the norm. By the beginning of the thirteenth century the manner in which an episcopal election should be held had been well established in the canon law and knowledge of the correct procedures was widespread, becoming ever more so during the course of the century. As would be expected, given that only canonically sound elections could be considered valid, most elections were (as far as we know) conducted in accordance with the requirements of the canon law and the instructions of the handbooks on the conduct of elections. The majority of thirteenth-century electoral procedures are relatively sparsely documented; just as modern historians have been drawn to the spectacular disputes rather than the minutiae of electoral procedure, so too contemporary chroniclers, who generally made substantial comment on episcopal elections only if problems arose. A detailed account of the election of Walter de Eynsham in 1228, which was probably written by one of the monks who elected him, describes at considerable length the procedure followed; their conduct appears

---

3 *EEA 12: Exeter, 1086-1257*, ed. F. Barlow (Oxford, 1996), p. liii.

4 See the *ODNB* entries for Quinel and Bitton, both by N. Orme.

5 Robert de Insula, prior of Finchale, became bishop of Durham in 1274. Prior Henry Woodlock was elected bishop of Winchester thirty years later.

canonically sound.[6] A handful of electoral records produced by cathedral chapters during the second half of the period have survived, amongst them the electoral roll compiled at Durham in 1283, during the election of Anthony Bek to that see.[7] The documents entered onto this roll follow the model provided by Lawrence of Somercote almost exactly. The contents of the Worcester *Sede Vacante* register (in which the earliest entries relate to the 1302 vacancy) are likewise in accordance with the theoretical requirements.[8] The evidence of such texts, when taken in conjunction with the production of electoral tracts, suggests that cathedral chapters were greatly concerned to hold elections that were procedurally sound. A handful of elections were questioned (and indeed quashed) on procedural grounds, such as the 1228 Durham election, which was overturned because the monks of Durham, unanimous in their choice of William of Stichill, acclaimed his election individually, rather than as one.[9] The scarcity of such cases is, however, striking and indicates that capitular efforts to hold procedurally sound elections were almost always successful.

There was, however, a subtle difference between a canonical election (into which category almost every election of this period falls) and a complication-free election; the latter was extremely rare. Many of the difficulties originated within the electoral bodies themselves for, far from being united in their wishes, cathedral chapters were often hotbeds of dissent. This was dramatically illustrated during the Winchester dispute of 1238-44, when intense royal pressure ensured that internal differences came to the fore. Following the appointment of a new prior in 1239, the monks became divided into two factions. The first of these was led by Prior Andrew, who 'drew almost half the stars in his train and, corrupting the hearts of many' persuaded them to back the royal candidate.[10] A second group formed around another monk, Benedict de Burgh, who supported the candidacy of William de Raleigh and who led a group of monks to Rome to fight his case.[11] By 1241, tensions between the two groups had escalated to such a degree that Prior Andrew assented to the imprisonment and maltreatment of those members of the convent who backed Raleigh's cause.[12] Disagreements between brethren rarely became this bitter, but divided elections were common; it was unusual for the outcome of an election to be unanimous. Usually the

6 *Gervase*, II, pp. 115-24.

7 *Records of Antony Bek, Bishop and Patriarch, 1283-11*, ed. C. M. Fraser (Durham, 1953), pp. 180-90; *Durham Annals and Documents of the Thirteenth Century*, ed. F. Barlow (Durham, 1945), pp. 54-63.

8 *Reg. Sede Vacante*, pp. 1-79.

9 *Script. Tres*, pp. 36-7.

10 *CM*, III, p. 622.

11 *Rôles Gascons*, ed. F. Michel and C. Bémont (5 vols, Paris, 1885-), I, pp. 115, 161; *CPR 1232-1247*, p. 401.

12 *CM*, IV, pp. 107-8, 159-60; *Reg. Inn. IV*, no. 137.

minority would give their assent to the choice of the majority, thus securing his election, but on occasion two results would be declared, with both sides refusing to admit defeat. Twenty years after the Winchester dispute, the monks of that see held another election, at which the majority of the electors chose their former prior, William de Taunton, abbot of Milton, and the minority elected the current prior, Andrew of London.[13] As a result of their inability to agree, both elections were quashed at Rome and a papal provision was made.[14]

If the monks of Winchester Cathedral found it difficult to agree about their choice of bishop, the problem was far greater for the chapter members of England's two double sees, Bath and Wells, and Coventry and Lichfield. For much of the twelfth century, the monks of Bath and the canons of Wells had shared the right to elect their bishop, with the monks taking precedence. Then, when the see became vacant in 1174, the uneasy peace that had held for the past century broke down, and the canons alone elected the new bishop. Difficulties again arose in 1191, although a temporary rapprochement occurred in 1204, resulting in the election of a local man, Jocelin of Wells.[15] He gradually altered the balance of power between Bath and Wells until the former's primacy was little more than nominal, with Wells becoming the *sedes praesula* of the diocese. He also bequeathed his body to Wells – a breach with long-standing tradition which effectively made this the first church of the diocese.[16] Most significantly, in July 1242 he had compiled a selection of documents that supported the right of the canons to elect: the papal sanction of the election of Bishop Reginald (1174) by Wells alone, a papal confirmation of the right of Wells to elect independently, a decree that ordered joint elections to be held and the documents of his own election, in which the chapters had acted jointly.[17]

Although Jocelin appears to have intended that his actions would establish the rights of Wells to elect jointly with, and possibly independently of, Bath, it was inevitable that the latter see would not cede its rights so easily. Unsurprisingly, his death was followed by a disputed election. The monks of Bath elected Master Roger, the precentor of Salisbury Cathedral, on 6 February, having

---

13 *AM*, II, pp. 98-9.

14 *CPL*, I, p. 378; *Gervase*, II, p. 218. The case was complicated by the fact that William of Taunton lacked a dispensation for illegitimacy and should therefore have been postulated (*CPL*, I, pp. 377-8).

15 Everett Crosby, *Bishop and Chapter in Twelfth-Century England: A Study of the 'Mensa Episcopalis'* (Cambridge, 1994), pp. 48-65; Vincent, 'Jocelin of Wells', pp. 25-7.

16 Church, *Chapters*, pp. 240-41. For a dispute over the possession of a bishop's corpse, see *The Great Register of Lichfield Cathedral known as Magnum Registrum Album*, ed. H. E. Savage (Kendal, 1926), pp. 341-2 (no. 716). The monks of Coventry appear to have attempted to claim the body of William of Cornhill, who had been buried at Lichfield, but were prevented from bringing a legal case on this matter by the new bishop, Alexander of Stavensby.

17 Church, *Chapters*, p. 241. The inspeximus is printed as Appendix S, pp. 397-407.

invited the canons of Wells to be present as witnesses, but not to participate.[18] In consequence, although the canons seem to have had no objections to the person of the bishop-elect, they immediately appealed against the election on the grounds that their non-participation invalidated it.[19] Innocent IV confirmed the election in February 1244, 'without prejudice' to either see and in order that 'the church may not suffer'.[20] On 1 April a papal mandate ordered that, in future, elections were to be conducted jointly by Bath and Wells, with the votes of both chapters having equal weight, although the election and installation of the bishop were to take place at Bath.[21] This ruling seems to have been effective, for there were no further disputes between the two chapters on this subject. Nevertheless, the experiences of the chapters of Bath and Wells in the early 1240s illustrate the extent to which inter-capitular discord could influence the course of an election; under normal circumstances, the see should have been filled more rapidly, and without recourse to Rome.

The other double see, Coventry and Lichfield, faced similar difficulties throughout the thirteenth century.[22] When William of Cornhill died in August 1223, the monks of Coventry swiftly elected their prior. The canons of Lichfield appealed to Archbishop Stephen, who quashed the election; the Coventry monks then launched a counter-appeal to Rome. Honorius III's solution to the dispute was to make the first papal provision to an English diocese: Alexander Stavensby was provided to the bishopric of Coventry and Lichfield in April 1224.[23] In the wake of this contested election, the pope attempted to prevent further disputes by determining that elections should take place alternately at Coventry and Lichfield,[24] but the difficulties continued. No fewer than five candidates were elected during the 1238-40 vacancy. Robert Lexington,[25] a royal justice, and William of Manchester,[26] dean of Lichfield, were probably elected by the canons, but both resigned their claim to the bishopric. William Raleigh seems to have been elected by the monks;[27] as a canon of Lichfield he

18 *Bath Chartularies*, p. 42; *CM*, IV, p. 391.

19 *Wells MSS.*, I, p. 76.

20 *CPL*, I, pp. 205-6.

21 *CPL*, I, p. 208.

22 The complicated nature of the elections held in this diocese is reflected in the outlines provided by *Fasti 1066-1300*, XI, pp. xl-xli, 4-9. They will be explored in greater detail in the introduction to the forthcoming *English Episcopal Acta* volume for Coventry and Lichfield, 1208-95, drafted by the late Jeffrey Denton and currently in process of completion by Philippa Hoskin.

23 *AM*, III, p. 90; *Acta Stephani Langton Cantuariensis Archiepiscopi*, ed. K. Major (Oxford, 1950), nos. 61, 64; *Fasti 1066-1300*, XI, pp. 5-6.

24 *Registrum Album*, no. 761; *Fasti 1066-1300*, XI, p. xl.

25 *AM*, III, p. 149.

26 *CM*, III, pp. 541-2.

27 *CM*, III, p. 525.

may have been an acceptable compromise candidate, but he too declined the see. Subsequently a new licence to elect was issued jointly to the chapters of Coventry and Lichfield; their next choice was Nicholas Farnham, who also declined.[28] Finally, late in 1239, Hugh Patteshall accepted.[29]

Unfortunately, Patteshall's episcopate lasted less than three years, and another electoral dispute followed his death. This time, the monks and canons held a joint election, but the result was split: the dean and some of the canons of Lichfield, along with some of the Coventry monks, elected Richard, abbot of Evesham, whilst the remainder of the electors, including the prior of Coventry, favoured William de Montpellier. An appeal to Rome was the inevitable result of such dissent. Richard of Evesham died before the appeal was heard, William of Montpellier resigned his claim to the bishopric and Roger Weseham, dean of Lincoln, was provided to the bishopric.[30] The inability of the two chapters to hold harmonious elections meant that the diocese of Coventry and Lichfield enjoyed the dubious distinction of being the first diocese to have obtained two of its bishops by papal provision.

The next election appears to have passed off without major difficulty, and the longevity of Bishop Roger Meuland (1257-95) meant that Coventry and Lichfield avoided further electoral discord for several decades. The respite was only temporary. Whilst the Lichfield chronicler claimed that the election of Walter Langton (held at Lichfield in February 1296) was made 'harmoniously and peacefully',[31] the truth was rather more complicated. In the aftermath of the election, the prior and convent of Coventry planned to appeal against its outcome. The appeal was apparently dropped,[32] and Langton remained bishop of Coventry and Lichfield until his death in 1321. Yet the circumstances in which he and his predecessors were appointed serve as a stark reminder of the disruption that could be caused by divisions within the electoral body.

The Role of the King: Suggestion, Persuasion and Coercion

Far more frequently, however, it was not dissent but compromise that determined the course of elections, as the election of large numbers of curial candidates to English bishoprics suggests. Cathedral chapters often chose to comply with royal wishes by electing an individual whose name had been suggested to them

---

28 *AM*, III, p. 149; *CM*, III, pp. 541-2.

29 *Fasti 1066-1300*, XI, pp. 6-7.

30 *CPL*, I, pp. 203, 214, 218; *AM*, I, p. 121; *CM*, IV, pp. 171-2, 237, 423-6; *Fasti 1066-1300*, XI, p. 7.

31 *Anglia Sacra*, I, p. 441.

32 *Fasti 1066-1300*, XI, p. xl, citing Durham Cathedral Library MS. C. IV. 24, fos. 109v-112v.

by the king.[33] Although Gibbs and Lang questioned whether such men 'would have been elected by the better judgement and free choice of their respective cathedral chapters',[34] many chapters seem to have been perfectly content to appoint courtier bishops, and in some dioceses curial candidates were repeatedly favoured. This was especially common in dioceses where the cathedral chapter was made up primarily of non-residentiary secular canons, many of whom were themselves royal servants, but it also occurred in monastic sees; Winchester, for example, had a long tradition of electing such individuals, which only began to break down in the late thirteenth century. As late as 1280, Prior Adam actively sought out Edward I's advice on the election; he had initially wanted to consult with the king as soon as the bishop died and had to be persuaded by Chancellor Burnell to wait until the licence to elect was granted.[35] This was a system with many advantages for the diocese, which not only avoided a dispute with the crown, but also gained a representative who enjoyed good relations with the king and could use his connections for the benefit of his flock.[36] The Dominican preacher Hugh de St Cher complained that many bishops were chosen not by God, but because the electors believe that

> This man will preserve the rights of our church and successfully prosecute our business, he will go out to seek the asses not souls, and will defend our property, because he is powerful, or noble, or a great pleader.[37]

It seems certain that, despite the disapproval this provoked from certain sections of the church, chapters did take secular considerations into account when choosing their bishop. Thus we should be wary of seeing chapters who elected king's men simply as victims of an oppressive system which forced them to act against their will.

On the other hand, it is unlikely that so many royal servants would have gained promotion to the episcopate had it not been for the application of royal pressure (of varying degrees) to electoral bodies. Amongst the complaints against Henry III presented to Louis IX of France by the baronial reformers in January 1264 was the following allegation:

> And what is still more harmful, the lord king, at the persuasion of certain perverse men, frequently takes away, by prayer or by pressure, the right of free election

33 There are only four instances in which Henry III's candidate is known to have been elected, as Gibbs and Lang (*Bishops*, p. 88) note, but it seems clear that this was only the tip of the iceberg.

34 Gibbs and Lang, *Bishops*, p. 88.

35 The National Archives (TNA) SC1/24/195.

36 Vincent, *des Roches*, pp. 49-50.

37 Quoted in Ralph Bennett, *The Early Dominicans: Studies in Thirteenth-Century Dominican History* (Cambridge, 1937), p. 141.

> which by law they ought to have and were accustomed to have from of old, so that if perchance any do not listen to such requests, pressed upon them even for an unworthy candidate, they are often penalized by loss of their temporal goods, or in other instances the persons elected, no matter how canonically, are not admitted to favour until, through prolonged vacancy, everything that was of value has been exhausted.[38]

According to Matthew Paris, several chapters elected the royal candidate in order to avoid becoming victims of the king's wrath. In 1246, for example, the canons of Salisbury elected the royal justice William of York as their bishop because they wished to please the king and thus avoid danger to the diocese.[39] Four years later the monks of Winchester, worn down by the difficulties they had faced as a consequence of their election of William de Raleigh, agreed to elect the king's half-brother, Aymer de Lusignan, as his successor.[40] In Paris' version of events, such elections were unquestionable proof of the king's malign influence over the English Church, achieved through coercion.

Henry III and Edward I used a wide range of methods in order to bring about the election of their candidates, ranging from gentle persuasion to rather more heavy-handed tactics, although, somewhat inevitably, many of the more peaceful dealings between king and chapter have gone unrecorded. It was, for example, almost unheard of for the licence to elect to name the king's preferred candidate; there are only two surviving examples of such a written indication of royal preferences, and one further instance in which we can infer that royal wishes had been formally conveyed to the chapter. The first dates from the end of the reign of King John: in March 1215, he named the Abbot of Whitland (who was subsequently elected) in the licence granted to the canons of Bangor.[41]

In early 1243, Henry III apparently indicated in writing (although not in the licence) to the monks of Bath that he wished them to elect his treasurer, Peter Chaceporc, as their bishop; letters written by the cathedral convent refer to the letters written in his favour by the king and queen,[42] although the king subsequently (hastily and somewhat mysteriously) withdrew his request.[43] Then, in 1254, Henry issued a licence to elect to the canons of Carlisle, which stated that

38 *Documents of the Baronial Movement*, pp. 270-71.

39 *CM*, IV, p. 587.

40 *CM*, V, pp. 180-81.

41 *RLP*, pp. 130b, 132b.

42 *Bath Chartularies*, pp. 44-6.

43 *CR 1242-1247*, p. 59.

> [The canons] have the king's letters patent directed to Earl Richard and Master William de Kilkenny, or either of them present in the realm, to give the royal assent to the election of John, prior of Newburgh [and a royal chaplain] to be elected as bishop, and to make a restitution of the temporalities. But if they do not elect him, they are to send the person elected to the king.[44]

The circumstances in which this licence was granted were somewhat unusual, for the king was then in Gascony, but the naming of a favoured royal candidate at this stage of the electoral process was probably entirely conventional. The need to seek the *congé d'élire* from the king brought several leading members of the cathedral chapter to the royal court, where they could be informed of the king's wishes; indeed, the royal recommendation of Peter Chaceporc to the monks of Bath was also made to the delegation that travelled to Bordeaux to petition for licence to elect.[45] King John had promised that licence to elect would not be denied or delayed and, with two exceptions, this pledge was upheld by Henry III and Edward I. In 1228, Henry III repeatedly refused to grant *congé d'élire* to the monks of Durham, nominally because he wished the election to be peacefully carried out, but in reality because he was seeking the election of Luke, his treasurer. After three months, fearing that they would lose their right of election (as stipulated by canon law), the monks went ahead regardless, provoking a royal appeal based in part on the fact that *conge d'élire* had not been granted and had not been unjustly denied.[46] Nearly two decades later, in 1243 Henry III refused the monks of Norwich licence to elect; he did not accept that the see was vacant, because he refused to recognize the translation of their bishop, William Raleigh, to the bishopric of Winchester.[47]

These two cases were clearly anomalous. Nevertheless, securing this vital document was not always an entirely straightforward process and might take several days. The Canterbury chronicler thought that a delegation seeking licence to elect should petition the king on two or three successive days before they might be justified in proceeding to elect without royal permission.[48] His account of the archiepiscopal election that followed the death of Stephen Langton in 1228 includes a description of the monastic proctors' visit to court to seek licence to elect. A small group of monks, led by the prior and including several senior members of the chapter, arrived at court and was honourably received by the king. Henry did not immediately grant them their request, but instead 'asked for a short delay in replying ... asserting that he wished to deliberate on

---

44 *CPR 1247-1258*, p. 292.

45 *CR 1242-1247*, p. 52.

46 Evers, 'Disputes', pp. 65-71, and Appendix, pp. 1-18.

47 *CPR 1232-1247*, p. 409.

48 *Gervase*, II, p. 124.

this for at least one night, and to take council from the bishops and barons'. Early the next day, 'both the bishops and the leading men and other countless persons assembled as one at Westminster, with the lord king', and the prior again petitioned the king for permission to hold a free election. Henry granted their request, asking that they should choose unanimously and elect an individual whose promotion would benefit God, the church and the kingdom.[49]

This uniquely detailed account of the experiences of a monastic delegation seeking licence to elect raises almost as many questions as it answers. It seems that the granting of *congé d'élire*, although a routine procedure, was more than a mere formality. Moreover, it demanded the personal involvement of the king. That this was the case is also indicated by the fact that even when the king was overseas proctors had to make their petition to him; the task of issuing such licences was not amongst the business delegated to regents.[50] For example, in early 1243, following the death of Bishop Jocelin of Wells, a pair of delegations (one from Bath and the other from Wells) travelled to Bordeaux to seek licence to elect from Henry III.[51] Why was the king's personal involvement required? In broad terms, this requirement must surely reflect the importance of the matter in hand; it was fitting for the king to be personally involved in all stages of the appointment process for such a great office, and for this business to be conducted in a formal manner – hence the public issuing of the licence. Furthermore, it seems likely that the king was issuing more than formal permission to elect; he must surely have used this as an opportunity to indicate his wishes to the electors. That this was the case is surely indicated by Henry's insistence that he needed to 'deliberate on' the matter and seek advice from the bishops and barons. It seems unlikely that the king and his advisors were discussing whether or not to grant licence to elect, since the provisions of the 1214 charter left Henry with little choice in this matter. Far more plausible is the notion that the king was taking counsel on the rather more pressing question of who should be the royal candidate to fill the vacant see.

In many cases, it seems that such an informal indication of the king's wishes was sufficient to secure the election not only of a royal servant, but of a specific curial candidate. However, even once the delegation had left the court, the electors were not free from royal oversight. In 1256, following the election of Hugh Balsham as bishop of Ely, Henry III wrote to Archbishop Boniface, outlining his objections to this election. Amongst his complaints was that the election had been held before the arrival of the king's proctors, whose presence

---

49 *Gervase*, II, pp. 115-17.

50 See *CPR 1247-1258*, p. 206, relating to Henry III's visit to Gascony in 1253. The governance of the kingdom was entrusted to Queen Eleanor and Richard of Cornwall, but licence to elect and assent to elections were to be sought from the king in person.

51 *CPR 1232-1247*, pp. 354 (for Bath) and 367 (for Wells).

was required in order to ensure the promotion of a suitable individual, loyal and useful to the king and the kingdom.[52] It seems, therefore, that it was customary for royal proctors to attend elections, although it is unclear from this document whether they were present at the vote itself or withdrew immediately beforehand (as Somercote's insistence on the exclusion of outsiders would suggest).[53] What is clear is that, although elections were no longer held in the king's chapel (as had been commonplace in the twelfth century), they were still conducted under the supervision of the king's representatives, and this must have had a serious impact on the ability of cathedral chapters to act freely.

The role of royal proctors in securing the election of the king's candidate was also commented on by Matthew Paris in his account of the 1250 Winchester election. According to his account, the royal clerks Peter Chaceporc and John Mansell were sent to Winchester, to persuade, and if necessary force, the monks to elect Aymer de Lusignan, the king's half-brother, as William de Raleigh's successor.[54] On this occasion, however, the royal oversight went far beyond the conventional, for Henry himself took the extremely unusual step of personally visiting the see. On 30 October he took up residence at the episcopal manor of Marwell, less than ten miles from Winchester.[55] He then he moved to Winchester where, according to the *Chronica Majora*, he entered the chapter house and spoke to the monks in their chapter, as if he were a bishop preaching a sermon. Cowed by the king's threats, the monks decided to elect Aymer and named him as their bishop in the king's presence on the same day.[56]

Paris' account of the election is, in several ways, somewhat problematic. His chronology is the subject of some debate: Huw Ridgeway accepts his version of events, and states that the king arrived at Winchester on 4 November, the day on which the election took place,[57] whereas Michael Clanchy suggests that Henry delivered his address the following day, by which time Aymer had already been postulated.[58] It is also somewhat curious that Paris is the only chronicler to

---

52 *CR 1256-1259*, pp. 108-9.

53 *Somercote*, p. 30.

54 *CM*, V, pp. 179-80.

55 Theodore Craib (ed.), *The Itinerary of Henry III* (London, 1923), p. 216.

56 *CM*, V, pp. 180-83. Paris states that the monks publicly named Aymer as their bishop in the royal presence, which has sometimes been taken as meaning that Henry was present at the election itself. It seems more likely that the king left the monks whilst they held the election itself (in accordance with canon law), but returned for the public proclamation of their choice.

57 Huw Ridgeway, 'The Ecclesiastical Career of Aymer de Lusignan, Bishop-Elect of Winchester, 1250-60' in Brian Golding and John Blair (eds), *The Cloister and the World: Essays in Medieval History in Honour of Barbara Harvey* (Oxford, 1996), pp. 148-77, at p. 150. That the election took place on 4 November is confirmed by the annalists of Winchester (*AM*, II, p. 92) and Osney (*AM*, IV, p. 99).

58 Michael Clanchy, 'Did Henry III have a Policy?', *History*, 53 (1968), pp. 203-16, at pp. 206-7. Craib's *Itinerary*, p. 216, would seem to support Clanchy's view – he has Henry at Marwell on

comment on this unusual turn of events, and we are forced to ask unanswerable questions about his sources: how much of the sermon is Henry and how much is Matthew? Did the chronicler somehow manage to obtain a transcript of the king's actual speech or is the text we now have a considerably distorted version of what was originally said? The truth is probably somewhere between these two options. What seems to indicate that it conveys something close to Henry's sentiments is its measured approach; if Paris had forged the text, he would surely have produced something less conciliatory and more aggressive in tone.

It is the tone of the speech that is the most interesting aspect of this account, for it seems to reflect much of Henry's general approach to episcopal elections. In his sermon, Henry combined bribery and threats: 'mingled soft speeches, threats and promises', as Paris puts it. His counsellors were to prepare the way for him, and it does seem that the monks had essentially agreed to comply with the king's wishes by the time Henry arrived in Winchester; the king certainly believed that they had 'shown [themselves] favourable to [his] request'. His sermon ('sermo') continued in this vein, being based on a verse of Psalm 85: 'Mercy and truth are met together; righteousness and peace have kissed each other.' The psalm in question was an effective choice for the occasion, since it could be seen as a metaphor for the difficult relationship between Henry and Winchester from the late 1230s to 1250 and beyond. Although it essentially presents God as a merciful deity, his anger is an ever-present threat and the people live in fear. He will 'speak peace to his people', but only if they do not 'turn again to folly'. Righteousness and peace having kissed each other, the former will show the way forward and 'our land shall yield her increase'.

The monks had turned to folly before, in Henry's view, by electing William de Raleigh against his will, and the king reminded them that he 'was severe upon you' in response. Now, however, they were given the chance to repent and display their obedience by electing Aymer de Lusignan. If they failed to do so, 'He would forthwith ruin them all, according to the words of the poet: the man in power begs with a naked sword.'[59] Henry, like the God of the psalm, was offering love and prosperity, but only as a reward for obedience – the obedience a Christian owed to his God, and a subject owed to his king. The two types of loyalty were of course difficult to distinguish between; given the quasi-sacerdotal nature of medieval kingship, disobeying the king could indeed by construed as disobeying God.

The menacing undertone of the speech is neutralized by Henry's claim of a special affinity with the monks, based on his birth in the city and his baptism

4 November and Winchester the following day – but given that the two are only six miles apart, the evidence is inconclusive.

[59] The quotation was taken from Bernard Silvestris' *De mundi universitate*, as quoted by Peter of Blois in his dedication of a letter collection to Henry II. Richard Southern, *Scholastic Humanism and the Unification of Europe: The Heroic Age* (Oxford, 2001), p. 182.

in their church. They were bound to him 'by the ties of greater affection' and it was therefore especially fitting that they should pay him due obedience. The emphasis on Henry's own links to Winchester and on his kinship with Aymer ('fratrem meum uterinum') seems to suggest that by electing the latter as their bishop they will earn the special favour, almost the kinship, of the king. This would inevitably be expected to produce the increase in yield to which the psalm refers.

Just as this speech was divided between bribery and threats, so the crown used both tactics to persuade cathedral chapters to do its bidding. Thus Robert Grosseteste, writing to Archbishop Edmund shortly before the 1240 Hereford election, exhorted his superior to instruct the chapter 'about not fearing people's threats, and about guarding against bribes'.[60] Chapters were not infrequently given gifts in the run up to an election, such as the 'cope of good samite' given to the canons of Chichester shortly before they elected a successor to Richard Wyche.[61] In the course of the Winchester dispute of 1238-44, monks who were believed to be favourable to the royal cause tasted the fruits of royal favour; the hordarian Henry Corham, for example, received a royal gift of sixty beech poles to repair a weir,[62] whilst a man guilty of manslaughter was pardoned by the king thanks to the petition of Henry Byset, the curtarian.[63] During the same dispute, Henry III even paid the expenses of those members of the cathedral priory who went to Rome to oppose William Raleigh.[64] In 1298 Archbishop Winchelsey wrote to the monks of Ely cathedral, who were about to elect a new bishop; he was concerned that certain monks were being tempted by bribes, threats or 'carnal affections', and threatened all those guilty of conspiracy with excommunication.[65] Several members of the convent nevertheless elected the royal chancellor, Ralph de Walpole. On the other hand, chapters who fell foul of the king could be heavily penalized, as the canons of Carlisle discovered during the reign of Edward I: in 1280 they were amerced for 500 marks as a consequence of their failure to seek a second licence to elect when their first choice refused promotion to the episcopate.[66] It is easy to understand how chapters could have

60 *Grosseteste*, p. 284 (letter 83).

61 *CLR 1251-1260*, p. 120.

62 *CR 1237-1242*, p. 192. As hordarian, Corham was one of several Winchester obedientiaries who dealt with the financial affairs of the cathedral priory.

63 Ibid, p. 246.

64 See *CR 1232-1247*, p. 25, for royal authorization of a loan of up to 100 marks for the monks who went to Rome. After Raleigh's death, Henry demanded that his executors repay the costs of the election dispute from the episcopal revenues – half of the money being owed to the cathedral priory, the other half to the king in settlement of the loan he had made. See *CR 1247-1251*, p. 522.

65 *Reg. Winchelsey*, I, pp. 254-5; Rose Graham, 'The Administration of the Diocese of Ely during the Vacancies of the See, 1298-99 and 1302-3', *TRHS*, 4th series, 12 (1929), pp. 49-74, at p. 54.

66 *CPR 1281-1292*, p. 10. They were subsequently pardoned 200 marks of this fine.

been tempted to elect the royal candidate as their bishop and reap the benefits of such a choice.

The king could also use his right to control the temporalities of a vacant see as a tool in his battle to control episcopal elections. The custom of regalian right gave the king considerable rights of patronage,[67] which could be used to influence the chapter in a variety of ways. Most commonly, the king exploited his right to appoint to vacant prebends within secular chapters in order to bolster the careers of men whom he viewed as potential bishops. On several occasions, the royal candidate for a bishopric was presented to a prebend of that diocese only weeks or days before the election was held, presumably as a concession to the sensibilities of the chapter and the ideal of electoral freedom. Consequently, the canons could elect a man who was one of their brethren – but also one of the king's men. Thus Ralph de Neville was collated to the chancellorship of Chichester on 28 October 1222[68] and was elected as bishop of Chichester less than a week later.[69] During the vacancy that followed Neville's death, Robert Passelewe became archdeacon of Lewes on 5 March 1244;[70] he was elected as Neville's successor in April.[71] The same strategy was used by Edward I in 1280, when he was attempting to secure the bishopric of St David's for the wardrobe official Thomas Bek. He received a prebend in the cathedral chapter by royal presentation on 17 May[72] and was elected as bishop on 3 June.[73]

Such elections illustrate the use of royal patronage as a tool of persuasion, but it could also be used more forcefully if a chapter was refusing to cooperate with royal wishes. During the Winchester vacancy of 1238-44, Henry III made a series of appointments which were designed to force the monks of St Swithun's into compliance. Two priors were appointed in this manner. In 1239, Andrew le Breton was intruded against the wishes of the convent and of Archbishop Edmund, who excommunicated him.[74] In December 1243 Henry again took advantage of a prior's death to appoint to that office.[75] These appointments suggest that Henry was trying to control the cathedral monastery from the inside, and the fact that he created approximately twenty obedientiaries[76] (including two

67 Howell, *Regalian Right*, pp. 169-200.

68 *PR 1216-1225*, p. 349.

69 Royal assent to his election was give on 1 November (*PR 1216-1225*, p. 349).

70 *CPR 1232-1247*, p. 421.

71 Royal assent was given on 19 April (*CPR 1232-1247*, p. 423).

72 *CPR 1272-1281*, p. 370.

73 *Fasti 1066-1300*, IX, p. 49.

74 *CR 1226-1240*, p. 158; *AM*, II, pp. 323-4; *CM*, III, p. 622; *Reg. Inn. IV*, no. 137.

75 *CPR 1232-1247*, pp. 413-14; *AM*, I, p. 132.

76 Joan Greatrex, *Biographical Register of the English Cathedral Priories of the Province of Canterbury, c.1066 to 1540* (Oxford, 1997), p. 652.

sacrists,[77] a curtarian, a hostiller, a custos operum[78] and a hordarian[79]) supports this notion.

Kings could also use their rights over the revenues of a vacant diocese in order to influence the outcome of elections. Given that the crown was always in great need of money, the possibility of deliberate exploitation by royal officials was a constant concern. Sometimes this was encouraged by the king;[80] occasionally the king himself felt it necessary to restrain his officials.[81] It seems likely that, as Margaret Howell argued, the king rarely set out to deliberately despoil episcopal property; instead, 'he simply took what he required, just when he required it, with too little regard for the consequences'.[82] Nevertheless, the threat of royal destruction hung over electoral bodies and was occasionally put into practice, most spectacularly during the 1238-44 Winchester vacancy. When the monks' hostility to William of Savoy (Eleanor of Provence's uncle and the king's candidate for the bishopric[83]) first became known, 'the king destroyed the possessions and improvements of the bishopric, and often lay in the manors belonging to it, attended by a numerous company'[84] – a strategy that had the added advantage of reducing Henry's personal expenditure. Throughout the vacancy, Henry did his best to exploit the resources of the see. The temporalities were taken into royal custody only two days after des Roches died[85] and a month later the keepers of the see were ordered to assess a 'moderate aid' on the lands of the diocese.[86] The fine rolls are full of orders that the revenues of the bishopric be used to fund some royal act of patronage; payments recorded on the 1242-43

77 *CR, 1237-1242*, pp. 158, 231.

78 Ibid., p. 158.

79 Ibid., pp. 158, 192.

80 *CLR 1240-1245*, p. 210.

81 See, for example, *CPR 1232-1247*, p. 438.

82 Howell, *Regalian Right*, p. 145.

83 For his career, see Alain Marchandisse, 'Guillaume de Savoie: Un *Monstrum Spirituale et Belua Multorum Capitum* sur le Trône de Saint Lambert?', *Bulletin de la Société Royale le Vieux-Liège*, 13 (1997), pp. 657-70, 681-700.

84 *CM*, III, p. 494. The truth of this claim is somewhat difficult to uncover, given that Winchester was a favoured royal residence throughout the reign. Henry's itinerary shows that he made frequent visits to Winchester during the period under question – but this is unlikely to be of great significance, since he was a frequent visitor to the city, and there is no evidence to suggest that he stayed anywhere other than his own castle during the relevant visits. He was at Marwell for much of September 1238 and for a few days at Christmas 1238; this which would seem to go some way towards supporting Paris' claims, although the allegation that his aims were destructive is unproven. Craib, *Itinerary*, pp. 138-78, with the Marwell visits at pp. 139-41. An order to maintain the houses etc. of the see in the condition in which they were at the time of des Roches' death, given in August 1240, would seem to counter such claims. *CLR 1240-1245*, p. 488; Howell, *Regalian Right*, p. 145.

85 *CPR 1232-1247*, p. 224.

86 *CPR 1232-1247*, p. 225.

roll include forty shillings on a horse for Richard le Chaundler and fifty marks for a chapel at Westminster. In the final months of the dispute the king became particularly determined to squeeze as much revenue as possible out of the see, and in December 1243 he asked the keepers to sell the majority of the corn from the episcopal manors.[87] The following month they were ordered to 'send all the money they can get out of the issues of the bishopric after the king without delay'.[88] Margaret Howell calculated that Henry made profits of nearly £20,000 from the Winchester vacancy, and whilst his exploitation of episcopal vacancies as a source of income was on a much smaller scale than that of his twelfth-century predecessors, it is noteworthy that, during the years 1240-44, 20 per cent of royal income was derived from this source – primarily those at Canterbury and Winchester.[89] It is undeniable that the king could, if he so wished, make considerable financial gains from such circumstances, whilst simultaneously demonstrating to the English Church why it should do his bidding.

Henry III's exploitation of Winchester was remarkable, but in 1298 Edward I went even further and took Ely cathedral priory into royal custody, in an attempt to bully the monks into electing his chancellor as their bishop.[90] The monks protested vigorously, and before proceeding to hold an election, they appealed to Archbishop Winchelsey to defend them against this infringement of their rights. The archbishop responded by writing to the king to complain about the latter's actions; he claimed that as the priory was distinct from the bishopric, and was not vacant, Edward had no right to its custody.[91] Ecclesiastical concern about the dangers of such unlawful incursions by the custodians of vacant sees (as well as abbeys and priories) is reflected in the first three clauses of the *Articuli super cartas* (1300), by which the church sought protection from such arbitrary prises.[92]

Even after an election had received papal confirmation, it was possible for the king to use his control of the temporalities to express his displeasure at the appointment, typically by refusing to restore them. Both Henry III and Edward I

---

87 *Calendar of Fine Rolls*: www.finerollshenry3.org.uk. Robert Stacey, *Politics, Policy and Finance under Henry III, 1216-1245* (Oxford, 1987), pp. 220-23, discusses the financial value of episcopal vacancies to the crown and notes that 'the king's true financial advantages from episcopal vacancies were ... substantially greater than the direct monetary revenues which could be drawn from them'. These advantages included not only the opportunities for patronage noted above, but also the extensive provisions taken from Winchester to support the royal army during the 1242 Poitevin expedition. See also Howell, *Regalian Right*, pp. 142-6, on examples of such exploitation during other vacancies.

88 *CLR 1240-1245*, p. 210.

89 Stacey, *Politics*, p. 222.

90 Graham, 'Administration', pp. 52-3.

91 *Reg. Winchelsey*, I, p. 253.

92 Jeffrey Denton, *Robert Winchelsey and the Crown, 1294-1313: A Study in the Defence of Ecclesiastical Liberty* (Cambridge, 1980), pp. 195-6.

used this strategy on occasion, and although they always capitulated after a short while (typically within a matter of months) the new bishop faced an extremely difficult situation in the interim between consecration and the restoration to royal favour. The most striking illustration of this practice comes from Ralph Bocking's life of St Richard Wyche. On his return from Rome, Richard was greeted with hostility at court and prevented from taking possession of his see, where the royal officials were still in place. He took refuge with Father Simon of Tarring (on the border of the Chichester and Canterbury dioceses) for some time. Then, 'not wishing to seem laggardly or neglectful of his rights', he again sought out the king, and for some time followed the court, but whenever he attempted to present his petition, 'he received only insults from courtiers'.[93] Only after nearly two years of waiting did he finally receive the temporalities of his bishopric,[94] and the revenues owed to Wyche for the years during which the temporalities were withheld had still not been restored at the time of his death.[95]

Both Henry III and Edward I, then, took something of a carrot and stick approach to the cathedral chapters; electoral bodies made their choices knowing that to favour the royal candidate would bring them great advantages, and disregarding the king's wishes could have serious consequences. It is easy to understand why, faced with this choice, the majority of elections resulted in the election of a curial bishop. Nevertheless, it was far from unheard of for chapters to elect their own candidate, even when royal wishes had been clearly indicated to them. Even more striking, given the conventional assumption that a king thwarted in his attempts to secure a bishopric for a favoured royal servant would inevitably turn vicious, in neither reign did such a decision automatically lead to conflict. In 1253, for example, after the death of Robert Grosseteste, Henry III tried to persuade the canons of Lincoln to choose Peter d'Aigueblanche as their bishop, but they instead elected their dean, Henry Lexington. The king, despite his desire to see his favourite elected, could not find any just reason to reject the bishop-elect and thus reluctantly accepted the outcome. According to the *Chronica Majora*, Aigueblanche was rejected because he was a foreigner who resided abroad and did not understand English; furthermore, he was notorious for being unfaithful to the kingdom and for enriching himself to the detriment of his existing see.[96] Paris' account was almost certainly coloured by his personal

93 *Saint Richard*, pp. 98-101.

94 *CR 1242-1247*, p. 442.

95 This was one of the matters Wyche threatened to bring before 'the Court of the Most High' in his testament. See *Saint Richard*, p. 69; for the royal response, see *CLR 1251-1260*, p. 126; *CLR 1267-1272*, p. 156; Joseph Creamer, 'In the Footsteps of Becket: Episcopal Sanctity in England, 1170-1270' (University of Washington, PhD thesis, 2011), pp. 225-6.

96 *CM*, V, p. 422.

prejudices,[97] but it is striking that Henry chose not to challenge this slight to such a prominent and favoured figure. Indeed, it seems that Lincoln was not the only see to reject Aigueblanche, for Mathew Paris also reported attempts by the king to have him translated to Durham, London and Bordeaux. Yet on no occasion was an appeal made, nor does Paris insinuate underhand conduct on Henry's part in relation to any of these elections, as he would surely have done if there was anything to report.[98] Similarly, when the canons of Carlisle elected Thomas de Vipont as their bishop, instead of John of Newburgh, the royal chaplain who had been named in the licence to elect, Henry simply gave his assent to their choice.[99]

Such specific examples of chapters rejecting royal requests but still receiving royal assent to their choice are impossible to identify from the reign of Edward I, but it seems likely that such a sequence of events became more, rather than less common during the reign of Henry's son. The proportion of elections in which evidence of obvious royal intervention is lacking rose during the years 1272-1307; curial bishops became significantly less prominent, with diocesan clergy and monks being successfully elected far more frequently. It is of course possible that Edward was simply completely disinterested in episcopal appointments, yet the evidence would suggest that this was not the case. Given that, in general terms, Edward enjoyed a much tighter grip over ecclesiastical patronage than his father,[100] it seems extremely unlikely that Edward did not follow his father's policy of indicating his wishes to the chapter, although he may have been somewhat more willing to respect the wishes of electoral bodies, even where they conflicted with his own.

The Role of the King: Appeals

Given their differing priorities, it was inevitable that the tensions between kings and chapters would sometimes build to a level from which they could not be resolved informally and patched up, but instead had to be resolved through appeal to a higher authority: the papacy. Typically, the king was the catalyst for an appeal rather than the actual appellant; nevertheless, in such appeals his actions were clearly the primary cause of the litigation. By withholding his assent to an election, he could essentially force a chapter and their bishop-elect

97 See Richard Vaughan, *Matthew Paris* (Cambridge, 1958), for the chronicler's low opinions of Henry III, the papacy and foreigners.

98 *CM*, IV, p. 61 (for Durham); IV, p. 171 (London); V, p. 587 (Bordeaux); *EEA*, 35, p. xli.

99 *CPR 1247-1258*, p. 391. Gibbs and Lang, *Bishops*, pp. 87-8, gives a list of eleven occasions on which Henry III's choices were rejected by cathedral chapters; these include occasions on which the rejection led to an appeal.

100 Michael Prestwich, *Edward I* (London, 1997), p. 546.

to appeal to Rome, where royal representatives would subsequently present the king's counterclaims. Royal opposition to an election led to an appeal to the papal curia in eight of the vacancies that arose during the reign of Henry III: Durham (1228), Canterbury (1229), Winchester (1238-44, two appeals), Norwich (1239), Durham (1241), York (1255), Ely (1256) and Canterbury (1271). Two such appeals were made under Edward I: Carlisle (1278) and Ely (1299).[101]

Some patterns immediately emerge from this list of contested elections, most obviously the relative scarcity of appeals to Rome; whole decades passed without a royal appeal being launched, and only 8 per cent of the episcopal elections held in England between the death of John and the accession of Edward II were contested in this manner. Henry III provided the catalyst for slightly more appeals than his son: 11 per cent of the elections held during his reign were the subject of such appeals, whilst the figure was only 4 per cent under Edward I. Elections made by regular cathedral chapters were far more vulnerable in this respect; only one of the contested elections (York, 1255) related to a secular chapter. Similarly, the wealthiest, most politically significant chapters were vastly over-represented (only Carlisle could not be said to fit into this group, given the extreme poverty of the diocese, but this is probably best explained by its strategic importance). This final trend can be explained by the fact that the king inevitably displayed greater interest in appointments to such sees than to elections held in poorer, more marginal dioceses, but it may also suggest that such chapters were more willing to resist royal wishes and if necessary to fight their case at Rome.

If Stubbs' allegation that the thirteenth century was an age dominated by electoral litigation[102] is largely unwarranted, so too is the assumption that royal appeals were characterized by unsophisticated bluster and based solely on royal self-righteousness. Undoubtedly royal appeals were motivated by frustration at capitular refusal to do the king's bidding, but under the terms of the Freedom of Election charter, mere royal displeasure was not a valid reason to withhold assent to an election. Instead, the king must 'propose a reasonable objection and prove legitimately, on account of which we ought not to consent'.[103] Consequently, an appeal could only be successful if it was based on a sound knowledge of the canon law against which the soundness of the electoral procedure and the suitability of the bishop-elect was judged.[104]

---

101 All calculations in this and the following paragraph are based on the *Fasti Ecclesiae Anglicanae*.

102 Stubbs, *Constitutional History*, III, pp. 313-15.

103 *C&S*, I, p. 41.

104 For what follows, see Katherine Harvey, 'Objections to Episcopal Elections in England, 1216-1272', *Nottingham Medieval Studies*, 55 (2011), pp. 125-47, which discusses this topic in greater detail.

Royal objections based on procedural grounds were almost unheard of, and both examples of elections challenged on such terms took place during the reign of Edward I. The first of these was the 1278 Carlisle election. The canons had received licence to elect from the king[105] and elected M. William de Rotherfield, dean of York, who immediately declined the see. On the following day, they therefore held another election, and this time Ralph of Ireton, prior of Guisborough, was elected.[106] Edward I objected strongly to their actions, writing to Walter Giffard and demanding that the archbishop to do nothing to prejudice crown rights, since the chapter of Carlisle had held a second election without seeking a new licence.[107] Giffard died shortly afterwards, the chapter of York refused to confirm the election and both the canons of Carlisle and the king appealed to Rome. Nicholas III quashed the election due to this procedural flaw and provided Ireton to Carlisle.[108] Edward I also cited flaws in the letters notifying him that the majority of the Ely convent had elected their prior as their bishop in 1299 to justify refusing assent to this election, and assenting to that of the minority candidate John Langton. But whereas Edward's objections to the Carlisle election seem to have been genuinely technical, in the Ely case it seems clear that procedure was being used as a front to justify Edward's support for Langton – his chancellor.[109]

The provision of Ireton suggests one explanation for the crown's reluctance to launch such appeals, at least from the late thirteenth century onwards: if the procedure was flawed but the candidate suitable, then the situation could be resolved by a papal provision of the bishop-elect.[110] Such an outcome would clearly be disastrous for a king seeking the appointment of a completely different candidate. It also seems likely, given the solid knowledge of canonical procedure found within most cathedral chapters by the thirteenth century, that relatively few elections could have been challenged on such grounds; the majority of elections were probably entirely watertight in this respect. What is certain is that the crown had the ability to detect such flaws where they existed, for the king had access to a multitude of canon lawyers, including the masters of Paris and Oxford, who were pressed into royal service when the crown wished to oppose an election.[111] Consequently, it was possible for the king to present detailed cases

---

105 *CPR 1278-1281*, p. 280.

106 *The Chronicle of Lanercost, 1272-1346*, ed. H. Maxwell (Glasgow, 1913), pp. 18-19.

107 TNA SC 1/8/30.

108 *CPL*, I, p. 461.

109 *CPR 1292-1301*, p. 357.

110 Towards the end of the century, several York elections were quashed on procedural grounds and the candidate provided. See below, pp. 107-8.

111 *CPR 1232-1247*, pp. 438-9.

to the papacy, in which he typically highlighted the flaws in the bishop-elect most likely to lead to the quashing of the election.

In constructing such critiques, the king had at his disposal numerous descriptions of the model bishop, dating from apostolic times to the thirteenth century. The Apostle Paul set out the qualities required of a bishop in the first letter to Timothy: amongst other things, he must be 'of good behavior ... apt to teach ... not a novice'.[112] The Apostolic Rule was developed and enlarged upon throughout the Middle Ages, both in canon law and by theorists, but the central criteria remained maturity, morality and knowledge.[113] During the reign of Henry III, appeals focused on the unsuitability of the bishop-elect, highlighting the ways in which he deviated from these canonical and ideological traditions of good episcopacy. A relatively limited set of criticisms drawn from such models and proven to be efficacious at undermining would-be bishops cropped up again and again in the cases presented by royal proctors at Rome.

A key theme was the bishop-elect's background and family. A candidate's parentage was thought to be extremely relevant; many would-be bishops were afflicted by their parents' failure to marry and their own consequent illegitimacy. If properly dispensed by the pope, this was not a bar to the episcopal office, and several prominent members of the English episcopate were of illegitimate birth. Ralph de Neville was elected in turn to Chichester, Canterbury and Winchester, and although strong objections were brought against the latter pair of elections – strong enough to prevent him being translated to either – no one seems to have mentioned his illegitimacy; it was clearly well known that this problem had been dealt with.[114] An undispensed candidate might be the subject of a postulation (an appeal to the papacy to sanction the nomination of an individual who was somehow disqualified). Sewal de Boville, archbishop of York (1255-58) was one such individual; Henry III's appeal highlighted the problem of his birth, but Alexander IV granted a dispensation and confirmed the election.[115] But several would-be bishops lost their sees because of illegitimacy. When William of Taunton was elected to Winchester in 1262, it was found that his dispensation had been obtained surreptitiously, and that the convent should therefore have postulated him for papal approval, rather than electing him. His election was quashed, although he was subsequently granted a valid dispensation.[116]

A bishop's social status also depended on his parentage, and good birth was thought to be one of the attributes of a good bishop. Humble origins were

---

112 I Timothy 3: 1-7. A similar list of desirable episcopal qualities is given in Titus 1: 7-9.

113 Peltzer, *Elections*, pp. 48-53; Anton Weiler, 'The Requirements of the *Pastor Bonus* in the Late Middle Ages', *Dutch Review of Church History*, 83 (2003), pp. 57-83.

114 *CPL*, I, p. 70; *Royal and Other Historical Letters Illustrative of the Reign of Henry III*, ed. W. Shirley (2 vols, RS, 1862-66), I, p. 534.

115 *CPL*, I, p. 328; *AM*, III, p. 196; *CM*, V, p. 522; *Historians of the Church of York*, II, pp. 403-4.

116 *Gervase*, II, p. 218; *CPL*, I, pp. 378-9.

not a bar to being a successful and well-regarded member of the episcopate, as Robert Grosseteste demonstrated,[117] but they did make promotion to a bishopric considerably less likely. Servile origins were particularly frowned upon, and Henry III objected to would-be bishops of Norwich and Ely on this account.[118] The king displayed a strong preference for well-born candidates, and if a candidate of good family was pitted against one of lesser birth, the latter was likely to suffer. Ideas about the social hierarchy were undoubtedly a factor in the Winchester dispute, in which the king favoured two of the queen's uncles in turn, whereas the monks elected first Ralph de Neville and then William de Raleigh, both royal ministers born into local gentry families.[119] The letter Henry III wrote to the pope in support of Boniface of Savoy pointed out that the royal candidate was a man of noble character and birth, and consequently a suitable candidate for this wealthy see.[120] Noble birth was essential because it was equated with noble character, the latter being an essential characteristic of a good bishop.[121]

If parents could be an obstacle to a bishop's confirmation, children were potentially an even more serious problem. Stories of sexual misconduct became particularly powerful in the thirteenth century as attitudes to clerical marriage and priestly offspring hardened.[122] Walter of Eynsham was not the only would-be bishop to be accused of fathering children; Simon of Elmham, the prior of Norwich, who was elected to that see in 1237, was also said to be unchaste, as the existence of his daughter proved.[123] It was not, however, the existence of these children, but the fact that their respective fathers were in holy orders at the time of their conception that meant they could be cited in electoral appeals. The majority of career clerics had taken only minor orders and were thus not vowed to celibacy. Only if they also began to accrue benefices would their marital status become relevant – although there is some evidence to suggest that even in the early years of the thirteenth century some of the canons of Hereford Cathedral were married men. But children born to a would-be bishop before he took major orders were certainly not a bar to the episcopate, providing that

117 Richard Southern, *Robert Grosseteste: The Growth of an English Mind in Medieval Europe* (Oxford, 1992).

118 *CR 1256-1259*, pp. 108-9.

119 David Crook, 'William Raleigh', *ODNB*; Charles Young, *The Making of the Neville Family in England, 1166-1400* (Woodbridge, 1996), pp. 7-17.

120 *Rôles Gascons*, I, p. 159.

121 Stephen Jaeger, 'The Courtier Bishop in *Vitae* from the Tenth to the Twelfth Century', *Speculum*, 58 (1983), pp. 291-325, at p. 297.

122 Christopher Brooke, 'Gregorian Reform in Action: Clerical Marriage in England, 1050-1200', *Cambridge Historical Journal*, 12 (1956), pp. 1-21, at pp. 1-6.

123 *CPL*, I, p. 163.

his wife had subsequently died or entered a convent.[124] As late as 1257, the royal justice Simon Walton could be elected to Norwich without any mention being made of the fact that he had been married and had at least one child, a son whom he openly acknowledged as his legitimate heir; he may also have had a daughter.[125] Like illegitimacy, paternity could be used against a bishop-elect only in certain circumstances, but if the circumstances were right, then such claims were extremely potent. The emphasis that the canon law placed on the need for a bishop to be of good moral character meant self-control was essential, particularly if one was a member of a monastic order and had taken a vow of celibacy.

Other forms of immoral behaviour were also undesirable and consequently were frequently alleged by the king. According to the Apostle's Rule, a bishop should be gentle and not contentious, but Thomas Melsonby, elect of Durham, was accused of having caused 'all the dissent' between Bishop Richard Marsh and the cathedral priory of Durham, in a disagreement that had been referred to Rome and ended only with Marsh's death.[126] Gluttony was thought unseemly in a clergyman and thus Melsonby was accused of having eaten meat at prohibited times, and allowing his monks to do the same.[127] He was also said to have encouraged frivolous entertainments to which he should have put a stop; on one occasion, the jollity ended abruptly when an acrobat, permitted by the prior to walk a tightrope between the two towers of Durham Cathedral, fell to his death. According to the king, this sequence of events made Melsonby a murderer.[128] A man who could not be trusted to behave in a becoming manner prior to his promotion was clearly undeserving of his newly elevated status; the election should be quashed.

Just as a bishop should abstain from the company of women and from excessive drinking, it was necessary for him to be 'free from the love of money',[129] and thus a man who could be thought 'noted for avarice' was unfit for election.[130]

---

[124] Julia Barrow, 'Hereford Bishops and Married Clergy, c.1130-1240', *Historical Research*, 60 (1987), pp. 1-8; Nicholas Vincent, 'New Light on Master Alexander of Swerford (d.1246): The Career and Connections of an Oxfordshire Civil Servant', *Oxoniensia*, 61 (1996), pp. 297-309, at p. 306; Vincent, 'Jocelin of Wells', pp. 20-21. The existence of a wife could, however, remain problematic long after the election process was complete: Nicholas Farnham resigned the bishopric of Durham in 1249, amidst rumours that he had a wife whom he claimed to have repudiated before accepting his election. *EEA*, 29, p. xxvi.

[125] Vincent, 'Swerford', p. 305; *EEA 32: Norwich 1244-1266*, ed. C. Harper-Bill (Oxford, 2007), pp. xxxvii, 225-6.

[126] *Script. Tres*, p. lxxiii.

[127] Ibid.

[128] Ibid.

[129] I Timothy 3: 3.

[130] *Gervase*, II, p. 127.

Simony had been denounced since biblical times and consistently condemned in papal councils from the Council of Chalcedon (451) to the Fourth Lateran Council,[131] but despite (or perhaps because) of this, several putative bishops were accused of having bought their new position. Thomas Melsonby was accused of paying members of the English nobility to support his election and of granting Odo of Kilkenny, a royal clerk, a benefice to the same end; he was also said to have been on the receiving end of simoniacal transactions, having taken money and lands from postulants to Durham Cathedral Priory.[132]

One of the great ecclesiastical dilemmas of the thirteenth century was how far a bishop should be a man of the world. In the words of Nicholas Vincent, a bishop's success was determined by 'his ability to walk the tightrope that joined *regnum* and *sacerdotium*'.[133] A bishopric was an ecclesiastical office, requiring sincere religious faith; the model bishop was a man of great piety, perhaps even a potential saint. On the other hand, he was an important member of the English social elite, with many administrative responsibilities and a duty to engage in national affairs; according to the words of the king's licence to elect, it was necessary for the elect to be a man who was 'useful to the king and the kingdom' (*nobis et regno nostro utilis*).[134] Consequently, piety, even sanctity, was not enough – particularly from the perspective of the crown.

As a consequence of this debate, potential bishops were accused both of being too worldly and not worldly enough. Perhaps unsurprisingly, royal critiques usually favoured the latter approach. Henry III accused Hugh Balsham, the sub-prior of the Ely cathedral monastery, of being too unworldly to be a bishop; it would, he claimed, be unwise to entrust the guardianship of the Isle of Ely, a refuge of fugitives and rebels, to 'a simple denizen of the cloister, who was imbecile and inexperienced in warlike proceedings, and who never learned the shrewdness and sagacity of the court'.[135] The king exploited the fact that his scepticism about monk-bishops was shared by many contemporary churchmen.[136]

---

131 Simon Magus was condemned for simony in Acts 8: 9-24. For Chalcedon, see *Ecumenical Councils*, I, pp. 87-8 (c. 2) and for the Fourth Lateran Council, *Ecumenical Councils*, I, p. 264 (c. 63).

132 *Script. Tres*, p. lxxiii.

133 Vincent, 'Jocelin of Wells', p. 33.

134 *Records of Antony Bek*, p. 181.

135 *CM*, V, p. 619; *CR 1256-1259*, pp. 108-9.

136 For the debate over this issue, which rumbled on through the twelfth and thirteenth centuries, see Gaudemet, *Gouvernement*, pp. 81-5; Paul Oliger, *Les évêques réguliers* (Paris, 1958); John Cotts, 'Monks and Mediocrities in the Shadow of Thomas Becket: Peter of Blois on Episcopal Duty', *Haskins Society Journal*, 10 (2001), pp. 143-61; John Cotts, *The Clerical Dilemma: Peter of Blois and Literate Culture in the Twelfth Century* (Washington DC, 2009), pp. 176-213; Gibbs and Lang, *Bishops*, p. 6; *Giraldus Cambrensis opera*, ed. J. S. Brewer, J. F. Dimock and G. F. Warner (8 vols, RS, 1861-91), IV, p. 75; Brian Golding, 'Gerald of Wales and the Monks' in Peter Coss and Simon Lloyd (eds), *Thirteenth-Century England V* (Woodbridge, 1995), pp. 53-64; Powicke, *Langton*, p. 12; *Grosseteste*, p. 343 (letter 110); *CM*, III, p. 219.

Loyalty to the king was another problem that frequently raised its head during the course of electoral disputes. This was not simply because the king wanted to impose his men on the church; loyalty to the crown was a crucial quality if one was to hold a position that placed one at the forefront of national affairs and, in some sees, gave one control of castles vital to the defence of the realm. One of the criticisms levelled at Walter of Eynsham, archbishop-elect of Canterbury, was that he had been disloyal to the king's father at the time of the interdict. Loyalty to the crown was particularly important in the four border sees of Hereford, Coventry and Lichfield, Carlisle and Durham, and the king twice objected to candidates for the last of these sees on the grounds of suspected disloyalty. William of Stichill, elected to Durham in 1227, was accused of being Scottish,[137] whilst Thomas of Melsonby, elected there fourteen years later, was suspected of even greater disloyalty. Included in the list of objections Henry III made to this election were claims that, whilst prior of Coldingham (a daughter house of Durham Cathedral Priory, but situated in south-east Scotland), Melsonby had sworn an oath of allegiance to the Scottish king. Worse still, he had become a favoured councillor of the Scottish king Alexander II, advising against English interests; as bishop of Durham, he might encourage a French or Flemish invasion of the north of England.[138]

From this outline of the objections made by Henry III, it is clear that royal appeals were effective because they tapped into widely accepted, canonical models of episcopacy. Far from simply blundering in and demanding his own way, the king (with the help of his lawyers) was presenting very carefully considered arguments. Furthermore, he was doing more than using a generic set of accusations and hoping that at least one of them would turn out to be effective. It is rarely possible to prove or disprove individual allegations, but it is clear that, at the very least, the claims made were carefully tailored to fit the candidate's circumstances. Given his previous career, it was all too plausible that Thomas of Melsonby had pro-Scottish sympathies.[139] He was also said to have stirred up dissent against Bishop Richard Marsh, whose episcopate had been dominated by a bitter dispute with the monks. Most damningly, he was accused of using his position as prior of Durham to confer the church of Brantingham on Odo of Kilkenny, in order to secure the latter's support for his election; it was presumably hoped that Odo (a royal clerk) would petition King Henry on Melsonby's behalf. The archiepiscopal mandate for his induction, at the presentation of the prior and convent of Durham, was issued less than

137 Evers, 'Disputes', pp. 92-4 (transcription of MS record of the witness testimony at the archiepiscopal examination of the election). See also Powicke, *Henry III*, I, pp. 266-70.

138 *Script. Tres*, pp. lxxii-lxxiii.

139 D. E. R. Watt and N. F. Shead (eds), *The Heads of Religious Houses in Scotland from Twelfth to Sixteenth Centuries* (Edinburgh, 2001), p. 30. Coldingham Priory, a cell of Durham, was located in Berwickshire, within the diocese of St Andrews.

two months after Melsonby was elected.[140] Following appeals before both the archbishop of York and the pope, Melsonby (probably acting in accordance with papal wishes) resigned his claim to the bishopric.[141] On such scant evidence, and at such distance of time, it is impossible to judge whether the accusations made against him were justified or whether they led to the eventual failure of his candidacy. What is clear is that considerable effort went into explaining why such an outcome was necessary.

Furthermore, and despite the long list of accusations that might be levelled against a bishop-elect, there are some striking omissions – criticisms that one might expect to have been used, but do not seem to have been. For example, not a single bishop was accused of being under 30, despite maturity being one of the three principal attributes demanded of a would-be bishop by canon law.[142] William of Taunton, elected to Winchester in 1262, was reported to be excommunicate,[143] but no one ever seems to have thought to question the sincerity or orthodoxy of the religious beliefs of a bishop-elect. Nor were there any accusations of sodomy, despite the fact that hostility to and legislation against such practices became increasingly widespread from the twelfth century onwards, with the consequence that imputations of homosexuality became 'a powerful political weapon'.[144] Ill health and old age were respectively cited only once each as an indication of unsuitability,[145] and there were no suggestions of serious illnesses (such as leprosy and epilepsy), despite fears that an incumbent with such a disease would pollute his diocese.[146] In contrast to the experience of several eleventh-century Ottonian candidates for the episcopate, no thirteenth-century English bishop-elect was rejected for ugliness or puniness.[147] The exclusion of such allegations from royal depositions suggests both a sensitivity

---

140 *Calendar of the Durham Cathedral Muniments: Archiepiscopalia* (Durham, 2011), p. 19 (Archiepiscopalia 2.1.19).

141 *Durham Annals*, p. 9.

142 At least one of the thirteenth-century bishops was underage: Aymer de Lusignan, Henry III's half-brother, was no older than 25 (and may well have been younger) when he was elected to Winchester in 1250. Only Matthew Paris commented on his youth, and the election received papal confirmation. See Ridgeway, 'Aymer de Lusignan', pp. 150-51.

143 *CPL*, I, p. 378.

144 The Third Lateran Council (1179) was the first ecumenical council to legislate against sodomy; see *Ecumenical Councils*, I, pp. 217-18 (c. 11). More generally, see Robert Moore, *The Formation of a Persecuting Society*, 2nd edn (Oxford, 2007), pp. 85-8, and John Boswell, *Christianity, Social Tolerance and Homosexuality: Gay People in Western Europe from the Beginning of the Christian Era to the Fourteenth Century* (Chicago, 1980), pp. 277-8.

145 Thomas Melsonby was said to be plagued by kidney stones; *Script. Tres*, p. lxxiii.

146 Elaine Graham-Leigh, 'Hirelings and Shepherds: Archbishop Berenguer of Narbonne (1191-1211) and the Ideal Bishop', *EHR*, 116 (2001), pp. 1083-102, at pp. 1099-100; Moore, *Persecuting Society*, pp. 100-101.

147 Jaeger, 'Courtier Bishop', p. 299.

to the issues likely to result in the quashing of an election and the desire to avoid the inclusion of accusations that were patently untrue.

The effectiveness of Henry III's objections, and the importance of royal displeasure as a force in episcopal elections, is illustrated by his success rate. Of the nine candidates against whom royal complaints were presented to the papacy, only three received papal confirmation of their election: William Raleigh, Sewal de Boville and Hugh Balsham. Given such a promising precedent from his father's reign, it is somewhat surprising that Edward I provoked so few appeals. Overall, his approach to episcopal elections seems to have been rather different to that of Henry III, a difference reflected not only in the rarity of appeals, but also in the changing composition of the episcopate. Throughout Henry's reign, the majority of the English bishops had been former royal servants: ten of the seventeen in 1258, and eight out of seventeen at the time of his death (1272). Bishops who were also members of religious orders were rather rarer: there were only two in 1258, and five in 1272. By the time of Edward's death (1307), the bishop's bench looked rather different, with seven former members of the diocesan clergy, six regular bishops and only four *curiales*. The reign of Edward I, then, would seem to be the point at which the ability of English cathedral chapters to choose their own bishops reached its pinnacle; if there ever was a golden age of electoral freedom in England, it was between 1272 and 1307.

Since Edward I is usually seen as one of England's most formidable kings, this juxtaposition is somewhat unexpected. Of course, his approach was far from being entirely passive; like his father, he indicated his wishes to cathedral chapters and on occasion applied pressure to persuade them to comply with these wishes. His attempts to further the ecclesiastical career of his chancellor, Robert Burnell, were not entirely dissimilar to Henry III's efforts on behalf of his favourites. After an unsuccessful attempt to procure Canterbury for Burnell in 1270, Edward managed to have him promoted to Bath and Wells in 1274. When Canterbury fell vacant in 1278, the king worked hard to secure the appointment of his favourite. Once the monks had postulated Burnell, the king wrote to Nicholas III, describing the elect in glowing terms. An embassy was sent to the papal curia and one of its members, the distinguished Roman lawyer Francis Accursius, made a long speech in favour of Burnell's candidacy. Backing from other quarters was canvassed; amongst those who pledged their support was John Pecham. Ultimately the postulation was refused,[148] but this did not deter Edward from trying again when Winchester fell vacant in 1280. The monks postulated Burnell, 'at the instance of the king and queen', and another

---

[148] *CPL*, I, p. 456; *Reg. Nic. III*, no. 415; George Haskins and Ernst Kantorowicz, 'A Diplomatic Mission of Francis Accursius and his Oration Before Pope Nicholas III', *EHR*, 58 (1943), pp. 424-7; Richard Huscroft, 'The Career of Robert Burnell, Bishop of Bath and Wells and Chancellor of Edward I' (University of London, PhD thesis, 2001), pp. 85-6.

embassy embarked for Rome.[149] Only after this attempt also failed[150] did the king give up hope; Burnell was to remain at Bath and Wells until his death in 1292.

Nor was Robert Burnell the only one of Edward's *familia* to gain promotion to the episcopate. Of his six chancellors, only one did not become a bishop.[151] Four of his wardrobe clerks received bishoprics during his life time.[152] John Kirkby, the king's treasurer, received Ely in 1294.[153] Clearly Edward had not relinquished control of the episcopate, and yet his approach was more relaxed than we might expect, given that he substantially increased royal control over other forms of ecclesiastical patronage, including appointments to lesser benefices.[154]

We can only speculate as to why Edward avoided a major electoral dispute on the scale of those which his father fought with Durham and Winchester. Certainly he was not afraid of coming into conflict with the church, as his turbulent relationships with Archbishops Pecham and Winchelsey of Canterbury and Archbishop Corbridge of York, as well as Anthony Bek of Durham, demonstrate.[155] On the other hand, one of Edward's great virtues as a monarch – and in this he was considerably different to his father – was his ability to compromise and to hold back when necessary. Thus in 1286, when he was about to embark for Gascony, he compromised with the church in a dispute over the respective rights of secular and ecclesiastical jurisdiction, probably because he realized it was unwise to provoke discord when he was absent from the kingdom.[156] He also displayed rather more reluctance to take an aggressive stance with France than might be expected of such a war-like king.[157] His ability to work with, rather than against, parliament, at least in the early years of his reign, is also suggestive.[158] Against this backdrop, accepting, for example, the

---

149 Huscroft, 'Burnell', pp. 86-7; Cosgrove, 'Winchester', pp. 169-78.

150 The grounds on which this postulation was quashed are vague; the pope expressed his surprise that it had even been made, given the results of his inquiry after the 1278 Canterbury election, but unfortunately the extent and findings of that enquiry are unknown. It is, however, plausible that Burnell's personal life (he reportedly fathered several bastards) was the major sticking point. See Huscroft, 'Burnell', esp. pp. 85-6.

151 The bishops were Merton of Rochester, Burnell of Bath and Wells, Langton of Chichester, Greenfield of York and Baldock of London. The non-bishop was William Hamilton, who was dean of York. Edmund Fryde *et al.* (eds), *Handbook of British Chronology*, 3rd edn (Cambridge, 1986), p. 85.

152 Louth (Ely), Langton (Coventry and Lichfield), Bek (Durham) and March (Bath and Wells). Prestwich, *Edward I*, p. 154.

153 *The Chronicle of Bury St Edmunds, 1212-1301*, ed. A. Gransden (London, 1964), pp. 86-7.

154 Prestwich, *Edward I*, p. 546.

155 Ibid., pp. 250-58, 540-47, 562. See also throughout the biographies of some of the leading bishops: Douie, *Pecham*; Denton, *Winchelsey*; Fraser, *Anthony Bek*.

156 Prestwich, *Edward I*, pp. 257-8.

157 Ibid., pp. 334-5.

158 For Edward I and parliament, see Prestwich, *Edward I*, pp. 436-68, and John Maddicott, *The Origins of the English Parliament, 924-1327* (Oxford, 2010), pp. 277-331.

election of Robert de Insula, a monk of Durham, to that see in 1274 can be seen not as an act of capitulation, but as cold political calculation. Edward had more to lose by starting his reign with a major electoral dispute than by allowing the election of a monk-bishop.

Other personal differences between the father and son may also have influenced their respective electoral policies. One of the great problems of Henry's reign was his almost excessive devotion to his numerous favourites,[159] and it was his efforts to secure bishoprics for such men (most notably the Savoyard uncles) that led him into many of his conflicts with the church. Edward learnt from his father's mistakes, and his treatment of his associates was more masterful than affectionate; he avoided over-favouring his relatives, was renowned for his tight-fistedness and seems to have felt no obligation to provide liberal rewards to those loyal to him.[160] Henry's almost fanatical personal piety may also have been a factor, producing in him an interest in the church that was less pragmatic than Edward's, and more likely to leave him feeling betrayed when chapters failed to concur with his wishes. Edward's preoccupation with military matters also meant that his focus was rather different to his father's; it would be understandable if a king engaged in fighting a war was less inclined to provoke a battle at the Roman curia.

Despite the difference between the approaches of the two kings, there was much continuity in the role played by the crown between the years 1216 and 1307. Most elections were characterized by compromise between the crown and the cathedral chapter, with one accepting the candidate of the other in order to avoid conflict. If the wishes of the two were incompatible, the king could prove an extremely destructive force, exploiting his power in an attempt to ensure that his candidate ultimately triumphed.

The Role of the Archbishop

The king was not the only prominent figure with influence over the electoral process. Although Marion Gibbs wrote of 'the impotence of the metropolitan' and stressed his lack of absolute competence,[161] the archbishop's duty to examine

---

159 Huw Ridgeway, 'Foreign Favourites and Henry III's Problems of Patronage, 1247-58', *EHR*, 104 (1989), pp. 590-610.

160 Kenneth McFarlane, 'Had Edward I a "Policy" towards the Earls?', *History*, 1 (1965), pp. 145-69; Michael Prestwich, 'Royal Patronage under Edward I' in Peter Coss and Simon Lloyd (eds), *Thirteenth-Century England I* (1986), pp. 41-52; Carpenter, *Struggle*, p. 478. Andrew Spencer, 'Royal Patronage and the Earls in the Reign of Edward I', *Historical Research*, 93 (2008), pp. 20-46, which sees Edward's patronage in a more positive light than has been usual, concludes that he judiciously avoided extremes of avarice or prodigality.

161 Gibbs and Lang, *Bishops*, p. 83.

and confirm episcopal elections gave him at least as much scope as the king to determine outcomes. Just as an elect could not become a bishop without royal assent, metropolitan confirmation was an unavoidable part of the bishop-making process.

Like the king, the archbishop might try to influence the chapter's choice before the election was held, and Stephen Langton is known to have done this with a considerable degree of success. In 1218, he persuaded the monks of Worcester to elect William de Blois, the legatine candidate for the see.[162] He also procured the election of Benedict Sawston to Rochester (1214).[163] More typically, archiepiscopal intervention took the form of exhortations to elect a suitable candidate, rather than requests for the election of certain individuals (although the possibility that such requests were made verbally cannot be excluded). In 1280, for example, Archbishop Pecham urged the prior and convent of Winchester 'To appoint for themselves as pastor one who is praiseworthy and acceptable to God and man, and under whom they may live happily'. He explicitly forbade his official to put forward a candidate on his behalf[164] – although the fact that he thought it necessary to do so might suggest that candidates were sometimes suggested, for why would it be necessary to forbid something that never happened? When the convent's first choice, Robert Burnell, was rejected by the pope, another election was held, and Pecham again sent general advice: the monks should elect a person 'who hates greed and is so proven in chastity that he will be able to profit those in lesser office both by word and example'.[165]

If the chapter failed to elect a suitable candidate, or failed to observe the correct procedures, then the archbishop would discover these flaws during the examination process and could quash the election. Archiepiscopal objections to elections usually focused, as Archbishop Pecham claimed, on principle rather than personality.[166] It is perhaps as a consequence of this difference that metropolitan objections have generally been viewed more sympathetically than royal ones, and yet the distinction is not as great as has often been implied.

Just as kings insisted that their rights be upheld, so too did archbishops – a similarity most clearly reflected in the early thirteenth-century disputes between the archbishop of Canterbury and the monks of Rochester. The diocese of Rochester was an electoral anomaly for unlike any other English bishopric it was subordinate not to the crown, but to the archdiocese of Canterbury. Technically, therefore, the king had no right to intervene in its elections; licence

---

162 *AM*, IV, p. 410.

163 *Anglia Sacra*, I, p. 385.

164 *Reg. Pecham*, I, pp. 98-9.

165 Ibid., I, pp. 138-40.

166 Ibid., I, pp. 219-20.

to elect was given by the archbishop, who controlled both the spiritualties and the temporalities during a vacancy.[167] Given that the blame for electoral disputes is usually laid firmly at the feet of the king, one might expect Rochester to be unusually dispute free, but this was not so. The 1226 election was disrupted by a dispute between the Rochester monks and the priory of Christ Church Canterbury, which also claimed the right of election; Archbishop Langton seems to have exploited this dispute to ease the promotion of his favoured candidate, Henry of Sandford.[168]

It is, however, the next Rochester vacancy that demonstrates most effectively the potential for an archbishop to provoke discord. The see fell vacant in 1235 and the monks of Rochester quickly elected the eminently suitable M. Richard of Wendene, an episcopal official.[169] Here, the process rapidly came to a halt, for Edmund of Abingdon refused to confirm Wendene's election.[170] The monks appealed to Rome, and Gregory IX appointed two successive commissions to bring about an end to 'the cause between the prior and convent of Rochester and the archbishop of Canterbury in regard to the election of a bishop of Rochester'. Archbishop Edmund was refusing to confirm the election and taking its revenues for his own use; the monks had petitioned the pope to confirm the election or to sequestrate the revenues of the see. The dispute dragged on into March 1238, when papal confirmation of Wendene's election was finally given.[171]

Archbishop Edmund was clearly not acting on behalf of the monks of his cathedral, since he was engaged in a bitter dispute with them for much of his pontificate.[172] Nor was there any obvious reason for him to object to the future Bishop Wendene. Instead, his actions seem to have been driven by a desire to protect archiepiscopal rights, specifically his right of patronage to the see, in accordance with the bull granted to Canterbury by Alexander III, which permitted the archbishop himself to appoint the bishop.[173] He apparently suggested that the prior and convent of Canterbury had papal letters to support his claim.[174] If his motivations are a little murky, his actions are all too clear. When thwarted, the response of this archbishop was much the same as that of Henry III when he was unable to secure his choice in any other diocese: he

---

167 Crosby, *Bishop and Chapter*, p. 197, and see above, pp. 4-5.

168 *Flores Hist.*, II, p. 190; *Acta Stephani Langton*, no. 100; Crosby, *Bishop and Chapter*, p. 197; Powicke, *Langton*, p. 114.

169 *Flores Hist.*, II, p. 215. C. H. Lawrence suggests that the monks may have selected Wendene, who was 'eminently suitable to be bishop' and something of a scholar, in a calculated attempt to appeal to the archbishop's personal preferences (*Life of St Edmund*, p. 74). If so, they failed miserably.

170 *CM*, III, p. 306; *Hist. Angl.*, II, p. 377; *Flores Hist.* II, p. 215.

171 *CPL*, I, p. 169; *Flores Hist.*, II, p. 226; *CM*, III, p. 480.

172 *Life of St. Edmund*, pp. 70-80, 146-7.

173 Churchill, *Canterbury Administration*, I, p. 280.

174 Crosby, *Bishop and Chapter*, pp. 215-16.

seized their revenues.[175] A papal mandate issued to the Legate Otto in May 1237 orders that he should not

> Suffer the archbishop of Canterbury and his church to be molested in regard to papal, royal and other liberties and immunities which they enjoy; provided that the prior and convent of Rochester be not harassed on the authority of the present letters about the election of the bishop.[176]

A disgruntled archbishop, it seems, could do just as much damage to a disobedient chapter as a disgruntled king.

Nor was Rochester the only English diocese to suffer from archbishop-related electoral difficulties. Until the mid-1250s, the archbishops of Canterbury and York claimed the right to quash unsuitable elections and to provide an alternative bishop; on three occasions during the reign of Henry III they attempted to exercise this right, with varying degrees of success. Boniface of Savoy's first (and most successful) appointment was made in 1244, shortly after his own consecration as archbishop of Canterbury. The canons of Chichester, acting in accordance with royal wishes, had elected the king's clerk Robert Passelewe as their bishop, but when the elect was examined by Robert Grosseteste (on behalf of the archbishop), his theological knowledge was found to be wanting. His role in royal judicial proceedings was also a stumbling block, specifically his role in the notoriously oppressive forest eyre of 1244-45. Acting on the advice of his bishops, Boniface therefore quashed Passelewe's election and nominated Richard Wyche as bishop of Chichester. This nomination was upheld by Innocent IV, who consecrated him at Lyons in 1245, although the wording of the papal mandate made it clear that the postulation had been legitimized by papal plenitude, not the authority of the primate.[177]

Emboldened by the relative success of the Chichester affair, Boniface attempted a similar manoeuvre in 1256, when he decided to quash the election of Hugh Balsham in order to obtain the promotion of Adam Marsh to the bishopric of Ely. He was unable to obtain Marsh's appointment, as the case had already been appealed to Rome, but his intentions were clear. Most significantly for the electoral freedom of the English Church, Boniface inadvertently provoked a papal declaration (applicable to the entire Latin Church) that all

---

175 *Flores Hist.*, II, p. 215.

176 *CPL*, I, p. 162. Gregory IX's 1238 judgement in favour of the monks effectively ended the dispute; subsequently, they were allowed to elect their own bishop.

177 *CM*, IV, pp. 401-2, 412, 426; *Saint Richard*, pp. 166-74; *EEA, 22: Chichester, 1215-1253*, ed. P. M. Hoskin (Oxford, 2001), pp. xxxv-xxxvi; Daniel Williams, 'Aspects of the Career of Archbishop Boniface of Savoy, 1241-70' (University of Wales, PhD thesis, 1970), p. 255.

disputed elections were to be considered as *causae majores*, and therefore to be examined at the papal curia – a major step on the road to papal provision.[178]

Nevertheless, the following year Carlisle fell vacant, and Archbishop Sewal de Boville attempted an appointment of his own. The canons' first choice declined to take office;[179] their second choice, Robert de Chaury, was a royal servant presumably elected at Henry's bidding.[180] His promotion was complicated by his illegitimacy, for which the pope had to dispense.[181] Far more troublesome, however, was the opposition to Chaury's appointment from the new archbishop of York, Sewal de Boville. He instead postulated John of Exeter, the chancellor of York Minster (and future bishop of Winchester);[182] moreover, the Dunstable annalist claimed that Boville purposely delayed the second election so that he could postulate by lapse.[183] If so, then his intentions were thwarted by the pope, since in June 1257 Alexander IV issued an indult for Chaury, formally dispensed for illegitimacy, to be promoted to the episcopate.[184] But as with royal attempts to dictate the outcome of elections, the significance of these three examples is less about the result and more about the intent displayed.

Even after archiepiscopal claims to provide had been rendered obsolete by the growth of papal powers over disputed elections, the archiepiscopate remained a force to be reckoned with. Archbishops were not afraid to oppose the king; many royal candidates for the episcopate found their ambitions thwarted by the metropolitan's refusal to confirm their election. One of Boniface of Savoy's first acts as archbishop was to quash the election of Robert Passelewe – an act that horrified Henry III, who seems to have hoped that his uncle-in-law would display gratitude for his promotion by being little more than a puppet-archbishop.[185] John Pecham was a particularly fearsome critic of would-be curial bishops, as his approach to episcopal elections was heavily influenced by staunch opposition to pluralism. As Decima Douie noted, his refusal to confirm pluralists as bishops was his 'best weapon' against this offence.[186] In at least one case, he acted

178 See below, p. 136. For modern accounts of the 1256 Ely election, see Vincent, 'Thirteenth Century', pp. 36-9; Ullmann, 'Disputed Election', pp. 259-68; Lovatt, 'Hugh Balsham', pp. 60-65; Williams, 'Archbishop Boniface', pp. 262-5.

179 *CPR 1247-1258*, p. 535.

180 Henry Summerson, 'Fearing God, Honouring the King: The Episcopate of Robert de Chaury, Bishop of Carlisle, 1258-78' in Michael Prestwich, Richard Britnell and Robin Frame (eds), *Thirteenth-Century England X* (2005), pp. 147-54, at p. 148.

181 *CPL*, I, pp. 346-7.

182 *CPL*, I, pp. 372-3.

183 *AM*, II, p. 205.

184 *CPL*, I, pp. 346-7.

185 *CM*, IV, p. 509; Leland Wilshire, *Boniface of Savoy, Carthusian and Archbishop of Canterbury, 1207–1270* (Salzburg, 1977), pp. 36-7.

186 Douie, *Pecham*, pp. 105-6.

pre-emptively: in 1280, when the sees of Winchester, Exeter and St David's were all vacant, he wrote to Nicholas III to inform him that Anthony Bek (a likely royal candidate for one of these sees) had recently surrendered some of his benefices.[187] The following year, he wrote to Bek to warn him that he would not confirm his election to any bishopric unless he gave up even more benefices, thus freeing himself from the stain of pluralism.[188]

At least one bishop-elect, and possibly two, resigned their elections because of Pecham's refusal to confirm pluralists. John Kirkby, the acting vice-chancellor of England, was elected as bishop of Rochester in 1283, but Pecham objected to his election on the grounds that his pluralism made him an unsuitable candidate. Kirkby chose to resign his candidacy rather than fight for the bishopric, presumably because even if an appeal to Rome had been successful, Rochester's extreme dependence on Canterbury would have made his tenure of the see virtually impossible. In the long term, however, Kirkby was triumphant, for he acquired the far wealthier see of Ely in 1286.[189]

Similar pressures may also have been behind the resignation in 1280 of Fulk Lovel, archdeacon of Colchester, who refused his election to London on account of his bodily weakness and in deference to his conscience.[190] His attack of conscience could plausibly have related to his pluralism: in 1255 he had been dispensed to hold a third benefice with cure of souls, and at the time of his death he held the church of Leatherhead, in Surrey, along with a prebend at York.[191] Whether Lovel resigned because he held multiple benefices or because he was old and ill,[192] Pecham's campaign against pluralism certainly featured in this election, for Richard Gravesend, the chapter's second choice, was confirmed as bishop only after a detailed investigation of his benefice-holding had been completed.[193]

The Winchester vacancy of 1280-82 allowed Pecham considerable scope to demonstrate the options open to an archbishop who was unhappy with a

---

187 *Reg. Pecham*, I, pp. 137-8.

188 Ibid., I, p. 244.

189 *Reg. Pecham*, I, pp. 197-8; Michael Prestwich, 'John de Kirkby', *ODNB*; Douie, *Pecham*, p. 105.

190 *Reg. Pecham*, I, pp. 113-14.

191 *EEA, 38: London, 1229-1280*, ed. P. M. Hoskin (Oxford, 2011), p. lxii. Two antiquarian guides to St Paul's suggest that Lovel held no fewer than twenty benefices, which were together worth more than the bishopric, and that he therefore refused London due to financial reasons and Pecham's hostility to his pluralism. Richard King, *Handbook to the Cathedrals of England: St Paul's* (London, 1879), p. 140; W. M. Sinclair, *Memorials of St Paul's Cathedral* (London, 1913), p. 26. Unfortunately neither work gives references for this assertion and I have been unable to trace their source.

192 *Registrum Statutorum et Consuetudinum Ecclesiae Cathedralis Sancti Pauli Londiniensis*, ed. W. Sparrow Simpson (London, 1873), p. 387, n. 2.

193 *Reg. Pecham*, I, pp. 113-14, 165-7.

chapter's choice. It was rumoured that Pecham had tried to guarantee that the pope would quash the postulation of Robert Burnell by alerting the cardinal-bishop of Tusculum to the chancellor's unlicensed pluralism.[194] He then refused to confirm the outcome of the second election, on the grounds that the elect, Richard de la More, was an undispensed pluralist; by doing so, he forced de la More and the convent of Winchester to appeal to Rome.[195] Pecham told Cardinal Hugh of Evesham that for him, the dispute was about principle rather than personalities[196] and made clear his passionate desire to secure papal endorsement of his anti-pluralism crusade.[197] Many of Pecham's contemporaries felt that de la More (whose pluralism was extremely modest by the standards of the day) had been victimized by the archbishop. A group of his suffragans threatened to appeal because he had judged this case more harshly than others, and his own letters indicate that he feared he was being criticized for inconsistency at the curia.[198] The bishop of Palestrina defended de la More's appeal and argued that Pecham had been too vigorous in his opposition to the bishop-elect.[199] Cases such as this one suggest that, at least during the 1280s, the archbishop of Canterbury was more of a threat to free capitular election than the king.

Pecham's approach to elections was somewhat singular, but it seems likely that this was not the only example of archbishops and their representatives attempting to enforce impractically high standards. When Robert Passelewe's election was quashed in 1244, it was noted that he had been asked some 'very difficult questions' by Bishop Grosseteste as part of his examination.[200] It seems possible that the questions put to him were more difficult than usual. Nearly six decades later, in 1302, Archbishop Winchelsey refused to confirm the election of Robert de Orford as bishop of Ely, on the grounds that he was insufficiently learned to be promoted to the bishopric.[201] It is unlikely that Orford had attended university, and he was to display no particular interest in learning during his years as bishop of Ely.[202] However, Winchelsey's academic standards were undoubtedly high, perhaps even a little too high, for few potential bishops were likely to have had the sort of stellar academic career that he had himself enjoyed before being elected to Canterbury.[203] The Ely chronicler provides a detailed

194 Ibid., II, pp. 714-15; Cosgrove, 'Winchester', p. 170.

195 *Reg. Pecham*, I, pp. 166-7, 173-4; *AM*, II, pp. 394-5; Cosgrove, 'Winchester', p. 172.

196 *Reg. Pecham*, I, pp. 219-20.

197 Ibid., I, p. 282.

198 Douie, *Pecham*, pp. 106-7.

199 Cosgrove, 'Winchester', pp. 174-6.

200 *CM*, IV, p. 401.

201 *Anglia Sacra*, I, p. 640; Graham, 'Administration', pp. 49-74.

202 Dorothy Owen, 'Robert of Orford', *ODNB*.

203 Denton, *Winchelsey*, pp. 7-14.

account of Orford's appearance before the pope which suggested that, if not well educated, then the bishop-elect was certainly not unintelligent. According to this narrative, instead of relying on a learned counsel to represent him in the consistory court, Orford spoke for himself, giving an impressive account of the proceedings at Canterbury and earning his provision to Ely:

> 'The archbishop', he said, 'put three arguments to me. I gave this answer to the first, and this answer to the second. The third was very difficult and entangling, so, to avoid a conclusion, I did not respond with theology but with logic'. At this the pope and the cardinal burst out laughing, and the pope said, 'Certainly you answered well my son. I do not find you to be an empty vessel, as our brother of Canterbury wrote to us, instead I approve of you as a vessel full of goodness and knowledge.'[204]

It seems difficult to escape the conclusion that the archbishop had deliberately tried to outwit the monk, only to be thwarted by an unexpectedly sympathetic response from Boniface VIII.

The Role of the Papacy

Throughout the thirteenth century, papal intervention in elections was the exception rather than the rule. For much of this time, there were only three reasons for the pope to become involved in the electoral process: if the elect was seeking appointment to a metropolitan see, and therefore had to receive confirmation from the pope, as his immediate superior; if an episcopal election was disputed and could only be resolved with papal jurisdiction; or if a postulation had been made.

Papal confirmation of archiepiscopal elections could be a straightforward business if the election was uncontested and there was no question over the suitability of the elect or the validity of the electoral process. For example, the election of Boniface of Savoy as archbishop of Canterbury was almost entirely uncomplicated. However, the relative simplicity of this appointment was the product of an extremely rare conjunction of capitular, royal and papal interests; all three benefited from the election, and therefore all three were willing to accept it.[205] Only one other thirteenth-century Canterbury election was this straightforward, that of Robert Winchelsey,[206] and only two York elections

204 *Anglia Sacra*, I, p. 641.

205 Wilshire, *Boniface*, pp. 29-32.

206 Graham, *Winchelsey*, pp. 161-75.

(those of Godfrey de Ludham, elected in 1258,[207] and William Greenfield, elected in 1304[208]) were complication free.

Many of the complications were the product of disputes that had to be resolved by the pope. When Walter de Eynsham was elected to Canterbury in 1228, both the king and the suffragan bishops of the province made appeals to Rome. According to Roger of Wendover, Henry III refused his assent to the election for three reasons: firstly, Eynsham was useless to the king and to the kingdom; secondly, the father of the elect had been convicted of theft and had been hanged; and thirdly, his loyalty to the crown was questionable, as his opposition to King John during the interdict displayed. The suffragans claimed that the election was invalidated by their non-participation and for good measure they accused Eynsham of fathering children by a nun.[209] In such circumstances, it fell to the pope to examine the election and resolve the dispute, which in this case he did by quashing Eynsham's election and appointing Richard Grant in his place.[210]

On other occasions, it was the papal examination that uncovered problems with the election, which the pope then had to resolve. Five elections were held at York during the reign of Edward I and only the last of these was the subject of a straightforward papal confirmation. In the other four cases, the election was quashed on procedural grounds and the elect re-appointed. William Wickwane's election (1279) was quashed 'on account of informality', but he was then provided to the see 'in consideration of his character and learning'.[211] When John le Romeyn's election was examined in Rome in 1285, he was forced to resign, 'a doubt having arisen'. A new election was then held at the curia, in which the majority of the electors were not only canons of York but also members of the papal hierarchy; most of these men were non-resident at York and had not participated in the first election. Such an unconventional arrangement was possible only because it was the procedure rather than the outcome of the initial election that had been questioned. The second group of electors was not expected to make their own choice of archbishop, but rather to reaffirm the decision made by their counterparts in England. Thus Romeyn was re-elected and confirmed by Martin IV.[212] Henry of Newark's election (1296)

---

207 *CM*, V, pp. 701, 718.

208 *Fasti 1300-1541*, VI, p. 3.

209 *CM*, III, p. 157.

210 *Gervase*, II, p. 127.

211 *CPL*, I, p. 459.

212 *CPL*, I, p. 483. The electors appointed by the pope were 'A[ncher], cardinal priest of S. Prassede, H[ugh of Evesham], cardinal-priest of S. Lorenzo in Lucina, J[ordan], cardinal-deacon of S. Eustachio, and B. Camerarius, Percival de Lavania, Peter de Sabello, the pope's nephew, Neapolio Orsini, papal chaplains, John himself, the above-mentioned archdeacon, and Master Thomas de Abberbyri, canons of York, then at Rome'.

was nullified by his failure to go to Rome, and consequently quashed; he was then provided to the see by Boniface VIII in order to please Edward I.[213] Thomas of Corbridge, like Romeyn, resigned in Rome (in 1300); the reasons for this are unclear, but presumably related to procedural flaws since he was subsequently provided to the see.[214]

Episcopal elections were also referred to Rome, where their outcome would be determined by papal judgement, if their circumstances were in some way anomalous. Thus Henry III requested that the election of Robert Bingham, bishop of Salisbury (1228-46) be examined and confirmed by the pope because the see of Canterbury was then vacant.[215] More typical were the elections considered at Rome because they were the subject of bitter disputes in England. The papacy could both resolve disputes and perpetuate them, as the example of the 1238-44 Winchester dispute illustrates. Both king and convent appealed to Rome in 1239, and had the postulation of Ralph Neville been confirmed at this point, Henry would, however reluctantly, have been forced to accept this outcome. Instead, Neville's appointment was quashed, a new election was ordered[216] and the dispute continued for another five years. Only after September 1243, when Innocent IV ruled in favour of William Raleigh, could the final resolution of the dispute begin.[217]

The papal response to the Winchester dispute also encapsulates the papal attitude to the English crown. Post-1216, popes were only rarely, if ever, deliberately antagonistic to the crown and were often willing to comply with royal wishes – as with the quashing of Neville's election or the confirmation of Boniface of Savoy as archbishop. On occasion, it was even explicitly stated that an appointment had been made to please the king, as when Thomas of Corbridge was provided to York despite his failure to go to Rome in person.[218] But such rulings were made only if they were also agreeable to the pope. Neville's postulation was quashed not simply to please Henry III, but also because he does not seem to have been well regarded at the curia, where his bid for the archbishopric of Canterbury had also ended in failure.[219] Popes were also unafraid to make some rulings that were extremely unfavourable to the crown, such as the confirmation of William Raleigh's translation to Winchester.

---

213 *CPL*, I, p. 569.

214 *CPL*, I, p. 586.

215 *Reg. St Osmund*, II, pp. 111, 115-16.

216 *Reg. Grég. IX*, no. 4728.

217 *Reg. Inn. IV*, nos. 113-14.

218 *CPL*, I, p. 569.

219 His prospects were not helped by Simon Langton's strident criticisms; the archdeacon of Canterbury accused Neville of being 'an unworthy, unlearned courtier, bold of action and desirous of freeing England from subjugation to Rome'. *CM*, III, p. 207.

So far, only routine papal involvement in elections has been considered. There was, however, another category of papal involvement which had particular significance during the thirteenth century: papal supervision imposed in response to political difficulties. England received four legatine missions during the reign of Henry III: Guala (1216-18), Pandulph (1218-21), Otto (1238-41) and Ottobuono (1265-8).[220] The first two played a key role in the filling of episcopal vacancies during the early years of Henry III's minority, in accordance with their mandate to 'dispose of vacant sees to persons faithful to the king and to the Roman see';[221] chapters were obliged to elect those nominated by the legate. Guala engineered the election of Hugh of Beaulieu, a former royal ambassador, at Carlisle[222] and supported the translation of Richard Poore from Chichester to Salisbury.[223] The legate filled the resultant vacancy at Chichester by appointing Ranulph de Wareham, a Benedictine monk closely associated with the royalist cause.[224] At Worcester he ignored the monks' demands that they be allowed to elect one of their own number, instead securing the election of William de Blois, a member of a clerical dynasty with a long history of royal service.[225] Pandulph's role in episcopal appointments was less hands-on; he seems to have acted primarily as an overseer, most notably during the 1220-21 London vacancy, when he confirmed the election of Eustace de Fauconberg.[226]

Legate Otto's role in the 1230s was also considerably more limited than that of Guala. His legation coincided with the Winchester dispute, but his involvement was rather less than might have been expected. Papal mandates were issued ordering him to 'see that no person who is unacceptable to the king is provided'[227] and to bring about an agreement between the various dissenting parties,[228] and Bishop Grosseteste complained of the king's intervention to him,[229] but his role appears to have been confined to mediation, and he left England on 7 January 1241 – well before the dispute was resolved.[230] If the royal petition

220 Carpenter, *Struggle*, pp. 431-4; Lawrence, 'Thirteenth Century', pp. 130-32; *Guala*, pp. xl-xlii. A fifth legate, Gui Foulquois, served in 1263-64, but never managed to enter England.

221 *CPL*, I, p. 43.

222 *AM*, II, p. 291; *Guala*, p. 11.

223 *Guala*, pp. lii-liii.

224 *AM*, II, p. 289; *Guala*, pp. 15-16.

225 *AM*, IV, p. 410; *Guala*, pp. lii, 100.

226 *AM*, II, p. 294; *Hist. Angl.*, II, p. 248; *PR 1216-1225*, p. 282; *Chron. E1&E2*, I, p. 23.

227 *Original Papal Documents in England and Wales from the Accession of Pope Innocent III to the Death of Pope Benedict XI (1198-1304)*, ed. J. Sayers (Oxford, 1999), no. 237.

228 *Reg. Grég. IX*, nos. 5019, 5024.

229 *Grosseteste*, pp. 208-13 (letters 60, 61).

230 Francis Gasquet, *Henry III and the Church* (London, 1905), p. 189.

against Raleigh's postulation is to be believed, Otto's influence was so limited that this choice had been made directly against the counsel of the legate.[231]

During the final legation of Henry III's reign, Ottobuono's role was not to direct elections, but stop them taking place. In a move presumably intended to prevent the election of Montfortian rebels to vacant bishoprics, the legate was ordered to 'inhibit all prelates, chapters, convents, and colleges to proceed to any election, provision or collation ... all such elections, provisions and collations being hereby reserved to the pope [for the duration of the legation]'.[232] Thus, during the later stages of the political crisis of the 1260s, the pope had far greater direct control over English episcopal elections than at any other time prior to the age of provision. Clement IV exercised these extraordinary powers of provision to fill the sees of York (in 1266) and Winchester (in 1268). On the first occasion he set aside the capitular election and provided St Bonaventura, who refused the see; he then translated Walter Giffard from Bath and Wells to York.[233] On the second he translated Nicholas of Ely from Worcester to Winchester by papal provision.[234] Both of these appointments suggest that just as Guala's appointments had been designed to encourage peace following the difficult final years of John's reign so Clement IV was using episcopal appointments as a tool to encourage political stability. Both Giffard and Ely were amongst the commissioners appointed under the Dictum of Kenilworth and were thus at the forefront of efforts to reunite a divided country. Like most of the papal interventions made during the course of the thirteenth century, these appointments were politically astute and designed to minimize divisions between those involved in the electoral process (as well as the country as a whole), but they were also somewhat to the detriment of the electoral freedom of the cathedral chapters involved.

The Role of the Candidate

According to the strictures of the canon law, candidates for the episcopate could hardly be counted amongst the players in the electoral process; instead, they should be pawns in the hands of the active participants, and ultimately in the hands of God. The reality, however, was somewhat more complex, not least because a bishopric was something to which many ambitious men aspired. Adam of Eynsham, describing the appointment of St Hugh as bishop of Lincoln, wrote that many of the courtiers present at the election 'would certainly not

231 *CPR 1232-1247*, pp. 400-401.

232 *CPL*, I, p. 430.

233 *CPL*, I, p. 431; *AM*, IV, pp. 184, 194, 198; *CPR 1266-1272*, p. 19; *Chron. E1&E2*, I, p. 76.

234 *Reg. Clem. IV*, nos. 1327-8; *AM*, II, pp. 106, 375; IV, pp. 214, 216; *Gervase*, II, p. 247.

have refused a bishopric if pressed to accept it, either because according to the apostle it was a good work, or from motives of secular ambition, because of the distinction and authority it conferred'.[235]

The role of personal ambition in thirteenth-century elections is perhaps best illustrated by the example of the 1223 Carlisle vacancy, on which occasion two men can be seen to have actively sought their own promotion to this (not obviously desirable) see. The successful candidate, Walter Mauclerk, was a long-standing royal clerk, but was not the king's candidate, as preparations for a royal appeal against the election demonstrate.[236] Instead, Mauclerk appears to have used his position as sheriff of Cumberland to orchestrate his own election.[237] The election subsequently received royal confirmation,[238] and although Mauclerk was to prove himself a loyal, competent bishop of this border see, it is hard to escape the conclusion that the minority government had been outmanoeuvred by an ambitious individual.

The outcome of the election was rather less satisfactory from the perspective of Mauclerk's rival for the see. When news of Bishop Beaulieu's fatal accident reached the Cumbrian monastery of Holm Cultram, its abbot, Adam of Kendal, expected that he would be elected as bishop of Carlisle. In an attempt to ensure the desired outcome, he used his abbey's revenues to bribe the electors and local figures who he believed could influence their choice. The disappointment of failing to secure the see sent him out of his mind; he was forced to resign his abbacy and was confined at Holm Cultram until his death shortly afterwards.[239] Adam of Kendal was far from being the only aspiring bishop to be accused of simony; allegations of bribery were made against a number of thirteenth-century bishops.[240] The veracity of these and other similar stories is open to question, but they indicate a contemporary belief that those elected to bishoprics, far from being passive instruments of higher powers, were interested by and active in their own promotion.

On many other occasions, candidates shaped the course of the electoral process by fighting for a see to which they had been elected; once an election had been held, it was rare for the elect to renounce his election without a struggle. One of the chief reasons for the longevity of the 1238-44 Winchester electoral dispute was the tenacity of the two royal ministers elected to the see against the

---

235 *Magna Vita*, I, p. 93.

236 *RLC*, I, p. 560b; *PR 1216-1225*, p. 408.

237 Nicholas Vincent, 'Walter Mauclerk', *ODNB*. Mauclerk's actions should probably be understood in the context of Henry III's apparently impending majority. Margaret Norton, 'The Bishops of the Archdiocese of York, c.1200-c.1250' (Trinity College Dublin, PhD thesis, 2004), p. 111.

238 *PR 1216-1225*, p. 413.

239 *Scotichronicon, by Walter Bower*, ed. D. E. R. Watt *et al.* (9 vols, Aberdeen, 1987-98), V, pp. 24-37; *Holm Cultram*, pp. 133-4.

240 See above, p. 67.

king's wishes: firstly Ralph Neville and then William Raleigh. Neville attempted to secure Bishop Grosseteste's support for his promotion, although he was vigorously rebuffed;[241] Raleigh worked harder to secure his promotion, perhaps because of his 'excessive ambition'.[242] He appears to have gone to the papal curia,[243] where he reportedly spent 8,000 marks on securing papal confirmation of his postulation.[244] He also rejected the king's demands that he sign a written agreement to renounce his claim to Winchester,[245] stating that he would only do so by the order of the pope.[246] His conduct earned him the respect of Matthew Paris, who reported that, in French eyes, Raleigh was the latest in a series of holy bishops to be unjustly persecuted by the English crown.[247]

However, not every bishop-elect had the stamina and status necessary to stage such a fight, and on several occasions candidates were persuaded to renounce their election. When Hereford fell vacant in 1239, the canons elected Michael, a canon of Lichfield and a 'man commended by all', but he was persuaded to resign, since bad times were ahead, and the king would confirm only the elections of foreigners – or so Matthew Paris claimed. In his place, and at the king's insistence, Peter d'Aigueblanche, the treasurer and household clerk of William of Savoy (Queen Eleanor's uncle) was elected.[248] Several other bishops-elect, having travelled to Rome to present the case for their election, eventually found themselves obliged to resign their claims to episcopal office, presumably as an alternative to having their election quashed. This was the fate of John de Sancto Germano, elect of Worcester, whose election was opposed by Archbishop Winchelsey.[249] The elect and his electors fought their side, sending proctors to Rome[250] and securing royal support for Sancto Germano's decision to plead his own case at the curia.[251] But less than a week after he entered Rome,

241 *Grosseteste*, pp. 213-16 (letter 62).

242 *CPR 1232-1247*, p. 439.

243 *AM*, I, p. 112.

244 *CM*, IV, p. 346.

245 *CM*, IV, p. 159.

246 *AM*, II, p. 331.

247 *CM*, IV, pp. 296-7; the other members of this group were SS. Anselm, Thomas Becket and Edmund of Abingdon. Paris made his own comparison between Becket and Raleigh, pointing out that even the martyr was not barred by the king from obtaining the 'essentials of life' (*CM*, IV, p. 286).

248 *CM*, IV, p. 48; François Mugnier, *Les Savoyards en Angleterre au XIIIe Siècle et Pierre d'Aigueblanche, Évêque d'Héreford* (Chambéry, 1890), pp. 29-30; Nigel Yates, 'Bishop Peter de Aquablanca (1240-1269): A Reconsideration', *JEH*, 22 (1971), pp. 303-17, at p. 303.

249 *Reg. Sede Vacante*, p. 12; *Reg. Winchelsey*, II, pp. 631-4.

250 *Reg. Sede Vacante*, pp. 10, 14-15.

251 Ibid., p. 15; *CCR 1296-1302*, p. 550.

the would-be bishop resigned; within a fortnight, William Gainsborough had been provided to Worcester in his place.[252]

External pressures were not the only reason why several bishops-elect failed to retain their bishopric; some candidates voluntarily renounced their election. Sometimes this was because they had received a better offer. In February 1239, William Raleigh was elected as bishop of Coventry and Lichfield, but whilst he was deciding whether to accept this see, the monks of Norwich elected him to be their bishop. Finding himself doubly-elect, Raleigh rejected Coventry and accepted Norwich. Paris claimed that this decision was based on a preference for living in England, rather than on the Welsh borders,[253] although a more cynical observer might note that Norwich was by far the wealthier of the two dioceses.

As his subsequent career demonstrated, Raleigh was clearly not motivated by reluctance to become a bishop, but was simply unsure about accepting a certain see. But whilst the lure of the mitre drew many men in, others, lacking in episcopal pretensions, nevertheless found that they had been elected to a bishopric. Consequently, whilst some electoral processes were shaped by a candidate's ambition, others were defined by the reluctance of the bishop-elect to take the office offered to him. Nicholas Farnham was elected to Coventry and Lichfield in 1239, but refused this promotion because he was unworthy.[254] Two years later, he was elected to Durham, and again seems to have been reluctant to accept his election; both Paris and the Durham annalist state that Bishop Grosseteste had to persuade him to accept.[255] Farnham overcame his reluctance to accept his election and went on to spend nearly a decade as bishop of Durham, but others were more definite in their refusal. During the course of the thirteenth century, the opportunity to become bishop of Carlisle was turned down twice: by Robert de Sancta Agata in 1256, and again by William of Rotherfield in 1278.[256] When Fulk Lovel, archdeacon of Colchester, was elected bishop of London in 1280, he immediately resigned on grounds of old age and ill health.[257]

If ill health was a valid excuse for the resignation of a bishop-elect, there was one even better reason for failing to take up the office to which one had been elected: death. Richard Talbot was elected as bishop of London in 1262, but died before he could be consecrated.[258] A similar misfortune befell Salisbury in 1288, when Lawrence of Hakeburne died at Canterbury, whence he had gone to seek

---

252 *Reg. Sede Vacante*, p. 32; *CPL*, I, p. 604.

253 *CM*, III, pp. 525, 531-2; *Chronicle of Bury*, p. 10; *EEA*, 21, p. xxxii.

254 *CM*, IV, p. 134.

255 *CM*, IV, p. 87, *Script. Tres*, pp. 38-41; *EEA*, 29, pp. xxiv-xxv.

256 *CM*, V, p. 588; *Chronicle of Lanercost*, pp. 18-19.

257 *AM*, II, p. 393; IV, pp. 283, 478; *Chronicle of Bury*, p. 71; *Registrum Statutorum*, p. 387, n. 2; *Chron. E1&E2*, I, p. 89; *Reg. Pecham*, I, pp. 113-14.

258 *AM*, IV, pp. 131-2; *Gervase*, II, p. 216.

archiepiscopal confirmation of his election.[259] Unlike many other candidates, this unfortunate duo did not choose their role in the election process, but they certainly had a dramatic impact on its outcome.

Other Participants

Given the power and prestige enjoyed by a medieval bishop, it was inevitable that other individuals and groups would become involved in the electoral process, even though they had no formal role. Amongst the most prominent of these secular participants was the queen, and both Eleanor of Provence and Eleanor of Castile can be shown to have intervened in episcopal elections. The former may well have played a part in encouraging Henry III to promote the careers of her uncles, William and Boniface of Savoy; in the words that Matthew Paris attributed to the king, it was his desire 'that I might satisfy the wishes of the queen, my wife' that had led him to seek William's election to Winchester in 1238.[260] In 1242 she wrote to the chapters of Bath and Wells in order to second the king's request for the election of Peter Chaceporc.[261] In 1260, a group of Durham monks came to Winchester to seek *congé d'élire*. Whilst they were there, a messenger arrived from the queen (then at Marlborough), asking Henry to request that John Mansel (a trusted royal councillor) should be elected; a few days later, once the licence had been granted, the royal couple both wrote to the monks in his favour.[262] Over three decades later, in 1275, Eleanor of Castile supported Robert Burnell's election to the same diocese.[263] In 1288, she wrote to the canons of Salisbury to inform them of her support for William de la Corner's election; if they elected her candidate, and appointed her kinsman James of Spain to a prebend, they could be sure of her favour.[264]

Far from being frowned upon, the queen's participation in the electoral process was seen as a potential force for good and her support was sought by prominent churchmen. In the early 1240s, as the Winchester dispute reached its climax, Innocent IV wrote to Queen Eleanor, asking her to persuade her husband to drop his opposition to William Raleigh. At around the same time, Robert Grosseteste wrote to Archbishop Boniface, begging him to ask Eleanor

---

259 *Gervase*, II, p. 294; *Chronicle of Bury*, p. 91.

260 *CM*, V, pp. 180-84.

261 *Bath Chartularies*, pp. 45-6; Margaret Howell, *Eleanor of Provence: Queenship in Thirteenth-Century England* (Oxford, 1998), p. 41.

262 Howell, *Eleanor*, pp. 173-4.

263 TNA SC1/10/56.

264 BL Royal MS 12 D xi fo. 88.

to entreat Henry to relent.[265] Similarly, when king and archbishop clashed over the 1244 Chichester election, it was Eleanor who mediated between the two men; according to Paris, it was also Eleanor who pointed out to the angry king that Robert Passelewe (the royal candidate, whose election had been quashed by Boniface) would make a poor bishop, but was extremely good at making money for the crown.[266]

Other members of the royal family also made their influence felt. Richard, earl of Cornwall, tried to secure the bishopric of Ely for his kinsman, Roger de Meuland, in 1253. On that occasion, Henry III requested that his brother withdraw his petition to the monks; in return royal support would be given to Meuland's candidacy for the next available bishopric.[267] The king does not seem to have kept his word, for Meuland had to wait until 1257 to be elected as bishop of Coventry and Lichfield. The earl again petitioned in his favour, and Richard's influence was sufficient to allow the monks and canons to ignore the king's request that they elect his treasurer, Philip Lovell.[268] An even more striking example of such intervention occurred in 1270, when the future Edward I decided to try to persuade the monks of Canterbury to elect Robert Burnell as their archbishop. Arriving in Canterbury, he found that the election was already in progress; consequently, he broke into the chapter house and, using every means at his disposal, demanded that the monks should elect Burnell. They refused, being inspired by the Holy Spirit to elect their prior instead.[269]

Members of the nobility and gentry could also influence the outcome of elections; hence the complaint of the canons of Wells, who resented 'the power of the English nobles who meddle in every election'.[270] Royal ministers were particularly well placed for such intervention. It was surely not coincidental that Hubert de Burgh's brother and nephew both acquired bishoprics during the period when he was the most powerful man in England.[271] Robert Burnell, in his role as chancellor, was consulted over two elections in 1280: the prior of Winchester asked him for advice regarding the king's wishes for that see,[272] and the canons of London sought his assistance in smoothing over difficulties with their licence to elect.[273] In 1240, Gregory IX acknowledged the receipt of letters from nine English earls, all of whom had written to the pope in defence

265 *CM*, IV, p. 349; *Grosseteste*, pp. 290-92 (letter 86); Howell, *Eleanor*, p. 41.

266 *Royal Letters*, II, pp. 42-3; *CM*, IV, pp. 509-10; Howell, *Eleanor*, p. 42.

267 *CR 1253-1254*, p. 313.

268 *CM*, V, p. 613.

269 *Bartholomæi de Cotton*, p. 145, refers to Edward's violent response, although the local chronicler says nothing of violence: *Gervase*, II, p. 252. See also Huscroft, 'Burnell', pp. 26-8.

270 *Wells MSS*, I, p. 117.

271 *CM*, III, p. 121; Vincent, 'Thirteenth Century', p. 35.

272 TNA SC1/24/195.

273 TNA SC1/23/215.

of the royal stance on the Winchester election – although he claimed that their correspondence had arrived too late to influence his decision.[274] Local ties could also play a part. Walter de Cantilupe, elected to Worcester in 1236, was a member of a powerful baronial family which played an important part in national politics throughout the thirteenth century, but the monks who chose him as their bishop may have placed more stead on his local connections: the Cantilupes' power base was in Warwickshire and a Cantilupe bishop was a powerful asset in the ongoing struggle between the cathedral priory and another local family, the Beauchamps.[275] Lower down the social scale, it seems probable that Richard Blund's election as bishop of Exeter (1245) was not unconnected to the fact that he came from a prominent local family; his brother, Hilary Blund, had been provost and mayor of the city in the 1220s-1230s.[276]

Local secular officials could become embroiled in disputes. The mayor and citizens of Winchester were on the front line of the campaign against William Raleigh, keeping him out of the city and complying with royal orders not to supply him with provisions.[277] Their significance in this dispute is underlined by the penalties imposed on them by the bishop, who excommunicated the leading citizens and all the bailiffs in 1243.[278] The mayor had particularly roused the episcopal wrath, and when Raleigh entered his see in 1244, he was singled out for 'a heavier atonement and punishment'.[279] Other, less prominent individuals such as the sailors who took Raleigh overseas have barely left a trace on the records, but nevertheless played a vital role in the election.[280]

Interest in English elections was not limited to the English, and there are occasional examples of foreign rulers becoming involved in the electoral process. In August 1216, Alexander II of Scotland seized Carlisle. Shortly afterwards, he persuaded the canons to elect one of his clerks, an excommunicate, as their bishop.[281] Peter des Roches wrote to Frederick II on behalf of John Blund, elect of Canterbury, presumably in order to request that the emperor intercede with the pope on Blund's behalf.[282] The complexity and duration of the Winchester dispute meant that it acquired a uniquely cosmopolitan dimension. In 1244, William Raleigh was driven out of England by the king's harsh treatment of him, and went into exile. Arriving in France, he was welcomed by Louis IX, who

---

274 *Original Papal Documents*, no. 240.

275 Philippa Hoskin, 'Diocesan Politics in the See of Worcester, 1218-1266', *JEH*, 54 (2003), pp. 422-40, at pp. 434-5.

276 Frank Barlow, 'Richard Blund', *ODNB*.

277 *AM*, II, p. 331; III, p. 162; *CM*, IV, p. 266.

278 *AM*, II, p. 89; III, p. 162.

279 *CM*, IV, p. 390.

280 *AM*, I, p. 132.

281 *Guala*, p. 11.

282 Vincent, *des Roches*, p. 368.

sent a messenger to meet the new arrival at Abbeville. This royal representative 'received the bishop on the part of his master, the king, with joy and gladness of countenance, promising him in all things the king's advice and help, with every consolation and protection'. Furthermore, the mayor and commons of the city were to be ready to defend the bishop, by force if necessary, should the king of England send after him 'to do him harm'.[283] Towards the very end of the dispute, another of the queen's Savoyard uncles became involved. Unlike William and Boniface, Thomas, count of Flanders and Hainault, was not a rival to Raleigh but a defender; it was at his instance that formal permission for the bishop's return to England was granted.[284] The support of such figures must have been a boon to Raleigh, since it put additional pressure on Henry to concede defeat.

External intervention in the bishop-making process was not solely the preserve of the secular elites; prominent members of the ecclesiastical hierarchy were also keen to make their influence felt. By the thirteenth century, the right of the local clergy to participate in episcopal elections, and of the suffragan bishops of a province to elect their archbishop, had become virtually extinct. The last occasion on which such claims are known to have been made was in 1228, when the suffragan bishops of Canterbury appealed against the election of Walter de Eynsham, arguing that their non-participation invalidated the process.[285] Nevertheless, the fact that the English bishops lacked a formal role in the electoral process did not mean that they were unconcerned by the problems and practice of election.

Episcopal involvement sometimes took a general form, as members of the bishops' bench, acting either individually or in tandem, spoke out in favour of electoral freedom and against the king's intervention in ecclesiastical affairs. The question of electoral freedom was only once raised in the thirteenth-century ecclesiastical gravamina, at the Canterbury provincial council of 1257. Three clauses were dedicated to elections, each of them focusing on excessive royal influence:

> 3. Item, although elections in cathedral or conventual churches ought to be free, so many royal requests of such a kind intervene that the frightened electors more often give preference to human wishes over the divine will. The same thing happens with respect to churches or prebends when they happen to fall vacant, for the use of the royal clerks.

283 *CM*, IV, p. 295. The surviving records of thirteenth-century French government are unfortunately too sparse to allow Paris' claims to be either corroborated or disproved.

284 *CPR 1232-1247*, p. 433.

285 *CM*, III, p. 157.

> 4. Item, when elections have been made and the elect presented to the king, sometimes he delays his consent, opposing the elect or even the election without reasonable cause, so that thus the elect gives way through fear or the electors are compelled to acquiesce with the king's request, from which many dangers (both spiritual and temporal) befall the churches.
>
> 5. Item, when sometimes in a case allowed by the law the power of appointment devolves from the vacant cathedral or collegiate church to a higher power, the lord king tries to extend to this kind of case the privilege granted to him that the licence to elect should be sought from him before an election is held, to the detriment of his own salvation and the scandal of many, and also against the charter on elections granted by his father.[286]

That the bishops complained at all is of interest, since it provides a clear indication that discontent about the manner in which elections were conducted remained current until at least the mid-thirteenth century. On the other hand, the fact that they complained so infrequently about electoral freedom (against repeated complaints about, amongst other things, royal intervention in ecclesiastical justice)[287] suggests that it was not a primary concern. They may also have been deterred by a problem allegedly pointed out by Henry III, when four bishops (Boniface of Canterbury, William of Salisbury, Silvester of Carlisle and Aymer of Winchester) made an informal complaint to him at the Easter 1253 parliament: many of the English bishops owed their own bishopric to Henry, and by questioning the king's role in elections thus questioned their own position.[288]

However, formal representations were not the only means by which a bishop could become involved in elections and many of them intervened on a case-by-case basis. The motivations behind such interventions were mixed, with defence of electoral freedom being only one concern. The prime example of such principled involvement was, somewhat unsurprisingly, Robert Grosseteste, a vigorous exponent of electoral freedom whose collected letters include several examples of missives in which he reminds those involved in elections of the importance of canonical election. In 1238 he wrote three letters concerning the election at Winchester; two were addressed to the Legate Otto, asking him to ensure the freedom of the electors, whilst the third reminded Ralph Neville, the bishop-elect, of the need to avoid the stain of personal ambition.[289] Grosseteste

286 *C&S*, I, p. 540. The translation is mine.

287 For an overview, see William Jones, 'Bishops, Politics and the Two Laws: The Gravamina of the English Clergy, 1237-1399', *Speculum*, 41 (1966), pp. 209-45.

288 *CM*, V, p. 373.

289 *Grosseteste*, pp. 208-13 (letters 60-61); Gasquet, *Henry III*, pp. 180-81.

wrote a further letter about Winchester in 1243/4, expressing his concerns about the ongoing dispute and asking Archbishop Boniface to use his influence with the queen to bring about an end to the difficulties.[290] A fifth, slightly earlier, letter, addressed to Edmund of Abingdon and dating from late 1239 or early 1240, expressed concerns about secular intervention in elections, with particular reference to the forthcoming Canterbury election.[291]

Nor was Grosseteste the only bishop whose involvement in elections can be traced. Inevitably, episcopal intervention is most clearly demonstrable during major disputes; in such circumstances, it was fitting for senior ecclesiastical figures publicly to intervene. Indeed, they might even be ordered to do so. In the early stages of the Winchester dispute, Gregory IX wrote that the convent should select their candidate with the advice of Richard Wendene, bishop of Rochester, and Walter Mauclerk, bishop of Carlisle; he also required Archbishop Edmund of Abingdon and Bishop Robert Grosseteste to take a supervisory role.[292] As the dispute drew to a close, in 1244, Innocent IV requested that the archbishop-elect of Canterbury, the bishops of Worcester and Hereford, and Archdeacon Langton of Canterbury pressurize the king into restoring the temporalities of Winchester to Raleigh.[293] Although Paris' claim that Bishops Robert Grosseteste, Peter Aigueblanche and Walter Cantilupe pursued Henry III around the south of England in order to 'advise him to correct his faults'[294] is clearly inaccurate,[295] it seems that several of the bishops did write to Archbishop Boniface, 'devoutly praying us for peace' between Henry and William Raleigh.[296]

The bishops might also become involved in the examination of a bishop-elect and the process by which he was elected. Robert Grosseteste, examining the election of Robert Passelewe to Chichester (1244) on behalf of Archbishop Boniface, posed a serious of difficult theological questions to the would-be bishop, and quashed the election because the elect was unable to answer them.[297] This task might also be delegated to other senior churchmen. When Archbishop Boniface was notified of the election of Walter de Bronescombe as bishop of Exeter in March 1258, he was 'occupied at Westminster with state and private business'. Consequently, he deputized the examination of the candidate to Masters Eustace de Lenn, Pontius, rector of Lambeth church, Roger de

---

290 *Grosseteste*, pp. 290-92 (letter 86).

291 *Grosseteste*, pp. 283-5 (letter 83).

292 *Reg. Grég. IX*, no. 4728.

293 *Reg. Inn. IV*, nos. 505-7.

294 *CM*, IV, p. 286.

295 Not least because Aigueblanche was with the king at Windsor at the time of the alleged pursuit. See *EEA*, 35, p. xliv, and *The Royal Charter Witness Lists of Henry III (1226-72)*, ed. M. Morris (2 vols, Kew, 2001), I, p. 191.

296 *CM*, IV, p. 297.

297 *CM*, IV, p. 401; Williams, 'Archbishop Boniface', pp. 96-8, 255.

Canterbury and Michael de Bristol. Once Boniface had received their written report of the examination, he confirmed the election and notified his assent to Henry III.[298]

According to custom, the cathedral chapters of Christ Church Canterbury and St Mary's York had the right to confirm episcopal elections held during their respective provinces during archiepiscopal vacancies; attempts to exercise this right, or the withholding of capitular confirmation, affected a small number of thirteenth-century elections. Robert Wickampton was elected to Salisbury in 1271, during the archiepiscopal vacancy that followed the death of Boniface of Savoy. His election was confirmed by the Canterbury convent, but the suffragan bishops refused to consecrate him and he was therefore forced to seek confirmation of his position in Rome.[299] Seven years later, Archbishop Walter Gifford of York died shortly after the election of Ralph Ireton as bishop of Carlisle. The bishop-elect sought confirmation from the chapter at York, but was rebuffed.[300] Gilbert Segrave, bishop-elect of London, was more fortunate; he obtained confirmation from the Canterbury convent in 1313, when the archbishopric was vacant following the death of Robert Winchelsey.[301]

Non-episcopal members of the clerical elite might also be involved in the election itself; the role of the archdeacons was particularly significant in this respect. During the first half of the thirteenth century, the archdeacons of some monastic sees claimed the right to participate in elections, even though they did not belong to the cathedral convent. Typically, their involvement is noted in relation to electoral disputes. At Norwich, in 1236, John de Ferentino, archdeacon of Norwich, sent his proctor to the king to present his case 'against the election and the electors and the prior of the church of Norwich'.[302] The archdeacon's support for the king's appeal against Simon of Elmham was almost certainly a factor in its success. At Winchester, the archdeacons of Winchester and Surrey first claimed the right to elect in 1204, when they supported the candidacy of Richard Poore against that of the eventual victor, Peter des Roches.[303] By 1238, when the see again fell vacant, the archdeaconries were held by Hugh and Luke des Roches, nephews of the late bishop. Together they acted as supporters of the royal candidates for the see, William de Valence and Boniface of Savoy; Hugh probably went to Rome as one of the royal proctors.[304] The

298 *Reg. Bronescombe*, I, pp. 2-3.

299 *AM*, IV, pp. 239-43; *Gervase*, II, pp. 251-2.

300 *CPL*, I, p. 461.

301 *Fasti 1300-1541*, V, p. 1, citing Canterbury Cathedral Library, CCA-DCc-Register/Q (Sede Vacante Register 1292-1349), fo. 64.

302 *CPR 1232-1247*, p. 167.

303 Vincent, *des Roches*, pp. 49-52.

304 *EEA, 9: Winchester 1205-1238*, ed. N. Vincent (Oxford, 1994), pp. 171-3, 175-6.

cousins fought staunchly for their right to participate in the episcopal election; by January 1240, their dispute with the monks had come to a head and the pope intervened in an attempt to resolve their differences. The archdeacons, it seems, had excommunicated the monks, and Gregory IX appointed Cardinal Otto, the papal legate in England, to bring about a truce.[305] That the king exploited the differences between the monks and archdeacons is supported by Paris' account, which claims that he initially refused the monks a licence to elect, on the grounds that the archdeacons were bound to be present, but were not.[306] The significance of Luke des Roches as the king's ally, and hence a leading opponent of Raleigh, is indicated by the fact that he appears to have resigned when the new bishop's election was confirmed, despite the fact that he survived until 1253.[307]

The role of the English clergy in episcopal elections becomes harder to detect during the final decades of the thirteenth century. One reason for this is likely to be the crystallization of correct electoral procedure, meaning that there was no longer room for semi-formalized extra-capitular participation, which would almost certainly lead to the quashing of the election; the days when suffragan bishops and archdeacons could claim a right to elect were past. The rarity of major electoral disputes during the reign of Edward I also reduced the opportunities for bishops to act as mediators or overseers. Yet it is hard to believe that the ecclesiastical elites had lost interest in the identities of the bishops who would become their colleagues and rulers, and it therefore seems likely that, throughout this period, there were numerous informal (and now untraceable) interventions. How far these shaped the composition of the English episcopate can now be no more than a matter for speculation.

The final group of churchmen to play an important role in English episcopal elections were the cardinals resident at the papal curia. Their role in episcopal elections was somewhat ambiguous, largely because the relationship between the cardinals and the popes was somewhat unclear. As part of the pope's body, they were so closely united to the pope that they could be viewed as one and the same thing, and the pope and cardinals were commonly viewed as a single legal entity – although there was no doubt that the pope was the head of this body. It was widely argued that the pope should make no important decisions without taking the advice of the cardinals, and amongst the list of *causae ardue*, on which he was obliged to consult them, were 'all questions having to do with episcopal elections and translations'. On the other hand, the unity of the pope and cardinals was probably not such that he always followed their advice, and

305 *Reg. Grég. IX*, nos. 5019, 5024.

306 *CM*, III, pp. 493-4.

307 *EEA*, 9, pp. 176-7.

the idea that the pope could act without the cardinals if necessary gained ground during the thirteenth century.[308]

In certain circumstances, the role played by the cardinals comes into focus, most obviously when the pope delegated the examination of an election to a small number of cardinals. In 1228, a delegation of canons from Salisbury went to Rome to present the election of Robert Bingham to the pope. They informed the papal chamberlain and one of the cardinals of their business, and on the fourth day of their stay were ushered into the papal presence. After a brief audience, they were examined by three cardinals, who asked keen and searching questions about the elect and the process of the election. The next day, these cardinals presented their findings to a papal tribunal, at which the pope and many cardinals were present, and the election was confirmed.[309] A similar procedure must have been followed on a considerable number of occasions, including in 1304, when the papal mandate confirming the election of William Greenfield of York noted that an examination had been carried out by three cardinals.[310]

The perceived importance of the cardinals in determining the outcome of elections examined at Rome is also reflected in the volume of related correspondence directed to them by various other participants in the electoral process. Many of the letters sent to the pope were also copied to the cardinals, and additional letters were directed to cardinals who might be favourable to the cause in hand. For example, in 1256 Henry III directed letters to Ottobuono cardinal deacon of S. Adriano, M. Jordan the papal notary and Riccardo cardinal deacon of S. Angelo, asking for their backing in his appeal against Hugh Balsham, and reminding them of the disappointments he had recently suffered in elections at York and Dublin.[311] Archbishops also sent letters to members of the College of Cardinals, canvassing their support in electoral disputes. John Pecham wrote to the English cardinal Hugh of Evesham on at least two occasions during the Winchester dispute of 1280-82.[312] Robert Winchelsey's register includes several examples of letters to cardinals concerning electoral matters, both soliciting their aid and thanking them once it was forthcoming.[313] Perhaps the most significant indication of the extent to which cardinals could influence the outcome of an election is to be found in the register of Archbishop Henry Newark of York: at the beginning of his pontificate, despite being in a considerable amount of debt,

---

308 Norman Zacour, 'The Cardinals' View of the Papacy, 1150-1300', in C. Ryan (ed.), *The Religious Roles of the Papacy: Ideals and Realities, 1150-1300* (Toronto, 1989), pp. 413-38.

309 *Reg. St Osmund*, II, pp. 114-16.

310 *CPL*, II, p. 7.

311 *Diplomatic Documents Preserved in the Public Record Office*, ed. P. Chaplais (London, 1964), pp. 198-200; Vincent, 'Thirteenth Century', p. 38.

312 *Reg. Pecham*, I, pp. 219-20, 282.

313 *Reg. Winchelsey*, I, pp. 644, 670-73.

he established pensions to be paid to several cardinals as a token of his gratitude for their services at his election.[314]

***

To date, much historiographical emphasis has been placed on the king's role in major electoral disputes. Historians have largely accepted Matthew Paris' vision of the king as a royal bull in an ecclesiastical china shop, trampling over the rights of the church in order to promote the careers of his (usually foreign) favourites. Consequently, the crown has long been viewed solely as a disruptive force and as the major threat to the electoral freedom of the English Church. Yet whilst there is obviously some truth in this perception, it is hard to avoid the conclusion that Henry III and Edward I have been unfairly maligned- the son even more so than the father. The default royal approach was compromise-based, and for the most part this approach worked, resulting in appointments acceptable to all concerned.

Much of the miscomprehension surrounding medieval ecclesiastical elections has its roots in the assumption that the motivations of cathedral chapters were somehow purer than those of the king. In reality, their concerns were often just as pragmatic, even worldly; witness the entry on the Worcester *sede vacante* register which stated two reasons why John de Sancto Germano's right of election should be prosecuted:

> Namely, that the building of the Church of Worcester would be continued by him and the state of the monks of Worcester as regards their food and refection in the refectory would be improved.[315]

Just as the crown sought the promotion of candidates who would be useful and loyal to the king and the kingdom, so monastic chapters favoured bishops who had something to offer them – whether that something was royal favour or better dinners.

Such capitular pragmatism meant that outright conflict with the crown could often be avoided, but even when disputes did break out, the king's conduct was usually far more nuanced than has previously been admitted. Any participant in an election had to work within and around the framework provided by canon law and custom. Realizing that unsophisticated demands were unlikely to produce the desired outcome, the crown presented carefully constructed appeals calculated to appeal to ecclesiastical sensibilities.

---

314 *Reg. Romeyn*, II, pp. 296-300.

315 *Reg. Sede Vacante*, p. 14.

Nor should we deny the crown the justification of principle. According to the terms of John's charter (which had received papal confirmation), the king had a formal role to play in episcopal elections, granting licence to elect, giving assent to the election and controlling the temporalities.[316] Given the great power and political significance enjoyed by the episcopate,[317] it was also part of the king's duty to ensure that the men appointed to English bishoprics were loyal and useful to the kingdom. To allow the election of an unsuitable candidate was a dereliction of duty. Even Innocent III, a staunch defender of electoral liberties, had recognized this, ordering the Legate Nicholas to ensure that those appointed to bishoprics were 'not only distinguished in life and learning, but also loyal to the king, profitable to the kingdom, and capable of giving counsel and help'.[318] Innocent even suggested that 'any honourable request of his [King John's] which preserves the liberty of the church' should be granted.[319] To modern eyes, royal involvement in episcopal elections seems incompatible with the ideal of electoral freedom, but from a medieval perspective such intervention was not only acceptable, but also necessary.

If the crown sought to create an episcopate full of skilled administrators who would be loyal and useful to king and country, then the archiepiscopate (especially in the final decades of the thirteenth century) and the papacy typically favoured pious and learned bishops who would be effective diocesans. The aims of the king and the ecclesiastical elites were usually very different, and often divergent.[320] What they had in common was that both differed from the aims of the cathedral chapters to whose choices they were responding; this difference was particularly marked where monastic chapters were concerned. It was when cathedral convents tried to favour local men, especially members of the cathedral chapter, that they were most likely to experience difficulties in securing the confirmation of their choices.

Such difficulties were as likely to be the result of ecclesiastical objections as of royal complaints; Stubbs and his ilk somewhat underestimated the church's enthusiasm for electoral litigation. Archbishops, popes and squabbling cathedral chapters all found fault with capitular elections, and this frequently produced the same result as royal complaints: the quashing of such processes. Indeed, it might be argued that archbishops and popes posed an even greater threat to capitular freedom of choice than the monarchy, since they actually had the

316 *C&S*, I, pp. 40-41.

317 Richard Dobson, 'The Political Role of the Archbishops of York during the Reign of Edward I' in Simon Lloyd and Peter Coss (eds), *Thirteenth-Century England III* (Woodbridge, 1989), pp. 47-64.

318 *SLI*, pp. 166-7 (no. 62).

319 *CLI*, no. 939.

320 Denton, *Winchelsey*, pp. 41-2.

ability to overturn elections, where the king could only withhold his assent and hope that the pope shared his opinion of the elect.

The overemphasis on the role of the king has led to the marginalization of the other participants in elections. In order to understand these processes, we need to consider the quintet of core participants on an equal basis, for the actions of each could be decisive. In particular, it is time to restore the candidate to the picture, and to recognize that, whatever canon law demanded, these men were not simply pawns in the hands of the players; they actively sought to achieve (or, more rarely, to avoid) promotion to the episcopate. Similarly, elections were not solely the domain of these five major participants; very few vacancies were filled without other parties offering their opinions, and attempting to determine the outcome.

Throughout the thirteenth century, pragmatic compromise between large numbers of participants was the defining feature of episcopal elections. When compared to the idealistic vision of electoral freedom presented by the canon law, and favoured by certain chroniclers, such compromises may seem like a failure, but it is questionable whether the perfect form of such ideals could ever have existed in the real world – or whether any but the most idealistic actually wanted them to. Given the divergent, and sometimes contradictory, perspectives of these parties, the wonder is not that there were so many electoral disputes, but rather that there were so few. Yet even if Stubbs' vision of constant litigation has now been overturned, it is hard to escape the conclusion that the differences between participants were being patched over rather than resolved. The cracks that remained provided a fertile breeding ground for the roots of papal provision.

PART II
The Age of Provision

Chapter 4
The Age of Provision: Canon Law and Custom

In 1341, a canon of Lincoln travelled to Avignon to visit the papal curia. Under normal circumstances, such a journey would not be worthy of comment and would probably have gone unrecorded. This canon, however, was no ordinary canon, and his journey was no ordinary journey; indeed, it marked a turning point in English ecclesiastical history. Thomas Bek was bishop-elect of Lincoln and having heard rumours that his bishopric had been reserved, he went to Avignon to seek clarification of the situation. It was several months before his case was dealt with, but on 26 June 1342 he received papal confirmation of his election; consecration followed days later. Thomas Bek had secured his possession of England's largest bishopric.[1] Unbeknown to him, he had also secured for himself a place in history, as (virtually) the last pre-Reformation English bishop to owe his position to election by cathedral chapter.[2]

The transition from episcopal election to papal provision was one of immense significance for the English Church and, more broadly, for English government and society. Episcopal appointments were significant points of contact between the secular and ecclesiastical hierarchies; changes to this system thus raise a number of intriguing questions. What, for example, does the transition tell us about the changing nature of the papacy during the High Middle Ages? How does it affect our understanding of the internal dynamics of the English Church? What can we learn about the relationship between king and papacy – a topic of great significance given the events that were to unfold in the sixteenth century?[3] Yet this topic has, to date, received little attention from historians. There is a substantial body of work on the rise of provision and its impact on

---

1 *Murimuth*, pp. 120-21, 124; *CPL*, III, p. 52; William Stubbs, *Registrum Sacrum Anglicanum*, 2nd edn (Oxford, 1897), p. 75.

2 This description is usually applied to John Trilleck, bishop of Hereford (1344-60), but his election to the see was followed by his provision – the latter cancelled out the former. *CPL*, III, p. 95. For the handful of English bishops elected in the early fifteenth century, during the Great Schism, see below, p. 133.

3 J. T. Ellis saw the roots of the English Reformation in medieval hostility to papal interventions in English affairs, including provisions. John Ellis, *Anti-Papal Legislation in Medieval England, 1066-1377* (Washington DC, 1930).

lesser benefices,[4] but the nature and impact of this shift within the context of the English episcopate has never been studied in depth.[5]

The Development of Provision: the English Experience

In order to discover how the transition to provision came about, it is necessary to look back to the early years of the thirteenth century, at which time election by the cathedral chapter was considered the sole means by which a bishop could be appointed.[6] Indeed, the importance of election, and of electoral freedom, was restated in two key documents issued during the second decade of this century: King John's 1214 charter on freedom of election and the decrees of the Fourth Lateran Council (1215). The former provided a royal guarantee that 'there shall be free elections in perpetuity of all prelates'; the king would not 'deny or defer' licence to elect, nor would he refuse to confirm an election, unless there were legitimate grounds for doing so.[7] Canons 23-26 of the Lateran decrees focused on technical details of the electoral process (which was assumed to be the sole form of appointment), such as the permitted length of vacancy and forms of election.[8] The significance of these two texts is that neither allowed for any form of papal provision to take place; it was assumed that vacancies would be filled by capitular election. Indeed, the pontiff's only role in this process was the confirmation of those who were immediately subject to him.[9] That the dominance of election extended beyond the legal texts into the real world is demonstrated by the circumstances surrounding the appointment of Stephen Langton to the archbishopric of Canterbury in 1206. A disputed election

---

4 See, for example, Ann Deeley, 'Papal Provision and Royal Rights of Patronage in the Thirteenth Century', *EHR*, 43 (1928), pp. 497-527; Geoffrey Barraclough, *Papal Provisions* (Oxford, 1935); Louis Caillet, *La Papauté d'Avignon et l'Église de France: La Politique Bénéficiale du Pape Jean en France (1316-1334)* (Paris, 1975).

5 The best treatments of this topic are to be found in the following general works on the English Church: William Pantin, *The English Church in the Fourteenth Century* (Cambridge, 1955), pp. 48-75; William Pantin, 'The Fourteenth Century', in Lawrence, *English Church and the Papacy,* pp. 187-93; Peter Heath, *Church and Realm, 1272-1461* (London, 1988), pp. 92-6, 138-42. Smith, *Episcopal Appointments*, pp. 1-49, and Haines, 'Episcopate during the Reign of Edward II', pp. 657-709, provide valuable studies of the English episcopate during a crucial period for this transition.

6 Until the early twelfth century, election by 'the clergy and the people' had been the usual form; a bishop had to be selected, or at least approved of, by the local clergy and laity. See Peltzer, *Elections*, pp. 26-36; Duggan, 'Law and Practice', pp. 43-7; Richard Southern, *Western Society and the Church in the Middle Ages* (London, 1970), p. 156.

7 *C&S*, I, pp. 38-41.

8 *Ecumenical Councils*, I, pp. 246-8.

9 Ibid., p. 247. Of the English episcopate, only the archbishops of Canterbury and York were directly subject to Rome.

culminated in the examination of two would-be archbishops at Rome, and papal rejection of both the monastic and the royal candidates. Innocent III favoured Langton's appointment to the see, but rather than providing him, indicated his wishes to the Canterbury delegation then at the curia. The monks held another election, complied with papal wishes and thus the papal nominee was conventionally elected.[10] It is striking that, even though Pope Innocent decided who should be appointed, he did not think of making a provision and instead acknowledged the chapter's right to elect.

However, by 1223, when the bishopric of Coventry and Lichfield fell vacant, change was already in the air.[11] A dispute arose between the monks of Coventry and the canons of Lichfield, with both groups claiming the sole right to elect their bishop. An appeal was made to Rome, where Honorius III judged that the right to elect should be shared; on this occasion, he suggested, the rivals should delegate their powers of election to him, as a neutral arbiter. He then proceeded to appoint and consecrate Master Alexander of Stavensby. Although he was subsequently postulated by the canons of Lichfield, Stavensby was essentially the first English bishop to owe his position to a papal provision.[12] However, this mode of appointment remained a novelty throughout the reign of Henry III, and was used only seven more times prior to 1272. Two further provisions were made during the course of the 1220s, and five more followed by the end of the reign:

- Richard Poore to Durham, 1228
- Richard Grant to Canterbury, 1229
- Roger Weseham to Coventry, 1245
- John Gervase to Winchester, 1262
- Walter Giffard to York, 1266
- Nicholas of Ely to Winchester, 1268
- Robert Kilwardby to Canterbury, 1272

Only 11 per cent of the Henrician bishops (eight out of seventy-two) were appointed by papal provision. Under Edward I (1272-1307) this rate increased to 19 per cent; nine (out of forty-six) of the Edwardian bishops were appointed in this way:

- Ralph Ireton to Carlisle, 1278
- John Pecham to Canterbury, 1279

---

10 Christopher Holdsworth, 'Stephen Langton', *ODNB*.

11 William, prior of Goldcliff, had been provided to Llandaff by Pandulph (the papal legate) in 1219. *Fasti 1066-1300*, IX, pp. 14-15.

12 *Anglia Sacra*, I, pp. 437-8; Nicholas Vincent, 'Master Alexander of Stainsby, Bishop of Coventry and Lichfield, 1224–1238', *JEH*, 46 (1995), pp. 615-40, at pp. 628-9.

- William Wickwane to York, 1279
- John de Pontissara to Winchester, 1282
- Henry of Newark to York, 1296
- Ralph Walpole to Ely, 1299
- John Salmon to Norwich, 1299
- Thomas Corbridge to York, 1299
- William Gainsborough to Worcester, 1302

Despite the increased number of provisions made under Edward I, they appear to have been similar in form to those made during his father's lifetime. All seventeen papal appointments to English bishoprics between 1216 and 1307 were essentially responsive: the pope made a provision in order to settle an electoral dispute. Since disputes were most likely to occur in the wealthiest dioceses, it was to such sees that the majority of these early provisions were made. In none of these examples is the pope known to have previously made a reservation (that is, 'a declaration that a benefice should not be bestowed until the pope had been consulted'[13]). It is also important to note that, throughout the thirteenth century, this was only one of the ways in which electoral disputes were settled; on many occasions the pope simply ordered a new election to be held. On an election-by-election basis, it is hard to determine how the appropriate course of action (provision or new election) was chosen.

It was during the reign of Edward II that irrevocable steps towards the dominance of provision were taken. Between 1307 and 1327, fourteen of the twenty-six bishops (54 per cent) appointed owed their promotion to papal provision;[14] eleven of these were provided during the second half of the reign, following the election of John XXII to the pontificate. Equally significant was the increase in proactive provisions (that is, those in which a reservation was made, followed by a provision, with no dispute having occurred); eleven of the fourteen provisions of Edward II's reign were of this type. The papacy became increasingly willing to override the chapter's right of election. Although elections continued to take place and in a substantial minority of cases were upheld, the principle of appointment by election had been fatally undermined.

The process continued during the early years of the reign of Edward III. Twenty episcopal vacancies were filled between 1327 and 1344, twelve of them by a provision (60 per cent). As during the previous reign, a clear majority (ten) of these were proactive. Four vacancies were provoked by the translation of an

---

13 Colin Morris, *The Papal Monarchy: The Western Church from 1050 to 1250* (Oxford, 1989), p. 548.

14 Walter Reynolds is counted twice, since he was provided to both Worcester and Canterbury during this timeframe.

existing bishop to a new see,[15] and on each occasion the resultant vacancy was immediately filled by provision, without any opportunity for an election to be held. Although, even in the early 1340s, there remained several sees which had yet to acquire a bishop by provision,[16] the age of provision had begun. Whilst elections continued to be held by English cathedral chapters throughout the Middle Ages, the validity of the process was never upheld. Some of the men elected did succeed in becoming bishops, but in every such case their election was overturned by a subsequent provision. Consequently, almost every English bishop appointed between 1344 and the English Reformation was provided by the pope.[17] Therefore, it can accurately be stated that the process by which an English bishop was created was transformed during the first half of the fourteenth century.

This transformation was the product of a long-term process: papal control over the Latin Church had been increasing for well over a century. This process was somewhat haphazard, and should not be characterized as a deliberate policy of aggressive centralization;[18] nevertheless, the papacy became increasingly concerned with the control of ecclesiastical benefices. Initially the focus was on lesser benefices (especially cathedral prebends and parishes with the cure of souls), which served as an important source of patronage for the papacy. Innocent II (1130-43) was the first pope known to have directly intervened to secure the grant of a benefice for a particular clerk. Eugenius III (1146-53) ordered that benefices be conferred on named individuals on at least four occasions, and henceforth the numbers continued to grow.[19] The registers of Innocent III mention twenty-five mandates of provision issued by his predecessor Celestine III (there were probably many more),[20] whilst Innocent himself was commended for assigning canonries to many learned and worthy clerks. The first letters of provision were indications of papal wishes rather than orders; thus Innocent II's intervention in favour of Arias the clerk took the form of a request to the archbishop of Compostela. Even in the thirteenth century, it was technically possible for an instruction to collate to be ignored on legal grounds, such as the unsuitability of the candidate. In reality, however, a bishop who ignored such a request would face heavy pressure from the papacy to comply, and by the

---

15 This was itself a novelty, with translation having been extremely rare in the previous century – probably because only the pope could translate a bishop from one see to another.

16 Bath and Wells, Chichester, London, Rochester (where a provision had been made, but revoked, in 1317) and Salisbury.

17 A handful of bishops were elected during the Great Schism of the early fifteenth century. On post-1344 bishops, see Heath, *Church and Realm*, pp. 138-42, 218-20, 289-93.

18 Geoffrey Barraclough, *The Medieval Papacy* (London, 1968), p. 103.

19 Morris, *Papal Monarchy*, p. 547.

20 Ibid., p. 436.

thirteenth century popes were employing 'monitors' and 'executors' to enforce their wishes.[21]

Until the succession of Innocent IV (1243-54) direct papal provision to English prebends and parish churches was rare, but from this time onwards the system developed rapidly. Popes began to grant large numbers of expectatives,[22] and whilst relatively few foreigners seem to have been provided to English benefices, hostility against this group grew rapidly.[23] During the first half of the thirteenth century, the development of such practices had little impact on bishoprics, but, when Clement IV issued *Licet ecclesiarum* in August 1265, the move towards such provisions had begun in earnest. This constitution, by which all benefices vacated at the papal curia were reserved to the pope, also set out (for the first time in canon law) the classical theory that the pontiff has the right to full disposal (*plenaria dispositio*) by provision or reservation of all ecclesiastical benefices.[24] It was on this theory that all subsequent papal claims to provide were founded. The papacy's capacity for innovation was somewhat limited during the final decades of the thirteenth century by a succession of short-lived popes: eleven men were elected to the papacy between 1271 and 1305, and only one of them served for more than five years. Faced with strong opposition to *Licet ecclesiarum* at the Second Council of Lyon (1274), Gregory X actually made some concessions, notably by agreeing that any benefice having fallen vacant at the papal see (and thus having been reserved) could be collated by the normal patron if a provision had not been made within a month.[25] But with the election of Boniface VIII (1294-1303), the shift towards provision was back on course, and in *Praesenti declaramus* the definition of vacancies 'apud sedem apostolicam' was widened to include the benefices of papal legates and nuncios, as well of those of any cleric travelling to or from the curia who died within two legal days' journey of the court. The benefices of curial officials, wherever they died, were also reserved.[26]

---

21 Ibid., pp. 547-9.

22 An expectative gave a named individual a claim to the first suitable benefice to fall vacant; it was often ordered that he receive a pension in the interim. These writs enabled the pope (who would often not hear of a vacancy until after it had been filled by the local patron) to dispense patronage more effectively. The practice was banned at the Third Lateran Council (can. 8), due to distaste for a practice that gave one man a vested interest in another's death, but the papacy took advantage of its power to dispense from the decree, and issued expectatives in ever increasing numbers. *Ecumenical Councils*, I, p. 215; Morris, *Papal Monarchy*, p. 548.

23 Lawrence, 'Thirteenth Century', pp. 145-50.

24 *Licet ecclesiarum* (*Sext.* 3.4.2, *CIC*, II, p. 1021); John Wright, *The Church and the English Crown, 1305-1334* (Toronto, 1980), p. 6.

25 *Ecumenical Councils*, I, pp. 319-20 (c. 5), 323-4 (c. 18).

26 *Praesenti declaramus* (exact date unknown, 1294-1303, *Sext.* 3.4.34: *CIC*, II, p. 1031). Boniface VIII also issued *Piae Sollicitudinis* (5 May 1295, *Extravag. Comm.* 3.2.1: *CIC*, II, p. 1257), by which he confirmed *Licet ecclesiarum* and *Statutem*, in addition to *Si apostolica* (1298, *Sext.* 3.4.35: *CIC*, II,

Thus, at the time of Clement V's accession in July 1305, the papal right to reserve had been firmly established, yet its application to bishoprics remained limited. Within a week of his election, the new pope set about changing this, with the issue of the constitution *Etsi in temporalium*. Proclaiming that this constitution was issued for the good of the church, since 'there is nothing which hurts the church of God more than that unworthy persons should be appointed to the rule of souls', Clement confirmed his predecessors' rulings and made the first specific mention of archbishoprics and bishoprics as forms of benefice that would be reserved if they fell vacant at the curia.[27] It was during the pontificate of the lawyer-pope John XXII (1316-34), however, that the system of papal provision was finalized. His bull *Ex debito* (1316?) expanded the number of situations in which the pope had the right to provide still further. The benefices of lesser clerks were now included, and the phrase *vacante in curia* was expanded to include benefices void at the curia, whether by death, deprivation, resignation, the annulment of an election, the rejection of a postulation, translation, consecration, benediction or the provision by the pope of another benefice.[28] The contents of *Ex debito* were reiterated in *Ad regimen*, a codification of the whole system of reservations issued by Benedict XII in 1335; this constitution placed particular emphasis on the papal right to dispose of all the benefices vacated by anyone provided to a higher benefice.[29] The culmination of the legislation on this issue came in 1344, when Clement VI proclaimed that 'plenary powers of disposal of all churches, dignities, offices and ecclesiastical benefices are vested in the Roman pontiff'.[30]

The fourteenth-century transition from episcopal election to the provision of bishops was thus the culmination of a process that had begun nearly two hundred years earlier and encompassed the ecclesiastical hierarchy as a whole. The process had, ironically, been helped on its way by the growth of free election during the thirteenth century: electoral freedom led to disputes (within chapters or between king and chapter), which had to be resolved by the papacy. In the words of Jean Gaudemet: 'Electoral bodies condemned themselves.'[31] Electoral

p. 1031), which allowed the ordinary patron to appoint to parish churches with the cure of souls which had fallen vacant at the curia, if the pope died and during papal vacancies.

27 *Etsi in temporalium* (31 July 1305, *Extravag. Comm.* 3.2.3, *CIC*, II, pp. 1258-9); Menache, *Clement*, p. 37; Wright, *Church*, p. 8.

28 *Ex debito* (date unknown, *Extravag. Comm.* 1.3.4, *CIC*, II, pp. 1240-41); Wright, *Church*, pp. 9-11; Deeley, 'Provision', pp. 499-500.

29 *Ad regimen* (11 January 1335, *Extravag. Comm.*, 3.2.13, *CIC*, II, pp. 1266-7); Barraclough, *Provisions*, p. 9.

30 Guillaume Mollat, *The Popes at Avignon, 1305-1378* (London, 1963), p. 26. The last major pronouncement on this matter was made by Urban V in 1362/3, when he reserved all patriarchal, archiepiscopal and episcopal churches. Lunt, *Papal Revenues*, II, p. 231.

31 Jean Gaudemet, 'De l'Élection à la Nomination des Évêques' in J. Gaudemet, Église *et Société en Occident au Moyen Age* (Aldershot, 1984), XVII, pp. 26-9; Robert Helmholz, *The Oxford History of the*

disputes were a frequent occurrence in the thirteenth century and were typically resolved by appeal to Rome; particularly complex disputes (such as the one that took place at Winchester between 1238 and 1244) might even involve multiple appeals. The disputed Ely election of 1256 was to prove particularly significant in this respect, for it was as a result of Archbishop Boniface's attempts to overrule the monastic election and provide his own candidate (the Franciscan friar Adam Marsh) to the see that Alexander IV declared all electoral disputes to be *causae majores* and therefore subject to papal jurisdiction.[32] With the benefit of hindsight it is possible to see that such legislation was detrimental to the independence of national churches and would inevitably lead to greater papal interference in the election process. At the time, however, this ruling was extremely popular – so popular that, at the Second Council of Lyons (1274), Gregory X found it necessary to modify the ruling; henceforth, only a reasoned, written appeal against the decision of a metropolitan created a *causa major*.[33] In this manner papal involvement in episcopal appointments became normalized; from here it was a relatively short step to provision.

The transition to provision had been a long time in the making but the conclusion, when it came, was relatively swift, being completed within three decades; by the early 1340s the age of election was over in England. This was the inevitable result of the changes made to the appointment system over the last century or so, and events in England were echoed across Europe. Nevertheless, it is likely that the crystallization of the process in early fourteenth-century England was encouraged by the combination of a powerful and long-lived pope, John XXII (1315-34), and a relatively weak period of English kingship. Pope John was an extremely efficient organizer and a natural ruler; he was often inflexible and always convinced of his own rightness. He was also set on increasing papal power and independence;[34] it was therefore inevitable that he would do his utmost to develop papal control over appointments. England, on the other hand, was weakened by the difficult reign of Edward II and by the minority of Edward III, and thus unusually vulnerable to papal incursions.[35]

The rise of provision should not, however, be understood simply as a response to the problem of disputed elections, for it also had roots in the centralizing tendencies of the late medieval papacy. It was inevitable that as the power of

Laws of England: The Canon Law and Ecclesiastical Jurisdiction from 597 to the 1640s (Oxford, 2004), p. 93; Barraclough, 'Making of a Bishop', pp. 275-319; Menache, *Clement*, p. 38.

32 *Reg. Alex. IV*, no. 2230; Ullmann, 'Balsham', pp. 259-68.

33 *Ecumenical Councils*, I, pp. 320-21 (cc. 9-10).

34 Barraclough, *Papacy*, pp. 144-5.

35 Two recent biographies of Edward II provide nuanced depictions of the difficulties of that king's reign: Roy Haines, *Edward II* (Montreal, 2003), and Seymour Phillips, *Edward II* (London, 2010). Mark Ormrod, *The Reign of Edward III* (London, 1990), pp. 3-15, provides the best account of the regency of Isabella and Mortimer, and the establishment of majority rule.

the popes increased, they would seek to exercise more direct control over the appointments of their subordinates. This shift was partly justified by ideological factors, which explained why Clement IV was able to revive the ancient custom of *plenaria disposition*;[36] this classical theory was examined and developed by many early fourteenth-century canonists, who argued that the pope had direct jurisdiction over every diocese because bishops derived their own jurisdiction from him.[37] Wider ideas about the power of the papacy were also significant.[38] The pope derived both his power and his pontifical authority directly from God; indeed, God was Himself present on earth in the person of the pope, the vicar of Christ. Consequently, it was not necessary to hold an election in order to discover the will of God, for the pope could communicate divine will on appointments directly. Therefore, it was perfectly acceptable for the pope to select a man for office, delegating some of his powers to the appointee (to be exercised in accordance with papal wishes), for in doing so he was simply acting as the divine agent in the election.[39]

The papacy also attempted to justify the centralization of episcopal appointments in spiritual terms; papal provision was the best way to ensure that suitable candidates were promoted to the episcopate. Clement V explained that the constitution *Etsi in temporalium* was the product of such concern for the church:

> Though the caution of discretion should be had in the disposition of temporal goods, especially that they be disposed of worthily and in praiseworthy manner, nevertheless, in ecclesiastical matters it ought to be our intention to watch much more closely, so that for their utility and the praise of the divine name, according to the conditions and states of persons, there should be provided ecclesiastical persons of merit, since, according to canonical sanctions, there is nothing which hurts the Church of God more than that unworthy persons should be appointed to the rule of souls.[40]

John XXII expressed similar sentiments, declaring that the system of general reservations was designed to combat simony.[41]

---

36 In *Licet ecclesiarum* (*Sext.* 3.4.2, *CIC*, II, p. 1021).

37 Wright, *Church*, p. 11; Michael Wilks, *The Problem of Sovereignty in the Later Middle Ages* (Cambridge, 1963), pp. 331-411.

38 For the development of ideas about papal power in the thirteenth century, see John Watt, *The Theory of Papal Monarchy in the Thirteenth Century* (New York, 1965); Pennington, *Pope and Bishops.*

39 Diana Wood, *Clement VI: The Pontificate and Ideas of an Avignon Pope* (Cambridge, 1989), pp. 101-2.

40 *De praebendis et dignitatibus* (*Extravag. Comm.* 3.4.2, *CIC*, II, p. 102).

41 May McKisack, *The Fourteenth Century, 1307-1399* (Oxford, 1959), p. 274.

The introduction of papal provision also brought practical benefits to the papacy – benefits that were of particular value as its financial problems grew.[42] Patronage was an important source of power for all medieval rulers (whether secular or ecclesiastical), and the provisions system placed the pope at the heart of a Europe-wide network of patronage. Men seeking promotion went to the curia, and encouraged their friends to join them, in order that they too might enjoy the fruits of papal munificence.[43] Powerful individuals and institutions petitioned the pope to provide their favourites to appropriate benefices.[44] Those seeking preferment at the papal curia were obliged to spend a good deal of money in order to achieve their goal, and the income received by the papacy as a result of episcopal appointments made at the curia was a substantial boon.[45]

Rights and Responsibilities in the Age of Provision

In the mid-thirteenth century, following the issue of the Freedom of Election charter and the pronouncements of the Fourth Lateran Council, the identities of the core participants in the electoral process, as well as the rights and responsibilities of each of these participants, had been relatively well defined. However, the emergence of provision muddied the waters and in the decades leading up to 1344, when election and provision coexisted, there was a certain ambiguity over the rights and responsibilities of the core quintet. Many elections were held in conformity with the thirteenth-century model; these were conducted in the manner outlined in Chapter 1. If, however, a provision was made, then the roles of the key players were substantially altered.

Whilst the electoral system was dominant, the pope was a relatively minor player, an active participant in only a handful of anomalous elections. With the rise of provision, the pope became the most important figure in the appointment process, with ultimate responsibility for the creation of every English bishop. Despite (or perhaps because of) this papal supremacy, reconstructing the pope's rights and responsibilities is a difficult task, and one that must be based on an assemblage of fragments of information, rather than the more plentiful sources for the roles of the various participants in the age of election.

---

42 Barraclough, *Papacy*, p. 123.

43 See, for example, the letter of M. Stephen de Kettelburgh to M. John Lutterel, Chancellor of Oxford University, in which he urged him to come to the curia, because the pope 'freely provides them [suitable men at the curia] with great dignities and prebends'. *Snappe's Formulary*, ed. H. E. Salter (Oxford, 1923), p. 304. The letter is translated in Pantin, *English Church*, pp. 16-17.

44 Ernest Jacob, 'Petitions for Benefices from English Universities during the Great Schism', *TRHS*, 4th series, 27 (1945), pp. 41-59.

45 See below, pp. 145-6.

The first step on the road to the making of a provision was the reservation of the see, that is, the issue of a statement informing those concerned that the pope had reserved the right of appointment to himself. Initially, this was done on a case by case basis, with a new reservation issued shortly before, or immediately after, a see became vacant. Such a reservation applied only to a single vacancy in a single see.[46] This system of reservation was used throughout the period in question; from 1362 all English bishoprics were automatically reserved to the papacy, thanks to the general reservation made by Urban V.[47]

Once a reservation had been made, the new bishop had to be chosen; exactly how this was done is somewhat unclear. There might well be a papal candidate, chosen from the upper ranks of the ecclesiastical hierarchy or known to the pope by some other means, such as presence at the curia on diplomatic business. Even when a reservation had been made, the wishes of others might also be considered. If an election had been held, the bishop-elect might be presented to the curia (either in person or, more rarely, in writing). In the early years of the fourteenth century, elections were occasionally upheld by the pope even when a reservation had been made. More typically, if a provision had yet to be made, the election could be quashed, only for the bishop-elect to be provided to the see. The papacy might also consider petitions made by the king or by other powerful secular figures, such as the queen and members of the nobility.

Whilst the final choice rested with the pope, it is likely that the cardinals were deeply involved in the appointment process. The exact nature of the relationship between the pope and the cardinals was the subject of much discussion at this time,[48] but their place at the heart of papal administration and decision-making was unquestioned.[49] Amongst their customary duties was the examination of episcopal elections and postulations; the examination of the process of the election and the person of the elect was typically delegated to a small number of cardinals (usually three, but occasionally one or two) who would report their findings to the pope.[50]

Once all appropriate examinations had been carried out, the new appointment could be announced in a public consistory.[51] It was also necessary

---

46 See, for example, the reservation of Lincoln in April 1319, nine months before the death of John Dalderby: *CPL*, II, p. 424.

47 Lunt, *Papal Revenues*, II, p. 230.

48 On which see Zacour, 'Cardinals' View', pp. 413-38; Wood, *Clement VI*, pp. 96-121.

49 Guillaume Mollat, 'Contribution à l'Histoire du Sacré Collège de Clément V à Eugène IV', *Revue d'Histoire Ecclésiastique*, 46 (1951), pp. 22-112.

50 Ibid., pp. 91, 94.

51 The election of Simon Meopham as archbishop of Canterbury was confirmed in a public consistory in 1328; presumably provisions were published in the same manner. Roy Haines, 'An Innocent Abroad: The Career of Simon Mepham, Archbishop of Canterbury, 1328-33', *EHR*, 112 (1997), pp. 555-96, at p. 559.

for the provision to be announced in writing, in the form of bulls of provision. Such a bull announced the elevation of the new bishop, typically giving some details of the appointment process. Thus the bull by which William Bateman was provided to Norwich in 1344 stated that the see had been reserved, but the cathedral convent, ignorant of this reservation, had elected Bateman. The pope set his election aside but, having consulted the cardinals and considered the merits of the elect and the electoral process, provided Bateman to the see. He therefore committed to him 'the pastoral care and administration of the see, both in spiritualities and in temporalities'.[52] The bishop received a copy for himself; further copies were addressed to the cathedral prior and convent, the clergy and vassals of the see, the archbishop of the province and the king.[53]

The pope's final act in the appointment process was the consecration of the new bishop, a task he sometimes undertook himself (for example, Anthony Bek of Norwich was consecrated by Benedict XII in 1337[54]) but which was more frequently delegated.[55] Sometimes the task was delegated to one of the cardinals;[56] alternatively, the provisee might be issued with a mandate to be consecrated by 'any catholic bishop'.[57]

This expansion of papal powers over episcopal appointments inevitably altered the role played by the cathedral chapter in the bishop-making process. Throughout the thirteenth century, the chapter's role had been pivotal; except in exceptional circumstances, a bishop could only be appointed by means of canonical election. With the rise of provision, however, the chapter was marginalized and, technically, the monks or canons might have no say in the appointment of their bishop. Only in the final stage of the process, the enthronement, did they retain a formal role.

Yet, despite the dominance of provision, capitular election was not outlawed; chapters could still hold elections, and continued to do so throughout the fourteenth and fifteenth centuries.[58] If an election was held, the chapter was required to observe all of the customary formalities, such as seeking licence

---

52 *The Register of William Bateman, Bishop of Norwich, 1344-1355*, ed. P. E. Pobst (2 vols, Woodbridge, 1996-2000), I, p. 31; *Richard d'Aungerville, of Bury: Fragments of His Register and Other Documents* (Durham, 1910), pp. 3-4, has a transcription of Bury's bull of provision.

53 See, for example, the lists of bulls issued for the provision of John Stratford to Winchester in 1323. *CPL*, II, p. 230; Haines, *Stratford*, p. 22.

54 *CPL*, II, p. 541.

55 For a list of consecrations during the early fourteenth century, included the name(s) of the officiating cleric(s), see *Registrum Sacrum Anglicanum*, pp. 69-75.

56 See for the mandate ordering Ralph Baldock, bishop of London, to be consecrated by the cardinal-bishop of Sabina, *CPL*, II, p. 8.

57 For an example of such a mandate, see *CPL*, II, p. 198.

58 For a mid-fifteenth-century example of election in the age of provision, see Virginia Davis, *William Waynflete: Bishop and Educationalist* (Woodbridge, 1993), pp. 14-22.

to elect and following the correct electoral procedure as outlined in electoral tracts.[59] There was, however, no guarantee that an election would be upheld, even if it was canonically sound and the candidate was suitable; it was rapidly established that if a papal provision had been made before the election was held, then the provision automatically took precedence. This did not mean that elections had no value, for the chapter's candidate could be provided by the pope if he saw fit to do so. Nevertheless, where the thirteenth-century electoral body had firm rights and responsibilities, the position of the late medieval cathedral chapter was rather more uncertain.

The cathedral chapter was not the only victim of the rise of provision; the English king also found his rights over the election process, as enshrined in the Freedom of Election charter, were eroded. Whereas cathedral chapters were obliged to seek the *congé d'élire* before proceeding to election, the pope could make a provision without consulting the king. Furthermore, royal assent was not required in the case of appointments made at the papal curia, as Innocent III had made clear at the time of Stephen Langton's election. In that case, the pope had, initially at least, been willing to wait for John to give his assent, as a mark of respect, but he made it clear that this was not necessary:

> It has not been usual to wait for the prince's assent in elections celebrated at the Apostolic see, since it should be presumed that the Apostolic see, in matters to which it gives thorough consideration, would not act in prejudice of anyone, accustomed as it is to preserve justice for all.[60]

This may, as Cheney suggested, have been a custom of Innocent's own making, since very few elections had been held at the curia prior to his own pontificate,[61] but it set a firm precedent, the implications of which only became clearer as provision became commonplace. The king did, however, retain the right to give his assent to elections made by English cathedral chapters. He also continued to exercise control over the temporalities during a vacancy, and to restore them to the new bishop once an appointment had been made.

On the other hand, the prominence of the metropolitan in the electoral process declined substantially with the rise of provision. During the early years of the fourteenth century, before provision became the sole means of appointment, archbishops continued to examine and confirm elections, but their judgement was no longer final. If a provision was made, the archbishop's assent, and even

---

59 The continuing concern with correct electoral procedure is reflected in the fact that Lawrence of Somercote's tract, and other examples of this genre, continued to be copied during the later Middle Ages.

60 *CLI*, no. 725.

61 Cheney, *Innocent III and England*, p. 153.

consecration, counted for nothing; the papal appointment would be upheld. As the number of appointments made without papal involvement fell, so too did the level of archiepiscopal involvement in elections; whereas the suitability of capitular choices needed to be confirmed, a papal provision could be made without any input from the archbishop. Inevitably, the archiepiscopal right of consecration was also eroded, for the majority of papal provisees were consecrated at Avignon. Furthermore, bishops who were not consecrated at the papal curia often received papal permission to be consecrated 'by any catholic bishop'.[62] As a result of the rise of provision, English archbishops lost their place at the heart of the electoral process; by the later Middle Ages, a bishop could theoretically be appointed without any reference to the archbishop of the province, and this was increasingly the case in practice.

Legally, at least, the role of the candidate was largely unaltered, since his part in the process was supposed to be a passive one. There was one major change: under the system of election, only archbishops-elect and bishops-elect whose position was the subject of an appeal were obliged to go to Rome, but all papal provisees were required to make the journey to the papal curia. Only the pope could grant exemption from this duty.[63]

Custom in the Age of Provision: Ritual Changes

Just as the rise of papal provision affected the roles played by the core quintet of participants, so too were the customs surrounding the appointment process altered. The rituals surrounding episcopal appointments were less changed by the rise of provision than might be expected, for the simple reason that elections continued to be held. Consequently, the customary preparatory acts, as well as the rites of the election itself, were still performed on numerous occasions; indeed, some of the most detailed accounts of these rituals date from the early fourteenth century. These accounts suggest that the rites surrounding elections were unaltered by the growth of papal involvement, and indeed had changed very little over the last century. The postulation of John Stratford as archbishop of Canterbury, made in 1333, was the result of a process almost identical to that which had resulted in the election of Walter de Eynsham in 1228: licence to elect was sought from the king, the election itself involved devotional observances

---

[62] See for example, the mandate granted to Henry Burghersh, bishop of Lincoln, in 1329. *CPL*, II, p. 198.

[63] For example, Adam Orleton received a papal indult that he should not travel to the curia following his translation from Winchester to Worcester in 1333. *CPL*, II, p. 409.

(including a sermon and much chanting) and the identity of the new archbishop was immediately announced to the clergy and people.[64]

Expectations regarding the response of the bishop-elect to his promotion were slightly altered by the rise of provision. A show of reluctance was still commonplace; John of Stratford greeted the news of his promotion to Canterbury with a quote from Jeremiah (1: 6), 'I cannot speak for I am a child', and deliberated for six days. At this point he did not, as might have been expected in previous decades, accept his new role, but instead declared that he would neither consent nor dissent, instead submitting entirely to the pope's will.[65] A quarter of a century earlier, Walter Reynolds had greeted his election as bishop of Worcester in a similar fashion. Initially he played for time, responding to the chapter's request that he accept his election by claiming that 'he dare not answer so arduous a matter over hastily, but would do so as soon as he was able'. Then, after over a fortnight of deliberation, he offered a carefully worded acceptance of his election. Since neither he nor the prior and convent of Worcester had received confirmation of the rumoured papal reservation from any trustworthy source, Reynolds was disinclined to believe in its existence and therefore accepted the election. However, he added that he would 'obey and observe the apostolic commands, and if he should do or consent to anything to the contrary, he wills that the deed and the consent may be had for no deed and no consent'.[66] During the period when election and provision coexisted candidates were obliged to perform a careful balancing act, ensuring that they neither rejected election by the chapter nor did anything that might prejudice the pope against them.

The customs surrounding the consecration of a bishop were also somewhat altered, not least because it was no longer guaranteed to take place in England, but might instead be performed at the papal curia or (very rarely) elsewhere in Europe.[67] Between 1307 and 1344, only 62 per cent of new bishops (twenty-seven out of forty-four) were consecrated in England by the relevant archbishop or by another member of the bishop's bench;[68] 34 per cent (fifteen) were consecrated at the papal curia, either by the pope or by one of the cardinals; 4 per cent (two) were consecrated elsewhere in France.[69] Consequently, the English elites, who

---

64 Haines, *Ecclesia*, p. 32.

65 Ibid.

66 *Reg. Sede Vacante*, pp. 108-10. Reynolds' claims to ignorance of a valid reservation must, however, be questioned, since the *sede vacante* register records that it received a letter of reservation from Pope Clement himself on 5 October (ibid., p. 104).

67 Henry Burghersh (Lincoln, 1320) was consecrated at Boulogne by the bishops of Norwich, Exeter, Hereford and Terouanne; William Ayermin (Norwich, 1325) was consecrated at St Germain des Prés, Paris, by William, archbishop of Vienne, and several continental bishops.

68 Bishops who were translated from one see to another (a growing group) were not re-consecrated.

69 My calculations are based on the details given in *Registrum Sacrum Anglicanum*, pp. 70-75.

had traditionally been present at episcopal consecrations, were now excluded from a significant minority of such ceremonies.

The consecration ceremony was, however, still guaranteed to take place, whereas the rest of the electoral rituals could be completely sidelined. This was most likely to happen when a vacancy was created by a translation and immediately filled by a papal provision. Indeed, the sole portion of the bishop-making process still routinely carried out in England was the *adventus* and enthronement of the new bishop, which had to take place in his cathedral city. This ensured that, even though the emphasis on popular participation was somewhat reduced, all episcopal appointments were acclaimed by the clergy and people of the diocese. It seems plausible that the transition to provision gave the ritual of enthronement an extra degree of significance, for this was often the first chance the diocese (and indeed the chapter) had to see their new bishop, and to demonstrate their acceptance of him.

Custom in the Age of Provision: Financial Changes

Many of the rituals of election survived the rise of papal provision wholly unaltered or only slightly modified. Similarly, chapters continued to be faced by many of the traditional costs associated with episcopal appointments, including travel expenses and customary dues. Royal officials would still have expected to receive the traditional gifts and payments, and the king continued to insist that one of his clerks be provided to a prebend in the new bishop's cathedral chapter.[70] If such a provision could not be made immediately, then a pension would be paid to the clerk in question. Following his election as bishop of Worcester (1338), Wolstan de Bransford was obliged to pay 100 shillings a year (in two equal instalments, at Michaelmas and Easter) to Robert de Kyngestone.[71] John Kirkby, provided to Carlisle by John XXII, was similarly required to pay an annual pension to a royal clerk until he could give him a benefice.[72] If the new bishop was consecrated in England, the archbishop might also claim a benefice (and a pension in lieu until one could be found) for one of his *familia*; in 1339 Bishop Wolstan was paying a 100 shilling pension to Richard de Twyverton, Archbishop Stratford's crucifer, for this purpose.[73] Even if a provision was made,

---

70 This tradition was first recorded in 1280, in the memorandum of costs relating to the election of Oliver Sutton. *Reg. Ant. Linc.*, III, p. 305.

71 *A Calendar of the Register of Wolstan de Bransford, Bishop of Worcester, 1339-1349*, ed. R. M. Haines (London, 1966), pp. 11, 34, 283. For the king's nomination of Kyngestone, see *CCR 1339-1341*, p. 105.

72 *The Register of John Kirkby, Bishop of Carlisle 1332-52 and the Register of John Ross, Bishop of Carlisle 1325-32*, ed. R. L. Storey (2 vols, Woodbridge, 1993-95), I, p. 22.

73 *Reg. Bransford*, p. 24.

the archdeacon who officiated at the enthronement would still expect to receive the customary gifts. William de Gainsborough, provided to Worcester in 1302, handed over his palfrey and its saddle, various vestments, a gold cup and ten marks, only to find that the archdeacon's official was still unsatisfied.[74]

However, the rise of papal provision made commonplace a range of costs, previously owed by only a handful of new bishops, but now payable by an increasing number, and eventually by all. Every bishop who owed (or hoped to owe) his see to provision was expected to make the costly and arduous journey to the papal curia.[75] Once there, he was required to pay a range of dues, in order to secure his position.[76] By far the largest expense was the *servitia*, the fees owed by any bishop whose election (or postulation) was confirmed by the pope in consistory or who owed his position to translation or provision. A handful of thirteenth-century bishops had been obliged to make this payment (which was shared between the pope and the cardinals), but it became routine only in the early fourteenth century; from 1342 virtually every English bishop and archbishop paid *servitia*. Exemptions were granted only to certain papal officials or if a see fell vacant twice in the same year.[77] The amount of *servitia* paid by a bishop was determined by the value of his see and was roughly equivalent to one-third of the gross annual income of the bishopric.[78] Although this sum was nominally a gift, in practice it was rigorously enforced by the papacy; the appointee was bound in writing to pay, and by the time of John XXII there existed an *obligationes et solutiones* register in which was recorded the value of each see and the amount of *servitia* due. Furthermore, there were penalties for non-payment, including the obligation to reside at the papal curia, suspension and excommunication.[79]

---

74 *Reg. Sede Vacante*, p. 53.

75 The journey to Avignon was, however, considerably less difficult than the journey to Rome; in this respect, fourteenth-century bishops had an easier experience than their thirteenth-century predecessors. On the journey to Avignon, as experienced by mid-fourteenth-century diplomats, see Plöger, *Avignon Popes*, pp. 144-60.

76 For what follows, see William Lunt, *Financial Relations of the Papacy with England, 1327-1534* (Cambridge, Mass., 1962), pp. 169-306, in which pages he discusses the service taxes at much greater length than is possible here.

77 John Kirkby, bishop of Carlisle, may be the exception that proves the rule; Lunt found no evidence that he paid common services for the pope's confirmation of his election, and his register includes a letter to John XXII, thanking him for his benevolence and stating that he can pay only by his thanks. Lunt, *Financial Relations*, pp. 758-9; *Reg. Kirkby*, I, p. 32.

78 The payment of these common services was often recorded on episcopal registers; see, for examples, *Registrum Hamonis Hethe: Diocesis Roffensis, A. D. 1319-1352*, ed. C. Johnson (2 vols, Oxford, 1948), I, pp. 58-9, 80-81, and *The Register of Walter Langton, Bishop of Coventry and Lichfield, 1296-1321*, ed. J. B. Hughes (2 vols, Woodbridge, 2001-7), I, p. 44.

79 The Apostolic *Camera* might refuse to hand over the bulls of provision until the service taxes were paid, as John Foxhales, archbishop-elect of Armagh, discovered in the late fifteenth century. See

Several smaller payments were also demanded. Just as royal and archiepiscopal officials demanded payments for their services from thirteenth-century bishops, so fourteenth-century provisees had to pay for their bulls of provision or translation, for letters of permission for consecration elsewhere and for the archiepiscopal *pallium*. Two further payments were due from those bishops who were consecrated at Avignon: *sacra* (one-twentieth of the *servitia* payment) and *subdeacon* (one-third of the *sacra*).[80]

Throughout the thirteenth century the cost of obtaining a bishopric had been increased by the necessity of gift-giving, and this remained true throughout the later Middle Ages. Higher-ranking figures at the papal curia – the pope and cardinals, but also members of the papal administration and household, and certain papal relatives – expected to receive gifts from those seeking their favour. The surviving records of English royal diplomats indicate that the crown was willing to spend large sums on persuading the curia to judge in its favour.[81] Whilst it is impossible to find any direct evidence of gift-giving relating to episcopal appointments during this period, it seems inconceivable that such transactions were not of vital importance in such circumstances. Certainly rumours that some bishops had effectively purchased their sees continued to circulate; for example, Ralph of Shrewsbury, bishop of Bath and Wells (1329-63), was forced to deny rumours that he had offered bribes to the extent of 10,000 florins and that he had corrupted the papal curia with money.[82] To modern ears, however, his protestations sound a little hollow, given that his register also records that, before his election was confirmed, he offered the pope 2,000 florins and claimed that he would have offered more had the finances of the see permitted.[83]

If gift-giving at the curia is hard to trace, it is somewhat easier to find examples of new bishops demonstrating their gratitude to the cardinals who eased their promotion. Shortly after his appointment was confirmed by the pope, Hamo of Hythe, bishop of Rochester, established a pension of twenty silver marks for William, cardinal of S. Ciriaco, who had examined his election.[84]

Benignus Millett, 'John Foxholes, Franciscan, Archbishop of Armagh 1471-74', *Seanchas Ardmhacha: Journal of the Armagh Diocesan Historical Society*, 18 (1999/2000), pp. 22-9, at p. 25.

80 Lunt, *Papal Revenues*, I, p. 90. The *sacra* was divided amongst the officials of the papal curia, whilst the *subdeacon* (as its name suggests) went to the papal sub-deacons.

81 Plöger, *Avignon Popes*, pp. 209-18.

82 *The Register of Ralph of Shrewsbury, Bishop of Bath and Wells, 1329-1363: From the Original in the Registry at Wells*, ed. T. S. Holmes (2 vols, London, 1896), I, p. 52.

83 Ibid., I, p. 29. Exactly what this payment was for is unclear.

84 *Reg. Hethe*, I, pp. 59, 102. The circumstances of Bishop Hamo's appointment were somewhat unusual; his election received papal confirmation, even though a provision had been made on the following day. See *CPL*, II, pp. 188-9; Roy Haines, 'The Episcopate of a Benedictine Monk: Hamo de Hethe, Bishop of Rochester (1317-1352)', *Revue Bénédictine*, 102 (1992), pp. 192-207.

Throughout the thirteenth century, becoming a bishop had been an expensive business; as papal involvement became more common, it became a very expensive business. Furthermore, such costs could no longer be avoided, for whilst chapters had previously been able to avoid the necessity for a visit to Rome by electing an uncontroversial candidate, the journey to Avignon was now all but compulsory. These substantial costs must have hampered the ability of cathedral chapters to fight for internal candidates and ensured that wealthy candidates (or those with wealthy backers, able to pay for accommodation in Avignon and expensive gifts for *curiales*) were most likely to secure appointment to a bishopric. Very few bishops, however, were able to pay the common services from their own resources, and consequently several early fourteenth-century prelates received papal licences to contract loans (secured by the goods of the relevant church) to cover their expenses at the curia.[85] For example, Robert Orford of Ely (1302-10) was given permission to contract a loan of 13,000 florins to meet his expenses at Rome,[86] and Simon Meopham received a similar licence for a loan of £2,000.[87]

A consideration of the costs of election also underlines the fact that, whilst the pope himself undoubtedly came to exercise ultimate control over episcopal appointments, the rise of provision also gave those surrounding the pope a much greater degree of influence over the appointment process. Informal payments to the cardinals, in the form of pensions and other gifts, reflect the influence they were perceived to have over the appointment process. That they also received formal payments, sharing the common services with the pope,[88] indicates their formal role; in practice, many bishops may have owed their appointment more to the cardinals than to the pope himself. Papal officials, such as the papal chamberlain (who controlled access to the papal presence) and the bureaucrats who provided the documents of provision, probably received smaller, but still substantial, financial rewards; they came to play a role in the appointment process comparable to that of royal and archiepiscopal officials during the previous century.

***

The transition from episcopal election to papal provision was a substantial one, which altered the bishop-making process in substantial ways. The (hitherto relatively rare) participation of the papacy became a crucial part of the

85 Lunt, *Financial Relations*, p. 214.

86 *CPL*, I, p. 603.

87 *CPL*, II, p. 272.

88 Those cardinals who were present at the curia at the time of the appointment also received a share of the petty services, which were divided between the pope and cardinals in a ratio of 4:1. See Lunt, *Financial Relations*, p. 169.

appointment process, undermining the roles of the other core participants and ensuring that the appointment of English bishops was never an entirely English affair. Indeed, it was now possible for a bishop to be created with very little consideration for the traditional rights and responsibilities of the chapter, king or archbishop. This transition had much to do with the changing nature (specifically the increasing power) of the late medieval papacy. Ironically, however, it also had roots in the age of election, and not simply because the first steps towards the dominance of provision were taken during the thirteenth century. The rise of electoral freedom led to an increased number of electoral disputes, in which the protagonists demanded papal intervention – thus normalizing it and inadvertently aiding the development of the provision system.

The rituals of appointment were less substantially altered; indeed, many continued largely unaltered. Crucially, however, the traditional processes of election were no longer essential. These rituals had previously been used to demonstrate that an election was canonically sound and had received the assent of the people. Whilst the system of free election was upheld by the ecclesiastical authorities, especially the papacy, such proof was of great importance, and consequently great emphasis was placed on ritual elements. However, by the mid-fourteenth century, new papal ideologies and approaches to election meant that although the traditional rites were still frequently performed, they had become an option, rather than a necessity.

Filling an episcopal vacancy had always been an expensive task, but the rise of provision made the creation of a bishop an even greater financial burden for cathedral chapters and new bishops than had been the case in the thirteenth century. The obligation to pay customary dues to the crown remained, but to these was added a raft of new expenses: the cost of a journey to, and a potentially lengthy stay at, Avignon, along with a new set of customary dues and gifts owed to the pope and his officials. This extra burden had been faced by thirteenth-century chapters only in exceptional circumstances (that is, archiepiscopal elections and electoral disputes), but by the 1340s it was the avoidance of such costs that had become unusual.

Given the scale of the changes to the theory and custom of episcopal appointments, and the importance attached to traditional rights in medieval culture, it would be surprising if they had not provoked a considerable response in England. Forceful reactions were not limited to those whose right to participate in the electoral process was enshrined in law, but who now found themselves in danger of being marginalized, or even completely excluded, for bishop-making also concerned the wider population. It is to the scale and nature of the English response to the rise of papal provision that we must now turn our attention.

Chapter 5
The Age of Provision: Responses and Consequences

Throughout the thirteenth century, episcopal elections had been one of the primary causes of dissent between the English king and the church, as well as an important source of discord within the church. The ferocity of the electoral disputes of this period demonstrates the importance of episcopal appointments in medieval society, and the jealousy with which the participants in the electoral process guarded their rights. Against this background, it might be expected that the four key English participants in the electoral process would have reacted strongly to the manner in which the fifth party (the papacy) altered this process during the early decades of the fourteenth century. This chapter considers each of the members of this core quartet (king, chapter, archbishop and candidate) in turn, examining their responses to the rise of provision, along with the strategies they adopted in order to adapt to the new system. It then considers the changing position of subsidiary participants, such as the queen and aristocracy, asking how far their ability to influence appointments was affected. Wider responses to the rise of provision, both clerical and lay, are also discussed. The final section of this chapter analyses the consequences of the transition to provision, asking whether procedural changes and new ideologies had any substantial impact on the composition of the English episcopate.

Changing Roles: the Crown and the Rise of Provision

The earliest papal provisions, made during the first half of the reign of Henry III, do not seem to have been seen as a cause for concern by the king. In some respects this is surprising, but the circumstances surrounding the appointments of Alexander Stavensby, Richard Grant and Roger Weseham were conducive to royal acceptance. All three were appointed following appeals to Rome: at Canterbury because royal assent had been withheld, and at Coventry and Lichfield because of dissent between the two chapters. The pope was therefore simply fulfilling his responsibilities by settling electoral disputes over which his judgement had been sought.

Clement IV's decision to appoint Nicholas of Ely as bishop of Winchester in 1268 seems to have marked something of a watershed in royal attitudes to papal

provision; this is certainly the first occasion on which royal objections against such an appointment are known to have been made. The details of this protest are sketchy; indeed, our only indication that it was made is a passing reference in the next such royal protest.[1] The reasons for Henry III's unease are, however, easy to surmise, for this was the first instance in which a pope had taken the initiative and made a formal provision that overrode the traditional processes. No election had been held and consequently no royal assent had been given (or withheld); the pope had simply used his powers of provision to translate Nicholas from Worcester.[2]

The royal protest had little impact on the papacy, and in 1272 (at the very beginning of Edward I's reign) the problem arose again, following the death of Boniface of Savoy. On this occasion an election had been held, and the prior of Christ Church Canterbury, Adam Chillendene, was elected by the monks. Henry III had objected to the election, and Chillendene had resigned his claim to the archbishopric at Rome. Robert Kilwardby, a Domincan friar, was provided in his stead.[3] No practical obstacles were placed in the new archbishop's way by the crown; the temporalities of the archdiocese were restored to him on 12 December 1272, within days of his return to England.[4] Nevertheless, on the following day a large assembly was held in the chapel of St Stephen at Westminster, and in the presence of numerous dignitaries (including the archbishop-elect, Walter Merton, Robert Burnell and Bishop Walter of Exeter) a formal protest was made and read on behalf of the absent king:

> Whereas the cathedral churches in England that are vacant ought to be provided for of right and are wont of custom to be provided for by canonical election to be made principally by the colleges, chapters, and persons to whom the right of election pertains, after they have sought and obtained the king's licence therefore, and after the election has been celebrated, the person elected has to be presented to the king, so that the king may propound against him anything reasonable that he may have to propound; it seems to the king and his council that prejudice would be done to him and to the church of Canterbury, whereof he is patron and defender, in this behalf, especially if the matter were drawn into an example in other churches of England, if the pope should assume to himself the power of providing for that church, these things being omitted in this case, when no wrong [peccatum] has been found either in the matter or form of the election, and none is expressed in his letters; wherefore in order that the Roman church shall not proceed to such provisions henceforth, and so that if it do proceed to them, no

1 *CCR 1272-1279*, p. 39.

2 *Reg. Clem. IV*, nos. 1327-8.

3 *CPL*, I, p. 442.

4 *CPR 1272-1281*, p. 2; *AM*, II, pp. 112-13.

> prejudice shall arise to the king thereby, so that he shall be bound to render the temporalities of any cathedral church thus provided, the king at present grants to you, the elect of Canterbury, the temporalities of Canterbury, by special favour, and I, Itherius Bochardi, the king's clerk, protest, in the king's name, that the grant of temporalities made in like case to Nicholas, bishop of Winchester, but with a protest, which is now repeated in your person, shall not be drawn into a custom or example in future times.[5]

This defence of royal rights was, of course, made not by Edward himself but by a regency council, headed by Robert Burnell, whose task was to preserve the status of the crown pending the king's return to England. Yet whilst this text was not of Edward's making, he would certainly have approved of both its substance and its style. The protest is made in terms that echo the Freedom of Election charter; it seems strange that the earlier document is not mentioned, given that it had been confirmed by the papacy on two separate occasions, but instead 'custom' is invoked. The king is concerned to protect not only his own rights, but those of the church – a claim that was to be made repeatedly by English kings over the next fifty years. Edward is 'patron and defender' of the church of Canterbury and must therefore protest at this challenge to its right of election. The papal decision to provide is portrayed as an arbitrary one, for the papal letters expressed no faults in either the elect or the election;[6] according to custom, the election should therefore have been confirmed. The inconvenient truth of Henry III's opposition to Chillendene was not mentioned. The protest instead focuses on fears that this provision will set a precedent which will be followed in other vacancies, with the king being forced to accept the provisions of candidates to whom he has not given his assent.

Despite the gravity of these concerns (the validity of which was to be demonstrated with increasing frequency during the early years of the fourteenth century), no further formal protests against this new means of appointment are known to have been made during the reign of Edward I. The assertion that 'the challenge to the papacy in 1272 was not repeated after 1282' is, however, misleading,[7] for whilst there is no evidence for formal public protests of this kind, royal opposition to provision certainly did not die out after the 1270s.

---

[5] *CCR 1272-1279*, p. 39.

[6] It was, however, suggested by at least one chronicler that Chillendene resigned 'knowing and fully understanding that he would be rejected, because His Holiness the Pope, upon examination of him, did not consider him sufficiently literate'. *Chronicles of the Mayors and Sheriffs of London*, ed. H. T. Riley (London, 1863), p. 160.

[7] Cosgrove, 'Winchester', pp. 177-8. The phrasing of this statement is in itself problematic, since it implies that a protest was made in 1282, whereas Cosgrove himself acknowledges that there is no reason to suppose that this was so.

Indeed, Edward I was not the only king to be forced to deal with this thorny issue during the opening weeks of his reign. Within three months of Edward II's accession, the bishopric of Worcester became vacant and the new king decided to procure it for his treasurer, Walter Reynolds. Consequently, on the same day as he granted licence to elect, the king wrote to the monks of Worcester requesting that they elect his favourite.[8] Reynolds' candidacy seemed secure, until rumours reached England that Clement V had reserved the see – which he had indeed done over a week before the writ of *congé d'élire* had been granted.[9] The new king responded not by accepting the situation, but by ordering the monks to proceed to election without delay.[10] The Worcester *Sede vacante* roll includes an extraordinary letter from Edward II in which he justified this decision. He was strongly opposed to papal claims of the right to make appointments, which he believed infringed his rights over his kingdom. Reiterating King John's Freedom of Election charter , he wrote that the king must be allowed to confirm or quash elections 'for the elect may be a traitor or an enemy of the king or the realm, or he may be of another nation, so that he does not understand the language'. The kings of England, he claimed, had never renounced any of their temporal claims over elections, and therefore if the pope made reservations 'he would do it to the disinherison of the king and prejudice of his crown'. Furthermore, 'if the pope has his design in the matter, an election will never be made in any cathedral church in England'. There were, Edward thought, two flaws in the reservation, which would mean that any election held at Worcester was valid: the papal bull of reservation gave an incorrect place of death for Bishop Gainsborough and no notification of its existence had been made to the cathedral priory.[11]

It is significant that Clement V chose the first episcopal vacancy of Edward II's reign to attempt the reservation of, and proactive provision to, an English bishopric; this was a provocative act and one to which Edward was bound to respond aggressively. The letter cited above indicates exactly why the king objected to such provisions: they did not help the king, but threatened both his rights and his relationship with the episcopate. It was crucial to the well-being

---

8 *CPR 1307-1313*, p. 8; *Reg. Sede Vacante*, p. 104.

9 *Reg. Sede Vacante*, p. 104; *CPL*, II, p. 34. Bishop Gainsborough died at Beauvais on 17 September 1307, on the return journey to England. The see was reserved (presumably on the grounds that Gainsborough was within two legal days' journey of the curia at the time of his death) on 5 October. The *congé d'élire* was not sought until 14 October. It was given three days later, and the election was held on 13 November. The timescale would suggest that the monks (and the king) did not anticipate a reservation and thus proceeded along normal lines; a lapse of two months between the death of one bishop and the election of the next was certainly not unusual in the thirteenth century. Clement V benefitted from this relatively leisurely approach; as provision became more common, the process became substantially compressed.

10 *CCR 1307-1313*, p. 4.

11 *Reg. Sede Vacante*, pp. 104-7.

of the kingdom that the bishops were loyal Englishmen who were both willing and able to work with the crown, for they were not only ecclesiastical leaders but also great secular powers, with an important role to play in the government of the realm. Appointing a royal servant to a bishopric was also an important form of patronage for the crown. Had the pope insisted on appointing his own candidates to English sees, the consequences were potentially disastrous; it was therefore not only inevitable, but also necessary, for Edward II to object to such a possibility.

If the king's response to the 1307 reservation of Worcester illuminates the reasons why the crown might object to papal provision, the eventual outcome of this process explains why Edward II was able to set aside these objections. The election was carried out, and Reynolds elected but, when he heard of the reservation, the would-be bishop refused to accept the see pending a papal decision. Subsequently the election was annulled by the pope, only for Reynolds to be provided to Worcester 'at the request of the king'.[12] As Sophia Menache argued, Clement V had been outmanoeuvred by Edward II.[13] This outcome opened the king's eyes to the potential of provision: royal candidates could still be appointed to the episcopate, but via a more secure and prestigious means. With the rise of provision, the king only had to deal with one (generally accommodating) pope, rather than a horde of troublesome monks or canons.

Papal willingness to accommodate royal wishes was not a new phenomenon; even Innocent III, a staunch proponent of electoral freedom who frequently clashed with King John over the latter's interventions in episcopal appointments, had written that candidates for the episcopate should be 'not only distinguished in life and learning, but also loyal to the king, profitable to the kingdom, and capable of giving counsel and help'.[14] A century later, it seems that papal attitudes had not substantially altered; indeed, they may even have become more favourable to the crown. It was during the pontificate of Clement V (1305-14) that the rise of provision began in earnest; the English crown's acceptance of this rise was greatly assisted by the 'affectionate relationship' which this pope, a Gascon and former royal clerk, enjoyed with both Edwards.[15]

Later popes were also generally sympathetic to royal wishes. When John XXII provided John Ross (an auditor of causes in the sacred palace) to the bishopric of Carlisle and was thus unable to appoint William Airmyn (keeper of the privy seal, and the bishop-elect), he apologized to the king and queen, writing that he 'now prays the king to excuse him in regard to the said appointment' and promising

---

12 *CPL*, II, p. 34.

13 Menache, *Clement*, pp. 61-3.

14 *SLI*, p. 166 (no. 62).

15 Menache, *Clement*, pp. 247-78 (quote at p. 248); Jeffrey Denton, 'Pope Clement V's Early Career as a Royal Clerk', *EHR*, 83 (1968), pp. 303-14.

that he 'has Master William written on the tablets of his heart, and will promote him in due place and time'.[16] According to the Durham chronicler (admittedly a hostile source), the same pope admitted that he had to quash the election of a Durham monk in order to provide Queen Isabella's cousin, because he had to please the king and queen.[17] By the pontificate of Clement VI, the papacy had apparently become even more accommodating of royal wishes. His reported declaration that if the king of England asked for an ass to be made a bishop he would grant his request[18] is, unfortunately, almost certainly apocryphal, but he also expressed similar (if slightly less extreme) sentiments in writing. In 1344, amidst a groundswell of English opposition to papal provision, Clement wrote to Edward III, suggesting that this mode of appointment was actually more likely to result in the fulfilment of royal wishes than the traditional form. Elections, he pointed out, were rarely satisfactory to the monarch, because their outcomes were often contrary to his wishes; provision, on the other hand, meant that '[the king's] councillors could be promoted by the Roman Church'.[19] Clement VI was undoubtedly unusually willing to accommodate royal wishes regarding elections, but the papacy was not, in general, hostile to royal involvement in episcopal appointments. Once it became apparent that the rise of provision was not simply an attack on royal rights in this sphere, the papacy and the crown could begin to work together in order to ensure that at least the majority of episcopal appointments were satisfactory to both parties.

Consequently, after 1307, the crown's attitude to provision was largely positive, and royal campaigning on behalf of curial candidates was henceforth directed not only at the chapter, but also at the pope. This approach acknowledged the fact that capitular elections were not yet obsolete (for, even if a provision was made, the pope might decide to provide the bishop-elect), whilst removing the king's dependence on the whims of the chapter. For example, when Archbishop Robert Winchelsey died in 1313, Edward II hoped that Walter Reynolds would be translated from Worcester to Canterbury. The king probably indicated his wishes to the Canterbury monks, but his efforts were focused on a secret correspondence with Clement V. In a letter written towards the end of June 1313, Clement began by reprimanding Edward for seeking to influence the appointment process, but made it clear that he intended to comply with the royal request. He had reserved the see, he claimed, in order to ensure the preferment of one who would bring profit to the church of Canterbury, but also inspire the king's trust through high regard for the rights of kingship. The

---

16 *CPL*, II, pp. 468, 470.

17 *Script. Tres*, p. 99.

18 *Chronicon Angliae*, ed. E. M. Thompson (RS, 1874), p. 20.

19 BL Cotton MS Cleopatra E.II, fo. 47r/49r, cited in John Aberth, *Criminal Churchmen in the Age of Edward III: The Case of Bishop Thomas de Lisle* (University Park, Pa., 1996), p. 16.

new archbishop should also work for the peace of the king and of the realm, give faithful counsel to the king and be willing, when necessary, to assist the king with aids.[20] As a consequence of this correspondence, the election of Thomas Cobham (a perfectly suitable candidate) was quashed and Reynolds was provided.[21] The king's two-pronged approach was also apparent at Lincoln, in 1320. Edward II gave his assent to the canons' election of Anthony Bek,[22] but simultaneously (and successfully) petitioned John XXII for the provision of Henry Burghersh.[23] When the relationship between king and pope worked well, the system of provision was highly satisfactory to both parties.

There were, however, sporadic disagreements, usually because the pope ignored or misinterpreted royal wishes. For example, Adam Orleton was successively provided to three English sees: Hereford in 1317, Worcester in 1327 and Winchester in 1333. On each occasion his promotion provoked royal fury; in 1327 and 1333 this anger was manifested in a delay of several months before the temporalities were restored.[24] During the early 1320s John XXII made a series of provisions that infuriated Edward II;[25] relations between the two were just beginning to mend when, in 1325, a misunderstanding led John XXII to appoint William Airmyn to Norwich. The pope was hoping to please Edward II by providing Airmyn, a *curialis* who had been the royal candidate for Carlisle two years earlier; unfortunately, the king now favoured Robert Baldock. Consequently, the new bishop's personal property was seized and the temporalities withheld.[26] Papal accommodation of royal wishes eased the transition from election to provision, but such accommodation was not constant – and when thwarted, both Edward II and Edward III (as well as the Isabella-Mortimer regency government) made clear their opposition to both the provision and the provisee.

It was when the king feared that his wishes might not be accommodated by the pope that he was most likely to turn his attention to the chapter, as Edward

---

20 Denton, 'Walter Reynolds', pp. 317-28; Henry Richardson, 'Clement V and the See of Canterbury', *EHR*, 56 (1941), pp. 97-103, with Clement V's letter reproduced at pp. 101-3.

21 *CPL*, II, p. 115.

22 *CPR 1317-1321*, p. 413.

23 *Foedera, Conventiones, Literae et Acta Publica*, ed. T. Rymer, A. Clarke and F. Holbrooke (3 vols in 6, London, 1816-30), II.i, pp. 414, 418.

24 Roy Haines, *The Church and Politics in Fourteenth-Century England: The Career of Adam Orleton, c. 1275-1345* (Cambridge, 1978). On the crown's response to the Worcester provision, see *CCR 1327-1330*, pp. 238-9; CPR 1327-1330, p. 245. On Winchester, see Roy Haines, 'Looking Back in Anger: A Politically-Inspired Appeal against John XXII's Translation of Bishop Adam Orleton to Winchester (1334), *EHR*, 116 (2001), pp. 389-404.

25 Phillips, *Edward II*, pp. 449-50. The appointments in question were Rigaud of Asserio to Winchester (1319), Roger Northburgh to Coventry and Lichfield (1321), and John Stratford to Winchester (1323).

26 *CPL*, I, pp. 477, 479; *CCR 1327-1330*, p. 24; Grassi, 'William Airmyn', pp. 550-61.

II's actions following the death of Bishop Richard Swinfield of Hereford (1282-1317) demonstrate.[27] In mid-March, as soon as Edward heard of the bishop's death, he petitioned John XXII to provide the royal clerk Thomas Charlton.[28] The canons of Hereford did not receive the *congé d'élire* until 7 April, several weeks after the first royal petitions were sent to the pope,[29] and it seems that they never held an election. On 6 May, Edward dispatched further letters to Avignon, backing Charlton's candidacy and requiring Adam Orleton to turn down the bishopric if it was offered to him.[30] By now, however, he was beginning to suspect that papal compliance would not be easy to secure and thus three days later he wrote to the dean and chapter of Hereford, requesting that they elect Charlton.[31] Despite the royal efforts, Orleton was provided to Hereford on 15 May[32] – thus illustrating why the crown, where possible, preferred to secure papal, rather than capitular, backing for its candidates.

King and pope also clashed over the management of the temporalities of vacant bishoprics. According to the custom of regalian right, the king held the temporalities during an episcopal vacancy and restored them only when a new bishop had received archiepiscopal (or papal) confirmation. The restoration process usually involved the payment of a substantial sum by the new bishop, in return for which he would be given the corn and stock that remained to the king at the end of the vacancy. It was also an important symbolic gesture, signalling the end of the vacancy (from the secular perspective) and emphasizing the bishop's position as a tenant of the crown.[33] Given that the power to confer the temporalities was closely bound up with the power to confer the bishopric,[34] it was inevitable that this tradition would be threatened by the centralizing tendencies of the thirteenth-century papacy. When Innocent IV confirmed the election of Boniface of Savoy as archbishop of Canterbury in 1243, he granted him not only the spiritualities but also the temporalities of the see.[35] This was a deliberate challenge to the custom of regalian right and (from the royal perspective) set an unwelcome precedent for the conduct of future appointments. In the short term, it had limited impact and the king's

---

27 *Fasti 1300-1541*, II, p. 3.

28 Smith, *Episcopal Appointments*, p. 27.

29 *CPR 1313-1317*, p. 633.

30 *Foedera*, II.i, pp. 328-9.

31 *CCR 1313-1318*, p. 467.

32 *CPL*, II, p. 150.

33 Howell, *Regalian Right*, pp. 65-8.

34 Ibid., pp. 206-10.

35 *Gervase*, II, p. 200. Although a royal order to transfer the temporalities to Boniface does not seem to have been registered on the surviving rolls, one must surely have been issued, for it is very unlikely that the royal agents would have obeyed a papal mandate of this kind.

right to restore the temporalities went otherwise unchallenged for some years.[36] Towards the end of the century, however, the issue once more came to the fore. In 1272, Edward I's protest at the provision of Kilwardby included an implied threat that the king would not in future consider himself bound to restore the temporalities to bishops provided by the pope.[37] Then, in 1299, Boniface VIII, as part of his provision of John Salmon to the bishopric of Norwich, sent letters to Edward I and Archbishop Winchelsey ordering that the temporalities of the see be restored to its new bishop. Inevitably, Edward responded angrily, and Salmon was forced to formally renounce the papal claim to restore the temporalities and acknowledge that of the king.[38] Boniface nevertheless issued a similarly worded bull of provision for William Gainsborough of Worcester in 1302, leading to a similar renunciation; the new bishop was bound to make fine with the king for 1,000 marks, 'for his trespass in admitting an apostolic bull containing that the pope has committed to the said bishop the administration of the temporalities'.[39] In 1307, Edward II again protested that the kings of England had 'never relinquished anything which concerns his temporality and the right of the crown'.[40]

Such protests were doomed to failure; it was inevitable that future popes would use the precedent set by Innocent IV in 1243 to justify the expansion of their powers in this field. From 1303 onwards, bulls of provision consistently bestowed both spiritualities and temporalities. Consequently, the formal renunciation of the words of the bull by the provisee became part of regular procedure in England. The new bishop was required to admit that the relevant clauses were not inserted at his behest, and to pledge that he had not done, and would not do, anything prejudicial to the rights of the crown. He then renounced the papal letters, insofar as they claimed rights over the episcopal temporalities, and supplicated the king to restore them 'of his grace and mere liberality as king'.[41] The pope appears to have turned a blind eye to this practice; as with the other stages of the appointment process, crown and papacy managed to establish a compromise acceptable to both parties.

---

36 Stubbs, *Constitutional History*, III, pp. 317-19. The restoration of spiritualities and temporalities did, however, become standard in bulls relating to Scottish and Irish bishoprics.

37 *CCR 1272-1279*, p. 39.

38 *CPL*, I, pp. 583-4; *CPR 1292-1301*, p. 442.

39 *Calendar of the Fine Rolls Preserved in the Public Record Office: I, 1272-1307* (London, 1911), p. 449; Howell, *Regalian Right*, p. 208.

40 *Reg. Sede Vacante*, p. 106.

41 *C&S*, II, pp. 1226-7; *CPR 1292-1301*, p. 442.

Cathedral Chapters in the Age of Provision

If the rights of the English crown were potentially threatened by the transition to provision, the cathedral chapters had even more to lose. The years 1214-1307 had been something of a golden age of electoral freedom; it was not guaranteed that the chapters would manage to secure the bishop of their choice, but they were at least certain to be able to hold an election and thus to give a formal indication of their wishes, with a reasonable chance that these would be observed. By contrast, as provision became increasingly common chapters were increasingly sidelined and simply given a new bishop. Superficially, the monks and canons of England's cathedrals seem to have accepted their fate with little fuss; there were no open protests against this procedural shift. There are, however, hints that they were more than passive observers of the shift, with cathedral convents more likely to show their displeasure than secular chapters. This difference is not entirely unexpected, given that secular chapters had always been more tractable, but it was almost certainly reinforced by the fact that many canons were themselves aliens who owed their prebends to papal provision. By the reign of Edward III, the proportion of foreigners in English cathedral chapters ranged from one in six to 75 per cent, with the greatest concentrations being found in the wealthiest cathedral chapters, at Lincoln, Salisbury and York.[42]

The most powerful expression of capitular distaste for the provision system came from the pen of the Durham chronicler, Robert Graystanes (d.1333),[43] himself a victim of the changes to the bishop-making process. Having described in detail his promotion to the episcopate, and his subsequent demotion, he allowed himself to pen a brief diatribe against the provision system:

> How more effectively can he take away from them their [right of] election, granted by kings and confirmed by popes, than by granting the benefice conferred by his own bishop to another cleric, especially without trying the case; and this through their negligence to the king's prejudice? On the same ground the Pope could reserve all the bishoprics of England, and bestow them on cardinals and others who live outside the realm, and the realm would be impoverished by the carrying off of money, and it would be endangered by the lack of counsel, which is usually esteemed among the kingdom's bishops. Or he could confer them on foreigners, who would remain in the country. And the king would then be in danger, because so many foreigners would occupy bishoprics in England, with the

---

42 Lepine, *Brotherhood of Canons*, pp. 28-36; Edwards, *English Secular Cathedrals*, pp. 70-96; Scott Waugh, *England in the Reign of Edward III* (Cambridge, 1991), p. 145; Wright, *Church*, App. A.

43 The attribution of the chronicle to Graystanes is traditional, but the association between the bishop-elect and the chronicle is a rather tenuous one: it is known that the author of the Durham chronicle of this period was a monk called Robert, and Graystanes is the only Durham monk of the 1330s known to have borne that name. Meryl Foster, 'Robert Graystanes', *ODNB*.

> castles and all that pertains to them, because with [other] foreigners they could rise up against the king. Besides, the king swore to Magna Carta, of which one article is that elections should be free. There were many other things which the realm's magnates advised should be discussed concerning this matter.[44]

Graystanes' anger is palpable and, although the predicted influx of foreign bishops never materialized,[45] his fears were seemingly shared by many of his contemporaries. Whilst the ability of cathedral chapters to oppose the transition in any practical sense was limited, chapters do seem to have collaborated with royal efforts to thwart papal intentions on several occasions – as at Worcester in 1307.[46] It also seems that they were aware of the need for speed if an election was to be held before a provision was made.[47] Traditionally, preparations for election did not begin until after the funeral of the late bishop, but in the fourteenth century they were increasingly brought forward. When Louis de Beaumont of Durham died in 1333, the date of the election was set at least a week before his funeral was held,[48] and the licence to elect was granted the day after the burial; given that Edward III was then at Havering-atte-Bower, it is clear that the proctors must have left Durham at least a week earlier.[49] The 1332 Carlisle election is a particularly striking case of an election being conducted at high speed: there is only a week between the granting of licence to elect and royal assent to the election.[50] Indeed, it seems highly unlikely that the normal procedures could have been followed, since the king was then at Woodstock – a journey of more than 250 miles from Carlisle. Unfortunately the sources do not give any hint

---

44 *Script. Tres*, p. 122.

45 In the early fourteenth century, cardinals were still expected to reside at the curia and thus the roles of cardinal and English bishop were generally thought to be incompatible. An English bishop who became a cardinal would usually be obliged to resign his bishopric; Stephen Langton, who remained a cardinal even after his appointment as archbishop of Canterbury, was the exception who proved the rule. Robert Kilwardby resigned the same archbishopric in 1278, following his nomination as cardinal-bishop of Porto. Nearly a century later, in 1368, Simon Langham resigned the same office in order to become cardinal-priest of St Sixtus. Only in the fifteenth century were residence requirements relaxed, facilitating the careers of men such as Henry Beaufort, Thomas Wolsey and Lorenzo Campeggio. But even in the early sixteenth century, the majority of English bishops were Englishmen. See Christopher Holdsworth, 'Stephen Langton', Simon Tugwell, 'Robert de Kilwardby' and William Dohar, 'Simon Langham' *ODNB*; Aidan Bellenger and Stella Fletcher, *Princes of the Church: A History of the English Cardinals* (Stroud, 2001), pp. 1-84; and *Fasti 1300-1541*, passim.

46 *Reg. Sede Vacante*, pp. 107-8.

47 If this was achieved, there was some hope that the election would be preferred – as at Rochester in 1317.

48 *Calendar of the Durham Cathedral Muniments: Locelli* (Durham, 2012), p. 247 (Locelli VI: 11a).

49 *CPR 1330-1334*, p. 469.

50 The licence was granted on 11 May (*CPR 1330-1334*, p. 280) and assent on 18 May (*CPR 1330-1334*, p. 304).

of how such speed was possible, or why it was deemed necessary, but it seems probable that this was an attempt to ensure that the election took place before a provision was made. If this could be achieved, it was more likely (although not inevitable) that the bishop-elect would have his position confirmed.[51] This may be a further example of king and chapter working together to ensure that a valid election could take place; if so, their attempts were successful, since John Kirkby's election received papal confirmation, notwithstanding the existence of a reservation.[52]

A letter written by Wolstan de Bransford, bishop-elect of Worcester, in late 1327 strongly suggests that cathedral chapters were far more than passive partners in such joint efforts to prevent provisions. As in the previous examples, the election had been conducted at great speed: Bishop Cobham died on 26 or 27 August,[53] licence to elect was granted on 31 August[54] and royal assent to the election of Bransford, the prior of Worcester, was given on 8 September.[55] Archiepiscopal assent was given on 3 October[56] and the temporalities were restored five days later,[57] but the process then stalled. At some point between 8 October and 11 November, the bishop-elect wrote to the king and council, recounting the course of his election so far and complaining that Archbishop Reynolds and the monks of Christ Church Canterbury had received a papal bull and letters ordering them to obstruct the Worcester electoral process, and the promotion of Wolstan himself. He therefore petitioned the king to prevent the implementation of these orders for, having been confirmed in the temporalities, he should not be ousted.[58] On 11 November the justices and council informed the king that they had given their advice on this matter to the convent of Worcester[59] and also advised the king to grant the petition.[60] Within the week, a writ had been sent to the archbishop of Canterbury, ordering him not to do anything that would prejudice the crown without first consulting the king.[61] Letters in

---

51 See, for example, the election of Hamo de Hethe to Rochester (1317), which was upheld on the grounds that it took place the day before the pope provided a rival candidate. *Anglia Sacra*, I, pp. 356–77; Haines, 'Episcopate of a Benedictine Monk', pp. 192–207.

52 *CPL*, II, p. 403.

53 *Anglia Sacra*, I, p. 533.

54 *CPR 1327-1330*, p. 159.

55 Ibid., p. 165.

56 *Fasti 1300-1541*, IV, p. 56.

57 *CPR 1327-1330*, p. 179.

58 TNA SC8/208/10384.

59 TNA SC8/208/10383.

60 TNA SC8/208/10385.

61 *CCR 1327-1330*, pp. 328-9. The writ was dated 17 November; Reynolds had died the previous day.

Wolstan's favour were also dispatched to Avignon.[62] The combined efforts of the king and the would-be bishop were in vain: the election was quashed, and Adam Orleton was translated from Hereford to Worcester by papal provision.[63] Yet this failure should not obscure the fact that the cathedral chapters did not simply accept their fate.

Another significant indication that chapters were concerned to protect their rights is the fact that chapters continued to seek licence to elect from the king, and to hold elections even in the late fifteenth century, long after provision had become the only mode of appointment.[64] This was not overt resistance to the papacy, since it was permitted by that authority, and if the pope chose to provide another candidate (as frequently happened) chapters were obliged to accept his decision. In the reign of Edward III alone, there were at least twenty-seven occasions on which a bishop was elected by a cathedral chapter, only for his election to be superseded by the papal provision of another candidate.[65] It was, however, an effective means of regularly reasserting capitular claims to participation in the appointment process.

The Archiepiscopal Response

The English archbishops (and, indeed, the whole of the English episcopate) were rather quieter on the question of provision than might have been expected. Had Robert Grosseteste lived in the early fourteenth century he would surely have had much to say on this issue, but from the evidence of the surviving sources we are hard-pressed to uncover the views of any of the early fourteenth-century prelates. There is, however, some indication that Archbishop Reynolds was unwilling to cooperate in schemes to thwart papal provisions. In 1320, he refused to confirm the election of Anthony Bek as bishop of Lincoln because the see had been reserved by the pope.[66] His response to two elections held in the months before his death in November 1327 is also suggestive. A royal writ of 9 December recorded that the late archbishop had 'delayed proceeding to the confirmation' of John de Godeley as bishop of Exeter, despite royal urgings that he should do so.[67] Furthermore, Reynolds had confirmed the election of Wulstan de Bransford, but had 'wilfully refused to consecrate although

62 *CPL*, II, p. 487.

63 *CPL*, II, p. 265.

64 The truth of this statement is most easily seen from the pages of the *Fasti Ecclesiae Anglicanae*.

65 Ormrod, *Edward III*, p. 125.

66 *Fasti 1300-1541*, I, p. 1, citing Lambeth Palace Library: Register of Walter Reynolds, fo. 220.

67 *CCR 1327-1330*, p. 240.

frequently requested to do so on the king's behalf'.[68] It is possible that Reynolds was simply too ill to concern himself with such matters, but the fact that, in both cases, the regency government was attempting to force through elections in the face of papal reservations provokes suspicions that Reynolds was making a stand in favour of papal rights. Since Reynolds had himself been twice provided (to Worcester and Canterbury), it was perhaps inevitable that he should take a positive view of this process, for to question its use would have been to question his own appointment. As a consequence, the English Church lacked a prominent ecclesiastical opponent of provision during the crucial early years of John XXII's pontificate.

If Reynolds leaned towards support for papal provision, his northern counterpart, William Melton, archbishop of York (1316-40), appears to have been rather more suspicious of the practice. Melton, as the metropolitan of a significantly smaller province, with only two dioceses unequivocally subject to his control,[69] was involved in far fewer elections than Reynolds (three during a twenty-six-year episcopate), but the manner in which he dealt with them is intriguing. When, in 1325, the election of William Airmyn as bishop of Carlisle (which had been examined and confirmed by Melton) was overturned by the papal provision of John Ross, the archbishop offered no resistance.[70] But when Durham fell vacant in 1333, he took a rather different approach.

Having received the *congé d'élire*, the monks elected one of their brethren, Robert of Graystanes, a high-ranking member of the cathedral community (of which he was the probable chronicler) and a doctor of theology.[71] Edward III, however, had an alternative candidate in mind and petitioned both the chapter and the pope to favour Richard de Bury, a trusted royal administrator who was then resident in Avignon as envoy to the papal curia.[72] The speed with which the election had been conducted (well within a month of the previous bishop's death) was almost certainly due to the chapter's fear that a provision would be made, and the hope that their choice might be upheld, as sometimes happened, if they managed to move faster than the pope. On this occasion, however, their efforts failed: Richard de Bury was provided to the bishopric of Durham on

---

68 Ibid., pp. 238-9.

69 Episcopal elections to the Scottish diocese of Whithorn had traditionally been examined by the archbishop of York, but by the early fourteenth century its ties to the English archdiocese were beginning to weaken. See Keith Stringer, *The Reformed Church in Medieval Galloway and Cumbria: Contrasts, Connections and Continuities* (Whithorn, 2003).

70 He did, however, express his displeasure at the new bishop's failure to make the conventional profession of obedience to York: *Reg. Melton*, I, p. 86.

71 *Script. Tres*, p. 120; Foster, 'Robert Graystanes'.

72 *Script. Tres*, p. 120. On Bury, see Nigel Denholm-Young, 'Richard de Bury', *TRHS*, 4th series, 20 (1937), pp. 135-68; William Courtenay, 'Richard Bury (Aungerville)', *ODNB*.

14 October 1333, the day before the election of Robert Graystanes.[73] At the time of the election, they must have been unaware that this was the case, but they soon learned that they had been thwarted. On 31 October, having already made contact with the archbishop of York, they sought royal assent to their choice, only to be informed by the king that 'We understand that the pope has provided Richard of Bury, our familiar clerk, to that bishopric; we do not wish to offend the pope: therefore we cannot consent to your election.'[74] Only if John XXII refused to provide Bury would the king favour Graystanes, giving him 'all the grace he craved'[75] – although, given that such a refusal would almost certainly have been coupled with the provision of the papal choice, it is doubtful whether royal favour would have been much help to the bishop-elect.

According to the Freedom of Election charter, which King John had granted to the English Church in 1214, the king had the right to withhold assent to an election if he could 'put forth some reasonable excuse and lawfully prove it, by reason of which we should not consent'.[76] By the 1330s, the belief that a provision had been made would have constituted a 'reasonable excuse' for the withholding of royal assent, and one might therefore expect that the electoral process would have paused at this point, until firm knowledge of events in Avignon was available. From a papal perspective at least, Graystanes should have followed the example of Walter Reynolds and pledged to obey all apostolic commands.[77] Instead, he travelled on to York, where he consulted with the cathedral canons and some skilled lawyers.[78]

Despite the withholding of royal assent and the suggestion that a provision might have been made, Archbishop Melton decided to continue with the bishop-making process.[79] On 10 November the prior and convent of Durham made a formal request for confirmation of the election, and it was duly examined and confirmed by two archiepiscopal officials. The *Te Deum* was sung and the new bishop made his oath of obedience to the archbishop and diocese of York.[80] Mandates for the prior and convent of Durham and the laity and clergy of the diocese to obey their new bishop were issued on the same day.[81] Less than a week

73 *CPL*, II, p. 405.

74 *Script. Tres*, p. 120.

75 *Chronicle of Lanercost*, p. 284.

76 *C&S*, I, p. 41.

77 Reynolds was elected to Worcester in 1307; shortly after his election rumours of a papal reservation of the see began to circulate. Declaring that he was disinclined to believe these stories, he tentatively accepted his election, but promised to 'obey and observe the apostolic commands'. The rumours proved true and Reynolds was subsequently provided to the see. *Reg. Sede Vacante*, pp. 108-10.

78 *Script. Tres*, p. 120.

79 *Chronicle of Lanercost*, p. 284.

80 *Reg. Melton*, I, pp. 100-102.

81 *Reg. Melton*, I, p. 102.

later, on Sunday 14 November, Graystanes was consecrated in the chapel of the archiepiscopal palace at York; Melton officiated and was assisted by John Kirkby, bishop of Carlisle, and Roland Jorz, the former archbishop of Armagh, who acted as an auxiliary bishop at York in the early 1330s.[82] Bishop Graystanes was enthroned in his own cathedral by the archdeacon of York on Thursday 18 November.[83]

Given that, by mid-November, all those involved in the appointment process were aware that a papal provision had almost certainly been made, why did they continue with this process? William Melton would later vigorously protest his innocence of any wrongdoing in a letter to John XXII, in which he claimed that he had believed that Bury could not have been provided, since he had heard that the would-be bishop had died in Paris.[84] This sounds like a desperate attempt on the archbishop's part to redeem himself in papal eyes, by insisting that he was ignorant, rather than defiant. However, the archbishop had something of a history of crediting and acting on somewhat implausible rumours that he would have done better to ignore: in 1330 he became involved in a plot to free Edward II (who was rumoured to be still living) and perhaps even to restore him to the throne.[85] Given this, it not implausible that such a rumour was in circulation and that Melton, wishing to believe its veracity, acted as if it were fact.

FromMelton's actions in 1333, it is apparent that he preferred the election of Graystanes to the provision of Bury, but it is less clear whether his objections were to the method of appointment, the identity of the appointee or both. Although Melton had himself spent many years in royal service, and continued to hold government posts even after his promotion to the episcopate, his approach to episcopal office may have made him more sympathetic to the would-be monk-bishop than might be expected of a man who owed his own promotion largely to royal favour. The archbishop was Yorkshire born and bred, a pious and charitable man who was closely involved in the running of his diocese and greatly concerned with the well-being of his flock.[86] Having come into conflict with the previous bishop of Durham, he may also have been concerned that his replacement should be more manageable. Bury, like Beaumont, had royal favour on his side; furthermore, he was very closely associated with the new king, whereas Melton was irrevocably linked to Edward II. Melton may well have feared that Bury would be virtually unmanageable, whereas Graystanes would be relatively easy to control.

---

82 *Reg. Melton*, I, pp. 102-3; *Script. Tres*, p. 120.

83 *Reg. Melton*, I, p. 103; *Script. Tres*, pp. 120-21; *Murimuth*, p. 71.

84 *Historical Papers and Letters from the Northern Registers*, ed. J. Raine (RS, 1873), p. 372.

85 Roy Haines, 'Sumptuous Apparel for a Royal Prisoner: Archbishop Melton's Letter, 14 January 1330', *EHR*, 124 (2009), pp. 885-94.

86 Rosalind Hill, 'William Melton', *ODNB*.

If Melton's opinions of the candidates were shaped by the fact that he was nearing the end of his career, and more strongly associated with the last reign than the current one, his attitude to papal provision may also have been somewhat behind the times. His own promotion to the archbishopric of York, in 1316, had taken place when the rise of provision was still far from complete, and had been achieved by the traditional method of capitular election.[87] At the beginning of his archiepiscopate, the rise of provision was beginning to limit archiepiscopal powers over the appointment process, but metropolitans were still examining, confirming and consecrating new bishops on a frequent basis. It seems that Melton still expected, or at least wanted, to do these things. Nearly two decades after his election much had changed but Melton, in collaboration with the Durham monks and other clerics at York, nevertheless appears to have been working against the provisions system by attempting to push through the election process before a provision was made – a policy that had on several occasions been used by Edward II.[88] If this could be achieved, then the election might be upheld. Melton, along with the Durham monks, would have been given added optimism by the outcome of the Carlisle election of the previous year: John Kirkby, a member of the cathedral chapter, received papal confirmation of his election despite the fact that a papal reservation of the see had been made.[89] As with the Durham election, Melton examined, confirmed and consecrated the elect before the papal stance became clear.[90]

It is striking that Melton twice within two years finalized elections despite the fact that a reservation had been made. It seems implausible that the archbishop was unaware of both reservations or at least that he could not anticipate that they would be made. It might be argued that the canon law on reservation and provision had become so complicated by the 1330s that even an experienced archbishop (Melton had been at York since 1316) was confused by it.[91] But none of the early fourteenth-century archbishops of Canterbury ever made a similar mistake, and Archbishop Reynolds on two occasions apparently refused to cooperate in royal schemes to thwart papal provisions, once withholding his consent to an election and on another occasion refusing consecration to the

87 *Historians of the Church of York*, II, p. 415.

88 For example, at Worcester in 1307.

89 *CPL*, II, p. 403.

90 *Reg. Melton*, I, pp. 94-5. On this occasion the king cooperated with the hastening of the electoral process, giving his assent to Kirkby's election and restoring the temporalities of the see to him. *CPR 1330-1334*, pp. 304, 313.

91 Such confusion would not have been unprecedented. In a letter to Boniface VIII, dated 19 July 1302, Archbishop Winchelsey asked a series of questions on the application of the canon law, claiming that 'modern doctors of law put varying interpretations on the constitutions concerning elections' and asking that the pope 'therefore enlighten my ignorance'. *Reg. Winchelsey*, I, pp. 631-4. I have been unable to trace the papal response to this request.

elect.[92] It is hard to escape the conclusion that Melton's actions constituted a deliberate, if relatively non-aggressive, form of resistance to the rise of papal provision.

The Role of the Candidate: Continuity and Change

Throughout the thirteenth century, the ideal of the passive holy man obliged to accept his election to episcopal office in order to comply with divine will had been only rarely represented in real life. Unsurprisingly, this did not change after 1300 and candidates continued to play an important part in the electoral process. A very small number of those elected rejected their elections, amongst them Henry of Mamesfield, dean of Lincoln, who turned down that see in 1320.[93] Far more common, however, was the would-be bishop who tried to ensure that his ambition was fulfilled. Several bishops-elect undertook the journey to Avignon, hoping that their appointment would be confirmed by the pope. Anthony Bek, elected to Lincoln after Henry of Mamesfield's resignation of his claims, was willing to fight for the see and when Archbishop Reynolds refused to confirm the election, Bek went to the papal curia to plead his case.[94] Bek's election was quashed, but his brother Thomas's journey to Avignon (in 1341) was more successful, resulting in his confirmation as bishop of the same see.[95]

The rise of provision offered would-be bishops a new path to the episcopate. Until the late thirteenth century, ambitious men were dependent on the wishes of the chapter or the whim of the king, but there was now a third way: winning the favour of the pope. Of the thirty-five bishops provided to English sees between 1272 and 1344,[96] eleven were at Avignon at the time of their appointment. Several other provisees were or had been in royal diplomatic service and had thus visited the papal curia. Another three were papal servants: John Grandisson (Exeter, 1327) and William Bateman (Norwich, 1344) were English-born, whilst Rigaud d'Asserio (Winchester, 1319) was, like John XXII, a lawyer from Cahors, Gascony. It is clear that, during the early decades of the fourteenth century, being known to the pope greatly increased one's chances of obtaining a bishopric. Both Adam Orleton (successively bishop of Hereford, Worcester and finally Winchester) and John Stratford (bishop of Winchester and subsequently archbishop of Canterbury) owed their first bishopric to their

92 *CCR 1327-1330*, pp. 238-40.

93 *The Book of John Schalby*, ed. J. H. Srawley (Lincoln, 1949), p. 18.

94 Smith, *Episcopal Appointments*, p. 35, citing Lambeth Palace Library: Register of Walter Reynolds, fo. 220b; *CPL*, II, p. 198.

95 *CPL*, III, p. 52.

96 The following paragraph is based on the entries for these bishops from the *ODNB*.

personal presence at the curia when the see fell vacant; both were provided, and further promoted, despite royal opposition.[97]

Candidates who achieved promotion in this way were vulnerable to royal displeasure[98] and also to criticism from their contemporaries. Stories of simony continued to circulate during this period, feeding off the popular belief that the primary reason for the growth of provision was the papal desire to misappropriate English money.[99] More unusual were the scurrilous accusations made against Walter Maidstone, bishop of Worcester, by Adam Murimuth, a man well acquainted with happenings at the papal curia. He claimed that the new bishop was 'a man defamed throughout Europe for immoral behaviour, and in secret improperly familiar with the pope'.[100] The continuer of the Westminster *Flores* criticized Maidstone in similar terms.[101] Whether or not such rumours were true, they certainly contained a grain of truth, for popes as well as kings exploited their powers over episcopal appointments to further the careers of their favourites. The rise of provision meant that by the early fourteenth century an Englishman who aspired to become a bishop could be equally well advised to focus his attentions on Avignon as on Westminster.

The Queen and the Nobility

Individuals who had no formal role in the electoral process had, on occasion, played an important role in episcopal elections during the reigns of Henry III and Edward I, and this pattern continued during the reigns of Edward II and Edward III. Indeed, the role of the queen and aristocracy became far more pronounced.

Occasionally, the king, queen and leading nobles came together to support the election of a single candidate. For example in 1310, as soon as Ely became vacant, the king, queen and a number of barons wrote to the prior and convent on behalf of Boniface of Saluzzo, a kinsman of both the king and the earl of Arundel. A group of nobles, including Arundel (who became one of the lords ordainer) even stayed in Ely for the duration of the election in order to press Saluzzo's case.[102] In 1316, Edward, Isabella and several magnates wrote to the

97 Haines, *Career of Adam Orleton*, pp. 15-20; Haines, *Archbishop John Stratford*, pp. 21-2.

98 See above, p. 155.

99 This belief was rooted in a much broader tradition of criticizing papal venality, not least in satirical texts such as *The Holy Gospel according to the Silver Mark*. See Lawrence, 'Thirteenth Century', pp. 127-9; John Yunck, *The Lineage of Lady Meed: The Development of Medieval Venality Satire* (Notre Dame, 1963).

100 *Murimuth*, p. 19.

101 *Flores Hist.*, III, p. 177.

102 *Anglia Sacra*, I, pp. 641-2.

prior and convent of Winchester to urge the election of John Sandale.[103] Even during the turbulent early months of Edward III's reign, it was apparently possible for some sort of consensus to be reached, for numerous letters were sent to John XXII on behalf of Simon Meopham, archbishop-elect of Canterbury, amongst them petitions from Edward III and Queen Isabella, as well as a letter allegedly sent by common consent of the English magnates, in which they complained about the recent disruptive rule of certain prelates.[104]

At least as common, however, were vacancies during which queen and nobles acted independently of, or even in opposition to, the king. Isabella of France backed a different candidate to her husband on at least two occasions before 1327. In 1316, a vacancy arose at Durham, and Isabella successfully petitioned for the provision of her kinsman Louis de Beaumont although her husband favoured Thomas Charlton.[105] The following year, she attempted to procure Rochester for her chaplain, John Puteoli; Edward II supported the monastic candidate, Hamo de Hythe.[106] Her independent actions in this sphere are surely a testament to the poor relationship between king and queen, for they stand in stark contrast to those of her predecessors, the two Eleanors, who often sought to influence elections, but always in tandem with their respective husbands.

Prominent noblemen were similarly unafraid to back their own candidates for the episcopate, as was forcefully illustrated when Durham became vacant in 1316. A great number of nobles gathered in Durham, amongst them the earls of Hereford, Lancaster and Pembroke, Lords Ross, Hastings, Monte Alto, Holland and Paynel, and Henry de Beaumont, brother of the queen's candidate. Several candidates were proposed, amongst them Thomas Charlton by the king, John Walwayn by the Earl of Hereford and John de Kynardesley by the Earl of Lancaster, and threats were made about what would happen if the monks made the wrong choice: 'the heads of those who erred would be chopped off, if a monk were elected'.[107] Nevertheless, the monks elected Henry of Stamford, prior of Finchale;[108] his election was quashed and Louis de Beaumont, a kinsman of the queen, was provided.[109] When Beaumont came to England to be consecrated, his party (which included two cardinals) was attacked on the road. The bishop and his brother were taken into captivity and held until ransomed. The motivations

---

103 *The Registers of John de Sandale and Rigaud de Asserio, Bishops of Winchester (A.D. 1316-1323)*, ed. F. J. Baignent (London, 1897), p. xxxii.

104 *Concilia*, II, pp. 539-44; Haines, 'Meopham', p. 559.

105 *Script. Tres*, p. 98.

106 Smith, *Episcopal Appointments*, p. 32.

107 *Script. Tres*, p. 98.

108 Ibid.; *Fasti 1300-1541*, VI, p. 107, citing Durham Cathedral Muniments, Locelli 6 No. 4.

109 *CPL*, II, p. 136.

behind this outrage are obscure, but any of the disappointed parties would have had an obvious reason to organize such an attack on the new bishop.[110]

Not all noble interventions were characterized by attempts at intimidation; nor were all noble efforts focused on the cathedral chapter. Just as in previous reigns, prominent noblemen used their connections to the crown in order to further the ecclesiastical careers of their kinsmen. Simon de Montacute's rise to the episcopate (he was the royal candidate for Winchester in 1333, was provided to Worcester in the same year and translated to Ely in 1337) was largely attributable to his brother William's position as earl of Salisbury and boon companion of the young Edward III.[111]

Like the king, aristocrats quickly adjusted to the new ways and began to petition the pope in order to secure the provision of their preferred candidates. Thomas of Lancaster wrote to John XXII in favour of Thomas Cobham, who was provided to Worcester in 1317; the pope was, however, at pains to point out that he had not received the petition until after the provision had been made.[112] If a would-be bishop could not be present at the papal curia in person, the next best thing was to have a representative there, and the value of such representation was clearly demonstrated by the 1320 Lincoln vacancy. In March 1320, an embassy left England for Avignon; amongst its members was Bartholomew Badlesmere.[113] During the middle years of the reign, Badlesmere was one of Edward II's most trusted councillors,[114] powerful enough to persuade the king to find a bishopric for his nephew, Henry Burghersh. The latter had already been the royal candidate for Winchester in 1319, and in 1320 his uncle presumably persuaded the king that Burghersh would be a good choice for Lincoln. According to the *Vita Edwardi Secundi*:

> So at Bartholomew's instigation the king of England was persuaded on the young man's behalf to humbly entreat the lord pope to see fit to promote him to the said episcopal see. Both the king of France and Edmund, the king of England's brother, requested it, and everyone praised the youth, repeatedly recommending his person to the lord pope.[115]

---

110 The incident is discussed in detail by Michael Prestwich, 'Gilbert de Middleton and the Attack on the Cardinals' in Timothy Reuter (ed.), *Warriors and Churchmen in the High Middle Ages: Essays Presented to Karl Leyser* (London, 1992), pp. 179-94.

111 Roy Haines, 'Simon de Montacute, Bishop of William, Earl of Salisbury, Bishop of Worcester (1333-37), of Ely (1337-45)' in Nigel Saul (ed.) *Fourteenth-Century England I* (Woodbridge, 2000), pp. 37-71.

112 *CPL*, II, p. 441.

113 *Vita Edwardi*, p. 179.

114 John Maddicott, 'Batholomew Badlesmere', *ODNB*.

115 *Vita Edwardi*, pp. 178-9.

Adam Murimuth did not doubt that Lord Badlesmere had used his visit to the curia to promote his nephew's career. The chronicler states that the nobleman was sent to Avignon as a royal nuncio for some difficult negotiations, and that he spent fifteen thousand pounds of the king's money there, but returned 'having procured nothing useful to the king, but only the promotion of the said Lord Henry'.[116]

During the reign of Henry III, foreign rulers had occasionally intervened in electoral disputes, and this trend continued during the early fourteenth century. The king and queen of France (the brother and sister-in-law of Queen Isabella) petitioned the pope on behalf of both Louis de Beaumont[117] and Henry Burghersh.[118] It would be unsurprising if the rise of provision had led to the English crown making greater use of its European contacts, persuading continental counterparts to petition the pope on behalf of royal candidates. Yet whilst the rise of provision meant that more and more episcopal appointments had a transnational dimension, there does not seem to have been a resultant increase in such petitions. In this respect at least, the filling of episcopal vacancies remained an almost entirely English affair.

Whilst the queen and nobility certainly played an enhanced role in the appointment processes of the fourteenth century and engaged with the procedural developments in order to enhance the effectiveness of their interventions, it is difficult to link this change to the rise of provision. Rather, the difference would seem to be in the changing nature of English kingship. For the greater part of Henry III's reign (with the exception of the minority and the years of reform and rebellion) there had been little doubt that the primary political force in England was the king. Consequently, the crown had also been the primary secular influence over elections. During the first half of the fourteenth century, during the reign of Edward II and the early years of Edward III, the weakness of the crown led to a rise in factional politics and to periods of outright political crisis. It was this royal weakness that allowed a broader range of secular influences to be brought to bear on episcopal appointments during the early decades of the fourteenth century; that this shift coincided with the rise of papal provision was little more than coincidence.

Contacts with Avignon: Diplomatic Personnel

Since Anglo-Saxon times, English kings had been in regular contact with the pope. During the thirteenth and fourteenth centuries, the regularity of this

116 *Murimuth*, p. 31.

117 *CPL*, II, p. 414.

118 *Vita Edwardi*, pp. 178-9.

contact increased substantially, and proctors played an increasingly important role in the appointment process. Kings of England needed to convey their wishes on the subject of episcopal appointments to the Holy See, but they did not present their requests in person.[119] Instead, they either set out their case in writing[120] or, like the vast majority of petitioners from the thirteenth century onwards, appointed proctors (a proctor being 'an individual formally empowered, within certain limits, to transact business on behalf of another').[121] Proctors represented their clients in the various curial departments and courts; their activities and responsibilities therefore varied widely, but their ultimate goal was the same: to ensure that their client's petition was granted.[122]

Many of the proctors employed by the English crown were high-status Englishmen: aristocrats and prominent royal clerks.[123] Such men were sent to Avignon for the specific purpose of doing the king's business – of which electoral affairs composed a substantial part. In March 1320, for example, a delegation left England, 'going on the lord king's business to the court of Rome'.[124] Amongst its members were the king's half-brother Edmund of Woodstock, two of Edward's most trusted advisors, the elder Hugh Despenser and Bartholomew Badlesmere, and Adam Orleton, bishop of Hereford.[125] Officially, their aim was to secure the see of Lincoln for Henry Burghersh, Badlesmere's nephew; unofficially, they were also there to persuade John XXII to release Edward II from his oath to uphold the ordinances.[126] Orleton's participation in this affair is representative of a broader pattern: bishops were frequent participants in diplomatic service in general, and in missions to the curia in particular. Orleton was sent to the curia

119 Edward I met Gregory X at Orvieto in February 1273; the next English king to hold a personal meeting with a pope was Edward VII, in 1903. Plöger, *Avignon Popes*, p. 65.

120 From 1306 to 1358, correspondence sent by the king to the pope and cardinals was enrolled on the Roman rolls (TNA, C70); many of these documents are printed in *Foedera*. See Barbara Bombi, 'Petitioning between England and Avignon in the First Half of the Fourteenth Century' in Anthony Musson, Mark Ormrod and Gwilym Dodd (eds), *Medieval Petitions: Grace and Grievance* (York, 2009), pp. 64-81, at pp. 70-73.

121 Patrick Zutshi, 'Proctors Acting for English Petitioners in the Chancery of the Avignon Popes (1305-1378)', *JEH*, 35 (1984), pp. 15-29, at p. 15.

122 Donald Queller, 'Thirteenth-Century Diplomatic Envoys: *Nuncios* and *Procuratores*', *Speculum*, 35 (1960), pp. 196-213; Bernard Guillemain, *La Cour Pontificale d'Avignon (1309-1376): Etude d'une Société* (Paris, 1992), pp. 567-72; Zutshi, 'Proctors', pp. 15-29; Barbara Bombi, 'Andrea Sapiti: His Origins, and His Register as a Curial Proctor', *EHR*, 123 (2008), pp. 132-48, at p. 138.

123 Plöger, *Avignon Popes*, pp. 65-123.

124 *Vita Edwardi*, pp. 178-9.

125 Ibid.; *Foedera*, II.i, p. 418.

126 The ordinances were a set of forty-one clauses imposed on the king by a group of baronial reformers in 1311; Edward was, for example, forbidden to leave the kingdom or to go to war without baronial consent. For the text, see *English Historical Documents Vol. 3, 1189-1327*, ed. H. Rothwell (London, 1975), pp. 529-39.

on royal business on several other occasions, the first in 1307 (when he may well have been involved in promoting the election of Walter Reynolds to Worcester) and the last in 1333 (when he left Avignon only weeks before his translation to Winchester).[127] Such men influenced elections both in their official capacity, by promoting the king's wishes, and also in a personal capacity, displaying their abilities to the pope or informing him of the merits of their friends and relatives.

Men such as the members of the 1320 delegation undoubtedly became familiar with the papal curia and its ways, but they were generalists, engaging in diplomacy across Europe, and often lacking in any formal qualification for the role. By the early fourteenth century, the king also had access to more expert representatives, specializing in law and the complexities of papal bureaucracy, and permanently (or at least semi-permanently) resident at the curia.[128] During the early years of his reign, Edward II simultaneously employed three such representatives: Raymond Subirani (a professor of canon law from Toulouse), Adam Murimuth, an English civil lawyer, and Andrea Sapiti, a Florentine notary public. These men dealt with a wide range of royal business and also worked on behalf of other clients; Subirani's services, for example, were also engaged by Walter Reynolds, Hugh Despenser the younger, Richard of Bury (a future bishop of Durham), Philip IV of France and the Italian poet Francesco Petrarch.[129]

The role played by such men in the bishop-making process is illuminated by the survival of a register of Andrea Sapiti.[130] Sapiti handled the affairs of both Edward II and Edward III,[131] but the surviving register covers only the final years of his career, from 1330 until his death in 1338. Amongst the documents copied into the register are papal letters relating to the provision of Richard de Bury as bishop of Durham (1333)[132] and the conferring of the pallium of John Stratford, following his translation to Canterbury (1334).[133] The selection of miscellanea copied into the register, which was presumably chosen for its relevance to Sapiti's business, includes a model of the promise to pay common services which any bishop provided by the pope was obliged to make[134] and, intriguingly, King John's Freedom of Election charter.[135] The balance of the material included in the register suggests that English elections did not form the bulk of Sapiti's business, but he was clearly involved not only in presenting the king's petitions,

---

127 Haines, *Career of Adam Orleton*, pp. 8-40.

128 Bombi, 'Petitioning', p. 75; Zutshi, 'Proctors', pp. 15-29; Plöger, *Avignon Popes*, pp. 83-8.

129 Bombi, 'Petitioning', pp. 75-82.

130 *Il Registro di Andrea Sapiti, Procuratore alla Curia Avignonese*, ed. B. Bombi (Rome, 2007).

131 For his life and career, see *Reg. Sapiti*, pp. 15-48; Bombi, 'Sapiti', pp. 132-46.

132 *Reg. Sapiti*, pp. 148-9, 267-8, 307-10.

133 Ibid., pp. 188-90, 218-19.

134 Ibid., pp. 78-9.

135 Ibid., pp. 348-51.

but also in assisting new English bishops through the later stages of the appointment process.

Royal proctors were not the most prominent participants in the appointment process; they rarely attracted comment in the narrative sources, and it is difficult to study their activities in non-general terms, for there is very little surviving material relating to their handling of English elections. The evidence for the activities of non-royal proctors is even sparser. Given, however, that proctors of various kinds were actively engaging with the personnel and institutions of the papal curia, it is clear that they provided a crucial link between the key participants in the appointment process. By the early fourteenth century, their role had been developing for some time. With the rise of provision, as the focus shifted from cathedral chapter to the papal curia, and the king could no longer rely on personal discussions with the electors to ensure the success of his candidates, their involvement became both less sporadic and more important.

The Rise of Provision and the Wider Community

The chronicle evidence reflects the hostility of the wider English clergy to the provisions system. The Durham chronicler's attack on papal provision has already been noted above; his fears about the new system of appointment were echoed by many of his contemporaries. Adam Murimuth (a diplomat who spent several years at the papal curia)[136] was a particularly vociferous critic, writing of Clement V that:

> The same Clement made reservations of bishoprics, and particularly in the kingdoms of France and England, in order that he might extort private and common service. And he reserved to the collation of the apostolic see all benefices vacant by his promotions and by the death of his nuncios and chaplains dying anywhere.[137]

The same chronicler claimed that Clement VI overturned the election of John Trilleck (Hereford, 1344) and provided him purely out of avarice, so that he could misappropriate more English gold.[138] Other chroniclers made accusations of simony against the pope, particularly in relation to high profile provisions such as that of Walter Reynolds to Canterbury. On that occasion, Robert of Reading claimed that the archbishopric was purchased 'by means of a large amount of

---

[136] Charles Kingsford and Wendy Childs, 'Adam Murimuth', *ODNB*.

[137] *Murimuth*, p. 174. Murimuth was referring to the constitution *Etsi in temporalium*, issued a week after Clement V was elected pope.

[138] Ibid., p. 158.

gold and silver',[139] a charge echoed by the author of the *Vita Edwardi Secundi*;[140] the chronicler of the Yorkshire house of Meaux specified 32,000 marks as the sum paid.[141] The veracity of these claims is unproven, but the chroniclers clearly feared that the rise of provision would give secular powers, who could afford to pay such sums, even greater control over ecclesiastical appointments, to the detriment of the church.

English sermons on the subject of episcopal appointments seem to have been an extremely rare phenomenon, at least during the thirteenth and early fourteenth centuries, but there was one intriguing example, the tenor of which is similarly hostile to the transition and critical of the king's attitude to it. It was given by Henry de Hertley, chancellor of Oxford University, in 1313, in the wake of the translation of Walter Reynolds to Canterbury. Apparently drawing heavily on the Burton Annalist's account of the 1211 confrontation between King John and the legatine delegation, it references the legend of St Wulfstan's staff, used by John to defend his right to control episcopal appointments.[142]

The *Articuli Cleri* (1315)[143] suggest the intriguing possibility that the English Church still saw the English crown as the greatest threat to electoral freedom. Clause 14 was first presented to the king in 1309 and was restated in 1316; it asked that elections to ecclesiastical offices should be free. The royal response was a straightforward pledge that elections would be held freely.[144] The ecclesiastical perspective may have shifted in the following two decades, as provision became more prevalent; in 1316, it was probably still unclear that the days of electoral freedom were numbered. Alternatively, it is possible that the church hoped that increased papal participation in episcopal appointments would protect them from royal intervention and produce an episcopate composed of more churchmen and fewer *curiales*. Given that some of those elected subsequently had their appointments confirmed by provision, chapters may have believed that

139 *Flores Hist.*, III, pp. 155-6.

140 *Vita Edwardi*, p. 79.

141 *Chronica monasterii de Melsa*, ed. E. A. Bond (3 vols, RS, 1866-68), II, p. 329.

142 The sermon, which apparently survives in an unidentified Lambeth manuscript, was mentioned by Henry Wharton in a footnote to his *Anglia Sacra*, II, pp. 523-4. For the 1211 Burton account, see *AM*, I, p. 211. On the legend, see Emma Mason, 'St Wulfstan's Staff: A Legend and its Uses', *Medium Aevum*, 53 (1984), pp. 157-79.

143 The *Articuli Cleri* consisted of the clerical complaints presented at the Lincoln Parliament of 1315 and the replies to these complaints provided by the king. The backdrop was the refusal of the clergy to make the king a grant of taxation until their grievances had been satisfactorily addressed. The complaints and responses were drawn up in this form in the following year; the tax had been granted at the end of 1315, even though only some of the issues raised had been satisfactorily dealt with. Phillips, *Edward II*, pp. 268-9.

144 *Historical Papers and Letters from the Northern Registers*, p. 258. On the *Articuli Cleri*, see Jeffrey Denton, 'The Making of the "Articuli Cleri" of 1316', *EHR*, 101 (1986), pp. 564-595, especially pp. 583-4.

the rise of provision (a procedure that, at least in theory, effectively bypassed the king) would lead to more internal candidates (that is, monks and canons) being appointed to the episcopate. If so, they were to be disappointed. Certain chapters may also have decided that it was preferable for royal proctors to focus their efforts on the papal curia, if this would lead to a decrease in the scale of the pressure placed on chapters by royal and aristocratic parties seeking to ensure the election of their candidates. If the possibility of papal provision deflected some of this hostile attention away from vulnerable cathedral chapters, it would be unsurprising if they welcomed this consequence of the transition process.

If the evidence for clerical opposition to provision is somewhat sparse, lay objections are easier to trace. Much of the hostility was focused on the provision of foreign candidates to lesser benefices, access to which had previously been determined by social networks and the bonds of lordship. Such opposition dated back to the thirteenth century, when popular feeling against foreign provisees to English livings ran high. In 1231-32, for example, a Yorkshire knight named Robert Tweng took it upon himself to attack Italians on the roads and to plunder the barns of non-resident Italian clergy.[145] In 1241 the crown ordered an inquiry into the numbers of English benefices held by 'Roman clerks'.[146] Whilst antipathy to foreign clerics remained significant into the fourteenth century,[147] it was only in the 1340s that lay concerns about papal provision became a significant force. In 1343 the commons and temporal lords protested against alien benefice holders and complained to the pope about the same. In 1344 an ordinance forbidding the introduction of papal bulls of provision into the realm was passed – although the king refused to convert this into a statute and assured the pope that rumours of anti-papal legislation were untrue.[148] Clement VI responded by promising that 'as the universal pastor of all churches, he does not intend to make such provisions and reservations unless he believes them to be expedient for the churches themselves'. Despite his conciliatory tone, he was disturbed by the anti-papal activities taking place in England: the making of ordinances by royal councillors 'against the liberties of the church', the issuing of edicts 'in derogation of ecclesiastical liberty' and the 'seizure and imprisonment of many ecclesiastics'.[149]

---

145 Hugh MacKenzie, 'The Anti-Foreign Movement in England in 1231-2' in Charles Taylor (ed.), *Anniversary Essays in Mediaeval History by Students of Charles Homer Haskins* (Boston, 1929), pp. 183-203.

146 Lawrence, 'Thirteenth Century', p. 148.

147 As the statute of Carlisle, which forbade foreign clerics to take money out of the realm, demonstrated. *The Parliament Rolls of Medieval England, 1275-1504*, ed. C. Given-Wilson (16 vols, Woodbridge, 2005), II, pp. 459-61.

148 Heath, *Church and Realm*, p. 129.

149 *CPL*, III, p. 9.

In 1347 the commons were again complaining, this time because the ordinance was not being enforced, but only in 1351 was the Statute of Provisors passed.[150] Throughout the fourteenth century, there was a lack of specific lay opposition to episcopal provision, which can be attributed to two main factors. Firstly, much of the hostility to provision was primarily xenophobic; despite the fears of some chroniclers, only two of the English bishops of the fourteenth century were foreign born.[151] Secondly, influence over episcopal elections was essentially confined to the very upper echelons of lay society, and the queen and aristocrats, like the king, were able to petition the pope with some degree of success.[152] The growing numbers of papal provisions to lesser benefices, including parish churches, had more immediate impact and provoked a much stronger response.

It is clear that the rise of provision to the episcopate did not cause opposition on a scale which such a major change might be expected to provoke. In part this was because the process was gradual. It crept up on England and became a reality before it was even recognized as such, at least in some quarters. More significant, however, is the fact that dependence on the papacy was normal for medieval Englishmen; they expected and wanted the papacy to be part of their lives. As early as the twelfth century, Southern argued, 'there was no need for popes to seek for business – they were overwhelmed by it',[153] and the tendency of the English to seek papal judgements on a wide range of issues only increased during the course of the thirteenth century.[154] As discussed above, in the century preceding the rise of provision, kings, chapters and archbishops had sought papal resolution of electoral disputes; furthermore, it was a well-established principle that only the pope could translate bishops.[155] It is crucial to recognize that papal intervention in elections was far from being a fourteenth-century innovation. Consequently, the transition from election to provision may not have seemed as dramatic from a fourteenth-century perspective as it seems to modern eyes with the benefit of hindsight.

It is also questionable how far medieval understandings of papal power would have allowed for large-scale opposition to provisions. Each of the popes involved in this transition had inherited the primacy of St Peter; the pope was the ultimate

---

150 Heath, *Church and Realm*, p. 129; Cecily Davies, 'The Statute of Provisors of 1351', *History*, 38 (1953), pp. 116-33.

151 Louis de Beaumont (Durham, 1317) and Rigaud de Asserio (Winchester, 1319).

152 Louis de Beaumont was elected to Durham at the request of Queen Isabella; Simon Montacute owed his provisions in part to his brother, Lord Montacute; and Henry Burghersh's uncle secured the bishopric of Lincoln for his young nephew. *Script. Tres*, pp. 98-100; Haines, 'Simon de Montacute', pp. 37-72.

153 Southern, *Western Society*, p. 151.

154 Lawrence, 'Thirteenth Century', pp. 141-5.

155 Pennington, *Pope and Bishops*, pp. 85-100.

sovereign, with no earthly superior. His power was therefore unlimited, at least in theory. He possessed the 'plenitude of power', and this power was unchecked by the aristocratic and feudal bodies that limited that of lay monarchs.[156] Every bishop derived his power from the pope, without whom he could not exist; the relationship between the pope and the bishops was compared to that of the sun alongside the moon and stars.[157] Such ideas did not preclude the possibility of protests against papal provision or questioning of this policy; one thinks of Robert Grosseteste who, refusing to grant a canonry to a nephew of Pope Innocent IV, declared 'as an obedient son, I do not obey, I contradict, I rebel'.[158] Nevertheless, the atmosphere of this era was one in which both the clergy and the laity were conditioned not to challenge the papacy.

The Consequences of the Rise of Provision

The causes of and reactions to this change having been considered, it is now necessary to consider the effects of the transition. One might expect that increased papal control over episcopal appointments would change the character of the episcopate.[159] Figure 5.1 illustrates the composition of the English episcopate during the years 1258 (at the end of Henry III's personal rule and before provision became commonplace), 1272 (at the accession of Edward I), 1307 (at the accession of Edward II), 1327 (at the accession of Edward III) and 1344 (the end of the period under consideration). These years have been chosen to provide a cross-section of the episcopate at crucial stages on the road to papal provision. The bishops are categorized according to their primary career prior to their election/provision; hence they are described as either papal servants, members of the diocesan clergy, members of the religious orders (monastic or mendicant) or curial bishops (that is, royal servants). Inevitably many of the bishops could be assigned to multiple categories, for example in the case of the many royal servants who also held numerous benefices; such bishops have been placed in the category with which they were most strongly identified, so a full-time royal administrator has been described as curial, however many benefices he held.

---

156 Barraclough, *Papacy*, pp. 120-23; Stephen Ozment, *The Age of Reform, 1250-1550* (London, 1980), pp. 135-55.

157 Lawrence, 'Thirteenth Century', pp. 119-20.

158 Ibid., p. 119.

159 Unless otherwise stated, the material in this section is drawn from the *Oxford Dictionary of National Biography*; *Fasti Ecclesiae Anglicanae*; Alfred Emden, *A Biographical Register of the University of Oxford to 1500* (3 vols, Oxford, 1957-59); and Alfred Emden, *A Biographical Register of the University of Cambridge to 1500* (Cambridge, 1963).

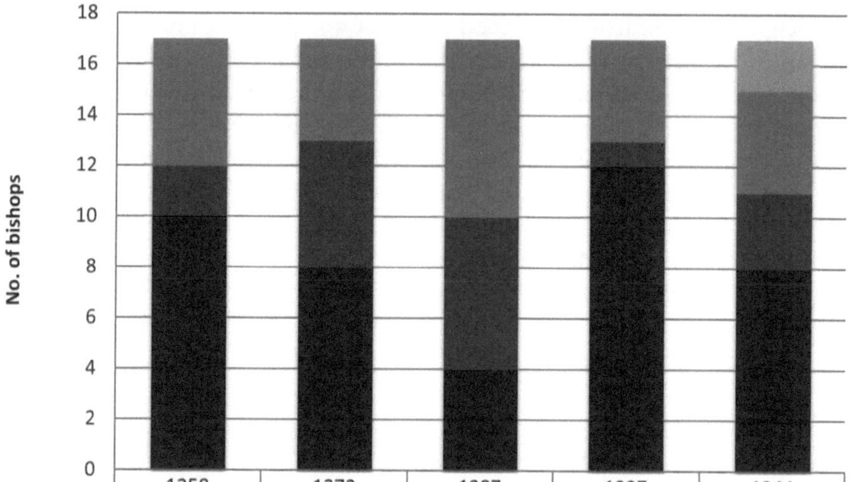

	1258	1272	1307	1327	1344
Papal	0	0	0	0	2
Diocesan	5	4	7	4	4
Regular	2	5	6	1	3
Curial	10	8	4	12	8

Figure 5.1 Career backgrounds of English bishops, 1258-1344

Curial bishops formed the largest single group in the episcopate at every stage, with the exception of 1307, at the end of Edward I's reign. Between 1258 and 1307 there had been a steady decline in the number of former royal curiales on the bishops' bench; the introduction of provision seems to have reversed this trend, at least temporarily, since by 1327 two-thirds of the bishops were former (or, indeed, current) royal servants. The rise of provision also halted the growth of the clerical (secular and monastic) groups, which had reached a peak under Edward I; career clerics, and especially monks, had usually been promoted as a result of free elections, and the increasing rarity of such processes was to their detriment. The balance between the curial and ecclesiastical groups became more equal during the early years of the reign of Edward III, mainly due to a brief run of free elections in the late 1330s and very early 1340s, but this period also saw the provision of two papal servants.[160]

Inevitably, this snapshot-based analysis conceals some of the more subtle changes in the composition of the episcopate. Increasingly, the curial members

[160] The pope at this time was Benedict XII (1334-42). His attitude to ecclesiastical appointments needs further study, but as a theologically trained Cistercian, he was a reforming pope in a very different mould to either his processor (John XXII) or successor (Clement VI, 1342-52). It is perhaps in his character that the explanation for this vaguely anomalous phase is to be found. Mollat, *Popes*, pp. 26-36.

of the episcopate were not administrators, as had been usual in the thirteenth century, but diplomats, whose careers had included long periods spent at the papal curia. Indeed, not all of those bishops who had previously been in royal service owed their promotion to the king. Many fourteenth-century bishops, amongst them Adam Orleton and John Stratford, owed their first bishopric to their personal presence at the curia when the see fell vacant; both were provided despite royal opposition.[161] It became increasingly possible for would-be bishops to bypass the crown and focus their quest for patronage directly on the pope. Significantly, this did not mean that the English were increasingly subject to foreign bishops, a change which would almost certainly have provoked strong protest from king and subjects; indeed, there were only two such appointments in the whole of the fourteenth century,[162] and even the handful of papal servants who received English bishoprics, such as John Grandisson (Exeter, 1327) and William Bateman (Norwich, 1344), were English born.[163]

In what other ways did the rise of provision impact on the composition of the English episcopate? The papacy clearly was responsible for the introduction of the mendicant orders into the English episcopate: although only very few English bishops of this period were friars, all of these were papal providees.[164] More generally, the standard of academic education amongst the episcopate seems to have improved. Roy Martin Haines has calculated that at least 50 per cent of the bishops promoted between 1307 and 1330 were graduates; just over 30 per cent held at least one doctorate, the majority of these in civil or canon law. Only a handful of the bishops were theologians.[165] How far this change can be attributed to the rise of provision is, however, questionable; the shift towards graduate bishops was part of a long-term process which became inevitable with the rise of the universities. But the predominance of lawyers might be linked to John XXII's own legal background.[166]

Two other intriguing patterns emerge when the composition of the episcopate during these years is considered. The average age at appointment to a bishopric seems to have dropped slightly as provision became dominant (see Figure 5.2); although the majority of the bishops appointed between 1327 and 1344 were in their forties or fifties, as had been the case in the previous three reigns, the proportion of vacancies filled by men in their thirties almost doubled, to around

---

161 Haines, *Career of Adam Orleton*, p. 17; Haines, *Archbishop John Stratford*, pp. 136-49.

162 Louis de Beaumont (Durham, 1317) and Rigaud de Asserio (Winchester, 1319).

163 On papal servants in the episcopate of Edward III, see Roger Highfield, 'The English Hierarchy in the Reign of Edward III', *TRHS*, 5th series, 6 (1956), pp. 115-38, at pp. 121-2.

164 They were Robert Kilwardby, archbishop of Canterbury 1272-79 and a former provincial of the Dominican order; John Pecham, his successor at Canterbury (1279-92), the prior of the Franciscan province of England; and William Gainsborough, bishop of Worcester, 1302-7, another Franciscan.

165 Haines, 'Episcopate', p. 671.

166 John Kelly, *The Oxford Dictionary of Popes* (Oxford, 1986), p. 214.

a quarter. The reasons for, and significance of, this shift are hard to pin down, but it might plausibly be linked to the young king's use of the provision process to promote his peers. Alternatively, or perhaps additionally, the rise of university education may have been important, with learned men being considered fit for episcopal office at a younger age than their less well-educated predecessors.

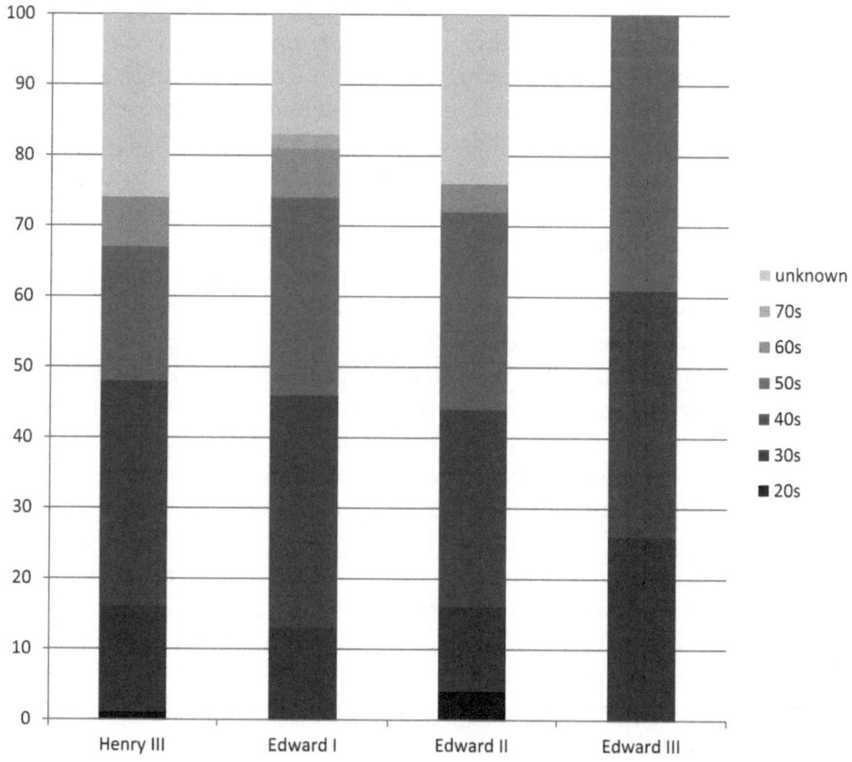

Figure 5.2 Age of English bishops at appointment, 1214-1344

The numbers of locally born bishops fell during the age of provision, as Figure 5.3 illustrates. Bishops born in the diocese to which they were appointed were always in the minority, consistently forming less than a third of the episcopate, but during the first half of the fourteenth century they became even rarer; 29 per cent of Edward I's bishops were born in the diocese to which they were later elevated, compared to only 14 per cent of those appointed between 1327 and 1344. Such a shift was surely inevitable with the rise of provision, for it was cathedral chapters who had favoured local men. The scarcity of foreign bishops shows that both king and pope recognized the importance of appointing

English men to English bishoprics, but they apparently did not consider regional ties to be significant.

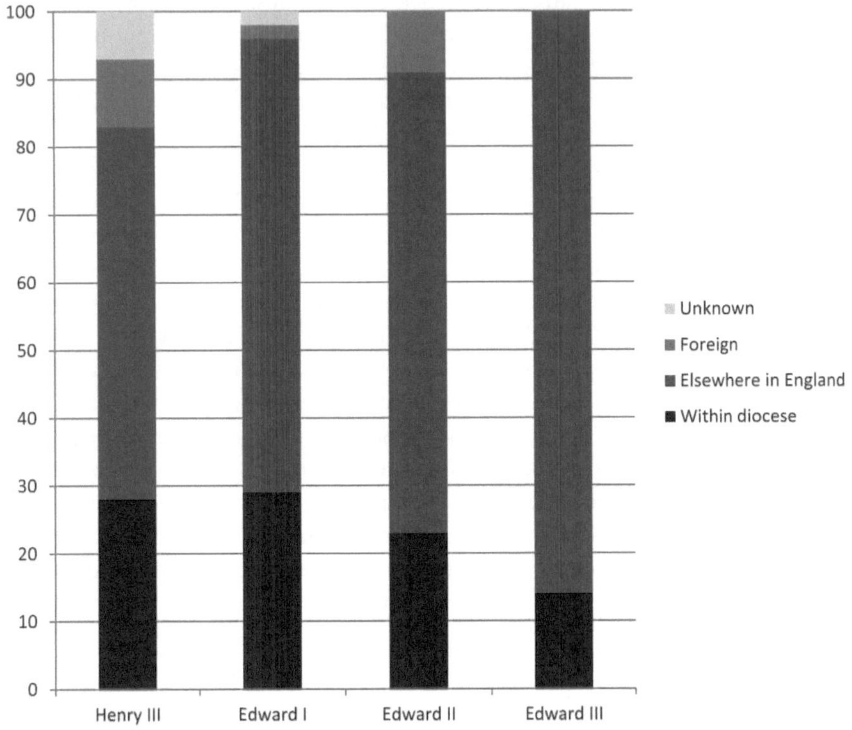

Figure 5.3 Birthplaces of English bishops, 1214-1344

It is striking that throughout the period under consideration episcopal dynasties were a common phenomenon. Thanks to the rise of clerical celibacy, father and son pairs were a rarity; the only certain example is to be found at the very beginning of the thirteenth century when Herbert and Richard Poore, sons of Richard of Ilchester, bishop of Winchester[167] were both promoted to the episcopate, and even they were born before their father was promoted to the episcopate. Other relationships were far more common: brothers, uncles and nephews, and kinsmen.[168] Most impressively, the kinship network headed by

167 *AM*, II, p. 65.

168 Medieval definitions of kinship were far broader than modern ones, with canon law recognizing four degrees of consanguinity, and affinity and civil law (which counted them differently) six. See Samantha Worby, 'The Influence of the Learned Laws on Common Law Kinship: An Introduction' in Helle Vogt and Mia Münster-Swendsen (eds), *Law and Learning in the Middle Ages:*

John de Gray, bishop of Norwich (1200-1214) produced no fewer than seven further bishops and one two-times bishop-elect. The Bek family produced four bishops over two generations, and the Gravesend, Stratford and Orleton-Trilleck families three. Still more families included two bishops, such as the Cantilupes (Walter of Worcester and his nephew, St Thomas of Hereford). The frequency with which family networks appear in the episcopate is hard to explain and there is no direct evidence of bishops directly intervening to secure bishoprics for their relatives, either before or after provision became commonplace. It was, however, common for bishops to raise younger kinsmen in their households, and to provide them with their first benefices, thus giving them a promising start to an ecclesiastical career. It is also plausible that both chapters and popes were inclined to take the successes of one bishop as a sign that another from the same family would be a good choice. It seems that fourteenth-century popes were unconcerned by potential nepotism within the English episcopate – which is perhaps unsurprising, given their tendency to promote their own relatives.[169]

If, however, the composition of the episcopate was in many respects unaltered by the rise of provision, there was one substantial change that must be almost entirely attributed to this procedural shift. The translation of a bishop from one see to another could only be performed by the pope, and an electoral body that wanted another diocese's bishop for their own had to postulate him for papal approval. Consequently, whilst election dominated, translations were extremely rare. Only four bishops were successfully translated during the first half of the thirteenth century, as illustrated in Table 5.1. The first pair of translations was carried out in exceptional circumstances, when England was subject to legatine control; the second pair resulted from two of the most dramatic electoral disputes of Henry III's reign. Translation was recognized as a possibility, but it remained a rarity.

Table 5.1 Translations between English dioceses, 1200-1249

Bishop	**From**	**To**	**Year**
Walter de Gray	Worcester	York	1215
Richard Poore	Chichester	Salisbury	1227
Richard Poore	Salisbury	Durham	1228
William Raleigh	Norwich	Winchester	1243

Proceedings of the Second Carlsberg Academy Conference on Medieval Legal History 2005 (Copenhagen, 2006), pp. 207-222.

169 Menache, *Clement*, pp. 48-52; Mollat, *Popes*, pp. 24-5; Wood, *Clement VI*, pp. 98-9, 204. Of the early fourteenth-century popes, only Benedict XII took a stand against nepotism; none of his relatives was made a cardinal and his nephew was warned that 'in our master natural affections have no voice' (Mollat, *Popes*, p. 29).

Despite the increased frequency of provisions, the rate of translation fell during the second half of the thirteenth century, as shown in Table 5.2. Both of these translations were reactive papal provisions, made in order to conclude disputed elections. In the second case, the vacancy created at Norwich was filled by the provision of the former bishop-elect of Ely, John Salmon.

Table 5.2 Translations between English dioceses, 1250-1299

Bishop	From	To	Year
Walter Giffard	Bath	York	1266
Ralph Walpole	Norwich	Ely	1299

In the early decades of the fourteenth century translations remained extremely rare, but by the 1330s the rise of translation had begun in earnest: three of the five translations made between 1300 and 1344 took place in that decade (Table 5.3).

Table 5.3 Translations between English dioceses, 1300-1344

Bishop	From	To	Year
Walter Reynolds	Worcester	Canterbury	1313
Adam Orleton	Hereford	Worcester	1327
John Stratford	Winchester	Canterbury	1333
Adam Orleton	Worcester	Winchester	1333
Simon Montacute	Worcester	Ely	1337

For the papacy, translation was a means to ensure that suitable bishops were provided to the most prestigious sees; a prelate could be trialled in a relatively low-key diocese and translated to a more powerful one only if and when he had proved his worth.[170] It also allowed the pope to use episcopal vacancies as a form of patronage; both Adam Orleton and John Stratford were more closely aligned with the papacy than the crown, and their translations should perhaps be seen as a reward for their loyalty. Furthermore, widespread acceptance that only the pope could translate may have meant that in the early stages of the transition

170 Translation down the episcopal hierarchy was virtually unheard of, although a very small number of bishops were thus demoted amidst the political chaos of the final years of Richard II's reign. Robert Swanson, *Church and Society in Late Medieval England* (Oxford, 1989), p. 10.

provisions were more easily accepted if they involved the movement of a bishop from one see to another.

From a royal perspective, translation offered hope for the further promotion of royal favourites who had initially been provided to one of the less desirable sees. The crown had long seen the potential of translation, but early attempts to have favourites translated to wealthier sees had usually been thwarted. Henry III's attempts to procure wealthier sees for Ralph Neville and Peter Aigueblanche, and Edward I's to secure the translation of Robert Burnell were all doomed to failure.

The transition to papal provision thus encouraged the rise of the episcopal careerist, initially appointed to one of the poorer English sees or to a Welsh bishopric, before being translated (in some cases twice) to a wealthier, more prestigious see. Without their knowledge, men like Adam Orleton and John Stratford were episcopal pioneers, providing an early blueprint for their late medieval successors. Whether the rise of translation benefitted the church as a whole or just the episcopate is something of a moot point but, for good or for bad, the rise of provision ushered in a new phase in the history of the English episcopate.[171]

***

Given the great energies that had been expended on the defence of electoral freedom during the course of the thirteenth century, one might expect that the fourteenth century would be characterized by a groundswell of protest against an innovation that threatened to destroy one of the cornerstones of ecclesiastical liberty. Yet if the English response to the rise of papal provision was rather muted, the reason is likely to be found in the fact that in practice the change was less dramatic than it appears in theory. Contemporaries, who lived through the transition rather than considering it in hindsight, reacted to the transition as they experienced it rather than as an abstract concept. Unlike the historian, they did not know what the eventual outcome would be; consequently, they responded to a series of piecemeal events, rather than a process with inevitable consequences.[172]

---

[171] For the significance of translation in late medieval England, see Joel Rosenthal, 'Even Money That Your Bishop Has Come And Gone: Episcopal Appointments and Translations in Fourteenth- and Fifteenth-Century England' in Linda Mitchell, Katherine French and Donald Biggs (eds), *The Ties That Bind: Essays in Medieval British History in Honour of Barbara Hanawalt* (Farnham, 2011), pp. 71-86, and for the impact of translation on a single diocese, Joel Rosenthal, 'The Bishops of Worcester in the Fourteenth and Fifteenth Centuries: Easy Come, Easy Go', *Midland History*, 37 (2012), pp. 17-44.

[172] For the dangers of projecting a sense of inevitability back into history, with particular reference to the medieval church, see Gary Macy, 'Was there a "The Church" in the Middle Ages?'

In practical terms, the changes were considerable but not overwhelming. Popes had always had the ability to overrule the other participants in the appointment process and although they had never before used this power so consistently, they did so in a way that permitted the compromises that had characterized thirteenth-century episcopal elections to continue. Whilst the mechanisms of episcopal appointment were substantially altered, the motivations of the parties involved changed considerably less. Chapters continued to hope for the promotion of one of their own, but with diminishing levels of success, largely due to the fact that papal criteria for episcopal suitability were not dissimilar to those of the crown. A vocal defender of ecclesiastical liberties, a Becket or a Pecham, was as troublesome to the papacy as he was to the king, whilst simple monks and canons generally lived their lives below the radar of princes secular and ecclesiastical. Not all popes were as accommodating of royal wishes as Clement VI, who, as already noted, reputedly declared that if the king of England asked for an ass to be made bishop, he would grant his request,[173] but royal and papal interests were largely compatible. Consequently, changes to the composition and quality of the English episcopate were limited, and the late medieval episcopal bench, 'whilst never completely homogenous, mostly reflected the tastes and policies of the king'.[174] The golden age of electoral freedom was over.

in Robert Swanson (ed.), *Unity and Diversity in the Church*, Studies in Church History, 32 (Oxford, 1996), pp. 107-16, especially pp. 113-14.

[173] *Chronicon Angliae*, p. 20.

[174] Heath, *Church and Realm*, p. 349.

PART III
The European Context

Chapter 6
Episcopal Appointments in a European Context

With the transition to papal provision now complete, English episcopal appointments ceased to be solely English affairs; it had become inevitable that each appointment would have a European element. Of course, even in the days when almost all vacant bishoprics had been filled without foreign influence or intervention, episcopal appointments had not been a solely English concern; instead, the topic was one that exercised both church and state across the entire breadth of Latin Christendom. Given that late medieval Western Europe was, in ecclesiastical terms, subject to a single spiritual ruler (the pope) and a single legal system, within which framework all episcopal appointments had to be made, it is unsurprising that the English experience was mirrored across Europe. In each province of the Catholic Church, capitular election had become the dominant form of appointment during the decades around 1200, only to be superseded by papal provision little more than a century later.[1]

Yet despite the rigidity of the framework provided by the canon law and enforced by the papacy, there remained scope for local variations in the manner in which bishops were appointed, and in the types of men chosen. For example, election by monastic convent was almost unheard of outside of England, for the

[1] In-depth English-language studies of European elections during this period are few and far between; for a recent exception see Peltzer, *Elections*, which covers the earlier decades of the thirteenth century. For (generally brief) outlines of thirteenth-century elections and the transition to provision, see John Dowden, 'The Appointment of Bishops in Scotland during the Medieval Period', *SHR*, 7 (1909), pp. 1-20; John Watt, *The Church and the Two Nations in Medieval Ireland* (Cambridge, 1970), pp. 155-6; John Watt, *The Church in Medieval Ireland* (Dublin, 1972), pp. 87-129; Peter Linehan, *The Spanish Church and the Papacy in the Thirteenth Century* (Cambridge, 1971), pp. 255-62; Joseph O'Callaghan, *A History of Medieval Spain* (Ithaca, 1975), pp. 490, 630; Glanmor Williams, *The Welsh Church: From Conquest to Reformation*, rev. edn (Cardiff, 1976), pp. 121-32; Giulio Silano, 'Episcopal Elections and the Apostolic See. The Case of Aquileia: 1251-1420', *Diretto e Potere Nella Storia Europea* (Florence, 1982), pp. 163-94; Malcolm Lambert, *Medieval Heresy*, 3rd edn (Oxford, 2002), pp. 307-9; Knut Helle (ed.), *The Cambridge History of Scandinavia: Prehistory to 1520* (Cambridge, 2003), pp. 449-50, 664; Pal Engel, *Realm of St. Stephen: A History of Medieval Hungary, 895-1526* (London, 2005), pp. 142-3, 313; Véronique Julerot, *"Y A Ung Grant Desordre": Élections Épiscopales et Schismes Diocésains en France sous Charles VIII* (Paris, 2006), pp. 50-56; Herminia Vilar, 'Canons and Cities: Cathedral Chapters and their Social Composition in Medieval Portugal', *e-journal of Portuguese History*, 5.2 (2007), pp. 1–19, at pp. 5-6; Etleva Lala, '*Regnum Albaniae*, the Papal Curia and the Western Visions of a Borderline Nobility' (Central European University at Budapest, DPhil thesis, 2008), section III.1.1.

simple reason that cathedral priories were something of an anomaly. Besides the ten English cathedral priories, only four European regular chapters enjoyed rights of episcopal election: St Andrews and Whithorn in Scotland, Downpatrick in Ireland and Monreale in Sicily.[2] Whilst attempts by secular rulers to influence ecclesiastical appointments were commonplace across Europe, their exact rights and responsibilities varied. Henry III and Edward I often influenced elections, but their Hungarian counterparts managed to maintain effective rights of nomination, a power they used to appoint large numbers of court priests to the episcopate. Only during the crisis of royal power that struck in the final decades of the thirteenth century did the Hungarian cathedral chapters manage to exercise their rights of election and to choose bishops drawn from their own ranks.[3] Archiepiscopal and papal influence also varied in both frequency and strength, not least because several ecclesiastical provinces (primarily, but not solely, in Italy) lacked a metropolitan and were instead directly subordinate to the papacy.[4]

A full-scale examination of the episcopal appointments of medieval Europe is clearly beyond the scope of this study; nevertheless, a consideration of some elements of this topic will allow us to determine how far the English experience was typical. This will both enhance our understanding of English appointments and demonstrate how far the findings of this study are relevant to Europe as a whole. To this end, this final chapter will consider episcopal appointments in France, Scotland and Italy during the thirteenth and early fourteenth centuries, highlighting the key features of their electoral history and comparing and contrasting their experiences with the English experience as described in the previous chapters. This trio of countries has been selected according to practical considerations (not least the existence of a relatively large body of existing historiography on this topic in either English or French, to which my findings about England can be compared), but also for historical reasons: they provide a range of political and ecclesiastical contexts, thus offering reasonable scope for comparison.

Late medieval France was, in broad terms, a very similar country to England, wealthy and with well-developed bureaucratic systems of both secular and

---

[2] Ian Cowan, 'The Organisation of Secular Cathedral Chapters' in Ian Cowan, *The Medieval Church in Scotland*, ed. James Kirk (Edinburgh, 1995), pp. 77-96, at p. 78; Edwards, *Secular Cathedrals*, p. 10.

[3] László Koszta, 'Conclusions Drawn from the Prosopographic Analysis of the Canons Belonging to the Cathedral Chapters of Medieval Hungary: 1200-1350' in Ana Jorge, Herminia Vilar and Maria Branco (eds), *Carreiras Ecleiásticas No Ocidente Cristão,* Séc. XII-XIV (Lisbon, 2007), pp. 13-28, at pp. 21-2.

[4] For a map of exempt dioceses outside of Italy, see Dauvit Broun, *Scottish Independence and the Idea of Britain: From the Picts to Alexander III* (Edinburgh, 2007), p. xiii, and also his comments on the topic at pp. 130-44.

ecclesiastical government.[5] It was, however, a less concrete entity than its cross-channel neighbour; the word 'France' meant different things to different people. Whilst royal government became increasingly centralized during this period, the power of the king was not equal in all parts of the kingdom.

Regional diversity remained important, with differences between the north of the country (the region of the langue d'oïl) and the south (the region of the langue d'oc) being especially marked.[6] The proportion of modern-day France under the rule of the French crown increased considerably over the course of the long thirteenth century, but even in the late 1320s substantial areas remained under the control of powerful dukes, including Gascony (held by the kings of England), Brittany and Burgundy.[7] An additional point of interest for the ecclesiastical historian is the number of French bishoprics. There were seventy-eight sees in total, divided into nine provinces, and the strength of royal control over these bishoprics varied by region.[8]

Scotland was also a country in which the strength of royal power varied from region to region. Norway did not cede control of the Western Isles until 1266,[9] and the need to bring peripheral regions such as Moray, Ross, Argyll and Galloway under royal control remained a priority for the Scottish crown throughout the late medieval period.[10] Following the death of Alexander III in 1286, the country experienced a lengthy period of political turmoil, including a serious attempt by the English to take control of the country.[11] Whilst the size of Scotland's episcopate was similar to that of England, consisting of thirteen bishoprics, in general ecclesiastical terms Scotland was less highly developed than either England or France.[12] It was also geographically even more distant

---

[5] Georges Duby, *France in the Middle Ages, 987-1460* (Oxford, 1993); Elizabeth Hallam and Judith Everard, *Capetian France, 987-1328*, 2nd edn (London, 2001).

[6] David Potter, 'Introduction' in David Potter (ed.), *France in the Later Middle Ages* (Oxford, 2002), pp. 3-8.

[7] The expansion of the kingdom is traced in a series of maps in Hallam and Everard, *Capetian France*, pp. 175 (1223), 284 (1259) and 352 (1328).

[8] For a map of the French bishoprics in the early fourteenth century, see Menache, *Clement*, pp. 94-5.

[9] Andrew Barrell, *Medieval Scotland* (Cambridge, 2000), p. 85.

[10] Ibid., p. 67.

[11] For recent political narratives, see, amongst others, Carpenter, *Struggle*; Michael Brown, *The Wars of Scotland, 1214-1371* (Edinburgh, 2004); Michael Brown and Steve Boardman, 'Survival and Revival: Late Medieval Scotland' in Jenny Wormald (ed.), *Scotland: A History* (Oxford, 2005), pp. 39-106; and Keith Stringer, 'The Emergence of a Nation State, 1100-1300' in Jenny Wormald (ed.), *Scotland: A History* (Oxford, 2005), pp. 38-76.

[12] For the development of ecclesiastical structures in Scotland during the twelfth and thirteenth centuries, see Geoffrey Barrow, *Kingship and Unity: Scotland 1066-1306* (London, 1981), pp. 60-83, and the collected papers of the late Ian Cowan in *The Medieval Church in Scotland*, ed. James Kirk (Edinburgh, 1995).

from Rome and Avignon than England, yet as a 'special daughter' of the papacy was in some senses more closely connected to it.[13]

Italy offers the opportunity to consider episcopal appointments in a very different environment, for late medieval Italy was extremely fragmented, in political, cultural and economic terms. The most consistently prominent political figure was the pope, who was a far more tangible presence in Italy than elsewhere in Europe; he claimed both spiritual and temporal control over the swathe of land in central Italy known as the Papal States. During the first half of the thirteenth century Frederick II, the Holy Roman Emperor, was a serious threat to papal ambitions (not least because he ruled much of southern Italy), but after his death imperial influence over Italy entered something of a decline. His successors as rulers of the south, firstly the Angevin kings and then, from the mid-1280s, the monarchs of a number of smaller kingdoms (notably Naples and Sicily), inevitably wished to play some role in the selection of bishops. Throughout the period in question, individual city states such as Venice and Milan were forces to be reckoned with, and their significance was heightened by the factional struggles between Guelphs (who favoured the papacy) and the pro-imperial Ghibellines.[14] Also of great significance for this study are the ecclesiastical divisions of late medieval Italy, notably the fact that it was divided into a total of 259 sees, a much larger number than were to be found in England, Scotland or even France.

France

According to a text inserted in the cartulary of Bourges Cathedral in the 1230s, at an unknown date in the late twelfth century King Philip Augustus of France and the Parisian master Peter the Chanter discussed the nature of good kingship. Realizing that the Chanter was about to reprimand him, the king interrupted him with a question about the quality of the episcopate: 'Tell me why ancient bishops ... were true saints, whereas one would be hard put to find a single modern bishop who is a saint.' Peter replied by contrasting the electoral practices of his contemporaries with those used in ancient times; in the past the electors (who were characterized by their humility and deep spirituality) depended on the wisdom of the Holy Spirit to guide their choice, but

---

13 For the origins of this special status, see Broun, *Scottish Independence*, pp. 130-44, and Andrew Barrell, 'The Background to *Cum universi*: Scoto-papal Relations, 1159-1192', *Innes Review*, 46 (1995), pp. 116-38.

14 For an overview, see the various essays in David Abulafia (ed.), *Italy in the Central Middle Ages* (Oxford, 2004). For the papal state, see Daniel Waley, *The Papal State in the Thirteenth Century* (London, 1961) and Peter Partner, *The Lands of St Peter* (London, 1972).

> In our modern elections, on the contrary, it is not the great wise man but the most stupid mentor, the devil, who arrives without being called, following banquets, drinking parties and secret meetings, convoked by his servants named 'Pride', 'Shame', 'Anger', 'Greed', Simony', 'uncontrollable Ambition' and others. It follows that he who is chosen by such negotiations does the work of him whose counsel has been accepted, living in pride, greed, exaltation and pomp.[15]

The criticisms made by the Chanter are strongly reminiscent of those levelled against the English Church by contemporary commentators across the Channel. Most striking to the English historian of elections are not, however, Peter's comments, but the fact that Philip Augustus allegedly greeted them 'with goodwill and entire agreement'.

Historians of medieval France have generally seen Philip's response to the Chanter as representative of his attitude to episcopal elections. His grant of rights of free election to French royal bishoprics and abbeys in 1190 (a quarter of a century before the English Church received a parallel concession), and a lack of obvious royal interference in elections led John Baldwin to judge him favourably in this respect.[16] Furthermore, comparisons of the conduct of elections in the English and French domains have often suggested that Capetian rule was far more conducive to ecclesiastical liberties than that of the Plantagenets[17] – a view shared by twelfth-century chroniclers such as Gerald of Wales[18] and William the Breton.[19] Yet not all of Philip's contemporaries were convinced that he was a defender of ecclesiastical liberties; the Englishman John aux Bellesmains, bishop of Poitiers (1162-82) and archbishop of Lyons (1182-93), was unimpressed when some English clerics complained about Richard I's treatment of the church, claiming that the Lionheart was 'a hermit' in comparison with the French king.[20] Recent studies have provided more nuanced comparisons, from

15 John Baldwin, 'Pierre le Chantre et Étienne de Gallardon: La Conjoncture de Regnum, Studium et Cancellaria au Tournant des XIIe et XIIIe Siècles', *Comptes-rendus des Séances de l'Académie des Inscriptions et Belles-Lettres*, 144 (2000), pp. 437-57. The translation is from John Baldwin, *Paris, 1200* (Stanford, 2010), pp. 78-9, 132-3.

16 John Baldwin, *The Government of Philip Augustus* (Berkeley, 1986), pp. 65-8, 176-7, 307-9.

17 Marcel Pacaut, *Louis VII et les Élections Épiscopales dans le Royaume de France* (Paris, 1957), p. 78; John Baldwin, 'Philip Augustus and the Norman Church', *French Historical Studies*, 6 (1969), pp. 1-30; Pascal Montaubin, 'Les Chapitres Cathédraux Séculiers de Normandie et la Centralisation Pontificale au XIIIe Siècle' in Sylvette Lemagnen and Philippe Manneville (eds), *Chapitres et Cathédrales en Normandie* (Caen, 1997), pp. 253-72, at p. 257; Jim Bradbury, *Philip Augustus: King of France 1180-1223* (London, 1998), pp. 203-5.

18 *Giraldus Cambrensis opera*, VIII, p. 301.

19 *Oeuvres de Rigord et de Guillaume le Breton: Historiens de Philippe Auguste*, ed. H. Delaborde (2 vols, Paris, 1882-85), II, pp. 219-20.

20 *Chronicles of the Reigns of Stephen, Henry II and Richard I*, ed. R. Howlett (4 vols, RS, 1884-89), II, p. 422.

which the English and French experiences emerge as different, certainly, but not completely polarized by differences in royal attitudes.[21]

As the post-1214 English narrative indicates, royal grants of electoral freedom were no guarantee that the crown would no longer play a role in the electoral process.[22] Just as in England, the French king maintained three crucial rights: granting of the licence to elect, assenting to the capitular choice and (in the majority of dioceses) holding the temporalities of the see during a vacancy.[23] These practices were widely accepted, although the last of them appears to have occasioned more opposition in France than in England. Most bishops took an oath of fidelity to the king within forty days of their consecration, as custom demanded,[24] but some objected, amongst them Hugh Mascaron, elected to Toulouse in 1287.[25] In France as in England, the king claimed the right of appointment to ecclesiastical benefices during an episcopal vacancy,[26] but whereas this claim seems to have been tolerated in England, it provoked much criticism on the continent. Nevertheless, in 1332 Philip VI reasserted his right to dispose of benefices up to the day when a new bishop took his oath to the king, and the papacy did little to prevent him from doing so.[27]

Furthermore, there is evidence to suggest that throughout the thirteenth century French kings endeavoured, with a considerable degree of success, to influence the choices made by cathedral chapters. As in England, it seems likely that royal wishes were indicated when the capitular representatives came to court to seek *congé d'élire*,[28] and chapters were often willing to comply with these wishes. Indeed, French chapters seem to have followed their English counterparts and on occasion deliberately elected men who they believed would be acceptable to the king, in order to enjoy the fruits of royal favour. For example, in 1257 the chapter of Le Puy (in the archdiocese of Bouges) reportedly elected Gui Foulquois (the future Clement IV) as their bishop on account of

21 Peltzer, *Elections*, pp. 238-58; Daniel Power, 'The Norman Church and the Angevin and Capetian Kings', *JEH*, 56 (2005), pp. 205-34.

22 Further indication of the truth of this statement can be found in Aragon, where Pedro II ceded all rights over episcopal elections in 1207 – but his successors 'continually interfered in elections to bishoprics and abbeys'. See Gaudemet, *Gouvernement*, p. 78; Jocelyn Hillgarth, *The Spanish Kingdoms (1250-1516)*, vol. 1: *1250-1410: Precarious Balance* (Oxford, 1976), p. 93.

23 Gaudemet, *Gouvernement*, pp. 77-8; Roland, *Chanoines*, pp. 165-92.

24 This custom was recorded by Maurice, bishop of Mans, at the time of his election in 1223: *Layettes du Trésor de Chartes*, ed. M. Teulet *et al.* (5 vols, Paris, 1863-1909), II, p. 1617.

25 Roland, *Chanoines*, p. 178.

26 See Howell, *Regalian Right*, pp. 169-78, for English examples.

27 Bernard Guillemain, *La Politique Bénéficiale de Bênoit XII, 1334-42* (Paris, 1952), pp. 68-74.

28 Gaudemet, *Gouvernement*, p. 77. Fernando Pico, 'The Bishops of France in the Reign of Louis IX (1226-1270)' (Johns Hopkins University, PhD thesis, 1970), p. 8, cites several examples of petitions for licence to elect in which it is implied (although never explicitly stated) that such an indication was expected.

his influence with the king.[29] Resisting royal wishes, on the other hand, could have negative consequences, and there are several examples of the temporalities being withheld until some powerful individual intervened on the new prelate's behalf – a practice that had the added advantage of enhancing royal revenue. In 1228, Cardinal Romanus interceded on behalf of the new bishop of Noyon, whose temporalities were being withheld; three years later Juhel de Tours made a similar plea for the new bishop of Mans.[30]

There is no French counterpart to the major Winchester dispute of 1238-44 and one reason why France was less prone than England to explosive electoral disputes prompted by disagreements between king and chapter may be found in the fact that the French cathedral chapters consisted of canons. The most spectacular English disputes involved monastic chapters, which were non-existent in Louis IX's kingdom. Nevertheless, electoral disputes were far from rare: during the reign of Louis IX alone, there were almost fifty elections (approximately one-fifth of the total) that either produced two bishops-elect or in which the choice of the majority was appealed.[31] Fernando Pico claimed that 'one in five, at any rate, is sufficient evidence of freedom in the electoral system',[32] which is true insofar as it indicates that royal wishes were not being imposed on the chapter; they were free to hold elections and to elect against royal wishes if they wished to do so. It is quite plausible that in some cases disputes were solely due to internal divisions within the chapter, just as disagreements between the English double chapters caused multiple appeals to Rome.

Nevertheless, it seems clear that the forceful expression of royal wishes was a relatively common cause of disputes which could be resolved only by an appeal to the papal curia. Such disputes typically occurred when approximately half of the chapter backed the royal candidate, whilst the other half favoured another candidate. Thus when the archbishopric of Sens fell vacant in 1241, the votes were split between Gilles Cornu, archdeacon of Sens, and Juhel de Mathéfélon, archbishop of Tours; two years later, Innocent IV ruled in favour of Cornu, the royal candidate.[33] Royal influence was even more apparent in another election of the 1240s, held at Noyon. Pierre Charlot, the bastard son of Philip Augustus, and Master Jean, dean of St-Martin de Tours, received an equal number of votes and consequently the case was appealed to Rome. The cardinals who examined the election took into account the memory of Charlot's father, and the requests of various members of the royal family (including Louis IX and Queen Blanche),

[29] Pico, 'Bishops', p. 9.

[30] Roland, *Chanoines*, p. 184.

[31] Pico, 'Bishops', pp. 12-15.

[32] Ibid., p. 17.

[33] *Reg. Grég. IX*, no. 268; *Reg. Inn. IV*, no. 270, 624; Roland, *Chanoines*, p. 169.

and decided in his favour.[34] The intervention of other secular powers could cause split elections, as at Metz in 1296-97. Some of the canons elected one of their number, Thiébaut de Bar, whilst others postulated Ferri de Lorraine, bishop of Orléans, who was the son of the Duke of Lorraine and the favoured candidate of Edward I. An appeal to Rome ended in the provision of a third man, Gérard de Réninge, archdeacon of Cambrai.[35] On other occasions, a minority of canons appealed against the choice of a royal candidate made by the majority of their brethren. At Poitiers in 1234, for example, a group of canons appealed against the election of the king's uncle, Pierre Charlot, treasurer of Saint-Martin de Tours, claiming that it had been achieved by threats and bribes.[36]

Given that the allegations made against candidates during electoral appeals were determined primarily by the requirements of canon law, it is unsurprising to find that the accusations made in France were very similar to those found in English appeals. Guillaume de Bussi, elected to Orléans in 1238, was, like his near-contemporaries Thomas Melsonby of Durham and Hugh Balsham of Ely, said to be unsuitable for a whole range of reasons: he was said to be of servile birth and violent temper (he had seized and imprisoned a clerk who had taken refuge in Reims Cathedral); he associated with women of bad character and engaged in an improper relationship with the Abbess of Avenay, with whom he had danced in public and sent inappropriate gifts. Despite these accusations, which were examined at Rome, his election received papal confirmation.[37] Other thirteenth-century elections were the subject of appeals based on canonical points including bad eyesight, extreme age, illiteracy, pluralism and having borne arms.[38]

Overall, despite the relative paucity of the sources (the lack of a French equivalent of the *Chronica Majora* and the chancery rolls is surely a great disappointment to any English medievalist seeking to compare England and France), it is possible to conclude that during the thirteenth century the French king enjoyed a degree of influence over episcopal elections roughly equivalent to that of his English counterpart, at least in the nine provinces (divided into seventy-eight sees) that were clearly located within the French kingdom. There may have been regional variations, with greater royal control in the northern

34 *Reg. Inn. IV*, no. 119; Roland, *Chanoines*, p. 170.

35 Michel Parisse, 'Une Élection Épiscopale Disputée à Metz en 1296-1297: de Bouchard d'Avesnes à Gérard de Réninge' in Wolfgang Haubrichs, Wolfgang Laufer and Reinhard Schneider (eds), *Zwischen Saar und Mosel: Festschrift für Hans-Walter Herrmann* (Saarbrucken, 1995), pp. 77-83.

36 *Reg. Grég. IX*, no. 2510; Pico, 'Bishops', pp. 17-18.

37 Charles Cuissard, 'Élection de Guillaume de Bussi, Éveque d'Orléans et Principaux Actes de Son Épiscopat, 1238-1258', *Mémoires de la Société Archéologique et Historique de l'Orléanais*, 25 (1894), pp. 573-82.

38 Pico, 'Bishops', pp. 18-19.

and eastern sees, which had traditionally been under greater royal scrutiny,[39] but the influence of the crown was felt across the kingdom. The role of the French archbishops is somewhat trickier to delineate, beyond the simple statement that their rights and responsibilities were those defined by canon law and therefore the same as those of their English peers: the metropolitan examined and confirmed the elect, received his oath of obedience and consecrated him. There are occasional hints of more complex archiepiscopal actions. On at least two occasions, which provide interesting parallels with the role of Boniface of Savoy in elections at Chichester (1244) and Ely (1256), French archbishops resolved electoral disputes by providing an alternative candidate: at Albi in 1228,[40] and again in 1242, when the archbishop of Aix provided to Sisteron.[41] In 1233, the canons of Périgieux transferred their right of appointment to the archbishop of Bordeaux; his choice was ratified by Gregory IX.[42] Each of these examples is drawn from southern dioceses, reinforcing the notion that royal influence was less marked in that area, but northern archbishops also intervened in elections. Eudes Rigaud, archbishop of Rouen, acted as a mediator in a disputed election at Chartres in 1260; by the time he left the city, the minority of candidates who had been opposed to the choice of the majority had agreed to change their minds, and Pierre de Mincy was unanimously elected.[43]

The actions of the bishop-elect were also of significance in the electoral process, and in France as in England two behaviours dominated: ambition and reluctance. Guillaume d'Auvergne was provided to Paris in 1228, having gone to Rome to oppose the election of the dean of Paris to that see;[44] a suspicious mind might suggest that his objections were not unconnected to his personal ambitions. In contrast, his predecessor at Paris, Guillaume de Seignelay, had been reluctant to accept his appointment and only did so because compelled by the pope.[45] In a display of *nolo episcopari* especially becoming of a Franciscan friar, Eudes Rigaud was apparently 'dragged and forced to the archbishopric of Rouen'.[46]

---

39 Ibid., pp. iii-v, 22-37.

40 Ibid., p. 12.

41 Edouard Baratier, 'Nominations et Origines des Évêques des Provinces d'Aix et Arles', *Les Évêques, les Clercs et le Roi (1250-1300)*, Cahiers de Fanjeaux, 7 (Toulouse, 1972), pp. 115-45, at pp. 121-2.

42 *Reg. Greg. IX*, no. 1471; Pico, 'Bishops', p. 13.

43 Adam Davis, *The Holy Bureaucrat: Eudes Rigaud and Religious Reform in Thirteenth-Century Normandy* (Ithaca, 2006), p. 143.

44 Bernard Plongeron, *Le Diocese de Paris* (Paris, 1987), p. 135.

45 Ibid., p. 133.

46 *The Chronicle of the Twenty-Four Generals of the Friars Minor*, cited by Davis, *Holy Bureaucrat*, p. 159.

It was the fifth core participant in the electoral process, the papacy, that was responsible for the development of new mechanisms for appointment during this period. During the early years of the thirteenth century, papal interventions in French elections were rare and typically related to archiepiscopal elections or disputed episcopal elections. Archbishops would have their elections examined and (where appropriate) confirmed at the papal curia as a matter of course; many were also consecrated by the pope. Eudes Rigaud, for example, was consecrated by Innocent IV at Lyon in 1248.[47] Faced with an electoral dispute, the pope had three options: to confirm one of the candidates, to order a new election to be held or to make a provision. During the reign of Louis IX, the first two of these options were favoured,[48] but papal provision does seem to have been slightly more frequent in France than in England. The earliest known provisions to French bishoprics were made during the pontificate of Innocent III; he nominated three bishops who had not been the original choice of the cathedral chapter.[49] Another early provision was made at Chartres in 1219, after Honorius III rejected two successive bishops-elect;[50] like the first English provision, of Alexander Stavensby to Coventry and Lichfield in 1224, this was clearly a responsive provision. Similar responsive provisions followed in other sees, for example at Paris in 1228, when Guillaume d'Auvergne objected to the election and was himself appointed,[51] and at Rouen in 1231, 1244 and 1282.[52] There was also a somewhat anomalous proactive appointment made by Innocent IV to the bishopric of Maguelone in 1247, on the grounds that the previous incumbent had died at the papal curia.[53] As in England, it was in the wealthiest and most powerful sees that the majority of early provisions were made.

Throughout the thirteenth century, election by cathedral chapter remained the normal mode of appointment for French bishops, and even where there was papal involvement, this did not preclude the possibility that capitular wishes would be respected. Of the forty-five bishops appointed to Norman sees during the course of the thirteenth century, only five were not the choice of at least

[47] Davis, *Holy Bureaucrat*, p. 31.

[48] Pico, 'Bishops', pp. 12-15.

[49] Pascal Montaubin, 'Innocent III et les Nominations Épiscopales en Italie' in Andrea Sommerlechner (ed.), *Innocenzo III. Urbs et Orbis* (2 vols, Rome, 2003), pp. 778-811, at p. 803, n. 85.

[50] Pico, 'Bishops', p. 12.

[51] Plongeron, *Paris*, p. 135.

[52] Montaubin, 'Normandie', p. 258. For the archbishops of Rouen in the thirteenth and fourteenth centuries, see Vincent Tabbagh and Pierre Bony (eds), *Fasti Ecclesiae Gallicanae*, vol. 2: *Diocèse de Rouen* (Turnhout, 1998), pp. 77-101.

[53] Bernard Guillemain and Catherine Martin, 'Les Élections Épiscopales de la Province de Narbonne entre 1249 et 1317' in *Les Évêques, les Clercs et le Roi (1250-1300)*, Cahiers de Fanjeaux, 7 (Toulouse, 1972), pp. 107-13, at p. 108.

part of their cathedral chapter.[54] Furthermore, the popes were not yet taking advantage of opportunities to appoint that would have been seized upon by their early fourteenth-century counterparts. Five Norman bishops were granted papal permission to resign their sees (on grounds of ill health and/or advanced age) during the 1230s and 1240s, but in none of these cases was the bishopric concerned reserved; instead, the pope allowed capitular elections to be held.[55]

As in England, it was in the years around 1300 that the number of papal provisions to bishoprics began to increase and pro-active provisions became widespread. At this stage, provisions remained more common in the wealthiest, most powerful sees, with less prominent dioceses typically enjoying opportunities to elect into the fourteenth century. Édouard Baratier's study of episcopal appointments in the provinces of Aix and Arles between 1250 and 1317 illustrated this pattern particularly well. The two archiepiscopal sees, along with the bishoprics of Marseille and Avignon, fell vacant twenty-four times during this period; on fifteen occasions the vacancy was filled by provision, on seven occasions by election and on two occasions the method is unclear. In contrast, the minor bishoprics of Gap, Sisteron, Carpentras, Apt and Frejus acquired twenty-five new bishops during the same period; twenty of them were elected and only four provided (for one election, at Sisteron, the method is unclear).[56] The pattern of appointments in the province of Narbonne during the years 1288-1317 was very similar.[57]

The rise of papal provision in France was greatly eased by royal acceptance of, and even encouragement of, the practice. Whereas English kings, at least initially, were sceptical about this new practice, fearing that it would be detrimental to their rights, but there is no evidence that French kings engaged in protests of the kind made by Edward I and Edward II at the beginning of their respective reigns. During the pontificate of Clement V, at the time when Edward II was fretting about the papal reservation of Worcester, Philip the Fair was developing a close alliance with the papacy which allowed him a great deal of influence over episcopal appointments. In August 1306, he thanked the pope for the appointment of three royal candidates to bishoprics: Pierre de Belleperche to Auxerre, Guillaume Bonnet to Bayeux and Nicolas de Lusarches to Avranches.[58] Whereas Edward II (and even Edward III) often tried to use both systems, seeking the election of a certain candidate whilst simultaneously petitioning

54 Montaubin, 'Normandie', pp. 257-9.

55 Ibid., pp. 257-8.

56 Baratier, 'Nominations', pp. 119-20. For a late thirteenth-century (1280) election at Carpentras, see Maurice Caillet, 'Élection, Confirmation et Consécration d'un Évêque de Carpentras au XIIIe Siècle', *Mélanges Raoul Busquet: Questions d'Histoire de Provence (XIe-XIXe Siècles)* (Vaison-la-Romaine, 1956), pp. 90-107, which includes some of the documents of the election.

57 Guilemain and Martin, 'Élections', p. 110.

58 Menache, *Clement*, pp. 81-2.

the pope for his provision, Philip was apparently keen to prevent the holding of elections. In 1308, faced with the prospect of an election at Auxerre, he wrote to Clement to inform him of the dangers of such a process, with the result that the see was reserved; a similar situation arose at Laon, where Philip was concerned to secure a bishop who 'would jealously labour for the honour of the king and the kingdom'.[59] Of course, royal wishes were not always granted. Philip struggled to find a see for Jean d'Auxois, a collector of subventions and an *enquêteur*; Clement V refused to appoint him to Auxerre in 1308, although he did become bishop of Troyes in 1314. Similarly, Pierre de Laon was the unsuccessful royal candidate for Orléans in 1312.[60]

The rate of provision increased further during the pontificate of John XXII and the dominance of this procedure quickly became far more marked in France than in England. Between 1316 and 1334, Pope John made 230 provisions to French bishoprics;[61] only thirteen elections were upheld.[62] Yet, despite these striking figures, election was not an irrelevancy, even to the papacy. Elections continued to be held, and very occasionally they received papal confirmation, even when a reservation had been made. In 1328, the canons of Angoulême elected Ayquelin de Blaye, archdeacon of Angoulême, and their choice received papal ratification. Unanimous elections received papal confirmation on several occasions, perhaps because unanimity was seen as an expression of divine will. Particularly impressive candidates, such as the scholar Pierre de Luc, archbishop of Bordeaux from 1332, and royal candidates such as Etienne de Bourret (elected bishop of Paris in the same year) also had their elections confirmed.[63]

The rise of provision continued during the pontificate of Benedict XII, and of the fifty-eight episcopal vacancies that arose between 1334 and 1342, only nine were filled by capitular election. These nine elections were held in seven sees, all of them located in the west of the country; three of them were in Brittany. Reservation became a routine procedure, which demanded no special circumstances: sees were usually reserved as soon as they fell vacant or occasionally before the death of a bishop (as at Castres and Albi). Although elections continued to be held, it was increasingly rare for their outcomes to be upheld. Occasionally an election would be quashed, only for the elect to be provided; in this way Philippe de Melun became bishop of Châlons-sur Marne, Bernard de Canvet bishop of Albi and Bonabes de Rochefort bishop of Nantes. More commonly, bishops-elect had their promotions overturned to make way

---

59 Ibid., p. 82. Note the similarity between Philip's words and the language of the English licence to elect.

60 Joseph Strayer, *The Reign of Philip the Fair* (Princeton, 1980), p. 94.

61 Caillet, *Papauté*, pp. 52-4.

62 Ibid., pp. 38-9.

63 Ibid., pp. 38-43.

for the provision of another. When Guillaume de Machecoul was elected bishop of Nantes in 1340, the election was overturned in favour of Olivier Salahadin, dean of Paris, who had only tenuous links to Brittany.[64]

As in England, the rise of provision was accompanied by an increase in the number of translations, and this gave the pope the opportunity to provide to the see that he had made vacant. However, bishoprics were rather more numerous in France than on the other side of the Channel, allowing for the easy creation of lengthy chains of translation and provision (in England such movements rarely involved more than a pair of sees, at least before the fifteenth century). Thus whereas death remained the primary cause of English vacancies, the same was not true in France. In 1339, for example, there were thirteen episcopal vacancies, at least eight of them the result of translations. One see that did become vacant as the result of a bishop's death was Sens, and Benedict XII responded not by making a provision, but by translating the bishop of Châlons to Sens. Châlons was then filled by the translation of the bishop of Arras; the bishop of Nevers was moved to Arras and the bishop of Boulogne was translated to Nevers.[65]

It is clear that by the 1330s the transition to provision was essentially complete, although, as in England, it was not until the pontificate of Urban V that the general reservation of benefices across the Latin Church made provision the only possible means of promotion to the episcopate. The French response to this transition appears, if anything, to have been even more understated than the English reaction.[66] In both countries, provisions to minor benefices provoked the strongest opposition, with ordinary lay patrons proving considerably more tenacious than either ecclesiastical patrons (who seem to have been more reluctant to oppose the pope) or those who had a stake in appointments to major benefices.[67] Protests against the provision of bishops, either practical or in writing, appear to have been few and far between.

French kings undoubtedly accepted the transition for the same reasons as their English counterparts, quickly realizing that the new system could ease the promotion of their favourites to the episcopate. The pope did not always grant the king's wishes: when Philip VI (1328-50) asked for the appointment of his chancellor, Guillaume de Sainte-Maure, to the archbishopric of Rouen, his request was turned down on the grounds that the duties of an archbishop were incompatible with those of a chancellor.[68] Nevertheless, in the mid-fourteenth century there existed a tacit agreement between king and pope by which royal

---

64 Guillemain, *Politique Bénéficiale*, pp. 39-41.

65 Ibid., p. 42.

66 On which, see above, pp. 149-85.

67 Guillemain, *Politique Bénéficiale*, pp. 65-7.

68 Raymond Cazelles, *La Société Politique et la Crise de la Royauté sous Philippe de Valois* (Paris, 1958), p. 384.

candidates would usually be provided. Thus Jean de Vienne was provided to Thérouanne in 1330 and then translated to the archdiocese of Reims in 1334, 'at the wish of the king'.[69] Royal influence on the composition of the episcopate was particularly marked in the north of the country, in the langue d'oïl region; in this area (excluding Brittany and Burgundy, where ducal influence remained strong) at least half of the bishops were involved in royal administration in one form or another. For elite royal servants, promotion to the episcopate was a natural stage in their career progression, and many combined episcopal and secular duties for some years.[70]

As in England, cathedral chapters continued to hold elections. According to the canons of Saint Pères, such a course of action was compatible with papal policy; they claimed that the chapters of Mirepoix and Lavaur, both cathedrals created by John XXII, had received papal promises that they might elect their bishops 'in perpetuity'.[71] The veracity of such pledges remains unverified, but the perception that the papacy was still open to the possibility of capitular elections being held (reinforced by rare examples of such elections being confirmed) would have gone some way to explaining a lack of capitular resistance towards the transition.

Strayer has suggested that the ecclesiastical response to provision, and the role of the crown in this transition, was conditioned by a relatively good relationship between the French Church and the king. 'Since the secular clergy trusted the king at least as much as they trusted the papacy, there was no great opposition to royal intervention in the choice of bishops, cathedral dignitaries and canons'; when chapters found their rights of election under threat from Rome, they preferred that the king should choose their bishops (typically by indicating his wishes to the papacy), rather than the pope.[72] In this respect the French chapters responded differently to their counterparts across the Channel. English cathedral convents continued to resist the wishes of the crown even in the early fifteenth century.[73]

Strayer proceeds to list the reasons papal choices were rarely satisfactory to the French Church, focusing on the appointment of Italians to French benefices. Clement V's appointments of his rather incompetent kinsmen, including Bernard de Fargues (a disastrous archbishop of Rouen), were particularly

---

[69] Ibid., p. 389; *Lettres Communes, Jean XXII (1316-1334)*, ed. G. Mollat (16 vols in 15, Paris, 1904-47), nos. 51983, 64141; Pierre Desporte (ed.), *Fasti Ecclesiae Gallicanae*, vol. 3: *Diocèse de Reims* (Turnhout, 1998), p. 172.

[70] Cazelles, *Philippe de Valois*, p. 385.

[71] Guillemain, *Politique Bénéficiale*, p. 43.

[72] Strayer, *Philip the Fair*, p. 241.

[73] See, for example, the dispute provoked by the election of Alexander Tottingdon as bishop of Norwich in 1406: C. Harper-Bill, 'Alexander Tottingdon' in *ODNB*.

problematic.[74] However, the majority of foreign provisees received only minor benefices[75] and, as in England, virtually all of the papally provided bishops were native-born and royally sanctioned. Of the ninety-three provisions made to major benefices (bishoprics and abbeys) by Benedict XII, only nine involved foreigners. Of these, two were from the Iberian Peninsula (and were appointed in the south-west of France), three were from the Rhône-Alps region (which had very close links with France) and two originated from the Empire. Only two Italians were appointed, one of them an abbot, the other Bertrand Acciajoli, bishop of Boulogne.[76]

Indeed, the transition to provision appears to have had little impact on the episcopate, which continued to be composed primarily of prominent members of the diocesan clergy,[77] royal servants and the scions of noble families, the last mentioned having been consistently more prevalent in the French episcopate than in England. For example, a study of the province of Narbonne between 1249 and 1317 suggested that at least 60 per cent of incumbents, and possibly as many as 80 per cent, were of noble birth. Amongst their number were St Louis d'Anjou (son of Charles II of Sicily and Marie of Hungary) Bertrand de l'Isle-Jourdain (illegitimate grandson of the count of Toulouse), and scions of numerous other great Languedocian families.[78] Also considerably more numerous in France than in England were mendicant bishops; twenty-five such individuals had been appointed by 1302.[79]

If the unchanging composition of the episcopate helped to reconcile the French people to the rise of provision, it is also worth considering the links between France and the papacy, for the ties between the two were in some respects at least much closer than those between England and the papacy. Even before the papal curia moved its base to Avignon in 1305, it had been a frequent visitor to France, especially the region around Lyon. There were also links between the French Church and the papal curia in terms of personnel.

---

74 Strayer, *Philip the Fair*, p. 241.

75 On the appointment of Italian clerks to French and English benefices, see Pascal Montaubin, 'Étrangers en Chrétienté: Clercs Italiens en France et en Angleterre (fin XIIe-mi XIVe Siècle)', *Actes des Congrès de la Société des Historiens Médiévistes de l'Enseignement Supérieur Public* 30 (1999), pp. 233-44.

76 Guillemain, *Politique Bénéficiale*, p. 58.

77 For the promotion of members of the cathedral chapters to the episcopate, see Hélène Millet, *Les Chanoines du Chapitre de Laon, 1272-1412* (Rome, 1982), pp. 217-21 (6.5 per cent of Laon canons became bishops in 1272-1305, rising to 13 per cent in 1305-48), and Robert Gane, *Le Chapitre de Notre-Dame de Paris au XIVe Siècle au XIVe Siècle* (Saint-Étienne, 1999), pp. 151-4 (from where 22 per cent of canons became bishops and 4 per cent archbishops).

78 Bernard Guillemain and Catherine Martin, 'Origines Sociales, Intellectuelles et Ecclésiastiques des Évêques de la Province de Narbonne entre 1249 et 1317', *Les Évêques, les Clercs et le Roi (1250-1300)*, Cahiers de Fanjeaux, 7 (Toulouse, 1972), pp. 91-106, at pp. 94-5.

79 Jacques Paul, 'Les Religieux Mendicants Évêques en France au XIIIe siècle', *Dal Pulpito alla Cattedra: i Vescovi degli Ordini Mendicanti nel '200 e nel Primo '300* (Spoleto, 2000), pp. 249-303.

Even before papal provision became commonplace, some chapters seem to have considered the wishes of the papacy when holding elections, as in the province of Narbonne, where eight papal chaplains were elected between 1249 and 1317.[80] The promotion of bishops to the ranks of the cardinals was also reasonably common, provoking vacancies that were increasingly filled by provision,[81] but also (given the crucial role played by the cardinals in papal government, including the filling of benefices) increasing the level of influence exercised by the French at the curia. Medieval Englishmen were used to papal involvement in their affairs; medieval Frenchmen were even more accustomed to frequent dealings with the papacy.

Yet if the French were more accepting of provision than the English in the years around 1300, their attitude changed dramatically in the early fifteenth century. By the late fourteenth century, although elections continued to be held, provision was well established as the sole form of episcopal appointment. The traditional form of appointment was given a new lease of life by the Great Schism, and opposition to provision revived. In the decades after 1400 the right to election was reasserted in France by a series of royal ordinances, and especially by the Pragmatic Sanction of Bourges (1438). The revival of election was short-lived and under Louis XI (1461-83) there was a shift back towards provision; by the end of the century, provision was once again the dominant mode of appointment.[82]

Scotland

If in Philip Augustus, France reportedly had a king with far greater respect for ecclesiastical, and specifically electoral, freedoms than England's King John, the kingdom to the north was ruled by a man who reportedly made Angevin attitudes to episcopal election appear reasonable. William the Lion (1165-1214) kept the Scottish Church under extremely close control; G. W. S. Barrow wrote of him that 'in comparison with royal treatment of the Scottish church in his time, the Constitutions of Clarendon read like a Gregorian tract'.[83] The most spectacular demonstration of William's attitude to episcopal elections is to be found in the St Andrews dispute of 1178-88. Following the death of Bishop Richard in May 1178, the canons of the cathedral priory elected as their bishop John, a member of an episcopal family with close personal connections to the

80 Guillemain and Martin, 'Origines', p. 97.

81 Guillemain and Martin, 'Élections', pp. 111-12; Baratier, 'Nominations', p. 131; Guillemain, *Politique Bénéficiale*, p. 40.

82 On episcopal appointments in fifteenth-century France, see Julerot, *Grant Desordre*.

83 Geoffrey Barrow, 'The Reign of William the Lion' in Geoffrey Barrow, *Scotland and its Neighbours in the Middle Ages* (London, 1992), pp. 67-89, at p. 87.

see. The king reacted furiously and nominated his chaplain Hugh, before having him consecrated by a group of Scottish bishops later in the year. Several appeals to Rome, two legatine missions to Scotland, the imposition of an interdict on the kingdom and the excommunication of the king, and the intervention of Henry II of England all failed to bring the dispute to a close; on several occasions it appeared to have been resolved only to re-erupt and only came to a definite conclusion with the appointment of John to Dunkeld, and the death of Hugh at the papal curia. Of particular interest during this dispute is William's behaviour; whilst King John made threats of violence against Stephen Langton, he never dared to carry them out, whereas the Scottish king attacked the would-be Bishop John's supporters and burned the property of his uncle, Bishop Matthew of Aberdeen, who was forced to flee the country.[84]

Although there was no Scottish parallel to the pledges of electoral freedom made by John and Philip Augustus, the kingdom does seem to have been influenced by the Europe-wide shift towards greater electoral freedom for cathedral chapters, and royal intervention became rather less forceful during the thirteenth century. This is not to say that Alexander II and Alexander III had any less interest in, or influence over, ecclesiastical matters than their forebears; instead, they had to focus their efforts on persuading chapters to elect their candidates using non-violent means. As in England, chapters had to seek licence to elect from the king before holding an election and obtain royal assent to their choice afterwards;[85] Scottish kings also claimed custody of the temporalities during an episcopal vacancy.[86] Along with the carrot of royal favour, and the stick of royal displeasure, these customary powers could be used to influence the outcome of episcopal elections and thus the crown retained a considerable amount of control.

Indeed, in the early thirteenth century, it seems to have been believed that Scottish bishoprics were in the gift of the crown, as one remarkable case indicates. In 1219, the papal Legate Pandulph was ordered to establish an inquiry into allegations surrounding Bishop William of Glasgow. It was rumoured that 'when chaplain of the king of Scotland, he gave 100 marks to Philip de Valon,

---

[84] The dispute would reward detailed consideration, but has yet to be the subject of such a study. See *Scottish Annals from English Chroniclers, AD 500 to 1286*, ed. A. O. Anderson (London, 1908), pp. 271–304; *Early Sources of Scottish History, AD 500 to 1286*, ed. A. O. Anderson (2 vols, Edinburgh, 1922), II, pp. 299–306, 343; *Melrose*, pp. 20-26; *Scotia Pontificia: Papal Letters to Scotland Before the Pontificate of Innocent III*, ed. R. Somerville (Oxford, 1982), pp. 88-139; *FES*, pp. 378-9; Paul Ferguson, *Medieval Papal Representatives in Scotland: Legates, Nuncios and Judges-Delegate, 1125-1286* (Edinburgh, 1997), pp. 56-63; Barrell, '*Cum universi*', pp. 120-38; Archibald Duncan, 'John', *ODNB*.

[85] John Dowden, *The Medieval Church in Scotland: Its Constitution, Organisation and Law* (Glasgow, 1910), p. 23.

[86] Gordon Donaldson, 'The Rights of the Scottish Crown in Episcopal Vacancies', *SHR*, 139 (1966), pp. 27-35.

the king's chamberlain, and promised a much larger sum to the queen to procure his appointment to the see by the king'.[87]

The result of the investigation is unknown, but William continued as bishop of Glasgow until his death in 1232, which suggests that the claims were found to be unsubstantiated. Nevertheless, that they were made, and seriously considered by the ecclesiastical authorities, suggests that royal control over elections remained strong enough for such rumours to seem plausible. This impression was reinforced by the fact that the holding of elections at court[88] (a practice that ended south of the border in 1214 and had been increasingly infrequent through the reign of King John) seems to have survived a little longer in Scotland. For example, Gilbert of Moray, bishop of Caithness (1222/3-45), was elected 'in the presence of the lord king and the chief men of his army'.[89]

As in England, many elections resulted in the election of royal servants, amongst them Gilbert of Sterling, clerk of the liverance and bishop of Dunkeld (1236-49), David Bernham, the royal chamberlain, who became bishop of St Andrews in 1239,[90] and William Fraser, royal chancellor and bishop of St Andrews from 1279. Nor were the Scottish kings afraid to engage in electoral disputes on behalf of their candidates. For example, in 1235 Alexander II supported the election of Gilbert, a monk of Melrose, as bishop of Galloway; his support for Gilbert was crucial in securing the latter's position as bishop, despite a dispute that rumbled on for six years.[91] Then, in 1253, the chapter of St Andrews elected Robert de Stuteville in opposition to the wishes of Alexander III, who favoured his chancellor Gamelin. Royal representations in favour of the latter were made at Rome, with the result that the election was overturned, and the pope instead appointed a third man, Abel, archdeacon of St Andrews. When Abel died only a few months later, the king secured the bishopric for Gamelin.[92]

The Scottish king had to deal with a challenge that neither his English nor French counterparts had to face: ruling over a kingdom that was directly subject to the papacy. Despite repeated attempts to secure the creation of a metropolitan see in Scotland, the country did not obtain its first archbishopric (at St Andrews) until the late fifteenth century. According to the papal bull *Cum universi*, Scotland was the 'special daughter' of the Apostolic See and thus the

87 *CPL*, I, p. 70.

88 For the evidence that elections were held at the royal court in late twelfth-century Scotland, see John Dowden, 'The Scottish Crown and the Episcopate in the Medieval Period', *SHR*, 7 (1909), pp. 130-40, at p. 133.

89 *Scotichron.*, V, p. 115.

90 Marinell Ash, 'David Bernham, Bishop of St Andrews, 1239-1253' in David McRoberts (ed.), *The Medieval Church of St Andrews* (Glasgow, 1976), pp. 32-44, at p. 34.

91 Andrew Barrell, 'Scotland and the Papacy in the Reign of Alexander II' in Richard Oram (ed.), *The Reign of Alexander II, 1214-49* (Turnhout, 2005), pp. 157-78, at p. 173.

92 *FES*, p. 380; Dowden, 'Scottish Crown and the Episcopate', p. 134.

pope had the right to examine, confirm and consecrate all Scottish bishops – that is, to perform the duties more usually carried out by the archbishop of the province in question.[93] In practice, however, this right was often delegated, at least in part, to existing members of the Scottish episcopate. In this manner, the bishops of Glasgow, Moray and Caithness were ordered to examine the bishop-elect of Aberdeen, and the process of his election. If they were satisfied by their findings, they were to consecrate him, receive his oath (according to the form of a simultaneously issued bull) and ensure that he received the obedience of the clergy and people of the diocese. If the elect or the election were found to be wanting, they were to annul the election and order another to be held.[94] Following a seven-year vacancy at Argyll, in 1248 the bishops of Glasgow and Dunblane were ordered to cancel any uncanonical elections that had been made to the see; furthermore, if the canons failed to elect within three months, the bishops were empowered to appoint and consecrate an individual of their choice.[95]

Despite frequently being entrusted with the exercise of archiepiscopal powers, the bishops were not given free rein to act as if they were archbishops. Power was delegated on an election by election basis, and the bishops appointed to examine and consecrate varied on each occasion, presumably to prevent any single bishop from achieving the status of an acting archbishop. Furthermore, the pope always had the opportunity to confirm capitular choices himself or to veto undesirable candidates. He also retained certain rights over dispensations. Thus, when an illegitimate canon named Geoffrey was postulated to the see of Dunkeld in 1236, the examination of the candidate was delegated to three of the Scottish bishops, but their power to dispense him for illegitimacy was quite clearly derived from Rome.[96] As the thirteenth century progressed, papal intervention became more commonplace and from the middle of the century onwards, papal provision became steadily more significant as a mode of appointment. Sometimes elections simply received papal confirmation, as in the case of Hugh of Aberdeen (1272)[97] and John of Brechin (1298).[98] On other occasions, elections were annulled, only for the former bishop-elect to be provided to the see, as happened at Aberdeen in 1282. Henry, precentor of Aberdeen, was unanimously elected by the chapter, but Martin IV annulled the

---

93 For the text of *Cum universi*, see *Anglo-Scottish Relations, 1174-1328: Some Selected Documents*, ed. E. L. G. Stones (London, 1965), pp. 14-16.

94 *CPL*, I, p. 182.

95 *CPL*, I, p. 251.

96 *CPL*, I, p. 157.

97 *CPL*, I, p. 442.

98 *CPL*, I, pp. 575-6.

election because the elect was not in holy orders. This defect was remedied and Henry was then reappointed.[99]

Just as the pope was not always willing to ratify the choices of English and French chapters, either by confirmation or provision, he sometimes rejected Scottish bishops-elect. One of the earliest papal provisions to a Scottish bishopric was made to Glasgow in 1259.[100] The cathedral chapter elected Nicholas Moffat, archdeacon of Teviotdale, who went to Rome to seek papal consecration. He was thwarted in his efforts to secure his bishopric,

> partly because he was unwilling to pay a sum of money which the pope and cardinals demanded from him (for he did not wish to seem to have entered into the sheepfold save by the door), and partly because those who had accompanied him, apparently for his assistance, on the contrary opposed him with all their might.[101]

Foremost amongst his opponents was Robert de Prebenda, canon of Glasgow and bishop-elect of Dunblane, who was 'so far blinded in his pride as to imagine that if the election of the other were quashed, he himself might easily be able to mount up to the see of Glasgow'.[102] Robert's ambitions were also left unsatisfied; he was consecrated as bishop of Dunblane and John de Cheam was provided to the bishopric of Glasgow. Alexander III's considerable protests against this provision went unheeded, and once the king realized that his requests that the provision be overturned would not be heeded, he was soon reconciled to the new bishop. When the new bishop returned to Scotland in 1260, the king received him 'kindly' and facilitated his enthronement.[103] The peaceful ending of the dispute should not, however, be allowed to obscure two interesting aspects of the royal reaction to this dispute. The first is the mere fact that objections were made; as in England, the king was clearly deeply suspicious of this new method of appointment. Secondly, Alexander's objections focused not on the identity of the new bishop, but on Pope Alexander IV's attempts to restore the temporalities of the see at the time of the consecration, following which Cheam attempted to draw the revenues of his see immediately. When the Scottish Alexander protested that this was contrary to the customs of his kingdom, according to which the temporalities should not be restored until the new bishop had sworn fealty to the crown, the pope countered with another

---

99 *CPL*, I, p. 465.

100 For a biographical study of the provisee, including details of his appointment, see Evan Balfour-Melville, 'John de Cheam, Bishop of Glasgow', *SHR*, 27 (1948), pp. 176-86.

101 *Melrose*, pp. 92-3.

102 Ibid., p. 93.

103 Ibid.

mandate for the restoration of the temporalities, under threat of papal censure; this was to be enforced by two English bishops, Gravesend of Lincoln and Bitton of Bath.[104] Ultimately, Alexander IV backed down, ordering John of Cheam to present himself to the king (a safe conduct having been granted) and 'on taking the said oath, to receive the temporalities at the king's hands, revoking whatever may have been done by the above bishops [i.e. Gravesend and Bitton] against the king or his realm'.[105]

This papal bull relating to Cheam was preserved in the royal archive at Edinburgh Castle and was recorded in a 1282 inventory of this store, the primary aim of which was to make a record of received correspondence relating to the rights of and agreements made by the king of Scots in relation to external parties such as the pope, and the kings of England and Norway. Amongst this collection was a document (no longer in existence) in which M. Richard of Lanark reported to William of Dumfries, a clerk of Alexander III, that 'certain bulls were in the Roman curia', according to which the king was not obliged to grant any possessions of any bishopric to a new bishop until the prelate had sworn fealty to the crown.[106] The similarities between Scottish concerns about royal rights over episcopal temporalities and English royal complaints about papal attempts to restore the temporalities to newly provided bishops are striking.

The fourteenth century saw the rapid expansion of papal provision to Scottish sees; by the middle of the century, elections were still being held, but were significant only as a means of suggesting a candidate to the pope.[107] Thus James Ben, archdeacon of St Andrews, was elected to that see in 1328; his election was quashed, but he was then provided. Election alone was rarely enough to secure the papal provision of a candidate, and Ben's case illustrates the importance of some factors familiar from the examination of English provisions. His chances were greatly improved by the backing of Robert I, and by his presence at the curia at the time that the see fell vacant.[108] As in England, the rise of provision aided rather than hindered the appointment of royal candidates, for the pope was usually willing to provide the candidate suggested to him by the monarch. In the late fourteenth and fifteenth centuries, the majority of bishops were chosen by the king, a practice restated by a papal indult of 1487, which allowed a space of six months between the death of one bishop and the provision of the next,

104 Balfour-Melville, 'John de Cheam', pp. 179-80.

105 *CPL*, I, p. 372.

106 *The Acts of the Parliaments of Scotland, 1124-1707*, ed. T. Thomson (12 vols, Edinburgh, 1814-74), I, pp. 107-110.

107 Andrew Barrell, *The Papacy, Scotland and Northern England, 1342-1378* (Cambridge, 1995), pp. 191-204.

108 *FES*, p. 381.

in order that royal nominations might be made. Consequently, there was little serious secular resistance.[109]

To turn again to the entire period under consideration, in practical terms, the direct relationship between Scotland and the papacy appears to have had relatively little impact on the manner in which elections were conducted or the nature of the bishops appointed. Nor did the pope take advantage of this unusual relationship to quash more elections or to introduce provision at an earlier date. The Scottish experience of election and the transition to provision was broadly similar to the English.

There were, however, some further peculiarities in the Scottish electoral experience which provide interesting contrasts with England. These electoral peculiarities occurred primarily in the two anomalous sees – Whithorn and Sodor – which were subject to, respectively, the archbishops of York and Nidaros, being exempt from the direct papal oversight that covered the rest of Scotland.[110] The atypical status of these sees must have created an unusually fluid relationship between political and ecclesiastical allegiance, which might plausibly have led to increased electoral complexity, and yet the reasons for this cannot be solely attributed to the influence of foreign metropolitans, not least because similar problems occurred in sees such as Argyll, which were wholly integrated into the ecclesiastical fabric of medieval Scotland.

In the definition of the electoral body, Scotland seems to have lagged some way behind its neighbour. By the early thirteenth century the sole right of the English cathedral chapters to elect their bishops was quite firmly established in the vast majority of sees. In the handful of dioceses where rights of participation were subject to dispute (for example at Winchester, where the archdeacons elected for the final time in 1238, at Canterbury, where the suffragans of the province argued for their participation into the 1230s, and in the double sees of Coventry and Lichfield and Bath and Wells) final settlements were in place by the middle of the century. In contrast, disputes of this kind persisted in Scotland into the early fourteenth century, most notably at St Andrews. Until the early twelfth century, the dominant religious community in the city had been the priory of the Culdees, a community of Celtic monks, which had been attached to the cathedral since the mid-tenth century.[111] Then, in 1144, a community of Augustinian canons was established as the cathedral chapter; it was apparently

[109] Dowden, *Medieval Church*, pp. 26-7; Alexander Grant, *Independence and Nationhood: Scotland, 1306-1469* (London, 1984), p. 93.

[110] For overviews of the relationship between these dioceses and their metropolitans, see Oram, 'In Obedience and Reverence', pp. 83-100; Sarah Thomas, 'The Diocese of Sodor between Nidaross and Avignon-Rome, 1266-1472', *Northern Studies*, 41 (2009/10), pp. 22-40.

[111] Geoffrey Barrow, 'The Clergy at St Andrews' in Geoffrey Barrow, *The Kingdom of the Scots: Government, Church and Society from the Eleventh to the Fourteenth Century* (London, 1973), pp. 212-32, at p. 212.

envisaged that the regular canons would eventually replace the Culdees. The Augustinians were to have the right of election, which there is no evidence that the Culdees had ever exercised. The first known example of Culdean participation in a St Andrews election dates from 1239, when they took part at the insistence of the king. From this date onwards, the Culdees made further vigorous claims to participate, unsuccessfully seeking papal confirmation of this right.[112] In 1254, the proctor, provost and chapter objected to the election of the dean of Dunkeld, which was subsequently overturned by Innocent IV.[113] The following year, the prior and convent of St Andrews received a papal indult that

> no prejudice shall arise to them and their church from their having, at the request of the king and of Master Gamelin, bishop elect, admitted under protest two of the Culdees of St Mary's ... to take part in the election of the late David [de Bernham], bishop of St Andrews [1239-53].[114]

The Culdees took part in no further elections, but in 1298 their provost, William Comyn, appealed against the election of William Lamberton on the grounds of his non-participation. Having renounced this appeal, in order to avoid prolonging the vacancy, he secured a papal decree which ordered that this renunciation would not prejudice his right, or that of his successors, to participate in future elections.[115] Only in 1332 did the Culdees finally abandon their quest for electoral rights at St Andrews.[116]

The Culdees were able to repeatedly reassert their claims because they enjoyed the backing of powerful men, including the king, and because many of them were themselves members of powerful families; far from being oppressed Celtic holy men, they were active players in the contemporary politics and ecclesiastical affairs.[117] Equally significant, however, was the wider Scottish context, and the ongoing St Andrews debate must be set alongside even more striking examples of blurring in the boundaries of electoral bodies. In several dioceses, the lack of a properly constituted chapter meant that election by the clergy and people survived long after it had been prohibited by the canon law. Not until the 1340s did Argyll have a cathedral chapter of the type that existed in every English diocese. Instead, four members of the diocesan clergy served as the electoral body: the deans of Glassary, Lorne, Kintyre (representing the clergy of the diocese) and Lismore (representing the city and cathedral). When

---

112 Ibid., pp. 212-15, 226-8.

113 *CPL*, I, p. 297.

114 *CPL*, I, p. 319.

115 *CPL*, I, p. 578.

116 Dowden, *Medieval Church*, pp. 22-3.

117 Barrow, 'St Andrews', pp. 215-25.

the cathedral chapter was first established, confusion reigned and a dispute occurred: Martin of Argyll was elected by the chapter, but Angus of Ergadia claimed the see on the grounds that he had been elected 'according to ancient and approved custom by the clergy of the city and diocese of Argyll'. The pair engaged in litigation at the papal curia and Martin's election was confirmed only after the death of Angus.[118]

Elsewhere, the people of the diocese elected alongside the clergy. Two elections were held at Whithorn in 1235. Gilbert, novice-master at Melrose Abbey, was elected first, 'as well by the clergy as by the entire population of Galloway, with the exception of the prior and convent of Whithorn'.[119] The latter group then elected Odo, one of their brethren, and went to York to seek his consecration. Somewhat surprisingly, Walter de Gray rejected the capitular candidate and instead confirmed and consecrated Gilbert,[120] despite the uncanonical nature of the electoral process. His decision was probably influenced by Alexander II's support for Gilbert; the Scottish king had only recently conquered Galloway, and the appointment of a bishop who was favourable to the Scottish crown was one means of encouraging regional stability. The failure of the Whithorn chapter to seek archiepiscopal permission to hold an election also seems to have rankled with Archbishop Gray and may have made him ill-disposed towards Odo from the start.[121] The election of 1253 was slightly more orthodox: the elect of the clergy and people was again confirmed, but this time only after he had been re-elected by the Whithorn chapter at York.[122]

Rival electorates were also an issue in the province of Sodor. The right of election had been granted to the monks of Furness Abbey in Cumbria by Olaf, king of Man, when he founded the house in 1134. Their rights were confirmed by Innocent IV in 1244, but were intermittently challenged during the early thirteenth century, before being finally overturned in 1275 by King Alexander III (who acquired the patronage of the see from the king of Norway according to the terms of the Treaty of Perth in 1266).[123] The king of Man and the Isles had actively supported the electoral rights of the clergy and people. When Luke, archdeacon of the Isles was elected by 'the entire chapter of Man' in 1248, he

118 Ian Cowan, 'The Church in Argyll and the Isles' in Ian Cowan, *The Medieval Church in Scotland*, ed. James Kirk (Edinburgh, 1995), pp. 129-43, at pp. 136-7.

119 *Melrose*, p. 61.

120 Ibid.; *FES*, p. 169.

121 Anne Ashley, 'Odo, Elect of Whithorn, 1235', *Transactions of the Dumfries and Galloway Natural History and Antiquarian Society*, 37 (1958), pp. 62-9; Richard Oram, *The Lordship of Galloway* (Edinburgh, 2000), pp. 179-84; Barrell, 'Scotland and the Papacy', p. 173; Oram, 'Whithorn and York', pp. 96-8.

122 Robert Brentano, 'The Whithorn Vacancy of 1293-94', *Innes Review*, 4 (1953), pp. 71-83, at p. 72.

123 *Scottish Annals*, pp. 381-2; Cowan, 'Church in Argyll and the Isles', pp. 130-31.

went to Norway to seek confirmation and consecration, only for the king to insist that a new election must be held, in his presence, by all the clergy and people. This second election never took place, because the king and the bishop-elect were both drowned when their ship sank on the journey back to Man. The next bishop, Richard of Natherton (1253-75), was appointed at the papal curia by the archbishop of Nidaros. After the Isles were transferred to Scottish hands, the electorate remained unconventional in its composition.[124] In 1275, Alexander III withheld assent from the election by the clergy and people, and instead nominated his own candidate to the archbishop of Nidaros.[125] Alan de Wigtown (1303x1305-1322) was imposed by Anthony Bek, bishop of Durham and lord of Man,[126] against the wishes of the Furness monks, who continued to claim rights of appointment. After a straightforward election by an unknown party in 1324,[127] Bernard, abbot of Arbroath and chancellor of Robert I, was appointed in 1327 by Robert I in order to increase his control in the west of Scotland. At around the same time, the canons of Snizort and the clergy of Skye elected Cormac Cormacii; they were still trying to secure his consecration in Nidaros in the summer of 1331, around which time Bishop Bernard died. The dispute was brought to an effective conclusion by the papal provision of Thomas de Rossay (1341-48).[128] Even after provision became the sole means of appointment, the clergy of Man continued to claim the right of election, in the absence of a full-scale cathedral chapter.[129]

The crown's acceptance of election by electors who did not belong to the cathedral chapter is easy to understand, since it gave the king greater scope for influence, offering him the chance to influence two separate groups of electors. More surprising is the papal acceptance of such practices, given the vigour with which the canon law of elections was enforced in England. (One thinks of the monks of Durham, who had their unanimous election of William Stichill quashed because they had acclaimed him separately, rather than as one.) The explanation must surely be found in papal pragmatism. In England, where the cathedral chapters were all in place by the early twelfth century (and many long

124 *FES*, p. 261.

125 Ibid.; *Scottish Annals*, pp. 381-2.

126 Bek had been created lord of Man by Edward I in 1290, at the time of the Treaty of Birgham. He was appointed as lieutenant of Queen Margaret and Prince Edward, who were expected to marry. Although the marriage never took place, because of Margaret's premature death, Bek retained at least nominal control of Man until the end of his life (barring a brief period in the late 1300s when the island was in the hands of Piers Gaveston). See Geoffrey Barrow, *Robert Bruce and the Community of the Realm of Scotland*, 4th edn (Edinburgh, 2005), pp. 38-9, 252-3.

127 *FES*, pp. 261-2.

128 Sarah Thomas, 'Rival Bishops, Rival Cathedrals: The Election of Cormac, Archdeacon of Sodor, as Bishop in 1331', *Innes Review*, 60 (2009), pp. 145-63.

129 *FES*, pp. 262-3.

before this), it was possible to focus on the detail. In Scotland, where the process of the formation of many of the cathedral chapters did not begin until the thirteenth century,[130] such an approach was impossible to enforce and thus the papacy (and, in the case of Whithorn and Sodor, the archbishops) rarely tried.

Another peculiarity of the Scottish electoral experience was the extent to which foreigners were involved in its episcopal appointments. There are some examples of foreign rulers intervening to support the wishes of the Scottish king; William Landallis was provided to St Andrews in 1342 on the recommendation of David II of Scotland and Philip VI of France.[131] Other interventions were far more substantial. Papal authority over Scotland was delegated to a string of legates, many of whom were also involved in English affairs. The 1244 appointment of Master Martin, a papal nuncio in England, to examine disputed elections at Moray and Argyll provoked protest from Alexander II, who complained that electoral disputes were being taken outside the realm. Innocent IV pledged that election cases would no longer be committed outside the realm, by either the pope or his legates; if it was necessary to do so, the case should be heard in Durham or Carlisle, rather than in York.[132]

Alexander's complaints should be placed within the context of York's claims to exercise jurisdiction over the Scottish Church. Although these claims had effectively been put to rest by *Cum universi*,[133] the crown remained sensitive to any attempts by York metropolitans to exercise influence within their kingdom. Any suggestion that an archbishop of York might serve as legate in Scotland was particularly repugnant, evoking memories of the last such mission, during the St Andrews dispute of the 1180s. The archbishop of York was far from being the only Englishman to play a role in Scottish appointments. In 1260, during the dispute that followed the provision of John de Cheam to Glasgow, the bishops of Lincoln and Bath were appointed by Alexander IV to ensure that the king restored the temporalities to the new bishop, although he subsequently admitted that this infringed on the king's rights and the ancient customs of the realm.[134]

English kings intervened in Scottish elections to a far greater extent than Scottish kings intervened in English elections, largely due to English claims of over-lordship in Scotland. Henry II was a significant player in the St Andrews dispute of 1178-88. The legatine mission of 1180 was based at the English garrison in Edinburgh Castle; once its failure became apparent, the bishop-elect and his uncle, Bishop Matthew of Aberdeen, fled to the protection of

---

130 Cowan, 'Secular Cathedral Chapters', pp. 78-96.

131 Barrell, *Papacy, Scotland and Northern England*, p. 192.

132 Ferguson, *Representatives*, pp. 97-8, 199-200.

133 For their twelfth-century history, see Barrell, '*Cum universi*', pp. 116-17.

134 *CPL*, I, p. 372.

the Angevin king, then in Normandy. In spring 1181 William the Lion was summoned to a meeting with Henry II and Bishop John, at which a peaceful settlement was sought, although not obtained.[135]

During the reign of Henry III, relations between the two kingdoms were for the most part extremely cordial,[136] but this did not prevent the English king intervening in Scottish appointments. In 1259, the pope asked Henry to use his influence with his son-in-law Alexander III to ensure that the new bishop of Glasgow, John of Cheam, could return to the country. In March 1260 Henry, who was then at St Omer (where Cheam had probably recently arrived), wrote to Alexander, Queen Margaret, Robert Bruce and the whole Council of Scotland to exhort the acceptance of the new bishop 'since the pope's order cannot be invalidated'.[137] Henry did not always take such a philosophical approach when the papacy encroached on his own rights.

Henry's involvement took the form of friendly advice, but after the death of Alexander III in 1286 and the beginning of the Anglo-Scottish wars, English incursions became more forceful. Between 1286 and 1306, fourteen bishops were appointed to Scottish sees; two of these appointments, to Sodor and Caithness, were made through the influence of Edward I. Five appointments were made under John Balliol, all of them in 1295-96, although Barrow suggests that they reflect the choices of the council of twelve rather than of Balliol himself.[138] The ability of the English crown to appoint to Scottish sees was somewhat limited by papal attitudes to such activities. In 1306, William Lamberton, bishop of St Andrews (1272-1316), and Robert Wishart, bishop of Glasgow (1271-1316), both close allies of Robert Bruce who had played a prominent role in the rebellion against English rule, were captured and imprisoned by the English.[139] Edward I promptly tried to have them replaced, nominating Geoffrey de Moubray to Glasgow and William Comyn to St Andrews,[140] but his ambitions died with him the following year. Edward II released Lamberton, who returned to Scotland; he continued to oppose Wishart and tried unsuccessfully to bring about his deposition and the appointment of Stephen Segrave.[141] Throughout his reign, Edward continued to make attempts to dictate the fate of Scottish bishoprics, with varying degrees of success. In 1318, he procured the provision

135 Duncan, 'John'.

136 Michael Brown, 'Henry the Peaceable: Henry III, Alexander III and Royal Lordship in the British Isles, 1249-1272' in Bjorn Weiler and Ivor Rowlands (eds), *England and Europe in the Reign of Henry III, 1216-1272* (Aldershot, 2002), pp. 43-66.

137 *CR 1259-1261*, p. 277; Balfour-Melville, 'John of Cheam', p. 179.

138 Geoffrey Barrow, 'The Scottish Clergy in the War of Independence', *SHR*, 131 (1962), pp. 1-22, at pp. 4-5.

139 Menache, *Clement*, p. 272.

140 *FES*, pp. 190, 381.

141 Menache, *Clement*, p. 273.

of John Egglescliffe, one of his penitentiary friars, to Glasgow; the capitular election was quashed to allow the appointment to be made.[142] Generally, however, John XXII was unsympathetic to Edward's Scottish ambitions. Also in 1318, Edward revived the scheme for the deposition of William Lamberton, falsely claiming that Clement V had agreed to this and proposing Thomas Rivers as a suitable replacement. John replied that he could find no evidence for his predecessor's agreement and that he was unable to make such an appointment. Six years later, in 1324, Edward petitioned that Egglescliffe should not be translated from Glasgow and that no Scottish prelate should be appointed to a Scottish bishopric. Unsurprisingly, the pope refused to grant this outrageous request, pointing out that English clerics such as Egglescliffe were unable to reside in their sees and therefore failed to carry out their pastoral duties.[143]

Scottish magnates also sought to influence the outcome of episcopal elections, and they appear to have done so more often, and with greater success, than their counterparts south of the border. Aristocratic power seems to have been incorporated more into the functional structures of Scottish royal government than it was in England, and this was especially marked in peripheral areas where royal control was less secure. For example, John Balliol and the Comyn family played a central role in the 1254 Whithorn election. Henry, abbot of Holyrood was elected with the support of the Comyn councillors, but Balliol wrote to the archbishop of York to object.[144] His actions were presumably justified by the fact that although he was not lord of Galloway, his wife, Dervorguilla, was one of the three heiresses to Galloway. He claimed to act in defence of his 'ancient liberties', and those of the people of Galloway, against the papal introduction of capitular election;[145] Oram has described his actions as 'self-interested and isolated'.[146] Ultimately, the Comyn candidate triumphed, being confirmed by Archbishop Gray in February 1255.[147]

The Balliols were involved in the next Whithorn election in 1294, which produced a dispute in which Robert Bruce, lord of Annandale, was also involved.[148] Thomas Dalton was elected by the cathedral chapter; he was a Bruce clerk, and his appointment had the backing of his employer. King John Balliol countered with a letter to Archbishop Romeyn of York, in which he complained

---

142 *FES*, pp. 190-91.

143 Sarah Layfield, 'The Pope, the Scots and their "Self-Styled" King: John XXII's Anglo-Scottish Policy, 1316-1334' in Andy King and Michael Penman (eds), *England and Scotland in the Fourteenth Century: New Perspectives* (Woodbridge, 2007), pp. 157-71, at pp. 166-7.

144 *FES*, p. 169.

145 Amanda Beam, *The Balliol Dynasty, 1210-1364* (Edinburgh, 2008), pp. 59-62.

146 Oram, *Lordship*, p. 157.

147 *The Register, or Rolls, of Walter Gray, Lord Archbishop of York*, ed. J. Raine (Durham, 1872), pp. 120-22.

148 For what follows see Beam, *Balliol Dynasty*, pp. 129-32, and Brentano, *Whithorn*, pp. 71-83.

that Thomas had been elected 'not by inspiration or even charitable nature, but through certain promises [and] simony'.[149] Ultimately though, like his father four decades earlier, Balliol was forced to concede defeat, withdrawing his objections due to 'the requests of the venerable nobles both distinguished and great', and restoring the temporalities to the new bishop in May 1295.[150]

Whithorn is the diocese in which noble involvement in elections is best documented but, to judge from the composition of the episcopate, it was certainly not the only diocese in which noble influence was felt either directly or through the king. Abraham's election as bishop of Dunblane, which took place at an unknown date between 1210 and 1214, was surely related to his position as chaplain of the powerful Earl of Strathearn.[151] Gilbert of Dunkeld (1229x30-36) was previously chaplain of Bishop Hugh de Sigillo;[152] Albin of Brechin (1246-69) was probably the illegitimate grandson of Earl David, and thus a distant kinsman of the king.[153] Robert Wishart of Glasgow (1271-1316) was a nephew of William Wishart, the royal chancellor, and was elected at the king's request;[154] Henry Cheyne of Aberdeen (1282-1328/9) had close links to the Comyn family;[155] and there were several others. In Scotland as in England and France, personal connections to powerful individuals certainly did not hinder one's chances of securing a bishopric.

The paucity of biographical information relating to the majority of Scottish bishops of this period makes it difficult to produce a meaningful analysis of the composition of the episcopate. Nevertheless, it is possible to make some general points about the similarities and differences in the composition of the English and Scottish episcopates. As in England, many of Scotland's bishops were former or current royal administrators, although the proportion appears to be somewhat lower: sixteen of the ninety-nine bishops successfully appointed to Scottish sees between 1214 and 1344 are known to have been in royal service, whereas even at the nadir of the curial bishop in England (c.1307), the proportion was a little over 20 per cent. In 1327, 70 per cent of English bishops were former or current *curiales*. Diocesan clergy, including members of the cathedral chapter in question, were frequently elected to both English and Scottish sees.

One pre-episcopal career path occurred a number of times in the Scottish episcopate, but never in England. On several occasions during the first half of the thirteenth century, the chaplains of powerful men were promoted to the

---

149 *Northern Registers*, pp. 104-5, App. C, no. 20.

150 Beam, *Balliol Dynasty*, p. 132.

151 *The Paradox of Medieval Scotland Database:* www.poms.ac.uk/db/record/person/749.

152 www.poms.ac.uk/db/record/person/468.

153 www.poms.ac.uk/db/record/person/407.

154 www.poms.ac.uk/db/record/person/2134; Archibald Duncan, 'Robert Wishart', *ODNB*.

155 www.poms.ac.uk/db/record/person/1983; Norman Reid, 'Henry Cheyne', *ODNB*.

Scottish episcopate, amongst them Robert, bishop of Ross (1214-49), the chaplain of William the Lion, and Gilbert of Dunkeld (1229x30-36), chaplain of Bishop Hugh de Sigillo. In contrast, only one royal chaplain was suggested as a possible English bishop,[156] and he failed even to be elected. The contrast is striking, but difficult to explain, for a royal chaplain would seem a promising candidate for the episcopate, a presumably pious man who was also loyal to the king and familiar with the ways of the world.

The relatively large numbers of monks and Dominican friars elected to Scottish sees also comes as something of a surprise to the English historian. The proportion of regular bishops is not dissimilar to the English ratio: twenty-one of the ninety-nine bishops appointed in Scotland, compared to around a quarter of the incumbent bishops in England. However, in England regular bishops were almost always elected by and from within monastic convents, and no secular chapter ever freely elected a bishop of this kind (although a very few were imposed by legates or provided by the pope). Given that Scotland had only two regular chapters (the Premonstratensian canons at Whithorn and the Augustinian canons at St Andrews) and eleven dioceses where the electoral bodies consisted of secular canons and/or the clergy and people, one might plausibly expect to find very few bishops belonging to religious orders. Yet, between 1214 and 1344, five Tironensians, six Augustinians, four Cistercians and six Dominicans acquired Scottish bishoprics, the majority of them by episcopal election. A further four regulars were elected or nominated (one each from the Augustinian, Premonstratensian, Cistercian and Dominican orders), only to have their elections quashed by the pope. In none of these cases does there appear to have been any sign of opposition based on the elect's membership of a religious order; the English hostility to monk-bishops does not seem to have infected Scotland. Furthermore, like France, Scotland embraced the idea of the friar-bishop in a way that England never did.[157] It is likely that these variations were caused in part by differences in the extent to which the religious orders were incorporated into wider political and ecclesiastical structures.[158] The majority of the Scottish monks elected came from powerful houses with close links to the crown, such as Arbroath, Melrose and Holyrood,[159] whereas

---

[156] John of Newburgh, chaplain of Henry III, was suggested by the king as a potential bishop of Carlisle in 1254. See *CPR 1247-1258*, p. 292.

[157] Robert Swanson, 'Mendicant Bishops in the British Isles in the Thirteenth and Early Fourteenth Centuries', in *Dal Pulpito alla Cattedra: i Vescovi degli Ordini Mendicanti nel '200 e nel Primo '300* (Spoleto, 2000), pp. 306-47.

[158] On the power of Scottish monasteries, see Richard Oram, 'Prayer, Property and Profit: Scottish Monasteries, c.1100-c.1300' in Sally Foster, Allan Macinnes and Ranald MacInnes (eds), *Scottish Power Centres: From Early Middle Ages to the Twentieth Century* (Glasgow, 1998), pp. 79-99.

[159] See Geoffrey Barrow, 'The Royal House and the Religious Orders' and 'Benedictines, Tironensians and Cistercians' in Geoffrey Barrow, *The Kingdom of the Scots: Government, Church*

the English Benedictine cathedral priories which provided most of the English monk-bishops were somewhat more independent.

Cultural differences may also have played an important part in perpetuating this difference. It seems that scepticism about the suitability of monks for episcopal office was a particularly English trait, which was possibly rooted in a peculiarly English conception of the model bishop. The great wealth of many of the English bishoprics, combined with their sheer physical size, meant that administrative ability was of great value in a member of the episcopate. Members of the regular clergy had, or at least were widely perceived as having, very little administrative experience; to put such a man in a position where he was expected to provide secular services to both his diocese and the realm was an act of questionable wisdom. Consequently, the English (or at least those who did not belong to or have considerable sympathy for the religious orders) were reluctant to accept such men as bishops. Elsewhere in Europe, in countries where bishoprics were much poorer (Scotland) or rather more numerous (France), and where the responsibilities and powers of the bishops were somewhat diluted, the electorate and the king could afford to be more open-minded about regular bishops.

Italy

As home of the Holy See, and of the pope himself throughout the thirteenth century, Italy's position vis-à-vis the papacy was even more peculiar than Scotland's; inevitably, this had an impact on the manner in which its episcopal appointments were handled. In contrast to England, Scotland and France, the country lacked a single powerful monarch and was instead extremely politically fragmented. It was also divided in ecclesiastical terms, since it consisted of 259 sees, many of them tiny in size. Forty-two per cent of these dioceses (eighty-one bishoprics, along with twenty-eight archbishoprics), the majority of them in central Italy, were directly subject to Rome.[160] Consequently, as in Scotland, archiepiscopal jurisdiction over elections was limited, whilst papal influence was unusually direct. A study of Italian episcopal appointments therefore offers the opportunity to discover how far the electoral experience differed when central royal government was lacking and papal control was considerably stronger.

Broadly speaking, the answer is that little changed. According to Robert Brentano, 'in Italy as in England, the thirteenth century was one of mixed

and Society from the Eleventh to the Fourteenth Century (London, 1973), pp. 165-87, 188-211, for the connections between the royal family and the religious houses in the twelfth and thirteenth centuries.

160 Montaubin, 'Nominations Épiscopales en Italie', pp. 778-9.

capitular election and papal provision; and in Italy as in England disputed elections provoked papal action'.[161] There were, however, some significant differences, particularly in relation to the introduction of provision. In England the first papal provision to a bishopric was made in response to an electoral dispute in the late 1220s; the first Scottish provision seems to date from the 1250s. In Italy, the practice made its debut somewhat earlier, during the pontificate of Innocent III (1198-1216). On numerous occasions Innocent refused to accept the choices made by Italian electors. Often he ordered a new election to be held; this was usually done in the conventional fashion in the vacant diocese, but occasionally a new election was supervised by papal proctors or held at the papal curia.[162] Neither of these practices was unfamiliar to English electors of the early thirteenth century, since Stephen Langton was elected at Rome and numerous elections were held under the watchful eye of a succession of legates. But in Italy, even at this early date, Innocent III was not only rejecting capitular choices or seeking to influence them, but also overruling capitular rights of election altogether. On at least nineteen occasions he appointed a new bishop to a vacant see. Like the first English provisions, these early Italian provisions were responsive, in the sense that they typically followed one or more elections with problematic outcomes. At Penne, for example, the provision followed the papal rejection of two successive capitular candidates, in 1199 and 1200. At Fondi, two uncanonical electoral processes resulted in the election of the same unfit candidate, Giovanni de Pastena, and when a third election produced another unsuitable elect, a provision was made.[163]

Despite the early introduction of provision, direct appointments by the pope remained rare for some time, and Montaubin argues that it is unwise to see the origins of later general reservations in the pontificate of Innocent III.[164] Elections were held throughout the thirteenth century, often without major dispute or excessive papal involvement. Thus when the archbishop of Bari died in 1280, the canons of his church were able to hold a free election. Their choice fell upon the legist Romnoaldo, chaplain to the cardinal bishop of Ostia; he accepted, and his election received papal confirmation shortly afterwards.[165] Nor did a see's first experience of provision necessarily spell the end of its opportunities to elect; at Città di Castello, bishops were provided in 1252 and 1265, but the next bishop was elected, in 1280.[166]

---

161 Robert Brentano, *Two Churches: England and Italy in the Thirteenth Century*, rev. edn (Berkeley, 1988), p. 213.

162 Montaubin, 'Nominations Épiscopales en Italie', p. 799.

163 Ibid., pp. 800-802.

164 Ibid., pp. 803-4.

165 Brentano, *Two Churches*, p. 216.

166 Ibid., p. 218.

Nevertheless, it is impossible to escape the conclusion that provision became commonplace in Italy when it was still a novelty elsewhere. In the archdiocese of Aquileia,[167] the century began (in 1204) with a free election, although since the chapter's choice, Volcher, was already bishop of Pavia, the pope had to authorize his translation. When Volcher died in 1218, an election was held, with some of the canons favouring one of their brethren, whilst others chose Bertold of Merano, a Hungarian archbishop. Honorius III declared the election to be void, due to a procedural flaw, and exercised his right, as the immediate superior, to appoint the new archbishop. His choice was Archbishop Bertold.

Aquileia was, it must be admitted, something of an oddity: its archbishop held the title of 'Patriarch' and it had strong historical links to Germany, from whence many of its previous prelates had originated. It is nevertheless striking that only two decades into the thirteenth century, and ten years before the first English provision was made, this Italian see had been subject to a translation and a reactive provision. In 1251, it experienced its first proactive provision: Innocent IV, apparently without justifying his actions, appointed Gregory of Montelongo, a kinsman of Innocent III and an extremely effective papal legate. From this point onwards, every patriarch of Aquileia was appointed by the pope; elections were not held or were quashed, or simply disregarded.

As an archdiocese located in a politically sensitive region, it would be expected that Aquileia would be at the vanguard of the transition to provision, and the shift did indeed take place relatively early. In addition, the fact that no elections were held after 1251 is indicative of an unusually decisive shift (although it was echoed at Tivoli, where provisions were made continuously from 1265[168]). Nevertheless, studies of a number of other Italian dioceses located within the Patrimony suggest that the Italian transition advanced more rapidly than was the case in England. In Perugia, the first provision was made in 1254, when Innocent IV rejected the capitular choice and appointed Master Bernardus, a papal chaplain. During subsequent vacancies, elections were held, but these typically resulted in split decisions and always ended with a papal provision.[169] During the course of the thirteenth century, at least three bishops of Anagni were elected and at least three were provided (the means of appointment is unclear for the other four). The last bishop to be elected seems to have been Pietro di Brunaco in 1290.[170] In Rieti, the first known provision was made in 1252, when Innocent IV appointed Tommaso, corrector of papal letters, to the

---

167 For what follows, see Silano, 'Aquileia', pp. 179-86.

168 Pascal Montaubin, 'Entre Gloire Curiale et Vie Commune: le Chapitre Cathédral d'Anagni au XIIIe Siècle', *Mélanges de l'École Française de Rome. Moyen-Age, Temps Modernes*, 109 (1997), pp. 303-442, at p. 321.

169 Giulio Silano, 'The Apostolic See and the Elections of the Bishops of Perugia in the Duecento and Trecento', *Medieval Studies*, 50 (1988), pp. 488-511.

170 Montaubin, 'Anagni', pp. 319-20.

bishopric. Clear evidence of papal provision survives for all but one of the eight subsequent bishops, but in 1339 the canons succeeded in having their election of Tommaso II confirmed. After this late aberration, the bishops of Rieti all owed their appointment to the papacy.[171]

As in England, the Italian experience varied from diocese to diocese; some sees experienced provision much earlier than others and some had been subject to a string of provisions by the early fourteenth century, whilst for others election remained a possibility. This all changed for a considerable number of Italian dioceses on 13 September 1319, when John XXII published a general reservation of all churches, including episcopal and archiepiscopal ones, within the lands of the Roman Church.[172] Such general reservations had previously been made in other countries, including England for a brief period in the 1260s and the French province of Narbonne during the pontificate of Innocent IV (when the threat of heresy was at its peak). They typically had limited practical impact, with only one nomination being made in Narbonne and two in England.[173] The Italian reservation was much wider ranging and was enforced with considerably more enthusiasm, foreshadowing the eventual Europe-wide reservation of 1362.

Given that the papacy had secular as well as ecclesiastical interests in Italy, it was inevitable that the papal approach to Italian ecclesiastical vacancies would be influenced by political and financial concerns. As late as the pontificate of Benedict XII, papal provisions to Italian bishoprics were most numerous in the Papal States. The southern sees were mostly extremely poor, located within the kingdom of Naples, and therefore of less interest to the papacy. The northern sees (such as the archbishoprics of Milan and Ravenna) were very wealthy and the pope frequently made provisions, but his political influence was weaker and therefore his ability to provide was sometimes impeded.[174]

In many respects, papal interventions in Italian elections echo those of secular rulers elsewhere in Europe – but where monarchs had influence over the church, the papacy had authority and its actions were largely irreversible. Consequently, when the Angevin kings of England prolonged episcopal vacancies in order to maximize their financial gain, they came under heavy papal pressure to cease doing so. In Italy, the popes benefited from the fruits of vacant benefices whose last holder had been appointed by papal action, and thus frequently prolonged vacancies past the three months permitted by canon law[175] – but since the pope was above canon law, he could do so with impunity.

---

171 Robert Brentano, *A New World in a Small Place: Church and Religion in the Diocese of Rieti, 1188-1378* (Berkeley, 1994), pp. 146-7.

172 Silano, 'Perugia', p. 492.

173 Guillemain and Martin, 'Élections', p. 108.

174 Guillemain, *Politique Bénéficiale*, p. 99.

175 Silano, 'Perugia', p. 493.

Similarly, just as English (and French and Scottish) kings sought the promotion of men whose appointment would bolster their authority within the kingdom and objected to the elections of potentially disloyal and troublesome individuals, papal policies were shaped by the contemporary political situation. Successive popes pressed the nominations of bishops who were sympathetic to papal ambitions, in order to counter the power of secular opponents, especially the Staufen.[176] The divisions between the Guelph (pro-papal) and Ghibelline (pro-imperial) factions had a significant impact on papal policy, with Guelphs frequently being provided to sees whose loyalty to the pope was questionable. Thus Johannes, archdeacon of Aquileia, was provided to Perugia in 1288; he was a relative of Innocent III and a member of a leading anti-imperial family.[177] Sees in regions loyal to the pope, such as Anagni and Rieti, were more likely to be allowed to elect their own bishops than those in regions such as Tuscany whose sympathies inclined towards the emperor.[178]

The influence of secular powers was not solely indirect, for they also tried to influence the choices made by cathedral chapters and the appointments made by the pope. In early thirteenth-century Sicily, the rights of the king were extremely similar to those of other western rulers. According to the terms of an imperial-papal agreement, made at Messina in 1212, elections were to be canonically free; nevertheless, the king was to be notified as soon as a see fell vacant and had to give his assent to the capitular choice before the new bishop could be enthroned. He also enjoyed rights over the property of vacant churches. As in England and France, royal pledges of electoral freedom did not mean that the king would no longer be able to secure the promotion of his candidates.[179] The influence of secular powers over cathedral chapters and the papacy is also suggested by the appointment of men such as Bertold, the last German patriarch of Aquileia (1218-51), who was elected by part of the cathedral chapter, only to have his election quashed and be provided by Honorius III. It seems unlikely that Bertold's illustrious kin (he was the brother of Otto VII, duke of Merano, of bishop Ecbert of Bamburgh and of Gertrude, queen of Hungary) had nothing to do with his appointment.[180]

More direct evidence of secular intervention comes from early fourteenth-century Siena, where a single Guelph family, the Malavolti, produced four of the five bishops of Siena who held office between 1282 and 1370. The surviving documentation of the election of the fifth, the Dominican Roger of Casole (1307-17) gives a valuable insight into the manner in which an election was held

176 Brentano, *Two Churches*, p. 213.

177 Silano, 'Perugia', p. 502.

178 Montaubin, 'Anagni', pp. 321-2; Brentano, *New World*, pp. 321-2.

179 Matthews, *Sicily*, pp. 309-10.

180 Silano, 'Aquileia', p. 179.

in an Italian city state. On 7 July 1307, the General Council discussed a report that Bishop Renaldo Malavolti was dying. The communal officials stated that

> the canons ... fear that after the death of the same bishop force will be used against them concerning the election of the future shepherd, and they also fear the dissipation and usurpation of the properties of the said episcopate ... And the will of the aforesaid canons and each of them should be free in the election ... There is also concern lest the magnates of the city of Siena and other men of the same city may easily come to blows and arms.

The councillors then discussed how they should handle this situation and agreed that it was necessary for them to intervene in the election, although it was suggested that their participation should be solely verbal. The Nine, along with a small group of men chosen by them, should have full authority to do whatever they thought necessary in this matter. It seems hard to doubt that the city's rulers had a great deal of influence over the election, which resulted in the appointment of another Malavolti bishop.[181]

The Sienese fears that the magnates might come to blows seem less ridiculous when one considers the consequences of the Perugian vacancy of 1329. The chapter held an election and chose Hugolinus Guelfoni, abbot of St Peter, who was subsequently provided by the pope. Nevertheless, a week after the election was held, Vinciolus de Vinciolis reported to the communal council that he had written to Pope John, requesting the nomination of Alexander de Vinciolis as bishop of Perugia. Alexander was the Perugian ambassador to Avignon and may well have been Vinciolus' son. The proposal gained some support amongst the councillors, but was fiercely opposed by Odo Ungari. The disagreement spiralled into a long-term dispute between the two families, which culminated in the murder of Odo Ungari. His murderers, amongst them Cecchinus de Vinciolis, were obliged to seek sanctuary in the convent of St Dominic to protect themselves from the wrath of the people, and were then banished from the city for over twenty years.[182] It was surely to avoid such contention that the commune of Florence, from the thirteenth century onwards, repeatedly passed laws that forbade Florentines to accept election to the bishoprics of Florence or Fiesole.[183]

Secular authorities could also support ecclesiastical bodies in their opposition to provision. As elsewhere in Europe, the most common form of resistance

---

181 William Bowsky, *A Medieval Italian Commune: Siena Under the Nine, 1287-1355* (Berkeley, 1981), pp. 271-2, with the quote at p. 271.

182 Silano, 'Perugia', pp. 506-7.

183 David Peterson, 'An Episcopal Election in Quattrocento Florence' in James Sweeney and Stanley Chodorow (eds), *Popes, Teachers and Canon Law in the Middle Ages* (Ithaca, 1989), pp. 300-325, at p. 303.

was the continued holding of elections. John XXII's general reservation of 1319 prohibited capitular elections within the papal territories, but chapters defied this ban and continued to elect, sometimes repeatedly.[184] Sicily (perhaps unsurprisingly for a kingdom that, in 1296, forbade its king to enter into any pact with the pope) was particularly resistant to papal interference in episcopal appointments, as three examples from the year 1305 illustrate. At Mazara and Siracusa, the chapters flatly refused to accept papal nominees and instead elected their own bishops, who were quickly confirmed by the archbishop. At Monreale, the canons choose Arnau de Rassach, but he was rejected by Benedict XI, who also excommunicated the electors. Frederick III of Sicily intervened on their behalf and persisted with his negotiations into the pontificate of Clement V, who subsequently confirmed Arnau's election and reversed the excommunication.[185]

The pattern found across Europe of elections continuing to be held in the fifteenth century, long after provision had become the sole means of appointment, was echoed across Italy.[186] Occasionally, though, Italian resistance to provision took a more dramatic turn. An early fourteenth-century bishop of Montemarano found himself barred from entering his see by his canons, who acted with lay assistance. Still more shocking was the response to the provision of Francesco as bishop of the southern see of Bisaccio. When he attempted to take possession of his see, his vassals refused either to receive him or to provide him with food. He was then taken into a wood, stripped naked, beaten and tied to a tree. Freed after two days and a night, he was refused assistance by Robert, king of Naples, and was forced to return to Avignon.[187] This violent attack, which was without parallel in England, Scotland or France, is one of the most striking examples of local variations in the appointment of medieval bishops; it certainly serves as a salutary reminder that whilst the broad narratives of each of these countries are very similar, the experiences of individual dioceses could be very different.

***

A thirteenth- or fourteenth-century Englishman witnessing an electoral process in Scotland, France or Italy would have seen much that was familiar to him, and a foreign observer of an English election would also have found the experience not dissimilar to the elections he had seen in his own country. In many respects, the English story of the rise of electoral freedom and the transition to papal provision is also a pan-European narrative. For each of the countries considered

184 Silano, 'Perugia', pp. 506-7; Guillemain, *Politique Bénéficiale*, p. 101.

185 Clifford Backman, *The Decline and Fall of Medieval Sicily* (Cambridge, 1995), pp. 191-2.

186 For a fifteenth-century election, see Peterson, *Election*, pp. 300-325.

187 Guillemain, *Politique Bénéficiale*, p. 101.

in this chapter, many of the key themes in this narrative are the same ones as occur again and again in England: divided chapters, secular influence, increasing papal intervention. On the other hand, our traveller might well have noticed minor divergences which piqued his curiosity, for just as there were differences between the electoral experiences of the English dioceses, so too were there local variations across the rest of Europe. By considering these variations, and comparing the English experience to that of other countries within Latin Christendom, it is possible to enhance our understanding of the English appointments that form the primary focus of this volume.

When considered in isolation, England often seems to deviate considerably from the model of canonical election provided by the papacy; there was too much secular intervention and too many electoral disputes. When England is compared to other countries, it becomes apparent that many of the English practices were echoed across Europe. In both Scotland and France, kings exercised exactly the same rights as in England: granting *congé d'élire*, giving assent to the outcome of the election and holding the temporalities during the vacancy. Each of these kings, along with a host of other powerful secular and ecclesiastical figures (from foreign rulers to city councils and aristocrats), expected to be able to influence the outcome of elections and were often successful in doing so. Such interventions often caused disputes and appeals to the papacy, but were not the sole cause of such happenings; the members of chapters across Europe were quite capable of disagreeing with each other, electing unsuitable candidates or making procedural mistakes without help from outsiders.

Furthermore, some of elections held in some parts of Europe deviated from canonical norms to a far greater extent than in England. Election by the clergy and people was all but extinct in England by the reign of King John; their role in the appointment of a new bishop had become a ceremonial one, involving popular acclamation of the capitular choice. Only very rarely, and at the very beginning of our period, did non-chapter members claim rights to election, most notably at Canterbury in 1228, when the suffragans of the province objected their exclusion, but had their claims quashed by the pope. In Scotland, however, it was almost normal for the clergy and/or people to elect in some dioceses, and the pope generally seems to have turned a blind eye, presumably because the structures of the Scottish Church were insufficient to enable this rule to be enforced. In Italy, too, unconventional electoral bodies survived, and at Ravenna, in contrast to Canterbury, the archbishop continued to be elected by his suffragans throughout the thirteenth century.[188] The papal ability to override canon law meant that in certain areas of Italy its strictures were often overruled, notably in the tendency for vacancies to stretch beyond three months – the

188 Brentano, *Two Churches*, p. 217.

canonical limit usually enforced elsewhere. Election-related violence also seems to have been somewhat more commonplace in Italy than in the rest of Europe.

The Italian experience reinforces the impression that secular intervention was not the only threat to capitular freedom of election; indeed, it could plausibly be argued that kings were only a secondary problem and that the papacy posed a much great danger. English kings (and their Scottish and French counterparts) could only seek to influence and could always have their interventions overruled. On the other hand, the papacy (which shared many of the concerns and motivations of secular rulers) could intervene more freely and directly, since it had canon law and righteousness on its side. There is considerably irony in the fact that, as Innocent III demanded that secular rulers cease to intervene in episcopal elections, in order that cathedral chapters might elect freely, he was developing the very method of direct appointment that would ultimately lead to the demolition of capitular rights. If church–state electoral disputes of the kind found elsewhere in western Europe did not tend to occur in thirteenth-century Italy, it was less because Italy lacked a powerful monarch to cause such ruptions and more because the papal word was final in a way that the king's was not.

The chronological variations in the introduction of provision across Europe also raise interesting questions about how far each country was aware of what was happening in the others and whether these variations were significant in shaping reactions to papal policy. Given that there was a good deal of interaction between European countries,[189] it seems implausible that the English had no knowledge of the changes taking place elsewhere. Yet if such knowledge was widespread, it is curious that they were not more aware and prepared when provision arrived in England. It also seems strange that it did not attract more comment in the chroniclers; Matthew Paris for one would surely have had something to say about the rapid growth of provision in Italy had he known about it.

Finally, it is apparent that despite the many similarities in the procedures of the elections held across Europe the resultant episcopates varied in their composition. The dominance of administrators in the English episcopate was apparently unique, at least amongst the four countries considered here; curial bishops were found everywhere, but generally in smaller numbers. On the other hand, England had few aristocratic bishops, and few mendicant bishops; both groups were common elsewhere. To fully explain such variations would require much deeper analysis, but it is likely that the answer is to be found in part in differing conceptions of the role of the bishop and thus of the qualities required of a bishop. Brentano argued that the incumbents of English sees were 'manor

[189] For an interesting study of the way in which interactions with other countries shaped a nation, see David Ditchburn, *Scotland and Europe: The Medieval Kingdom and its Contacts with Christendom, c.1215-1545*, vol. I: *Religion, Culture and Commerce* (Edinburgh, 2001).

bishops', whereas their Italian counterparts were 'city and chapter bishops'.[190] If his analysis is correct (and there is no immediate reason to doubt its accuracy), this would go some way to explaining the differences in the types of men elected. Another answer may be found in the unusually small number of dioceses in England, which meant that the episcopate offered the king only limited scope for patronage. The French king, with dozens of sees at his disposal, could afford to let a few of them go to friars and the scions of noble families, but the English king was obliged to weigh his choices far more carefully.

Ultimately, many of the questions this chapter has provoked could only be answered as part of a larger and more detailed consideration. Nevertheless, it has demonstrated that whilst the English episcopal appointments considered in this study were part of a European-wide process of development, there were also some important differences. Some of these anomalies resulted from the early centralization of the English Church and government, which had some negative consequences (at least from certain perspectives): the disputes between king and chapter, the administrator bishops and the close observation on canon law. On the other hand, comparisons also indicate that England was, in some ways, rather lucky. If the thirteenth century appears as a golden age of electoral freedom in England when placed alongside the twelfth century, this impression is only reinforced if thirteenth-century England is compared to thirteenth-century Italy; at least English cathedral chapters had only to contend with Henry III and Edward I, and were not faced with constant papal intervention at such an early date.

---

[190] Brentano, *Two Churches*, pp. 218-19.

Conclusion

Over a period of two hundred years, from the mid-twelfth to the mid-fourteenth centuries, the processes by which English bishops obtained office were transformed. Henry II exercised effective rights of nomination over the bishoprics in his kingdom. Elections were held, but they typically served simply to ratify the royal choice; if the king wanted an individual to be promoted to the episcopate, he could be confident that the electorate would comply. Yet within three decades of Henry's death, his son John issued a charter that promised freedom of election to the English Church, and in doing so ushered in a century of relative freedom of choice for the cathedral chapters. Henry III and Edward I could express their wishes – and might do so forcefully – but they could no longer guarantee the promotion of a favoured kinsman or servant. By the time of Edward II's accession, just under 100 years after the Freedom of Election charter, a new method of appointment – papal provision – had become sufficiently common for the new king to suspect that 'if the pope has his design in the matter, an election will never be made in any cathedral church in England'.[1] By the mid-1340s, when Edward's son Edward III was less than two decades into his lengthy reign, the elder man's prophecy had been (more or less) fulfilled. True, cathedral chapters would continue to hold elections for centuries to come, but their validity was no longer recognized. The wishes of the pope, or at least his methods of appointment, would henceforth always prevail.

How, then, did such a radical transformation come about, in a relatively short time? Jean Gaudemet argued that the blame lay with the cathedral chapters: 'electoral bodies condemned themselves' by becoming embroiled in frequent disputes (both internal and with other participants in the bishop-making process) which led to appeals and thus to the increased involvement of the papacy in episcopal appointments.[2] There is clearly much truth in this analysis and yet it seems flawed on at least two counts. Firstly, whilst chapters must take responsibility for disputes that were the product of internal divisions, to blame them for all appeals is to suggest that they should have made the appointments demanded of them by other parties, particularly the crown. Given that to do so would have been to ignore the demands of canon law, and to disregard the ideal of free canonical election, it seems unreasonable to expect such flexibility from the electoral bodies.

---

1 *Reg. Sede Vacante*, pp. 104-7.

2 Gaudemet, 'De l'Élection à la Nomination', pp. 27-8.

In addition, the increasing frequency of appeals to Rome was not simply the product of the capitular inability to please all of the people all of the time. Instead, it reflected a broader change in society. During the course of the twelfth and thirteenth centuries, European administrations, both secular and ecclesiastical, became increasingly bureaucratic in their nature. Innocent III (1198-1215) is estimated to have issued about 25,000 letters during the course of his pontificate,[3] whereas Boniface VIII (1294-1303) probably issued around 50,000 letters a year.[4] At the same time as, and partly as a consequence of, these developments, administrations also became increasingly legalized, and new appellate procedures were developed whereby the dissatisfied might seek justice from a higher power. The existence of these procedures led to the formation of a litigious society, in which the wealthy were able to challenge decisions or judgements on more or less valid grounds. Against this backdrop, it is unsurprising that those left dissatisfied by the outcome of an episcopal election sought the answer to their problems in the legal procedures on offer in Rome.

The dissatisfaction that resulted in appeals to the papal curia was the product of inevitable tensions between the ideological, spiritual and practical considerations that shaped appointment processes throughout the later Middle Ages. All of the parties involved in the making of a bishop hoped for the election of a suitable candidate; the appointment of an incompetent or scandalously unsuitable man was in no one's interests. However, ideas of exactly what made a good bishop were somewhat varied. In most appointment processes, pragmatism won; most churchmen were willing to accept that the bishop's great power, responsibilities and social standing meant that the choice of this individual could not depend solely on the wishes of a small group of monks or canons. The idea that a bishop should be 'useful to the king and the kingdom' was firmly entrenched in the medieval consciousness, and it was widely recognized that possessing this quality did not necessarily make one a poor bishop. Indeed, curial bishops, whether they resigned secular office upon promotion to the episcopate or combined royal service with their episcopal duties, could have a special value, acting as a useful hinge between church and state.[5] Throughout the age of election, chapters and popes considered (and frequently granted) the wishes of kings, and archbishops and popes confirmed elections that had clearly been made with secular influence. Everybody recognized the potential benefits to be gained from such a state of affairs and thus compromise was the order of the day.

---

[3] Othmar Hageneder, 'Die Register Innozenz III.' in Thomas Frenz (ed.), *Papst Innozenz III.: Weichensteller der Geschichte Europas* (Stuttgart, 2000), pp. 91-101, at p. 92.

[4] Michael Clanchy, *From Memory to Written Record: England 1066-1307*, 2nd edn (Oxford, 1993), pp. 60-61.

[5] For this notion, see William Pantin, 'Grosseteste's Relations with the Papacy and the Crown' in David Callus (ed.), *Robert Grosseteste* (Oxford, 1955), pp. 178-215, at pp. 204-8.

Of course, a system based on compromise rather than wholehearted agreement will sometimes break down; in this case, the consequence was electoral disputes, some of them spectacular. It is important not to downplay the significance of conflicts such as the major Winchester dispute of 1238-44; in the short term such events highlighted the major differences that existed between church and state, and in the long term the subsequent appeals to Rome helped to normalize papal intervention in episcopal elections, and paved the way for the rise of papal provision. On the other hand, vacancies involving major disputes and papal settlements were consistently much rarer than many general histories have implied. That disputed elections were more interesting than non-disputed processes and are therefore much better documented does not mean that they were normal.

The importance of electoral compromise in the thirteenth century is reflected in the composition of the English episcopate: a large proportion of the bishops were in some way connected to the crown, but a substantial number (usually less than half, but at times a little more) were local men, members of the local diocesan clergy and of the cathedral chapters themselves. Potentially, this balance could have been completely overturned by the rise of provision, with an influx of non-native papal administrators and relatives taking over England's cathedrals. Why did this scenario not become a reality? The answer lies primarily in the fact that even in the fourteenth century, as provision became rapidly more common, compromise remained the defining characteristic of the appointment process. The Avignon popes showed themselves willing to work with the English king; if anything, they were even more amenable to royal wishes than the English cathedral chapters. Consequently, after some initial difficulties, the crown quickly realized the potential of provision and accepted the new method rather than resisting it. The papacy also showed some sensitivity to the sensibilities of cathedral chapters, in the sense that whilst their electoral rights were significantly eroded, they were not completely unacknowledged. In permitting chapters to hold elections and present their candidates at the papal curia, the pope was offering the possibility (albeit a slender one) that capitular choices might still be upheld.

Like the age of election, the age of provision that followed was not free from disputes. Once the crown had been stripped of the effective powers of appointment it had enjoyed for much of the earlier Middle Ages, there was always the potential for royal choices to be thwarted. If this happened, complaints were inevitable, and Edward II and Edward III protested against unsatisfactory papal appointments just as Henry III and Edward I had resisted undesirable outcomes to capitular elections. If the disputes became less explosive in the fourteenth century, it was not necessarily because kings became less interested in the identities of new bishops or because the papacy was always more accommodating; rather, it was harder for the king to resist the wishes of

the head of the Latin Church, than for him to intimidate a group of monks or canons who were also his subjects.

In many respects, then, the story of episcopal appointments in thirteenth- and early fourteenth-century England is one of continuity, despite the dramatic alteration in the methods of appointment that took place during this period. Yet there were also important changes in the experiences of some of the key participants in the appointment process. The role of the archbishop underwent something of a transformation. In the early thirteenth century the metropolitan examined and confirmed every election that took place in his province; sometimes, he even chose the bishop himself. By the mid-fourteenth century, his place in the bishop-making process had all but disappeared; besides officiating at the occasional consecration, his position had been almost completely usurped by the papacy.

In addition, and despite the fact that cathedral chapters continued to hold elections throughout the fourteenth and fifteenth centuries, it is impossible to deny that their level of influence was considerably diminished by the rise of provision. Indeed, it is possible to argue that the thirteenth century, in particular the last few decades, was something of a golden age of electoral freedom. Although chapters were not guaranteed to secure the appointment of their candidate, they stood a reasonable chance; it was guaranteed that they would be able to hold an election and though considerable pressure might be put on them by external forces, they had the option to resist these pressures and hope to secure archiepiscopal or papal confirmation of their choice. When compared to the twelfth century (when the king dictated the majority of English appointments) and the fourteenth century (when there was no guarantee that an election would even be held, and almost all of those elections that did go ahead were quashed because a provision had already been made), the thirteenth century seems remarkably good.

It is also important to recognize that the king was not the only source of external pressures on the cathedral chapter, or indeed on the pope. It is clear that the candidate played a far more significant role in the electoral process than has usually been acknowledged; canon law may have demanded that the bishop-elect remain a somewhat passive figure, but the reality was rather different. Many men were desperate to secure a bishopric for themselves, and did everything in their power to do so. Others were equally reluctant to take on high ecclesiastical office and offered strong resistance to their appointment. A wide range of other powerful individuals, lacking a formal role in the appointment process, but deeply interested in its outcome, were frequently to be found putting their views across, sometimes in a manner not notably less forceful than the king's.

The majority of these trends were repeated across Europe; in broad terms, and often in specific ones, the electoral experiences of England were shared by its neighbours. Further comparative work on this topic, focusing on some of

the apparent differences between England, Scotland, France and Italy (and the rest of Latin Christendom) is much needed and would shed further light on the national experiences of each country. If there is a need for further analysis of the variations in the European narrative, it is equally important to remember that the dangers inherent in making generalizations about the whole of Europe equally apply to generalizations about the whole of England. Each of the seventeen English dioceses experienced the rise of canonical election and the subsequent transition to papal provision in a different way. Consequently, it is as important to look inwards as to look outwards; studies of individual dioceses, or even individual appointments, are in their own way as valuable as multinational comparative work.

To the modern eye, medieval episcopal appointments may seem a rather arcane topic, the products of a long-past world in which the church exercised immense power and the filling of an episcopal vacancy was a subject worth arguing over. Such reactions are, however, rather too glib. Elections continue to be held, in both secular and ecclesiastical contexts, throughout the modern world,[6] whilst the appointments of leading ecclesiastical figures, from the pope down, still generate a significant response. Current disagreements over the appointment of female and homosexual bishops are not dissimilar to medieval disputes about the characteristics that made men suitable or unsuitable for promotion to the episcopate. In some areas of the world, conflicts between church and state over rights of appointment continue, notably in China, where the Patriotic Association contests the Vatican's claim that the pope alone has the right to appoint bishops. In recent years the two parties have compromised by trying to find candidates who are acceptable to both parties, but since November 2010 three Chinese bishops have been consecrated without papal approval. One of these, Joseph Huang Bingzhang of Shantou, was excommunicated in July 2011.[7] The parallels between the experiences of modern China and late medieval Europe are clear. For as long as religious leaders continue to enjoy social, cultural and political influence, powerful men will seek to influence their appointments. On most occasions, a peaceful compromise will be reached, but when relations turn sour – whether in the medieval world or the modern – the consequences can be dramatic.

---

6 For the argument that medieval episcopal elections have much in common with modern democratic ones, see Peltzer, *Elections*, pp. 257-8.

7 *The Observer*, Sunday, 17 July 2011.

Appendix: Appointments to English Bishoprics, 1215-1344

Vacancies are judged to have begun with the death of a bishop, and to have ended with the restoration of the temporalities to his successor, this being (with a few exceptions) the point at which both royal and ecclesiastical (archiepiscopal/papal) assent had been given. For vacancies where one of these dates is unknown, I have substituted the nearest related event (for example consecration for restoration of the temporalities) and indicated this with a note. Where there is more than one possible date for a single event (for example where two chronicles give different dates for the death of a bishop), I have calculated the vacancy length using the date that, based on the circumstantial evidence, I consider to be more likely. Where the potential discrepancy is greater than two weeks, I have highlighted this in the notes.

Province of Canterbury

Bath & Wells

Bishop	Time in office	Length of vacancy (days)	Background	Chapter member	Mode of appointment	Circumstances of appointment
M. Roger of Salisbury	10/5/1244-21/12/1247	539	Precentor of Salisbury	No	Capitular election	Elected by monks of Bath; canons of Wells appealed. Henry III supported Peter Chaceporc; his candidacy was withdrawn, but the king still withheld assent because of the split in the electoral body. Election confirmed by pope
M. William Bitton I	20/7/1248-3/4/1264	212	Archdeacon of Wells	Yes (Wells)	Capitular election	Postulated following a joint election; royal and papal assent given
M. Walter Giffard	1/9/1264-26/12/1266	151	Royal clerk	Yes (Wells)	Capitular election	Royal assent given. Archbishop Boniface in exile, therefore Giffard went to France to seek his assent
William Bitton II	4/2/1267-4/12/1274	68	Archdeacon of Wells	Yes (Wells)	Capitular election	Royal and archiepiscopal assent given without complication
Robert Burnell	15/2/1275-25/10/1292	73	Royal chancellor	Yes (Wells)	Capitular election	Royal candidate elected; royal and archiepiscopal assent given without complication
M. William de Marchia	19/3/1293-19/6/1302	145	Treasurer of the exchequer	Yes (Wells)	Capitular election	Royal assent given; see of Canterbury vacant, therefore election confirmed by prior and convent of Canterbury
Walter de Haselschawe	12/9/1302-11/12/1308	85	Dean of Wells	Yes (Wells)	Capitular election	Royal and archiepiscopal assent given without complication

Bishop	Time in office	Length of vacancy (days)	Background	Chapter member	Mode of appointment	Circumstances of appointment
John de Drokensford	15/5/1309-9/5/1329	155	Keeper of the wardrobe	Yes (Wells)	Capitular election	Royal candidate elected. Royal and archiepiscopal assent given without complication, but Archbishop Winchelsey arranged the consecration to coincide with parliament, in an unsuccessful attempt to prevent the bishops attending the latter. Drokensford chose to attend parliament and the consecration was delayed
M. Ralph de Salopia	22/7/1329-14/8/1363	74	Chancellor of Oxford University	Yes (Wells)	Capitular election	Royal and archiepiscopal assent given and consecration carried out. Regency government nevertheless sought to have Robert Wyville (Queen Isabella's secretary) provided, but papal confirmation of the election was given in 1330

Canterbury

Archbishop	Time in office	Length of vacancy (days)	Background	Chapter member	Method of appointment	Circumstances of appointment
M. Richard le Grand	24/3/1229-3/8/1231	258	Chancellor and head of the schools of Lincoln Cathedral	No	Papal provision	Monks elected their prior, Walter of Eynsham, but the king and the bishops of the Canterbury province launched appeals on the grounds of his unsuitability. The election was quashed by the pope and Richard le Grand (probably the candidate of the suffragans) was provided
M. Edmund of Abingdon	4/2/1234-16/11/1240	916	Treasurer of Salisbury Cathedral; theologian	No	Capitular election	Three unsuccessful elections were held; each of them received royal assent. Ralph Neville, bishop of Chichester, was postulated, but the pope rejected him. Next, the prior of Canterbury, M. John of Sittingbourne, was elected, but he resigned at the papal curia. M. John le Blund, a theologian and king's clerk, had his election quashed for pluralism. The successful candidate, M. Edmund of Abingdon, was nominated by Gregory IX (probably on the advice of Simon Langton), who instructed the Canterbury monks to elect him. They did so, and the election received royal assent

Archbishop	Time in office	Length of vacancy (days)	Background	Chapter member	Method of appointment	Circumstances of appointment
Boniface of Savoy	27/2/1244-18/7/1270	1,199[1]	Bishop-elect of Belley; uncle of Queen Eleanor	No	Capitular election	Unanimous election by way of compromise; royal assent given, and king petitioned pope for confirmation of the election. Length of vacancy primarily due to lengthy papal vacancy following the death of Gregory IX
M. Robert de Kilwardby	12/12/1272-5/6/1278	878	Dominican provincial of England; theologian	No	Papal provision	Adam of Chillendene, prior of Canterbury, elected in September 1270, despite pressure from Prince Edward to elect Robert Burnell. King withheld his assent. Chillendene went to Rome, but the papal see remained vacant until September 1271. Chillendene resigned his claim to Gregory X, who had apparently persuaded him to do so. Kilwardby provided; crown protested, but royal assent given
John Pecham	30/5/1279-8/12/1292	359	Prior of the Franciscan province in England; theologian	No	Papal provision	See vacant following Kilwardby's appointment as cardinal of Porto. Convent postulated Robert Burnell, bishop of Bath and Wells and the royal chancellor, whose election received royal assent. Pope quashed the election and provided Pecham
M. Robert de Winchelsey	4/2/1293-11/5/1313	58	Archdeacon of Essex; regent-master at Oxford	No	Capitular election	Elected by the cathedral convent, apparently without external intervention. Royal assent given and election confirmed at Rome

Archbishop	Time in office	Length of vacancy (days)	Background	Chapter member	Method of appointment	Circumstances of appointment
Walter Reynolds	3/1/1313-16/11/1327	237	Royal chancellor; bishop of Worcester	No	Papal provision	Papal reservation of see made shortly before Winchelsey's death. Convent elected Thomas Cobham, a royal diplomat and serial pluralist, but this election was quashed due to the reservation. The royal candidate, Walter Reynolds, was translated from Worcester to Canterbury by papal provision
M. Simon de Meopham	19/9/1328-12/10/1333	309	Archdeacon of Shropshire; canon of Chichester and Llandaff	No	Capitular election	Elected by the convent; possibly the Lancastrian candidate. Royal assent and papal confirmation were given without complication
M. John of Stratford	5/2/1333-23/8/1348	116	Bishop of Winchester; royal chancellor	No	Papal provision	Stratford, the royal candidate, was postulated by the monks of Canterbury. He was translated from Winchester by papal provision even before the royal and capitular letters arrived at the papal curia

Chichester

Bishop	Time in office	Length of vacancy (days)	Background	Chapter member	Mode of appointment	Circumstances of appointment
M. Richard Poore	7/1/1215-9/5/1217	2,696	Dean of Salisbury	No	Capitular election	Perhaps the royal candidate; he certainly came from a curial family and had powerful connections. There had already been failed attempts to elect him to Winchester (1205) and Durham (1213) when the canons of Chichester elected him in 1215. Royal assent and archiepiscopal assent given
M. Ranulph of Wareham	17/12/1217-14/9/1222	222	Prior (elect?) and episcopal official of Norwich	No	Capitular election	Elected by the canons in accordance with the wishes of the Legate Guala. Royal assent given. Archbishop Langton in exile, therefore probably confirmed by Guala
Ralph Neville	3/11/1222-1/2/1244	50	Keeper of king's great seal	Yes	Capitular election	Neville was the royal candidate. He was presented to the chancellorship of Chichester Cathedral by the king very shortly before he was elected as bishop of Chichester by the canons. Royal assent and archiepiscopal confirmation given with difficulty

Bishop	Time in office	Length of vacancy (days)	Background	Chapter member	Mode of appointment	Circumstances of appointment
M. Richard Wyche	21/7/1246-2/4/1253	902	Chancellor of Edmund of Abingdon	No	Capitular election	Canons elected the king's candidate Robert Passelewe, a justice of the forest. Royal assent given. Archbishop Boniface examined the election and, on the advice of Robert Grosseteste (who participated in the examination), quashed it. He then nominated Richard Wyche, who was duly elected by the canons. King refused to give assent, therefore Wyche sought and obtained papal confirmation. Consecrated at the papal curia, but on return to England king withheld temporalities for over a year. Restored to grace and received temporalities July 1246
M. John of Climping	27/5/1253-22/5/1262	55	Chancellor of Chichester Cathedral	Yes	Capitular election	Elected by the canons; royal assent and archiepiscopal confirmation given without complication
M. Stephen of Bersted	20/6/1262-21/10/1287	c.29	Canon of Chichester	Yes	Capitular election	Elected by the canons; royal assent and archiepiscopal confirmation given without complication
M. Gilbert de Sancto Leofardo	24/6/1288-12/2/1305	247	Treasurer of Chichester	Yes	Capitular election	Elected by the canons; royal assent granted. Election confirmed by Archbishop Pecham, who Gilbert had formerly served as an archiepiscopal official

Bishop	Time in office	Length of vacancy (days)	Background	Chapter member	Mode of appointment	Circumstances of appointment
John Langton	16/7/1305-19/7/1337	154	Former (and future) royal chancellor	Yes	Capitular election	Langton was probably the royal candidate. He was elected by the chapter, and his election received royal assent and archiepiscopal confirmation
M. Robert of Stratford	21/9/1337-9/4/1362	64	Royal chancellor; chancellor of Oxford University	Yes	Capitular election	Elected by the canons, whose choice received royal assent. Archiepiscopal assent given by Archbishop Stratford, his brother

Coventry & Lichfield

Bishop	**Time in office**	**Length of vacancy (days)**	**Background**	**Chapter member**	**Mode of appointment**	**Circumstances of appointment**
M. Alexander Stavensby	20/5/1224-26/12/1238	275	Papal chamber clerk; theologian	No	Papal provision	Ongoing dispute between monks of Coventry and canons of Lichfield over their respective rights of election. They elected rival candidates, provoking an appeal to Rome. Pope ruled that both parties had right to elect, but suggested that the two chapters should, on this election, confer their powers of appointment on him. He provided Stavensby, who was subsequently postulated by the canons of Lichfield. King gave assent to the appointment just over a month after Stavensby's consecration (at Rome) and restored the temporalities
Hugh Patteshall	1/1/1240-7/12/1241	371	Royal chancellor	No	Capitular election	Monks of Coventry elected William Raleigh; he refused the see and instead accepted Norwich, to which he had also been elected. Monks then elected Nicholas Farnham; canons elected their dean, William of Manchester. When the dean declined, the two chapters united to persuade Farnham to accept, but he also declined. Hugh Patteshall was elected jointly by the two chapters. Royal assent and archiepiscopal confirmation given

Bishop	Time in office	Length of vacancy (days)	Background	Chapter member	Mode of appointment	Circumstances of appointment
M. Roger Weseham	25/3/1246-6/12/1256	1,569	Dean of Lincoln	No	Papal provision	Joint election produced a split result: the dean of Lichfield's party elected Richard of Evesham (the acting chancellor), whilst others backed William of Montpellier, a monk of Coventry. As a result, the king plundered Coventry and the monks dispersed for their safety. Evesham died, and a new election was held. William was elected again, despite the objections of the king and some of the canons. He went to Rome, where he resigned his claim. Pope provided Roger of Weseham, possibly through the influence of Robert Grosseteste. Temporalities were not restored for a further ten months, probably due to the king's displeasure at this appointment
Roger Meuland	17/2/1257-16/12/1295	73	Kinsman of Henry III	Yes (Lichfield)	Capitular election	Candidate of Richard, earl of Cornwall. Elected jointly by Coventry and Lichfield; royal assent and archiepiscopal confirmation given
Walter Langton	16/6/1296-9/11/1321	183	Treasurer of the exchequer	Yes (Lichfield)	Capitular election	Elected jointly by the two chapters; royal assent and archiepiscopal confirmation given. Consecrated overseas, whilst on royal service

Bishop	**Time in office**	**Length of vacancy (days)**	**Background**	**Chapter member**	**Mode of appointment**	**Circumstances of appointment**
M. Roger de Northburgh	12/4/1322-22/11/1358	154	Keeper of the wardrobe; archdeacon of Richmond	No	Papal provision	Dispute between Coventry and Lichfield over respective rights of election. Monks of Coventry elected Henry, their prior; canons of Lichfield appealed to Avignon. Edward II petitioned the pope for provision of Robert Baldock, but apparently changed his mind, as the pope provided Northburgh 'at his request'

Ely

Bishop	Time in office	Length of vacancy (days)	Background	Chapter member	Mode of appointment	Circumstances of appointment
John of Fountains	24/1/1220-6/5/1225	1,816	Abbot of Fountains Abbey (Cistercian)	No	Capitular election	Monks, probably under pressure from King John, elected Geoffrey de Burgh. Then, amidst the chaos of 1215, another election was held (possibly by a dissenting group amongst the electors) and M. Robert of York was elected. John restored the temporalities to him, but appealed against his election. The Pope annulled both elections and empowered the legate, the archbishop of Canterbury and the bishop of Salisbury to resolve the situation. They nominated John of Fountains, who was probably then elected by the convent. Royal assent given
Geoffrey de Burgh	2/6/1225-17/12/1228	27	Archdeacon of Norwich	No	Capitular election	Geoffrey, a former bishop-elect of Ely, elected by the monks, probably in compliance with the wishes of Hubert de Burgh, the king's chief minister. Royal assent and archiepiscopal confirmation given
Hugh of Northwold	26/5/1229-6/8/1254	160	Abbot of Bury St Edmunds (Benedictine)	No	Capitular election	Elected by the monks, and royal assent given. His transfer from Bury St Edmunds to Ely was deemed to be a translation and therefore papal confirmation was sought. Henry III wrote to Rome in his favour, and papal confirmation was given
M. William of Kilkenny	25/12/1254-21/9/1256	141	Keeper of the king's seal	No	Capitular election	Elected by the cathedral convent. Royal assent and archiepiscopal confirmation given

Bishop	Time in office	Length of vacancy (days)	Background	Chapter member	Mode of appointment	Circumstances of appointment
Hugh de Balsham	15/1/1258-15/6/1286	481	Sub-prior of Ely Cathedral	Yes	Capitular election	Elected by the monks, but the king (who hoped to procure the see for the Chancellor, Henry de Wengham) refused his assent and requested that Archbishop Boniface quash the election. Boniface did so, and proceeded to seek the election of Adam Marsh. This provoked the king into appealing to Rome, but the archiepiscopal examination of the election continued alongside the papal investigation. Royal and archiepiscopal proctors launched a scathing personal attack on Balsham's character at the papal curia, but the Pope rejected the archbishop's actions, recognized Balsham's election and consecrated him
John Kirkby	7/9/1286-26/3/1290	84	Royal treasurer	No	Capitular election	Probably the royal candidate, Kirkby was elected by way of inspiration. Royal assent and archiepiscopal confirmation given without difficulty
M. William of Louth	30/5/1290-25/3/1298	65	Keeper of the wardrobe	No	Capitular election	Elected by way of inspiration. Royal assent and archiepiscopal confirmation given

Bishop	Time in office	Length of vacancy (days)	Background	Chapter member	Mode of appointment	Circumstances of appointment
M. Ralph of Walpole	10/10/1299-20/3/1302	564	Bishop of Norwich	No	Papal provision	Heavy royal pressure was placed on the convent to elect the king's chancellor, John Langton. The result of the election (by way of scrutiny) was split; a majority voted for John Salmon, prior of Ely, but a substantial minority favoured Langton. Archbishop Winchelsey began an investigation into the circumstances of the election; Edward I refused assent to Salmon's election, allegedly on procedural grounds, but gave assent to Langton's election. Both elects travelled to Rome to present their cases; both were persuaded to resign their claims. Ralph Walpole, bishop of Norwich, was translated to Ely. Salmon was provided to Norwich in his place; Langton was given the archdeaconry of Canterbury
Robert Orford	4/2/1303-21/1/1310	321	Prior of Ely	Yes	Capitular election	Orford was elected by way of compromise and his election received royal assent. Archbishop Winchelsey quashed the election on the grounds of Orford's insufficient learning; Orford appealed to Rome. Boniface VIII's examination found that Winchelsey had been overly zealous in his questioning and the election was thus confirmed

Bishop	Time in office	Length of vacancy (days)	Background	Chapter member	Mode of appointment	Circumstances of appointment
John of Ketton	18/7/1310-14/5/1316	178	Almoner of Ely Cathedral Priory	Yes	Capitular election	King and nobles pressured convent to elect Boniface of Saluzzo, a royal kinsman. The monks spent two days discussing the matter, before proceeding to elect by way of compromise. The first set of seven electors was split between two candidates (Godfrey of Crowland, abbot of Peterborough, and Ralph of Fotheringhay, archdeacon of Ely); a second set was appointed and they chose Ketton. Royal assent was given, even though the king had set a notary to work, searching for flaws in the election, and appeared to be planning an appeal. This delayed, but did not prevent, the confirmation of the election by Archbishop Winchelsey
John of Hotham	20/7/1316-14/1/1337	67	Chancellor of the exchequer	No	Capitular election	Elected, probably at the king's request, by way of inspiration. Royal assent and archiepiscopal confirmation granted
M. Simon de Montacute	11/6/1337-20/6/1345	148	Bishop of Worcester	No	Papal provision	The king and his ministers made considerable difficulties about granting the licence to elect and it was only issued after six weeks of petitioning. Monks elected one of their number, John de Crauden, but the royal candidate, Simon de Montacute, was translated from Worcester by papal provision two days later. The election was therefore set aside

Exeter

Bishop	Time in office	Length of vacancy (days)	Background	Chapter member	Mode of appointment	Circumstances of appointment
William Brewer	25/11/1223-24/11/1244	78	Precentor of Exeter	Yes	Capitular election	Elected by the canons, probably at the request of his uncle William Brewer, a leading royal administrator. Royal assent and archiepiscopal confirmation given
M. Richard Blund	8/4/1245-26/12/1257	135	Chancellor of Exeter	Yes	Capitular election	Elected by the canons, who were possibly influenced by Blund's membership of a prominent Exeter family. Royal assent and archiepiscopal confirmation given
M. Walter de Bronescombe	6/2/1258-22/7/1280	70	Archdeacon of Surrey; chancellor of Exeter; royal clerk	Yes	Capitular election	Unanimously elected by the canons; royal assent and archiepiscopal confirmation given
M. Peter Quinel	11/10/1280-1/10/1291	81	Archdeacon of St David's	Yes	Capitular election	Elected by the cathedral chapter; royal assent and archiepiscopal confirmation given
M. Thomas Bitton	2/12/1291-21/9/1307	63	Dean of Wells	No	Capitular election	Elected by the cathedral chapter; royal assent and archiepiscopal confirmation given

Bishop	Time in office	Length of vacancy (days)	Background	Chapter member	Mode of appointment	Circumstances of appointment
M. Walter de Stapeldon	16/3/1308-15/10/1326	177	Precentor of Exeter; royal diplomat	Yes	Capitular election	Elected by the cathedral chapter, by fifteen votes to eight; royal assent given. King had presented M. Richard Plymstoke to the archdeaconry of Exeter, but Stapeldon refused to admit him, claiming that the archdeaconry was not vacant. Plymstoke retaliated by appealing against the election at the papal curia, but later withdrew his appeal. Archiepiscopal assent given
M. James Berkeley	8/1/1327-24/6/1327	85	Archdeacon of Huntingdon	Yes	Papal provision	Elected by the canons; his family connections to the Mortimers were probably significant. Royal assent given and king petitioned pope in Berkeley's favour. See had been reserved, but papal mandate to Archbishop Winchelsey to do as he saw fit. Winchelsey confirmed the election, but Berkeley was subsequently provided. Six weeks later, John XXII gave 'suppletion of the defect in the election by the chapter and confirmation by the archbishop'
John de Grandisson	9/3/1328-16/7/1369	259	Papal chaplain and diplomat	No	Papal provision	Canons elected John Godeley, dean of Wells, and royal assent was given. Archiepiscopal assent had not been given by the time of Archbishop Reynolds' death, and the crown tried to persuade the dean and chapter of Canterbury to confirm the election; they refused. Pope set aside the election, having provided John de Grandisson. The king accepted the new bishop and restored the temporalities

Hereford

Bishop	Time in office	Length of vacancy (days)	Background	Chapter member	Mode of appointment	Circumstances of appointment
M. Hugh de Mapenore	18/12/1216-16/4/1219	398[2]	Dean of Hereford	Yes	Capitular election	Elected against the wishes of King John, who appealed to the papal curia, claiming that the chapter was excommunicated at the time of the election. Pope delegated the case to Guala; he ruled in Hugh's favour shortly after John's death
Hugh Foliot	27/10/1219-7/8/1234	194[3]	Archdeacon of Shropshire	Yes	Capitular election	Elected by the canons; royal assent and archiepiscopal confirmation given
M. Ralph of Maidstone	30/9/1234-17/12/1239	54	Dean of Hereford	Yes	Capitular election	Elected by the canons; royal assent and archiepiscopal confirmation given
Peter d'Aigueblanche	11/9/1240-27/11/1268	269	Keeper of the king's wardrobe	Yes	Capitular election	Canons elected Michael, a canon of Lichfield, but he apparently resigned. A new election was held and Aigueblanche, the royal candidate, was elected. Royal assent and archiepiscopal confirmation given
John le Breton	14/4/1269-12/5/1275	138	Royal justice	Yes	Capitular election	Elected by the canons; royal assent and archiepiscopal confirmation given
M. Thomas de Cantilupe	26/6/1275-25/8/1282	45	Chancellor of Oxford University; former Chancellor of England	Yes	Capitular election	Elected by the canons; royal assent and archiepiscopal confirmation given

Bishop	Time in office	Length of vacancy (days)	Background	Chapter member	Mode of appointment	Circumstances of appointment
M. Richard of Swinfield	08/1/1283-15/3/1317	136	Archdeacon of London; member of Cantilupe's *familia*	Yes	Capitular election	Elected by the canons; royal assent and archiepiscopal confirmation given
M. Adam de Orleton	24/7/1317-28/9/1327	131	Royal diplomat (mainly missions to papal curia); auditor in the Sacred Palace	Yes	Papal provision	Chapter received licence to elect, but there is no evidence that an election was held, despite royal petitions for the election of Thomas Charlton. King also petitioned for Charlton's provision, but John XXII provided Adam Orleton. Orleton, who had been sent to the curia to promote Charlton's candidacy, accepted despite a royal mandate to decline the appointment. King did not challenge the provision any further and restored the temporalities
M. Thomas of Charlton	21/12/1327-11/1/1344	87[4]	Former keeper of the privy seal	Yes	Papal provision	See became vacant with the translation of Orleton to Worcester; Charlton provided immediately. No election held
M. John Trillek	29/3/1344-20/11/1360	78	Nephew of Adam Orleton; member of his *familia*	Yes	Papal provision	Elected by the canons; royal assent and archiepiscopal confirmation given. Election cancelled by the papal mandate that provided Trillek to the bishopric of Hereford

Lincoln

Bishop	Time in office	Length of vacancy (days)	Background	Chapter member	Mode of appointment	Circumstances of appointment
M. Robert Grossteste	16/5/1235-8/10/1253	68	Archdeacon of Leicester; lector of the Oxford Franciscans; theologian	Yes	Capitular election	Grosseteste was elected following considerable disagreement between the canons. Royal assent and archiepiscopal confirmation given
Henry of Lexington	1/4/1254-8/8/1258	175	Dean of Lincoln	Yes	Capitular election	Henry III tried to secure the see for Peter d'Aigueblanche, but the canons elected Lexington. Royal assent was given by Eleanor of Provence, acting on a mandate from her husband (who was then in Gascony); Archbishop Boniface confirmed the election
M. Richard of Gravesend	17/10/1258-18/12/1279	70	Dean of Lincoln	Yes	Capitular election	Elected by the canons; royal assent and archiepiscopal confirmation given
M. Oliver of Sutton	25/4/1280-13/11/1299	129[5]	Dean of Lincoln	Yes	Capitular election	Elected by the canons; royal assent and archiepiscopal confirmation given
M. John of Dalderby	18/3/1300-12/1/1320	127	Chancellor of Lincoln; theologian	Yes	Capitular election	Elected by the canons; royal assent and archiepiscopal confirmation given

Bishop	Time in office	Length of vacancy (days)	Background	Chapter member	Mode of appointment	Circumstances of appointment
Henry Burghersh	5/8/1320-?/12/1340	206	King's clerk; nephew of Bartholomew Badlesmere, a leading royal councillor	No	Papal provision	See reserved before Dalderby's death. Canons elected Henry Mansfield, their dean, but he declined the bishopric. A new election was held and Anthony Bek was elected; royal assent was given. Archbishop Reynolds refused confirmation, because a reservation had been made and Edward II was petitioning for the provision of Henry Burghersh. Bek's election was quashed and Burghersh provided
M. Thomas Bek	17/9/1342-2/2/1347	625[6]	Former official of Archbishop Melton; canon lawyer	Yes	Capitular election	Bek elected by the canons; royal assent given. Due to rumours of a reservation, Bek went to the papal curia, where he waited for approximately a year before being rewarded with papal confirmation of his election

London

Bishop	Time in office	Length of vacancy (days)	Background	Chapter member	Mode of appointment	Circumstances of appointment
Eustace de Fauconberg	23/3/1221-31/10/1228	56	Treasurer of the exchequer	Yes	Capitular election	Fauconberg was elected by the canons after considerable dispute. Royal assent given; election confirmed by legate
M. Roger Niger	27/4/1229-29/9/1241	179	Archdeacon of Colchester	Yes	Capitular election	Elected by the canons; royal assent and archiepiscopal confirmation given
M. Fulk Basset	16/3/1244-21/5/1259	900	Dean of York; baronial family	No	Capitular election	Elected by canons (majority of 23 to 14); royal assent given, despite Paris' claim that Henry III wanted the see for Aigueblanche. Canterbury vacant, therefore papal confirmation was sought, but the papal see was also vacant. When the election of Boniface of Savoy was confirmed, he was issued with (and complied with) a papal mandate to confirm the London election within fifteen days
Henry de Wengham	11/7/1259-13/7/1262	51	Royal chancellor	Yes	Capitular election	Elected by the canons, possibly in accordance with royal wishes, although there is no clear indication of this; royal assent and archiepiscopal confirmation given

Bishop	Time in office	Length of vacancy (days)	Background	Chapter member	Mode of appointment	Circumstances of appointment
M. Henry of Sandwich	15/1/1263-15/9/1273	186	Archdeacon of Oxford	Yes	Capitular election	Canons elected their dean, Richard Talbot; his election received royal assent and archiepiscopal confirmation, but he died a few days after the mandate for restoration of the temporalities was issued. A new election was held, and the canons chose Henry of Sandwich. His election received royal assent and archiepiscopal confirmation
M. John de Chishull	15/3/1274-7/2/1280	182	Royal treasurer; dean of St Paul's	Yes	Capitular election	Elected by the canons; royal assent and archiepiscopal confirmation given
M. Richard of Gravesend	17/5/1280-9/12/1303	100	Archdeacon of Northampton	Yes	Capitular election	Canons elected Fulk Lovel, archdeacon of Colchester, but he refused the election. At a second election, conducted by way of compromise, Richard of Gravesend was elected. Royal assent and archiepiscopal consent given
M. Ralph Baldock	1/6/1304-24/7/1313	175	Dean of St Paul's	Yes	Capitular election	Baldock was elected by the canons, and the election received royal assent and archiepiscopal confirmation. Consecration was postponed as three canons, all of whom had been excluded from the election, launched an appeal to Rome. They subsequently withdrew their claims and Baldock (who had travelled to the papal curia to present his case) received papal confirmation

Bishop	Time in office	Length of vacancy (days)	Background	Chapter member	Mode of appointment	Circumstances of appointment
M. Gilbert of Segrave	28/9/1313-18/12/1316	66	Precentor of St Paul's	Yes	Capitular election	Elected by the canons, perhaps through the influence of his brother, Lord Segrave. Royal assent and archiepiscopal confirmation given
M. Richard of Newport	31/3/1317-24/8/1318	103	Dean of St Paul's	Yes	Capitular election	Elected by the canons; royal assent and archiepiscopal confirmation given
M. Stephen of Gravesend	6/11/1318-8/4/1338	74	Canon of St Paul's	Yes	Capitular election	Elected by the canons; royal assent and archiepiscopal confirmation given
M. Richard Bentworth	24/5/1338-8/12/1339	46	King's clerk	Yes	Capitular election	Unanimously elected by the canons; royal assent and archiepiscopal confirmation given
M. Ralph of Stratford	13/2/1340-17/4/1354	67	King's clerk	Yes	Capitular election	Elected by the canons; royal assent given. The election was confirmed by John Stratford, archbishop of Canterbury and Ralph's uncle

Norwich

Bishop	Time in office	Length of vacancy (days)	Background	Chapter member	Mode of appointment	Circumstances of appointment
Pandulph Masca	9/8/1215-16/9/1226	295	Papal envoy	No	Capitular election	Elected by the monks, acting under the influence of papal proctors. Royal assent given. Consecration delayed until 1222, probably to avoid Pandulph becoming subject to the authority of Archbishop Langton
Thomas de Blundeville	21/11/1226-16/8/1236	67	Exchequer clerk; nephew of Hubert de Burgh, the justiciar	No	Capitular election	Elected by the monks; royal assent and archiepiscopal confirmation given
William Raleigh	26/7/1239-17/9/1243	1,074[7]	Royal justice	No	Capitular election	Monks elected their prior, Simon of Elmham; king withheld his assent, causing an appeal to Rome. The case was delegated to the Legate Otto and was eventually quashed by the pope. Papal mandate for a new election; monks elected William Raleigh. Royal assent and archiepiscopal confirmation given

Bishop	Time in office	Length of vacancy (days)	Background	Chapter member	Mode of appointment	Circumstances of appointment
M. Walter of Suffield	17/7/1244-19/5/1257	305[8]	Regent-master at Paris	No	Capitular election	Licence to elect initially refused, because Henry III refused to recognize Raleigh's translation to Winchester and therefore claimed that the see was not vacant. Once the licence was granted, the monks elected Suffield. Royal assent and archiepiscopal confirmation granted
M. Simon of Walton	11/8/1257-2/1/1266	84	Royal justice	No	Capitular election	Elected by the monks; royal assent and archiepiscopal confirmation given
Roger Skerning	17/3/1266-22/1/1278	75	Prior of Norwich	Yes	Capitular election	Elected by the monks; royal assent and legatine confirmation given
M. William of Middleton	15/3/1278-1/9/1288	53	Archdeacon of Canterbury; archiepiscopal official; royal clerk	No	Capitular election	Elected by the monks; royal assent and archiepiscopal confirmation given
M. Ralph of Walpole	7/2/1289-10/10/1299	160	Archdeacon of Ely; theologian	No	Capitular election	Unanimously elected by way of compromise; royal assent granted by Edward I, who was then in Aragon. Archiepiscopal confirmation given

Bishop	Time in office	Length of vacancy (days)	Background	Chapter member	Mode of appointment	Circumstances of appointment
John Salmon	19/10/1299-6/07/1325	9	Prior of Ely	No	Papal provision	See vacant because Ralph Walpole was provided to Ely. Salmon, who had been elected as bishop of Norwich but had resigned his claim at the papal curia, was provided to Norwich. No election was held. Consecrated by archbishop of Canterbury; temporalities were restored three days later
William de Airmyn	13/12/1326-27/3/1336	525	Keeper of the privy seal	No	Papal provision	Monks elected Robert Baldock, the royal chancellor. Royal assent and archiepiscopal confirmation given. Baldock resigned because William de Airmyn had been provided three days before his election. Claims that Airmyn had been provided at the request of Queen Isabella, but it seems likely that John XXII intended the provision to please Edward II, who had tried to procure Carlisle for him the year before. Royal displeasure meant that the temporalities were withheld for several months, until Airmyn restored to royal favour
M. Anthony Bek	9/7/1337-18/12/1343	469	Dean of Lincoln; papal chaplain, resident at the papal curia	No	Papal provision	Monks elected by way of compromise and chose one of their number, Thomas Hemenhale. Without securing royal assent, he went to Avignon to seek papal consent to his election. The see had been reserved and Anthony Bek had been provided, therefore Hemenhale was obliged to resign his claim to Norwich. He was, however, provided to Worcester

Bishop	Time in office	Length of vacancy (days)	Background	Chapter member	Mode of appointment	Circumstances of appointment
M. William Bateman	2/3/1344-6/1/1355	75	Royal proctor at papal curia; dean of Lincoln	No	Papal provision	Bateman was elected by way of inspiration, but his election was invalidated by the prior reservation of the see. Bateman, who was then at the papal curia, was provided a month after his election

Rochester

Bishop	Time in office	Length of vacancy (days)[9]	Background	Chapter member	Mode of appointment	Circumstances of appointment
M. Benedict of Sawston	22/2/1215-18/12/1226	243[10]	Precentor of St Paul's; Parisian master	No	Capitular election	Elected on recommendation of Stephen Langton, who confirmed the election and consecrated the new bishop
M. Henry of Sandford	9/5/1227-25/2/1235	142	Archdeacon of Canterbury; royal clerk	No	Capitular election	Monks of Rochester and monks of Christ Church Canterbury both claimed the right to elect. Langton settled in favour of the Rochester convent and confirmed the election of their candidate, Henry of Sandford
Richard Wendene	21/11/1238-12/10/1250	1,365	Official of Bishop Sandford	No	Capitular election	Monks elected Wendene, but Archbishop Edmund refused to confirm the election. Monks appealed to Rome and two papal commissions were appointed to resolve the dispute. Neither managed to do so; three years after his election, Wendene received papal confirmation
M. Laurence of Sancto Martino	9/4/1251-3/6/1274	179	King's clerk; archdeacon of Coventry	No	Capitular election	Monks elected Sancto Martino, probably at the request of the king. He was reluctant to do homage to the archbishop, fearing that this might be to the detriment of royal rights, but eventually agreed and received archiepiscopal confirmation at Lyons
Walter of Merton	21/10/1274-27/10/1277	140	Royal chancellor	No	Capitular election	Elected by the monks and received archiepiscopal confirmation

Bishop	Time in office	Length of vacancy (days)[9]	Background	Chapter member	Mode of appointment	Circumstances of appointment
John of Bradfield	29/5/1278-23/4/1283	214	Monk of Rochester	Yes	Capitular election	Elected by the monks and received archiepiscopal confirmation
M. Thomas of Ingoldisthorpe	26/9/1283-11/5/1291	156	Dean of St Paul's	No	Capitular election	Monks elected John Kirkby, the king's treasurer, but Archbishop Pecham objected to him on grounds of pluralism. Kirkby resigned his claim and a new election was held. Ingoldisthorpe was elected and received archiepiscopal confirmation
Thomas of Wouldham	6/1/1291-28/2/1317	240	Prior of Rochester	Yes	Capitular election	The monks elected Wouldham, but he refused the election. They obtained a new licence to elect, elected Wouldham again, and this time he accepted. Archiepiscopal confirmation and consecration
Hamo of Hythe	5/12/1317-4/5/1352	1011	Prior of Rochester	Yes	Capitular election	Monks elected Hamo, but on the following day a papal reservation of the see was made; John XXII probably intended to provide the queen's chaplain, Giovanni di Puzzuoli. After a protracted dispute at the papal curia, Hamo's election was nevertheless confirmed

Salisbury

Bishop	Time in office	Length of vacancy (days)	Background	Chapter member	Mode of appointment	Circumstances of appointment
M. Richard Poore	9/5/1217-22/7/1228	92	Bishop of Chichester	No	Capitular election	Translated to Salisbury at the instigation of Guala. Received royal assent
M. Robert of Bingham	3/4/1229-2/11/1246	255	Canon of Salisbury; theologian	Yes	Capitular election	Poore was translated to Durham. Bingham unanimously elected by the five canons to whom this task was delegated. Royal assent given; archbishopric of Canterbury vacant, therefore papal confirmation sought and given
William of York	29/1/1247-31/1/1256	88	Royal justice	No	Capitular election	Elected by the canons; royal assent and archiepiscopal confirmation given
M. Giles of Bridport	17/8/1256-13/12/1262	200	Dean of Wells; archdeacon of Berkshire	Yes	Capitular election	Elected by the canons; royal assent and archiepiscopal confirmation given
Walter de la Wyle	10/4/1263-4/1/1271	118	Succentor of Wells	Yes	Capitular election	Elected by the canons; royal assent and archiepiscopal confirmation given

Bishop	Time in office	Length of vacancy (days)	Background	Chapter member	Mode of appointment	Circumstances of appointment
M. Robert of Wickhampton	15/8/1274-24/4/1284	1319	Dean of Salisbury	Yes	Capitular election	Elected by the canons; royal assent given. Canterbury was vacant, and the prior and convent of Canterbury Cathedral confirmed the election. Both the king and the suffragan bishops refused to recognize their confirmation(the latter appealed to Rome) and thus Wickhampton received neither temporalities nor consecration. He went to Rome to seek papal confirmation, but the Holy See was also vacant and his election was not confirmed for over three years. Only after this was he consecrated and allowed to take full possession of the see
M. Walter Scammel	10/8/1284-25/9/1286	108	Dean of Salisbury; king's clerk	Yes	Capitular election	Elected by way of scrutiny (24 out of 33 votes); royal assent and archiepiscopal confirmation given
M. Henry of Braunstone	15/3/1287-11/2/1288	171	Dean of Salisbury; king's clerk	Yes	Capitular election	Elected by the canons; royal assent and archiepiscopal confirmation given

Bishop	Time in office	Length of vacancy (days)	Background	Chapter member	Mode of appointment	Circumstances of appointment
M. William de la Corner	26/2/1289-10/10/1291	381	King's clerk	Yes	Capitular election	Chapter elected Lawrence of Hakeburne, one of the canons, by way of scrutiny. He died before receiving archiepiscopal confirmation. A new election was held and William de la Corner (who had come second in the original election) was elected. Royal assent and archiepiscopal confirmation given
Nicholas Longespee	16/12/1291-18/5/1297	67	Treasurer of Salisbury Cathedral; son of earl of Salisbury; royal kinsman	Yes	Capitular election	Elected by the canons; royal assent and archiepiscopal confirmation given
M. Simon of Ghent	7/8/1297-2/4/1315	81[11]	Archdeacon of Oxford	Yes	Capitular election	Elected by the canons; royal assent and archiepiscopal confirmation given
M. Roger Martival	18/7/1315-14/3/1330	107	Dean of Lincoln	Yes	Capitular election	Elected by the canons; royal assent and archiepiscopal confirmation given

Bishop	Time in office	Length of vacancy (days)	Background	Chapter member	Mode of appointment	Circumstances of appointment
Robert Wyville	10/6/1330-4/9/1375	88	Secretary of Queen Isabella	Yes	Papal provision	Wyville was provided by John XXII. The canons had received licence to elect, but there is no direct evidence that they proceeded to election. Another canon, Nicholas Ludlow, was referred to as 'bishop-elect of Salisbury'; it is unclear what claim, if any, he had to this title, but it is possible that he had been elected by the chapter

Winchester

Bishop	Time in office	Length of vacancy (days)	Background	Chapter member	Mode of appointment	Circumstances of appointment
William de Raleigh	10/9/1244-1/9/1250	2285	Bishop of Norwich; former royal justice	No	Capitular election	Monks postulated Ralph Neville but Henry III, who wanted the see for Queen Eleanor's uncle, refused his assent. Following an appeal to Rome, the postulation was quashed by the pope. The pope twice issued a mandate for a new election to be held; following the second of these, a new election was held in May 1240 and William Raleigh was postulated. The king, who now wanted the see for another of Eleanor's uncles, again refused his assent, provoking another appeal to the papal curia. A long papal vacancy prolonged the dispute, but Innocent IV ruled in Raleigh's favour in September 1243. Henry III appealed against this confirmation, but the appeal was rejected in February 1244. Not until September 1244 was a reconciliation achieved and the temporalities restored
Aymer de Lusignan	14/1/1251-4/12/1260	136[12]	Half-brother of Henry III	No	Capitular election	Henry III commanded the monks to elect his half-brother; they complied. Aymer's youth meant that he had to be postulated and papal confirmation of his appointment was given. He was not consecrated until 1260, shortly before his death

Bishop	Time in office	Length of vacancy (days)	Background	Chapter member	Mode of appointment	Circumstances of appointment
M. John Gervase	18/10/1262-19/1/1268	683	Chancellor of York Minster; papal chaplain	No	Papal provision	Capitular election produced a split result: the majority favoured William de Taunton, abbot of Milton and previously prior of Winchester, whilst a minority voted for the current prior, Andrew of London. Both elections were quashed by the pope, who provided John Gervase (who was already at the curia). The temporalities were restored to him reasonably quickly, but only in return for a fine of £2,000
M. Nicholas of Ely	2/5/1268-12/2/1280	103	Bishop of Worcester; former baronial chancellor	No	Papal provision	No election was held. Gervase died at the papal curia and the see was immediately filled by the translation of Nicholas. The temporalities were restored and, unconventionally, the new bishop made a second profession of obedience to Canterbury
M. John de Pontissara	11/8/1282-4/12/1304	911	Archiepiscopal proctor at papal curia; king's clerk	No	Papal provision	Monks postulated Robert Burnell, bishop of Bath and Wells and the king's chancellor; pope refused to admit the postulation and reserved the see, but then issued a mandate for a new election to be held. The monks elected Richard de la More, archdeacon of Winchester. Royal assent given; archiepiscopal confirmation withheld on grounds of pluralism. Following an appeal to Rome, More resigned his claim and the pope provided Pontissara

Bishop	Time in office	Length of vacancy (days)	Background	Chapter member	Mode of appointment	Circumstances of appointment
Henry Woodlock	12/3/1305-29/6/1316	98	Prior of St Swithun's	Yes	Capitular election	Monks elected Woodlock; royal assent and archiepiscopal confirmation given without difficulty
John de Sandale	23/9/1316-2/11/1319	87	Royal chancellor	No	Capitular election	Elected by the convent; royal assent and archiepiscopal confirmation granted
Rigaud d'Asserio	17/4/1320-12/4/1323	167	Auditor of the Sacred Palace; papal nuncio in Britain	No	Papal provision	King petitioned pope for the provision of Henry Burghersh, but granted *congé d'élire* to the monks. They elected Adam of Winchester, one of their brethren, but Rigaud d'Asserio had already been provided and the election was therefore ruled invalid
M. John de Stratford	28/6/1324-5/2/1333	443	Royal diplomat	No	Papal provision	Bishop Rigaud died at the papal curia. Edward II petitioned for the provision of Robert Baldock, but John de Stratford (who was at the curia and had delivered the royal letters in favour of Baldock) had already been provided. Royal objections meant that Stratford remained in Avignon for several months and only received the temporalities a year after his provision

Bishop	Time in office	Length of vacancy (days)	Background	Chapter member	Mode of appointment	Circumstances of appointment
M. Adam de Orleton	23/9/1334-18/4/1345	230	Royal diplomat	No	Papal provision	See became vacant by translation of Stratford to Canterbury. Pope provided Orleton, who was translated from Worcester. An appeal was made by John Pebrehave, of the diocese of Winchester, citing Orleton's activities at the time of Edward II's deposition, but John XXII did not take the charges seriously and Orleton was not required to go to Avignon. King objected and refused to restore temporalities for nearly a year

Worcester

Bishop	**Time in office**	**Length of vacancy (days)**	**Background**	**Chapter member**	**Mode of appointment**	**Circumstances of appointment**
Sylvester of Evesham	8/4/1216-16/7/1218	49	Prior of Worcester	Yes	Capitular election	Elected by monks and received royal assent. Langton still in exile; Sylvester therefore sought and received consecration from the pope
William of Blois	10/9/1218-18/8/1236	56	Archdeacon of Buckingham	No	Capitular election	Monks wanted to elect one of their own number, but Guala forbade them to do so. They made an unsuccessful appeal to the king's council and were obliged to elect the legate's candidate, William of Blois. Election confirmed by legate and royal assent given
Walter de Cantilupe	27/9/1236-12/2/1266	40	King's clerk	No	Capitular election	Elected by monks; received royal assent and archiepiscopal confirmation
M. Nicholas of Ely	18/6/1266-2/5/1268	126	Baronial chancellor; archdeacon of Ely	No	Capitular election	Elected by monks; received royal assent and archiepiscopal confirmation
M. Godfrey Giffard	13/6/1268-26/1/1302	42	Chancellor of England	No	Capitular election	See vacant by translation of Bishop Nicholas to Winchester. Giffard elected by monks; received royal assent and archiepiscopal confirmation

Bishop	Time in office	Length of vacancy (days)	Background	Chapter member	Mode of appointment	Circumstances of appointment
William of Gainsborough	4/2/1303-17/9/1307	371	Franciscan friar; retained at papal curia by Boniface VIII, where he lectured in theology and served as a royal proctor	No	Papal provision	John de Sancto Germano, a member of the cathedral priory, elected by way of compromise. Royal assent given, but archiepiscopal confirmation withheld because of the elect's rumoured reluctance to accept his election and because of doubts over the validity of the electoral procedure. Convent appealed to Rome, seeking confirmation of the election or the right to hold a new election if the first was quashed. Sancto Germano went to Rome, but quickly resigned. Gainsborough provided. No royal or archiepiscopal objections to his appointment
Walter Reynolds	5/4/1308-3/1/1314	201	Royal treasurer	No	Papal provision	Hearing rumours that the see had been reserved, Edward II urged the monks to hold an election as soon as possible. Reynolds, the royal candidate, was elected but refused to accept the see because a reservation had been made. The election was annulled and Reynolds provided
Walter Maidstone	17/2/1314-7/4/1317	45	King's clerk	No	Papal provision	See became vacant by translation of Reynolds to Canterbury. Maidstone, who was at Avignon on king's business, provided
M. Thomas of Cobham	20/11/1317-27/8/1327	227	Royal diplomat	No	Papal provision	Monks received licence to elect, but Cobham (who was probably the royal candidate) had already been provided

Bishop	Time in office	Length of vacancy (days)	Background	Chapter member	Mode of appointment	Circumstances of appointment
M. Adam de Orleton	2/3/1328-1/12/1333	188	Bishop of Hereford	No	Papal provision	Monks elected Wolstan de Bransford, their prior, whose election received royal assent and archiepiscopal confirmation. Preparations for his consecration were underway when news of Orleton's provision reached England. Crown tried to secure Bransford's consecration, but Archbishop Reynolds did not comply. King strongly objected to the provision and issued two prohibitions to Orleton, as well as petitioning the pope in Bransford's favour. John XXII replied that, having provided Orleton, he could not comply with royal requests to confirm the election. Temporalities restored circa five months after provision
M. Simon de Montacute	15/5/1334-11/6/1337	105[13]	Archdeacon of Canterbury; curial family	No	Papal provision	See became vacant by translation of Orleton to Winchester. Montacute, the king's candidate for Winchester, was instead provided to Worcester. No election held
Thomas de Hemenhale	25/7/1337-24/13/1338	44	Monk of Norwich	No	Papal provision	See vacant due to translation of Montacute to Ely. Hemenhale (who was at the curia, having recently resigned his claim to the bishopric of Norwich) was provided
Wulstan de Bransford	17/2/1338-6/8/1349	55	Prior of Worcester	Yes	Capitular election	Elected by monks; received royal assent and archiepiscopal confirmation

Province of York

Carlisle

Bishop	Time in office	Length of vacancy (days)	Background	Chapter member	Mode of appointment	Circumstances of appointment
Hugh of Beaulieu	25/8/1218-4/6/1223	1,509	Former abbot of Beaulieu (Cistercian)	No	Capitular election	See had been vacant since July 1214. In 1216 the city was captured by Alexander king of Scots, who procured the election of one of his clerks. In April 1217 the English crown complained to the pope, who ordered Guala to quash the election. Hugh was elected on Guala's orders; the election received royal assent
Walter Mauclerk	27/10/1223-29/6/1246	145	Royal justice	No	Capitular election	Elected by the canons, probably on his own initiative. King wrote to archbishop indicating that the election lacked royal assent and asking him not to proceed to confirmation. King also appointed a proctor to oppose Mauclerk at the papal curia. Appeal apparently withdrawn; royal assent and archiepiscopal confirmation given
M. Silvester of Everdon	8/12/1246-24/3/1254	163	Royal clerk; keeper of the great seal	No	Capitular election	Silvester of Everdon elected, but declined. The monks sought a new licence to elect and elected him again. Royal assent and archiepiscopal confirmation given

Bishop	Time in office	Length of vacancy (days)	Background	Chapter member	Mode of appointment	Circumstances of appointment
M. Thomas de Vipont	24/12/1254-?/10/1256	275[14]	Rector of Graystoke, Cumbria	No	Capitular election	King sought the see for his chaplain, but the canons elected Vipont; received royal assent and archiepiscopal confirmation
Robert de Chaury	29/9/1257-?/10/1278	350[15]	Chamberlain of the exchequer; archdeacon of Bath	No	Capitular election	Canons elected Robert de Sancta Agata, archdeacon of Northumberland, but he declined the see. A new licence to elected was issued, Robert de Chaury was elected and the king gave his assent. Archbishop Sewal of York objected, instead postulating M. John of Exeter, the chancellor of York, but Alexander IV dispensed Chaury for illegitimacy and confirmed his election. Temporalities restored, even though the archbishop had 'shown himself difficult', since the king and pope had both consented to the election
Ralph of Ireton	10/7/1280-1/3/1292	626[16]	Prior of Guisborough (Augustinian)	No	Papal provision	Canons elected William Rotherfield, dean of York, but he declined the see. The next day another election was held and Ireton was elected. King wrote to Archbishop Giffard asking him not to do anything to prejudice royal rights, since licence to elect had not been sought for the second election. Giffard died and the dean and chapter of York refused to confirm the election, so the canons appealed to Rome. Election quashed on procedural grounds, but Ireton provided

Bishop	Time in office	Length of vacancy (days)	Background	Chapter member	Mode of appointment	Circumstances of appointment
John de Halton	18/6/1292-1/11/1324	110	Cellarer of Carlisle Cathedral Priory	Yes	Capitular election	Elected by canons; royal assent given; archiepiscopal confirmation given by the vicar-general on behalf of John le Romeyn, who was then overseas
M. John de Ross	20/6/1325-11/5/1332	232	Auditor of Causes in the Sacred Palace	No	Papal provision	Canons elected William Airmyn, the royal candidate, and his election received royal assent and archiepiscopal confirmation. However, the see had been reserved and John de Ross provided; the election was therefore invalid. Airmyn resigned his claim and the temporalities were restored to Ross
John de Kirkby	9/7/1332-3/12/1352	59[17]	Prior of Carlisle	Yes	Capitular election	Kirkby elected by the canons; election received royal assent and archiepiscopal confirmation; Kirkby was consecrated. His position was insecure for several months, as the see had been reserved, but John XXII confirmed the election

Durham

Bishop	Time in office	Length of vacancy (days)	Background	Chapter member	Mode of appointment	Circumstances of appointment
M. Richard Marsh	29/6/1217-1/5/1226	3,355	Chancellor of England	No	Capitular election	See vacant since 1208. Richard Poore elected 1213, but election quashed. John de Grey, bishop of Norwich, postulated in 1214 at the direction of the legate, but Grey died. Morgan, the bastard son of Henry II, was elected in 1215 at the king's suggestion, but the election was quashed on grounds of illegitimacy. John may also have tried to secure the translation of Peter des Roches from Winchester. Richard Marsh was elected at the direction of Guala and received royal assent
M. Richard Poore	22/7/1228-15/4/1237	814	Bishop of Salisbury	No	Papal provision	Henry III sought the see for Luke, his treasurer, and refused to grant the licence to elect. On the last day of the three months in which they were canonically allowed to hold an election, the monks elected William Stichill. Royal assent was withheld and the election was quashed on procedural grounds by the pope. Pope refused to allow a new election, but instead required the Durham proctors to name several candidates, of whom he would pick one. Richard Poore was translated from Salisbury to Durham by papal provision

Bishop	Time in office	Length of vacancy (days)	Background	Chapter member	Mode of appointment	Circumstances of appointment
M. Nicholas of Farnham	10/2/1241-2/2/1249	1,397	Royal physician	No	Capitular election	Monks elected their prior, Thomas Melsonby. The king objected to the election, claiming that Melsonby was manifestly unsuitable. Case examined by Archbishop Gray of York and at the papal curia; Melsonby resigned. Papal mandate for a new election to be held. Farnham elected; royal assent and archiepiscopal confirmation given
M. Walter Kirkham	2/10/1249-9/8/1260	243	Dean of York; royal clerk	No	Capitular election	Elected by the monks. Henry III had wanted the see for Aymer de Lusignan and royal assent was withheld for several months but then granted. Archiepiscopal confirmation
Robert of Stichill	5/12/1260-4/8/1274	118	Prior of Finchale (Durham cell)	Yes	Capitular election	Elected by monks; royal assent and archiepiscopal confirmation given
Robert de Insula	8/11/1274-7/6/1283	96	Prior of Finchale	Yes	Capitular election	Elected by monks; royal assent and archiepiscopal confirmation given
Antony Bek	4/9/1283-3/3/1311	89	King's clerk; archdeacon of Durham	No	Capitular election	Monks elected Bek, the king's candidate. Royal assent and archiepiscopal confirmation given
Richard Kellawe	20/5/1311-10/10/1316	78	Prior of Holy Island (Durham cell)	Yes	Capitular election	Edward II tried to secure the election of a kinsman of Antonio Pessagno, his Genoese banker, but the monks elected Kellawe. Royal assent and archiepiscopal confirmation given

Bishop	Time in office	Length of vacancy (days)	Background	Chapter member	Mode of appointment	Circumstances of appointment
Louis de Beaumont	4/5/1317-24/9/1333	206	Cousin of Queen Isabella; held numerous English benefices	No	Papal provision	Various candidates were suggested: Thomas Charlton by the king, Louis de Beaumont by the queen, John Walwayn by the Earl of Hereford and John de Kynardesley by the Earl of Lancaster. The monks elected Henry Stamford, prior of Finchale. The king withheld his assent; the prior of Durham appealed to the pope to confirm the election, but it had already been quashed. Beaumont was provided in accordance with Isabella's request
Richard of Bury	7/12/1333-14/4/1345	75	Royal diplomat	No	Papal provision	Monks elected Robert Graystanes, their sub-prior. King refused assent, as Richard de Bury had been sent to the papal curia to seek provision; royal assent to the election would only be given if this provision was not made. Archbishop Melton nevertheless confirmed the election and consecrated Graystanes, but Bury had been provided the day before the election, which was consequently invalid. King granted temporalities; Melton sought pardon from king and pope for consecrating Graystanes

York

Archbishop	Time in office	Length of vacancy (days)	Background	Chapter member	Mode of appointment	Circumstances of appointment
M. Sewal de Boville	4/5/1256-1/5/1258	370	Dean of York	Yes	Capitular election	Canons elected Sewal; Henry III refused his assent because the elect was illegitimate. Pope granted him a dispensation and confirmed the election
M. Godfrey de Ludham	1/12/1258-12/1/1265	215	Dean of York	Yes	Capitular election	Elected by the canons; royal assent and papal confirmation given
Walter Giffard	26/12/1266-25/4/1279	713	Royal chancellor; bishop of Bath and Wells	No	Papal provision	Canons elected William of Rotherfield, their dean, but the pope quashed the election. He provided Bonaventura, who declined the see. He then provided Walter Giffard, translating him from Bath and Wells
M. William de Wickwane	28/10/1279-26/8/1285	186	Chancellor of York Minster	Yes	Papal provision	Wickwane elected by 18 out of 21 electors. Royal assent given, but pope quashed the election 'on account of informality'. Wickwane was then provided

Archbishop	Time in office	Length of vacancy (days)	Background	Chapter member	Mode of appointment	Circumstances of appointment
M. John le Romeyn	12/4/1286-11/3/1296	229	Precentor of Lincoln	Yes	Capitular election	John le Romeyn elected by chapter and royal assent given. He went to Rome but, 'a doubt having arisen', had to resign. A new election was held at the papal curia, in which most of the electors were not only canons of York but also members of the papal hierarchy. Romeyn was re-elected, and the election was confirmed by the pope. Temporalities promptly restored
M. Henry of Newark	21/6/1297-15/8/1299	468	Dean of York; king's clerk	Yes	Papal provision	Newark was elected by the chapter; royal assent given. Newark's election was quashed because he failed to go to the papal curia to seek confirmation, but he was provided to the see in order to please the king
M. Thomas of Corbridge	30/4/1300-22/9/1304	259	Sacrist of St Mary and the Holy Angels, York	Yes	Papal provision	Corbridge elected by a majority of the canons; royal assent given. Corbridge resigned his election in Rome, probably due to doubts over the validity of the electoral procedure, but was then provided to the archbishopric. Temporalities restored by king without complications

Archbishop	Time in office	Length of vacancy (days)	Background	Chapter member	Mode of appointment	Circumstances of appointment
M. William of Greenfield	31/3/1306-6/12/1315	556	Royal chancellor; dean of Chichester	Yes	Capitular election	Greenfield elected by the canons, and received royal assent. Went to papal curia to seek confirmation; his stay was lengthened because of the delay in electing a successor to Benedict XI, but he received confirmation and consecration from Clement V soon after the latter's election
William Melton	8/10/1317-5/4/1340	672	Treasurer of the wardrobe	Yes	Capitular election	Melton, the king's candidate, elected by 17 out of 23 canons. Royal assent given but an appeal was made by M. Pandulf de Sabellis, papal notary, canon of York, and George de Yporegia, canon of Southwell, on unknown grounds. A lengthy papal vacancy delayed the examination of Melton's election, but his election was confirmed by John XXII. Temporalities restored two weeks later

Archbishop	Time in office	Length of vacancy (days)	Background	Chapter member	Mode of appointment	Circumstances of appointment
M. William de la Zouche	19/9/1342-10/7/1352	897	Treasurer of the exchequer; dean of York	Yes	Papal provision	Edward III wanted the see for William Kilsby, keeper of the privy seal; when the canons elected Zouche (by twelve votes to five) he was deprived of the treasurership. King petitioned pope in Kilsby's favour and stopped Zouche leaving England, supposedly because he had not sought royal assent. Only when the pope threatened to excommunicate those detaining the archbishop-elect was Zouche able to leave for the curia. Having been kidnapped and ransomed on his way to Avignon, he had to wait until June 1342 for judgement of his case. Election quashed, and Zouche provided and consecrated. Temporalities restored reasonably soon afterwards

Notes

1 The exact date of the restoration of the temporalities is unknown; this is the shortest possible length of the vacancy, but it may have been two to three months longer.

2 The date of the restoration of the temporalities is unknown; I have therefore taken Mapenore's consecration as the end point of this vacancy.

3 The date of the restoration of the temporalities is unknown. I have therefore taken Foliot's consecration as the end point of the vacancy. The chronicles offer two different dates for this ceremony, of which I have taken the earlier – but the discrepancy between the two is less than a week.

4 Orleton was translated to Worcester, and Charlton provided to Hereford, in late September 1327. At that time, the temporalities of the bishopric of Hereford were already in royal hands, having being confiscated by the crown during the ongoing dispute between Orleton and Edward II. Following Charlton's appointment, the temporalities were speedily restored, but Edward III resisted the appointment of Orleton to Worcester and withheld the temporalities of that see for some months. It therefore being impossible to date the end of Orleton's tenure at Hereford according to control of the temporalities, I have dated the start of this vacancy from the day of his translation.

5 The date of the restoration of the temporalities is unknown. I have taken the date of archiepiscopal confirmation as the end point of the vacancy; given that royal assent had already been given, the temporalities would probably have been restored within a few days.

6 The exact date of Henry Burghersh's death is unknown; he certainly died in December 1340, probably towards the end of the month, since the licence to elect was issued on 4 January 1341. The vacancy may therefore have been a few days, or even two to three weeks, longer than the figure given here.

7 Exactly when Raleigh received the temporalities is unclear; they were still in royal custody on 4 June 1239, but had probably been returned by 26 July, which I have taken as the end of the vacancy.

8 Since Henry III objected to the translation of William Raleigh from Norwich to Winchester, he did not receive the temporalities of the latter see until after Suffield was fully established at Norwich. I have therefore taken Raleigh's provision to Winchester as the starting point of the Norwich vacancy – although Henry III would not have agreed with me.

9 Rochester's anomalous position as a fief of the archbishopric of Canterbury means that information about the temporalities of the see is sketchy. Only for Hamo of Hythe (1319-52), to whom the temporalities were restored by the king, is the date on which this was done recorded with any certainty. Therefore, for the other Rochester bishops, the vacancy is calculated from the death of the old prelate to the consecration of the new.

10 The date of Sawston's consecration is uncertain; it is possible that he was actually consecrated on 25 January 1215.

11 The date of Bishop Longespee's death is uncertain, with different dates given in difference sources. I have based my calculation on the date given by the Salisbury obit. roll.

12 The date on which Aymer received the temporalities is unknown; I have therefore taken the date on which his election was confirmed by the pope as the start of his episcopate.

13 Due to royal objections to the translation of Adam Orleton from Worcester to Winchester, he did not receive the temporalities of his new see until well after Montacute

had received the temporalities of Worcester. I have therefore taken the date of Orlelton's translation to Winchester as the start date of the Worcester vacancy.

[14] The exact date of Bishop Silvester's death is unknown. He may have died as early as 2 February, but the see was certainly vacant by 24 March 1254; I have taken this date as the starting point of the vacancy.

[15] The exact date of Bishop Thomas' death is unknown, but the see was vacant by 14 October 1256, which date I have taken as the start of the vacancy.

[16] The exact date of Bishop Robert's death is unknown; the see was vacant by 23 October 1278, from whence I have calculated the length of the vacancy.

[17] The exact date of Bishop John's death is unknown. Licence to elect his successor was granted on 11 May 1332, which I have treated as the start of the vacancy.

Bibliography

Manuscript Sources

Bodleian Library

MS Laud misc. 647

British Library

Cotton MS Cleopatra E.II
Royal MS 12 D xi

The National Archives

SC1 [Ancient Correspondence]
SC8 [Ancient Petitions]

Primary Sources

Acta Stephani Langton Cantuariensis Archiepiscopi, ed. K. Major (Oxford, 1950).
The Acts of the Parliaments of Scotland, 1124-1707, ed. T. Thomson, 12 vols (Edinburgh, 1814-75).
Adae Murimuth Continuatio Chronicarum, ed. E. M. Thompson, RS, 93 (London, 1889).
Anglia Sacra, ed. H. Wharton, 2 vols (London, 1691).
Anglo-Scottish Relations, 1174-1328: Some Selected Documents, ed. E. L. G. Stones (London, 1965).
Annales Monastici, ed. H. R. Luard, RS, 36, 5 vols (London, 1864-69).
Bartholomæi de Cotton, Monachi Norwicensis, Historia Anglicana, ed. H. Luard, RS, 16 (London, 1859).
The Book of John Schalby, ed. J. H. Srawley, Lincoln Minster Pamphlets, 2 (Lincoln, 1949).
Calendar of the Close Rolls Preserved in the Public Record Office. Edward I, 5 vols (London, 1900-1908).
Calendar of the Close Rolls Preserved in the Public Record Office. Edward II, 4 vols (London, 1892).

Calendar of the Close Rolls Preserved in the Public Record Office. Edward III, 14 vols (London, 1896-1913).

Calendar of the Close Rolls Preserved in the Public Record Office. Henry IV, 5 vols (London, 1927-38).

Calendar of the Durham Cathedral Muniments: Archiepiscopalia (Durham, 2011).

Calendar of the Durham Cathedral Muniments: Locelli (Durham, 2012).

Calendar of Entries in the Papal Registers relating to Great Britain and Ireland, ed. W. Bliss *et al.*, in progress (London and Dublin, 1893-).

Calendar of the Fine Rolls Preserved in the Public Record Office, I: *1272-1307* (London, 1911).

Calendar of the Liberate Rolls Preserved in the Public Record Office. Henry III, 6 vols (London, 1916-64).

Calendar of the Manuscripts of the Dean and Chapter of Wells, ed. W. H. Bird and W. P. Baildon, 2 vols (London, 1907-14).

Calendar of the Patent Rolls Preserved in the Public Record Office. Edward I, 4 vols (London, 1893-8).

Calendar of the Patent Rolls Preserved in the Public Record Office. Edward II, 5 vols (London, 1893-1901).

Calendar of the Patent Rolls Preserved in the Public Record Office. Edward III, 16 vols (London, 1891-1916).

A Calendar of the Register of Wolstan de Bransford, Bishop of Worcester, 1339-1349, ed. R. M. Haines, Worcestershire Historical Society, 4 (London, 1966).

Cartularium Monasterii de Rameseia, ed. W. Hart and P. Lyons, RS, 79, 3 vols (London, 1884-93).*Charters and Documents Illustrating the History of the Cathedral, City and Diocese of Salisbury in the Twelfth and Thirteenth Centuries*, ed. W. R. Jones and W. D. Macray, RS, 97 (London, 1891).

Chronica Magistri Rogeri de Houedene, ed. W. Stubbs, RS, 51, 4 vols (London, 1868-71).

Chronica Monasterii de Melsa, ed. E. A. Bond, RS, 43, 3 vols (London, 1866-68).

The Chronicle of Bury St Edmunds, 1212-1301, ed. A. Gransden (London, 1964).*The Chronicle of Lanercost, 1272-1346*, ed. H. Maxwell (Glasgow, 1913).

Chronicles of the Mayors and Sheriffs of London, ed. H. T. Riley (London, 1863).

Chronicles and Memorials of the Reign of Richard I, ed. W. Stubbs, RS, 38, 2 vols (London, 1865).*Chronicles of the Reigns of Edward I and Edward II*, ed. W. Stubbs, RS, 76, 2 vols (London, 1882-83).

Chronicles of the Reigns of Stephen, Henry II and Richard I, ed. R. Howlett, RS, 82, 4 vols (London, 1884-89).

Chronicon Angliae, ed. E. M. Thompson, RS, 64 (London, 1874).

Chronicon de Lanercost, 1201-46, ed. J. Stevenson (Edinburgh, 1839).

Close Rolls of the Reign of Henry III Preserved in the Public Record Office, 14 vols (London, 1902-38).
Concilia Magnae Britanniae et Hiberniae, ed. D. Wilkins, 4 vols (London, 1737).
Corpus Iuris Canonici, ed. E. Friedberg, 2 vols (Leipzig, 1879-81).
Councils and Synods, with Other Documents Relating to the English Church, II: *A.D. 1205-1313*, ed. F. M. Powicke and C. R. Cheney, 2 vols (Oxford, 1964).
Cronica Johannis de Oxenedes, ed. H. Ellis, RS, 13 (London, 1859).
Decrees of the Ecumenical Councils, ed. N. P. Tanner, 2 vols (London, 1990). *Diplomatic Documents Preserved in the Public Record Office*, ed. P. Chaplais (London, 1964).*Documents of the Baronial Movement of Reform and Rebellion, 1258-67*, ed. R. F. Treharne and I. J. Sanders (Oxford, 1973).
Durham Annals and Documents of the Thirteenth Century, ed. F. Barlow, Surtees Society, 155 (Durham, 1945).
Eadmeri Historia Novorum in Anglia, ed. M. Rule (London, 1884)
Early Sources of Scottish History, AD 500 to 1286, ed. A. O. Anderson, 2 vols (Edinburgh, 1922).
The Ecclesiastical History of the English People, ed. B. Colgrave, R. Collins and J. McClure (Oxford, 1994).
English Episcopal Acta 9: Winchester 1205-1238, ed. N. Vincent (Oxford, 1994).
English Episcopal Acta 12: Exeter, 1086-1257, ed. F. Barlow (Oxford, 1996).
English Episcopal Acta 21: Norwich 1215-1243, ed. C. Harper-Bill (Oxford, 2000).
English Episcopal Acta 22: Chichester 1215-1253, ed. P. M. Hoskin (Oxford, 2001).
English Episcopal Acta 26: London, 1189-1228, ed. D. P. Johnson (Oxford, 2003).
English Episcopal Acta 29: Durham, 1241-1283, ed. P. M. Hoskin (Oxford, 2005).
English Episcopal Acta 30: Carlisle, 1133-1192, ed. D. M. Smith (Oxford, 2005).
English Episcopal Acta 32: Norwich 1244-1266, ed. C. Harper-Bill (Oxford, 2007).
English Episcopal Acta 35: Hereford, 1234-1275, ed. J. Barrow (Oxford, 2009).
English Episcopal Acta 38: London, 1229-1280, ed. P. M. Hoskin (Oxford, 2011).
English Historical Documents, vol. 2: *1042-1189*, ed. D. C. Douglas and G. W. Greenaway (London, 1953).
English Historical Documents, vol. 3: *1189-1327*, ed. H. Rothwell (London, 1975).
Flores Historiarum, ed. H. R. Luard, RS, 95, 3 vols (London, 1890).
Foedera, Conventiones, Literae et Acta Publica, ed. T. Rymer, A. Clarke and F. Holbrooke, 3 vols in 6 (London, 1816-30).

Gesta Abbatum Monasterii Sancti Albani, ed. H. T. Riley, RS, 28, 3 vols (London, 1867-69).
Giraldus Cambrensis opera, ed. J. S. Brewer, J. F. Dimock and G. F. Warner, RS, 21, 8 vols (London, 1861-91).
The Great Register of Lichfield Cathedral known as Magnum Registrum Album, ed. H. E. Savage, William Salt Society, Third Series (Kendal, 1926).
Historiae Dunelmensis Scriptores Tres: Gaufridus de Coldingham, Robertus de Graystanes et Willielmus de Chambres, ed. J. Raine, Surtees Society, 9 (London, 1839).
The Historians of the Church of York and its Archbishops, ed. J. Raine, RS, 71, 3 vols (London, 1879-94).
Historical Papers and Letters from the Northern Registers, ed. J. Raine, RS, 61 (London, 1873).
The Historical Works of Gervase of Canterbury, ed. W. Stubbs, RS, 73, 2 vols (London, 1870-80).
Jocelin of Brakelond: Chronicle of the Abbey of Bury St Edmunds, ed. D. Greenway and J. Sayers (Oxford, 1989).
Layettes du Trésor de Chartes, ed. M. Teulet *et al.*, 5 vols (Paris, 1863-1909).
The Letters and Charters of Cardinal Guala Bicchieri, Papal Legate in England 1216-1218, ed. N. Vincent (Woodbridge, 1996).
The Letters of Pope Innocent III (1198-1216) Concerning England and Wales: A Calendar, ed. C. R. Cheney and M. G. Cheney (Oxford, 1967).
The Letters of Robert Grosseteste, Bishop of Lincoln, ed. F. A. C. Mantello and J. Goering (Toronto, 2010).
Lettres Communes, Jean XXII (1316-1334), ed. G. Mollat, 16 vols in 15 (Paris, 1904-47).
Liber Quotidianus Contra Rotularis, ed. J. Topham (London, 1787).
The Life of St Anselm, Archbishop of Canterbury, by Eadmer, ed. R. W. Southern (Oxford, 1962).
The Life of St Edmund by Matthew Paris, ed. C. H. Lawrence (Stroud, 1996).
Magna Vita Sancti Hugonis, ed. D. L. Douie and H. Farmer, 2 vols (London, 1961).
Materials for the History of Thomas Becket, Archbishop of Canterbury, ed. J. C. Robertson and J. B. Sheppard, RS, 67, 7 vols (London, 1875-85).
Matthæi Parisiensis, Monachi Sancti Albani, Chronica Majora, ed. H. R. Luard, RS, 57, 7 vols (London, 1872-83).
Matthæi Parisiensis, Monachi Sancti Albani: Historia Anglorum, sive, ut Vulgo Dicitur, Historia Minor, ed. F. Madden, RS, 3 vols (London, 1866-69).
A Medieval Chronicle of Scotland: The Chronicle of Melrose, ed. J. Stevenson (Lampeter, 1991).
Memoriale Walteri de Coventria, ed. W. Stubbs, RS, 58, 2 vols (London, 1872-73).

Memorials of St Edmund's Abbey, ed. T. Arnold, RS, 96, 3 vols (London, 1890-96).

Oeuvres de Rigord et de Guillaume le Breton: Historiens de Philippe Auguste, ed. H. Delaborde, 2 vols (Paris, 1882-85).

Original Papal Documents in England and Wales from the Accession of Pope Innocent III to the Death of Pope Benedict XI (1198-1304), ed. J. Sayers (Oxford, 1999).

The Parliament Rolls of Medieval England, 1275-1504, ed. C. Given-Wilson, 16 vols (Woodbridge, 2005).

Patent Rolls of the Reign of Henry III, 6 vols (London, 1901-13).

Patrologia Latina, ed. P. Migne, 221 vols (Paris, 1844-65).

The Pontifical of Egbert, Archbishop of York, A. D. 732-766, ed. W. Greenwell, Surtees Society, 27 (Durham, 1853).

Radulfi de Diceto Decani Lundoniensis Opera Historica, ed. W. Stubbs, RS, 68, 2 vols (London, 1876).

Records of Antony Bek, Bishop and Patriarch, 1283-11, ed. C. M. Fraser, Surtees Society, 119 (Durham, 1953).

Recueil des historiens des Gaules et de la France, ed. M. Bouquet *et al.*, new edn directed by L. Delisle, 19 vols (Paris, 1869-80).

The Register of the Diocese of Worcester during the vacancy of the see, usually called 'Registrum sede vacante', ed. J. Willis Blund, Worcestershire Historical Society (Oxford, 1897).

Das Register Gregors VII, ed. E. Caspar, 2 vols in 1 (Berlin: Weidmannsche Buchhandlung, 1920-23).

Die Register Innocenz' III, ed. Othmar Hageneder *et al.*, 9 vols (Rome, 1968).

The Register of John Kirkby, Bishop of Carlisle 1332-52 and the Register of John Ross, Bishop of Carlisle 1325-32, ed. R. L. Storey, Canterbury and York Society, 79, 81, 2 vols (Woodbridge, 1993-95).

The Register of John Le Romeyn, Lord Archbishop of York, 1286-1296, ed. W. Brown, Surtees Society, 123, 128, 2 vols (Durham, 1913-17).

The Register of John Pecham, Archbishop of Canterbury 1279-92, ed. D. Douie, Canterbury and York Society, 64-5, 2 vols (Torquay, 1968-69).

The Register of Ralph of Shrewsbury, Bishop of Bath and Wells, 1329-1363: From the Original in the Registry at Wells, ed. T. S. Holmes, 2 vols (London, 1896).

Register and Records of Holm Cultram, ed. F. Grainger and W. Collingwood (Kendal, 1929).

The Register, or Rolls, of Walter Gray, Lord Archbishop of York, ed. J. Raine, Surtees Society, 56 (Durham, 1872).

The Register of Walter Bronescombe, ed. O. F. Robinson, Canterbury and York Society, 82, 87, 94, 3 vols (Woodbridge, 1995-2003).

The Register of Walter Langton, Bishop of Coventry and Lichfield, 1296-1321, ed. J. B. Hughes, Canterbury and York Society, 91, 97, 2 vols (Woodbridge, 2001-7).

The Register of William Bateman, Bishop of Norwich, 1344-1355, ed. P. E. Pobst, Canterbury and York Society, 84, 90, 2 vols (Woodbridge, 1996-2000).

The Register of William Melton, Archbishop of York, 1317-40, ed. R. Hill *et al.*, Canterbury and York Society, 70-71, 76, 85, 93, 101, in progress (Woodbridge, 1955-).

The Registers of John de Sandale and Rigaud de Asserio, Bishops of Winchester (A.D. 1316-1323), ed. F. J. Baignent, Hampshire Record Society, 8 (London, 1897).

Les Registres d'Alexandre IV, ed. B. de la Roncière, J. de Loye, P. de Cerival and A. Coulon, 3 vols (Paris, 1895-1959).

Les Régistres de Clement IV, ed. E. Jordan, 6 vols (Paris, 1893-1945).

Les Registres de Grégoire IX, ed. L. Auvrey, 4 vols (Paris, 1896-1955).

Les Registres d'Innocent IV, ed. E. Berger, 4 vols (Paris, 1884-1920).

Les Registres de Nicholas III (1277-1280), ed. J. Gay (Paris, 1938).

Il registro di Andrea Sapiti, Procuratore alla Curia Avignonese, ed. B. Bombi (Rome, 2007).

The Registrum Antiquissimum of the Cathedral Church of Lincoln, ed. C. Foster and K. Major, Lincoln Record Society, 27-9, 32, 34, 41-2, 46, 51, 62, 67-8, 10 vols (Hereford, 1931-75).

Registrum Epistolarum Fratris Johannis Peckham: Archiepiscopi Cantuariensis, ed. C. Martin, RS, 77, 3 vols (London, 1882-85).

Registrum Hamonis Hethe: Diocesis Roffensis, A. D. 1319-1352, ed. C. Johnson, Canterbury and York Society, 48-9, 2 vols (Oxford, 1948).

Registrum Roberti Winchelsey Cantuariensis Archiepiscopi, 1294-1313, ed. R. Graham, Canterbury and York Society, 50-51, 2 vols (Oxford, 1952-56).

Registrum Roffense, ed. J. Thorpe (London, 1769).

Registrum Statutorum et Consuetudinum Ecclesiae Cathedralis Sancti Pauli Londiniensis, ed. W. Sparrow Simpson (London, 1873).

Richard d'Aungerville, of Bury: Fragments of His Register and Other Documents, Surtees Society, 119 (Durham, 1910).

Roger Wendover's Flowers of History, ed. J. A. Giles, 2 vols (London, 1849).

Rôles Gascons, ed. F. Michel and C. Bémont, 5 vols (Paris, 1885-).

Rotuli Chartarum in Turri Londinensi Asservati, ed. T. D. Hardy (London, 1837).

Rotuli Litterarum Clausarum in Turri Londinensi Asservati, ed. T. D. Hardy, 2 vols (London, 1833-44).

Rotuli Litterarum Patentium in Turri Londinensi Asservati, ed. T. D. Hardy (London, 1835).

The Royal Charter Witness Lists of Henry III (1226-72), ed. M. Morris, 2 vols (Kew, 2001).
Royal and Other Historical Letters Illustrative of the Reign of Henry III, ed. W. Shirley, RS, 27, 2 vols (London, 1862-66).
The Rule of Saint Benedict in Latin and in English, ed. J. McCann (Tunbridge Wells, 1952).
Saint Richard of Chichester: The Sources for His Life, ed. D. Jones, Sussex Record Society, 79 (Lewes, 1995).
Scotia Pontificia: Papal Letters to Scotland before the Pontificate of Innocent III, ed. R. Somerville (Oxford, 1982).
Scotichronicon, by Walter Bower, ed. D. E. R. Watt *et al.*, 9 vols (Aberdeen, 1987-98).
Scottish Annals from English Chroniclers, AD 500 to 1286, ed. A. O. Anderson (London, 1908).
Selected Letters of Pope Innocent III concerning England (1198-1216), ed. C. R. Cheney and W. H. Semple (London, 1953).
The Shorter Latin Poems of Henry of Avranches relating to England, ed. J. C. Russell and J. P. Heironimus (Cambridge, Mass., 1935).
Snappe's Formulary, ed. H. E. Salter, Oxford Historical Society, 80 (Oxford, 1923).
Statutes and Customs of the Cathedral Church of the Blessed Virgin Mary of Salisbury, ed. C. Wordsworth and D. Macleane (London, 1915).
The Statutes of the Realm, 11 vols in 12 (London, 1810-28).
Tractatus universi iuris, duce, et auspice Gregorio XIII pontifice maximo in unum congesti, 25 vols (Venice, 1584-86).
Der Traktat des Laurentius de Somercote, Kanonikus von Chichester, über die Vornahme von Bischofswahlen entstanden im Jahre 1254, ed. A. von Wretschko (Weimar, 1907).
Two Chartularies of the Priory of St. Peter at Bath, ed. W. Hunt, Somerset Record Society, 7 (London, 1893).
Vetus Registrum Sarisberiense Alias Dictum Registrum S. Osmundi Episcopi: The Register of S. Osmund, ed. W. Jones, RS, 78, 2 vols (London, 1883-84).
Vita Edwardi Secundi, ed. W. Childs (Oxford, 2005).
Wells Cathedral: Its Foundation, Constitutional History, and Statutes, ed. H. Reynolds (Leeds, 1881).

Secondary Sources

Aberth, John, *Criminal Churchmen in the Age of Edward III: The Case of Bishop Thomas de Lisle* (University Park, Pa., 1996).
Abulafia, David (ed.), *Italy in the Central Middle Ages* (Oxford, 2004).

Ash, Marinell, 'David Bernham, Bishop of St Andrews, 1239-1253' in David McRoberts (ed.), *The Medieval Church of St Andrews* (Glasgow, 1976), pp. 32-44.

Ashley, Anne, 'Odo, Elect of Whithorn, 1235', *Transactions of the Dumfries and Galloway Natural History and Antiquarian Society* 37 (1958): 62-9.

Backman, Clifford, *The Decline and Fall of Medieval Sicily* (Cambridge, 1995).

Baldwin, John, *The Government of Philip Augustus* (Berkeley, 1986).

Baldwin, John, 'Master Stephen Langton, Future Archbishop of Canterbury: The Paris Schools and Magna Carta', *English Historical Review* 123 (2008): 811-46.

Baldwin, John, *Paris, 1200* (Stanford, 2010).

Baldwin, John, 'Philip Augustus and the Norman Church', *French Historical Studies* 6 (1969): 1-30.

Baldwin, John, 'Pierre le Chantre et Étienne de Gallardon: La Conjoncture de Regnum, Studium et Cancellaria au Tournant des XIIe et XIIIe Siècles', *Comptes-rendus des Séances de l'Académie des Inscriptions et Belles-Lettres* 144 (2000): 437-57.

Balfour-Melville, Evan, 'John de Cheam, Bishop of Glasgow', *Scottish Historical Review* 27 (1948): 176-86.

Baratier, Edouard, 'Nominations et Origines des Évêques des Provinces d'Aix et Arles', *Les Évêques, les Clercs et le Roi (1250-1300)*, Cahiers de Fanjeaux, 7 (Toulouse, 1972): 115-45.

Barlow, Frank, *The English Church, 1066-1154* (London, 1979).

Barlow, Frank, *William Rufus* (London, 1983).

Barraclough, Geoffrey, 'Bernard of Compostella', *English Historical Review* 49 (1934): 487-94.

Barraclough, Geoffrey, 'The Making of a Bishop in the Middle Ages: The Part of the Pope in Law and Fact', *Catholic Historical Review* 19 (1933/34): 274-319.

Barraclough, Geoffrey, *The Medieval Papacy* (London, 1968).

Barraclough, Geoffrey, *Papal Provisions* (Oxford, 1935).

Barrell, Andrew, 'The Background to *Cum universi*: Scoto-papal Relations, 1159-1192', *Innes Review* 46 (1995): 116-38.

Barrell, Andrew, *Medieval Scotland* (Cambridge, 2000).

Barrell, Andrew, *The Papacy, Scotland and Northern England, 1342-1378* (Cambridge, 1995).

Barrell, Andrew, 'Scotland and the Papacy in the Reign of Alexander II' in Richard Oram (ed.), *The Reign of Alexander II, 1214-49* (Turnhout, 2005), pp. 157-78.

Barrow, Geoffrey, 'Benedictines, Tironensians and Cistercians' in Geoffrey Barrow, *The Kingdom of the Scots: Government, Church and Society from the Eleventh to the Fourteenth Century* (London, 1973), pp. 188-211.

Barrow, Geoffrey, 'The Clergy at St Andrews' in Geoffrey Barrow, *The Kingdom of the Scots: Government, Church and Society from the Eleventh to the Fourteenth Century* (London, 1973), pp. 212-32.

Barrow, Geoffrey, *The Kingdom of the Scots: Government, Church and Society from the Eleventh to the Fourteenth Century* (London, 1973).

Barrow, Geoffrey, *Kingship and Unity: Scotland 1066-1306* (London, 1981).

Barrow, Geoffrey, 'The Reign of William the Lion' in Geoffrey Barrow, *Scotland and its Neighbours in the Middle Ages* (London, 1992), pp. 67-89.

Barrow, Geoffrey, *Robert Bruce and the Community of the Realm of Scotland* (4th edn, Edinburgh, 2005).

Barrow, Geoffrey, 'The Royal House and the Religious Orders' 'Benedictines, Tironensians and Cistercians' in Geoffrey Barrow, *The Kingdom of the Scots: Government, Church and Society from the Eleventh to the Fourteenth Century* (London, 1973), pp. 165-187.

Barrow, Geoffrey, 'The Scottish Clergy in the War of Independence', *Scottish Historical Review* 131 (1962): 1-22.

Barrow, Julia, 'Grades of Ordination and Clerical Careers, c.900-c.1200', *Anglo-Norman Studies* 30 (2008): 41-61.

Barrow, Julia, 'Hereford Bishops and Married Clergy, c.1130-1240', *Historical Research* 60 (1987): 1-8.

Bartlett, Robert, *England under the Norman and Angevin Kings, 1075-1225* (Oxford, 2000).

Beam, Amanda, *The Balliol Dynasty, 1210-1364* (Edinburgh, 2008).

Beck, Henry, 'Canonical Election to Suffragan Bishoprics According to Hincmar of Rheims', *Catholic Historical Review* 43 (1957): 137-59.

Bellenger, Aidan and Fletcher, Stella, *Princes of the Church: A History of the English Cardinals* (Stroud, 2001).

Benson, Robert, *The Bishop-Elect* (Princeton, 1960).

Bennett, Ralph, *The Early Dominicans: Studies in Thirteenth Century Dominican History* (Cambridge, 1937).

Bethell, Donald, 'English Black Monks and Episcopal Elections in the 1120s', *English Historical Review* 84 (1969): 673-94.

Blumenthal, Ute-Renate, *The Investiture Controversy: Church and Monarchy from the Ninth to the Twelfth Century* (Philadelphia, 1991).

Bombi, Barbara, 'Andrea Sapiti: His Origins, and His Register as a Curial Proctor', *English Historical Review* 123 (2008): 132-48.

Bombi, Barabara, 'Petitioning between England and Avignon in the First Half of the Fourteenth Century' in Anthony Musson, Mark Ormrod and Gwilym Dodd (eds), *Medieval Petitions: Grace and Grievance* (York, 2009), pp. 64-81.

Boswell, John, *Christianity, Social Tolerance and Homosexuality: Gay People in Western Europe from the Beginning of the Christian Era to the Fourteenth Century* (Chicago, 1980).

Bouchard, Constance, *Spirituality and Administration: The Role of the Bishop in Twelfth-Century Auxerre* (Cambridge, Mass., 1979).

Bowsky, William, *A Medieval Italian Commune: Siena Under the Nine, 1287-1355* (Berkeley, 1981).

Bradbury, Jim, *Philip Augustus: King of France 1180-1223* (London, 1998).

Brentano, Robert, *A New World in a Small Place: Church and Religion in the Diocese of Rieti, 1188-1378* (Berkeley, 1994).

Brentano, Robert, *Two Churches: England and Italy in the Thirteenth Century* (rev. edn, Berkeley, 1988).

Brentano, Robert, 'The Whithorn Vacancy of 1293-94', *Innes Review* 4 (1953): 71-83.

Brentano, Robert, *York Metropolitan Jurisdiction and Papal Judges Delegate (1279-1296)* (Berkeley, 1959)

Brett, Martin, *The English Church Under Henry I* (Oxford, 1975).

Brooke, Christopher, 'Gregorian Reform in Action: Clerical Marriage in England, 1050-1200', *Cambridge Historical Journal* 12 (1956): 1-21.

Broun, Dauvit, *Scottish Independence and the Idea of Britain: From the Picts to Alexander III* (Edinburgh, 2007).

Brown, Michael, 'Henry the Peaceable: Henry III, Alexander III and Royal Lordship in the British Isles, 1249-1272' in Bjorn Weiler and Ivor Rowlands (eds), *England and Europe in the Reign of Henry III, 1216-1272* (Aldershot, 2002), pp. 43-66.

Brown, Michael, *The Wars of Scotland, 1214-1371* (Edinburgh, 2004).

Brown, Michael and Boardman, Steve, 'Survival and Revival: Late Medieval Scotland' in Jenny Wormald (ed.), *Scotland: A History* (Oxford, 2005), pp. 77-106.

Buc, Philippe, *The Dangers of Ritual: Between Medieval Texts and Social Scientific Theory* (Princeton, 2001).

Bynum, Caroline, *Holy Feast and Holy Fast: The Religious Significance of Food to Medieval Women* (Berkeley, 1989).

Caillet, Louis, *La Papauté d'Avignon et l'Église de France: La Politique* Bénéficiale du Pape Jean en France (1316-1334) (Paris, 1975).

Caillet, Maurice, 'Élection, Confirmation et Consécration d'un Évêque de Carpentras au XIIIe Siècle', *Mélanges Raoul Busquet: Questions d'Histoire de Provence (XIe-XIXe Siècles)* (Vaison-la-Romaine, 1956), pp. 90-107.

Carpenter, David, 'Archbishop Langton and Magna Carta: His Contribution, His Doubts and His Hypocrisy', *English Historical Review* 126 (2011): 1041-65.

Carpenter, David, *The Minority of Henry III* (London, 1990).

Carpenter, David, *The Struggle for Mastery: Britain 1066-1284* (London, 2003).

Carruthers, Mary, 'On Affliction and Reading, Weeping and Argument: Chaucer's Lachrymose Troilus in Context', *Representations* 93 (2006): 1-21.

Cazelles, Raymond, *La Société Politique et la Crise de la Royauté sous Philippe de Valois* (Paris, 1958).

Cheney, Christopher, *From Becket to Langton: English Church Government 1170-1213* (Manchester, 1956).

Cheney, Christopher, *Pope Innocent III and England* (Stuttgart, 1976).

Cherry, John, 'The Medieval Episcopal Ring' in Janet Backhouse (ed.), *The Medieval English Cathedral* (Donington, 2003), pp. 208-17.

Chibnall, Majorie, 'Innocent II and the Canterbury Election of 1138' in Coloman Viola, *Mediaevalia Christiana (XIe-XIIIe siècles), Hommage à Raymonde Foreville* (Brussels, 1989), pp. 237-45.

Christelow, Stephanie, 'Chancellors and Curial Bishops: Ecclesiastical Promotions and Power in Anglo-Norman England', *Anglo-Norman Studies* 22 (1999): 49-69.

Church, Charles, *Chapters in the Early History of the Church of Wells* (London, 1894).

Churchill, Irene, *Canterbury Administration: The Administrative Machinery of the Archbishopric of Canterbury*, 2 vols (London, 1933).

Clanchy, Michael, 'Did Henry III have a Policy?', *History* 53 (1968): 203-16.

Clanchy, Michael, *From Memory to Written Record: England 1066-1307* (2nd edn, Oxford, 1993).

Constable, Giles, 'Moderation and Restraint in Ascetic Practices' in Giles Constable, *Culture and Spirituality in Medieval Europe* (Aldershot, 1996), X.

Cosgrove, Art, 'The Elections to the Bishopric of Winchester, 1280-2', *Studies in Church History* 3 (1966): 169-78.

Cotts, John, *The Clerical Dilemma: Peter of Blois and Literate Culture in the Twelfth Century* (Washington DC, 2009).

Cotts, John, 'Monks and Mediocrities in the Shadow of Thomas Becket: Peter of Blois on Episcopal Duty', *Haskins Society Journal* 10 (2001): 143-61.

Cowan, Ian, 'The Church in Argyll and the Isles' in Ian Cowan, *The Medieval Church in Scotland*, ed. James Kirk (Edinburgh, 1995), pp. 129-43.

Cowan, Ian, 'The Organisation of Secular Cathedral Chapters' in Ian Cowan, *The Medieval Church in Scotland*, ed. James Kirk (Edinburgh, 1995), pp. 77-96.

Craib, Theodore (ed.), *The Itinerary of Henry III* (London, 1923).

Crosby, Everett, *Bishop and Chapter in Twelfth-Century England: A Study of the 'Mensa Episcopalis'* (Cambridge, 1994).

Cubitt, Catherine, 'Wilfred's "Usurping Bishops": Episcopal Elections in Anglo-Saxon England, c.600-c.800', *Northern History* 25 (1989): 18-38.

Cuissard, Charles, 'Élection de Guillaume de Bussi, Éveque d'Orléans et Principaux Actes de Son Épiscopat, 1238-1258', *Mémoires de la Société Archéologique et Historique de l'Orléanais* 25 (1894): 561-620.

Dal Pulpito alla Cattedra: i Vescovi degli Ordini Mendicanti nel '200 e nel Primo '300 (Spoleto, 2000).

Davies, Cecily, 'The Statute of Provisors of 1351', *History* 38 (1953): 116-33.

Davis, Adam, *The Holy Bureaucrat: Eudes Rigaud and Religious Reform in Thirteenth-Century Normandy* (Ithaca, 2006).

Davis, Virginia, *William Waynflete: Bishop and Educationalist* (Woodbridge, 1993).

Deeley, Ann, 'Papal Provision and Royal Rights of Patronage in the Thirteenth Century', *English Historical Review* 43 (1928): 497-527.

Denholm-Young, Nigel, 'Richard de Bury', *Transactions of the Royal Historical Society*, 4th series, 20 (1937): 135-68.

Denton, Jeffrey, 'Canterbury Archiepiscopal Appointments: The Case of Walter Reynolds', *Journal of Medieval History* 1 (1975): 317-27.

Denton, Jeffrey, 'The Making of the "Articuli Cleri" of 1316', *English Historical Review* 101 (1986): 564-95.

Denton, Jeffrey, 'Pope Clement V's Early Career as a Royal Clerk', *English Historical Review* 83 (1968): 303-14.

Denton, Jeffrey, *Robert Winchelsey and the Crown, 1294-1313: A Study in the Defence of Ecclesiastical Liberty* (Cambridge, 1980).

Desporte, Pierre (ed.), *Fasti Ecclesiae Gallicanae*, vol. 3: *Diocèse de Reims* (Turnhout, 1998).

Ditchburn, David, *Scotland and Europe: The Medieval Kingdom and its Contacts with Christendom, c.1215-1545*, vol. I: *Religion, Culture and Commerce* (Edinburgh, 2001).

Dobson, Richard, 'The Political Role of the Archbishops of York during the Reign of Edward I' in Simon Lloyd and Peter Coss (eds), *Thirteenth Century England III* (Woodbridge, 1989), pp. 47-64.

Donaldson, Gordon, 'The Rights of the Scottish Crown in Episcopal Vacancies', *Scottish Historical Review* 139 (1966): 27-35.

Douie, Decima, *Archbishop Pecham* (Oxford, 1952).

Dowden, John, 'The Appointment of Bishops in Scotland during the Medieval Period', *Scottish Historical Review* 7 (1909): 1-20.

Dowden, John, *The Medieval Church in Scotland: Its Constitution, Organisation and Law* (Glasgow, 1910).

Dowden, John, 'The Scottish Crown and the Episcopate in the Medieval Period', *Scottish Historical Review* 7 (1909): 130-40.

Duby, Georges, *The Early Growth of the European Economy* (London, 1975).

Duby, Georges, *France in the Middle Ages, 987-1460* (Oxford, 1993).

Duggan, Anne, 'Law and Practice in Episcopal and Abbatial Election before 1215: With Special Reference to England' in Corinne Péneau (ed.), Élections et Pouvoirs Politiques du VIIe au XVIIe Siècle (Bordeaux, 2008), pp. 43-62.
Dunning, Robert (ed.), *Jocelin of Wells: Bishop, Builder, Courtier* (Woodbridge, 2010).
Edwards, Kathleen, *The English Secular Cathedrals in the Middle Ages* (Manchester, 1967).
Emden, Alfred, *A Biographical Register of the University of Cambridge to 1500* (Cambridge, 1963).
Emden, Alfred, *A Biographical Register of the University of Oxford to 1500*, 3 vols (Oxford: Clarendon Press, 1957-59).
Engel, Pal, *Realm of St. Stephen: A History of Medieval Hungary, 895-1526* (London, 2005).
Ellis, John, *Anti-papal Legislation in Medieval England, 1066-1377* (Washington DC, 1930).
Ferguson, Paul, *Medieval Papal Representatives in Scotland: Legates, Nuncios and Judges-Delegate, 1125-1286* (Edinburgh, 1997).
Flight, Colin, *The Bishops and Monks of Rochester, 1076-1214* (Maidstone, 1997).
Fraser, Constance, *A History of Anthony Bek, Bishop of Durham 1283-1311* (Oxford, 1957).
Fryde, Edmund *et al.* (eds), *Handbook of British Chronology*, Royal Historical Society Guides and Handbooks, 2 (3rd edn, Cambridge, 1986).
Gane, Robert, *Le Chapitre de Notre-Dame de Paris au XIVe Siècle au XIVe Siècle* (Saint-Étienne, 1999).
Gasquet, Francis, *Henry III and the Church* (London, 1905).
Gaudemet, Jean, Église et Société en Occident au Moyen Age (Aldershot, 1984).
Gaudemet, Jean, 'De l'Élection à la Nomination', *Concilium* 157 (1980): 23-30.
Gaudemet, Jean, *Le Gouvernement de l'Église à l'Époque Classique*, vol. II: *Le Gouvernement Local* (Paris, 1979).
Gibbs, Marion and Lang, Jane, *Bishops and Reform, 1215-1272* (London, 1936).
Golding, Brian, 'Gerald of Wales and the Monks' in Peter Coss and Simon Lloyd (eds), *Thirteenth Century England V* (Woodbridge, 1995), pp. 53-64.
Graham, Rose, 'The Administration of the Diocese of Ely during the Vacancies of the See, 1298-99 and 1302-3', *Transactions of the Royal Historical Society*, 4th series, 12 (1929): 49-74.
Graham, Rose, 'Archbishop Winchelsey: From his Election to his Enthronement', *Church Quarterly Review* 148 (1949): 161-75.
Graham-Leigh, Elaine, 'Hirelings and Shepherds: Archbishop Berenguer of Narbonne (1191-1211) and the Ideal Bishop', *English Historical Review* 116 (2001): 1083-102.
Gransden, Antonia, *Historical Writing in England*, 2 vols (London, 1974-82).

Grant, Alexander, *Independence and Nationhood: Scotland, 1306-1469* (London, 1984).

Grassi, John, 'William Airmyn and the Bishopric of Norwich', *English Historical Review* 60 (1955): 550-61.

Greatrex, Joan, *Biographical Register of the English Cathedral Priories of the Province of Canterbury, c.1066 to 1540* (Oxford, 1997).

Greatrex, Joan, *The English Benedictine Cathedral Priories: Rule and Practice, c.1270-c.1420* (Oxford, 2011).

Green, Judith, *Henry I: King of England and Duke of Normandy* (Cambridge, 2009).

Guillemain, Bernard, *La Cour Pontificale d'Avignon (1309-1376): Etude d'une Société* (Paris, 1992).

Guillemain, Bernard, *La Politique Bénéficiale de Bênoit XII, 1334-42* (Paris, 1952).

Guillemain, Bernard and Martin, Catherine, 'Les Élections Épiscopales de la Province de Narbonne entre 1249 et 1317', *Les Évêques, les Clercs et le Roi (1250-1300)*, Cahiers de Fanjeaux, 7 (Toulouse, 1972), pp. 107-13.

Guillemain, Bernard and Martin, Catherine, 'Origines Sociales, Intellectuelles et Ecclésiastiques des Évêques de la Province de Narbonne entre 1249 et 1317', *Les Évêques, les Clercs et le Roi (1250-1300)*, Cahiers de Fanjeaux, 7 (Toulouse, 1972), pp. 91-106.

Hageneder, Othmar, 'Die Register Innozenz III.' in Thomas Frenz (ed.), *Papst Innozenz III.: Weichensteller der Geschichte Europas* (Stuttgart, 2000), pp. 91-101.

Haines, Roy, *Archbishop John Stratford: Political Revolutionary and Champion of the Liberties of the English Church* (Toronto, 1986).

Haines, Roy, *The Church and Politics in Fourteenth-Century England: The Career of Adam Orleton, c. 1275-1345* (Cambridge, 1978).

Haines, Roy, *Ecclesia Anglicana: Studies in the English Church of the Later Middle Ages* (Toronto, 1989).

Haines, Roy, *Edward II* (Montreal, 2003).

Haines, Roy, 'The Episcopate of a Benedictine Monk: Hamo de Hethe, Bishop of Rochester', *Revue Bénédictine* 102 (1992): 192-207.

Haines, Roy, 'The Episcopate during the Reign of Edward II and the Regency of Mortimer and Isabella', *Journal of Ecclesiastical History* 56 (2005): 657-709.

Haines, Roy, 'An Innocent Abroad: The Career of Simon Mepham, Archbishop of Canterbury, 1328-33', *English Historical Review* 112 (1997): 555-96.

Haines, Roy, 'Looking Back in Anger: A Politically-Inspired Appeal against John XXII's Translation of Bishop Adam Orleton to Winchester (1334)', *English Historical Review* 116 (2001): 389-404.

Haines, Roy, 'Simon de Montacute, Brother of William, Earl of Salisbury, Bishop of Worcester (1333-37), of Ely (1337-45)' in Nigel Saul (ed.), *Fourteenth Century England I* (Woodbridge, 2000), pp. 37-71.

Haines, Roy, 'Sumptuous Apparel for a Royal Prisoner: Archbishop Melton's Letter, 14 January 1330', *English Historical Review* 124 (2009): 885-94.

Hallam, Elizabeth and Everard, Judith, *Capetian France, 987-1328* (2nd edn, London, 2001).

Harper-Bill, Christopher, 'John and the Church of Rome' in Stephen Church (ed.), *King John: New Interpretations* (Woodbridge, 1999), pp. 289-315.

Harvey, Katherine, 'Episcopal Emotions: Tears in the Life of the Medieval Bishop', *Historical Research* (Forthcoming)

Harvey, Katherine, 'The First Entry of the Bishop: Episcopal Adventus in Fourteenth-Century England' in Jeffrey Hamilton (ed.), *Fourteenth Century England VIII* (Woodbridge, forthcoming).

Harvey, Katherine, 'Objections to Episcopal Elections in England, 1216-1272', *Nottingham Medieval Studies* 55 (2011): 125-47.

Haskins, George and Kantorowicz, Ernst, 'A Diplomatic Mission of Francis Accursius and his Oration before Pope Nicholas III', *English Historical Review* 58 (1943): 424-47.

Heath, Peter, *Church and Realm, 1272-1461* (London, 1988).

Helle, Knut (ed.), *The Cambridge History of Scandinavia: Prehistory to 1520* (Cambridge, 2003).

Helmholz, Robert, *The Oxford History of the Laws of England: The Canon Law and Ecclesiastical Jurisdiction from 597 to the 1640s* (Oxford, 2004).

Helmholz, Robert, *The Spirit of Classical Canon Law* (Athens, Ga., 1996).

Highfield, Roger, 'The English Hierarchy in the Reign of Edward III', *Transactions of the Royal Historical Society*, 5th series, 6 (1956): 115-38.

Hillgarth, Jocelyn, *The Spanish Kingdoms (1250-1516)*, vol. 1: *1250-1410: Precarious Balance* (Oxford, 1976).

Holt, James, *Magna Carta* (2nd edn, Cambridge, 1992).

Hoskin, Philippa, 'Diocesan Politics in the See of Worcester, 1218-1266', *Journal of Ecclesiastical History* 54 (2003): 422-40.

Howell, Margaret, *Eleanor of Provence: Queenship in Thirteenth-Century England* (Oxford, 1998).

Howell, Margaret, *Regalian Right in Medieval England* (London, 1962).

Hyams, Paul, 'What did Henry III of England Think in Bed and in French about Kingship and Anger?' in Barbara Rosenwein (ed.), *Anger's Past: The Social Uses of an Emotion in the Middle Ages* (Ithaca, 1998), pp. 92-124.

Jacob, Ernest, 'Petitions for Benefices from English Universities during the Great Schism', *Transactions of the Royal Historical Society*, 4th series, 27 (1945): 41-59.

Jaeger, Stephen, 'The Courtier Bishop in *Vitae* from the Tenth to the Twelfth Century', *Speculum* 58 (1983): 291-325.

Jared, Lauren, 'English Ecclesiastical Vacancies during the Reigns of William II and Henry I', *Journal of Ecclesiastical History* 42 (1991): 362-93.

Johnson, David, 'Bishops and Deans: London and the Province of Canterbury in the Twelfth Century', *Historical Research* (Forthcoming)

Jones, William, 'Bishops, Politics and the Two Laws: The Gravamina of the English Clergy, 1237-1399', *Speculum* 41 (1966): 209-45.

Julerot, Véronique, 'La Confirmation des Élections Épiscopales à la fin du Moyen Âge: Origine et Enjeux', *Revue Historique de Droit Français et Étranger* 81 (2003): 173-94.

Julerot, Véronique, 'La Première Entrée de l'Évêque: Réflexions sur son Origine', *Revue Historique* 308 (2006): 635-75.

Julerot, Véronique, *"Y A Ung Grant Desordre": Élections Épiscopales et Schismes Diocésains en France sous Charles VIII* (Paris, 2006).

Kelly, John, *The Oxford Dictionary of Popes* (Oxford, 1986).

King, Richard, *Handbook to the Cathedrals of England: St Paul's* (London, 1879).

Kipling, Gordon, *Enter the King: Theatre, Liturgy and Ritual in the Medieval Civic Triumph* (Oxford, 1998).

Knowles, David, 'The Canterbury Election of 1205-6', *English Historical Review* 53 (1938): 211-20.

Koszta, Laszlo, 'Conclusions Drawn from the Prosopographic Analysis of the Canons Belonging to the Cathedral Chapters of Medieval Hungary (1200-1350)' in Ana Jorge, Herminia Vilar and Maria Branco (eds), *Carreiras Ecleiásticas No Ocidente Cristão,* Séc. XII-XIV (Lisbon, 2007), pp. 13-28.

Lambert, Malcolm, *Medieval Heresy* (3rd edn, Oxford, 2002).

Latham, Ronald, *Revised Medieval Latin Word-List, from British and Irish Sources* (Oxford, 1980).

Lawrence, Hugh, *The English Church and the Papacy in the Middle Ages* (rev. edn, Stroud, 1999).

Lawrence, Hugh, 'The Thirteenth Century' in Hugh Lawrence, *The English Church and the Papacy in the Middle Ages* (rev. edn, Stroud, 1999), pp. 117-56.

Layfield, Sarah, 'The Pope, the Scots and their "Self-Styled" King: John XXII's Anglo-Scottish Policy, 1316-1334' in Andy King and Michael Penman (eds), *England and Scotland in the Fourteenth Century: New Perspectives* (Woodbridge, 2007), pp. 157-71.

Lepine, David, *A Brotherhood of Canons Serving God: English Secular Cathedrals in the Later Middle Ages* (Woodbridge, 1995).

Lepine, David, 'High Solemn Ceremonies: The Funeral Practice of the Late Medieval English Higher Clergy', *English Historical Review* 61 (2010): 18-39.

Leyser, Karl, 'England and the Empire in the Early Twelfth Century', *Transactions of the Royal Historical Society*, 5th series, 10 (1960): 61-83.

Linehan, Peter, *The Spanish Church and the Papacy in the Thirteenth Century* (Cambridge, 1971).

Lovatt, Roger, 'Hugh Balsham, Bishop of Ely 1256/7-1286' in Rosemary Horrox and Sarah Rees-Jones (eds), *Pragmatic Utopias: Ideals and Communities, 1200-1360* (Cambridge, 2001), pp. 60-83.

Lunt, William, *Financial Relations of the Papacy with England, 1327-1534* (Cambridge, Mass., 1962).

Lunt, William, *Papal Revenues of the Middle Ages*, 2 vols (New York, 1934).

McFarlane, Kenneth, 'Had Edward I a "Policy" towards the Earls?', *History* 1 (1965): 145-59.

Maciejewski, Jacek, '*Nudo Pede Intrat Urbem*: Research on the *Adventus* of a Medieval Bishop through the First Half of the Twelfth Century', *Viator* 41 (2010): 89-100.

MacKenzie, Hugh, 'The Anti-Foreign Movement in England in 1231-2' in Charles Taylor (ed.), *Anniversary Essays in Mediaeval History by Students of Charles Homer Haskins* (Boston, 1929), pp. 183-203.

McKisack, May, *The Fourteenth Century, 1307-1399* (Oxford, 1959).

McLaughlin, Megan, *Sex, Gender and Episcopal Authority in an Age of Reform, 1000-1122* (Cambridge, 2010).

Macy, Gary, 'Was there a "The Church" in the Middle Ages?' in Robert Swanson (ed.), *Unity and Diversity in the Church*, Studies in Church History, 32 (Oxford, 1996), pp. 107-116.

Maddicott, John, *The Origins of the English Parliament, 924-1327* (Oxford, 2010).

Marchandisse, Alain, 'Guillaume de Savoie: Un *Monstrum Spirituale et Belua Multorum Capitum* sur le Trône de Saint Lambert?', *Bulletin de la Société Royale le Vieux-Liège* 13 (1997): 657-70, 681-700.

Mason, Emma, 'St Wulfstan's Staff: A Legend and its Uses', *Medium Aevum* 53 (1984): 157-79.

Matthew, Henry and Harrison, Brian (eds), *Oxford Dictionary of National Biography*, 61 vols (Oxford, 2004).

Matthews, Donald, *The Norman Kingdom of Sicily* (Cambridge, 1992).

Mauss, Marcel, *The Gift: The Form and Reason for Exchange in Archaic Societies*, trans. Wilfred Halls (London, 1990).Menache, Sophia, *Clement V* (Cambridge, 1998).

Miller, Maureen, 'The Florentine Bishop's Ritual Entry and the Origins of Medieval Episcopal *Adventus*', *Revue d'Histoire Ecclésiastique* 96 (2002): 5-28.

Millet, Hélène, *Les Chanoines du Chapitre de Laon, 1272-1412* (Rome, 1982).

Millett, Benignus, 'John Foxholes, Franciscan, Archbishop of Armagh 1471-74', *Seanchas Ardmhacha: Journal of the Armagh Diocesan Historical Society* 18 (1999/2000): 22-9.

Mollat, Guillaume, 'Contribution à l'Histoire du Sacré Collège de Clément V à Eugène IV', *Revue d'Histoire Ecclésiastique*, 46 (1951): 22-112.

Mollat, Guillaume, *The Popes at Avignon, 1305-1378* (London, 1963).

Montaubin, Pascal, 'Les Chapitres Cathédraux Séculiers de Normandie et la Centralisation Pontificale au XIIIe Siècle' in Sylvette Lemagnen and Philippe Manneville (eds), Chapitres et Cathédrales en Normandie (Caen, 1997), pp. 253-72.

Montaubin, Pascal, 'Entre Gloire Curiale et Vie Commune: le Chapitre Cathédral d'Anagni au XIIIe siècle', *Mélanges de l'École Française de Rome. Moyen-Age, Temps Modernes* 109 (1997): 303-442.

Montaubin, Pascal, 'Étrangers en Chrétienté: Clercs Italiens en France et en Angleterre (fin XIIe-mi XIVe Siècle)', *Actes des Congrès de la Société des Historiens Médiévistes de l'Enseignement Supérieur Public* 30 (1999): 233-44.

Montaubin, Pascal, 'Innocent III et les Nominations Épiscopales en Italie' in Andrea Sommerlechner (ed.), *Innocenzo III. Urbs et Orbis*, 2 vols (Rome, 2003), pp. 778-811.

Moore, John, *Pope Innocent III (1160/61-1216): To Root Up and to Plant* (Turnhout, 2003).

Moore, Robert, *The Formation of a Persecuting Society* (2nd edn, Oxford, 2007).

Moorman, John, *Church Life in England in the Thirteenth Century* (Cambridge, 1946).

Morey, Adrian and Brooke, Christopher, *Gilbert Foliot and his Letters* (Cambridge, 1965).

Morris, Colin, *The Papal Monarchy: The Western Church from 1050 to 1250* (Oxford, 1989).

Mugnier, François, *Les Savoyards en Angleterre au XIIIe siècle et Pierre d'Aigueblanche, Évêque d'Héreford* (Chambéry, 1890).

Nagy, Piroska, *Le Don des Larmes au Moyen Âge* (Paris, 2000).

Nagy, Piroska, 'Religious Weeping as Ritual in the Medieval West' in Don Handelman and Galina Lindquist (eds), *Ritual in its Own Right: Exploring the Dynamics of Transformation* (Oxford, 2005), pp. 117-37.

Neve, John le *et al.*, *Fasti Ecclesiae Anglicanae 1066-1300*, 11 vols (London, 1968-), compiled by Diana Greenway: I: *St Paul's, London* (1968); II: *Monastic Cathedrals* (1971); III: *Lincoln* (1977); IV: *Salisbury* (1991); V: *Chichester* (1996); VI: *York* (1999); VII: *Bath & Wells* (2001); X: *Exeter* (2005); compiled by Julia Barrow: VIII: *Hereford* (2002); compiled by Matthew Pearson: IX: *The Welsh Cathedrals* (2003); compiled by Christopher Brooke, Jeffrey Denton and Diana Greenway: XI: *Coventry and Lichfield* (2011).

Neve, John le *et al.*, *Fasti Ecclesiae Anglicanae 1300-1541*, 12 vols (London, 1962-5), compiled by H. P. F. King: I: *Lincoln* (1962); compiled by Joyce Horn: II: *Hereford* (1962); III: *Salisbury* (1962); V: *St Paul's, London* (1963); VII: *Chichester* (1964); IX: *Exeter* (1962); XII: *Introduction, Errata and Index* (1965); compiled by Bridgett Jones: IV: *Monastic Cathedrals* (1963); VI: *Northern Province* (1963); VIII: *Bath & Wells* (1964); XI: *The Welsh Dioceses* (1965).

Norton, Peter, *Episcopal Elections 250-600: Hierarchy and Popular Will in Late Antiquity* (Oxford, 2007).

O'Callaghan, Joseph, *A History of Medieval Spain* (Ithaca, 1975).

Oliger, Paul, *Les Évêques Réguliers* (Paris, 1958).

Oram, Richard, *The Lordship of Galloway* (Edinburgh, 2000).

Oram, Richard, 'In Obedience and Reverence: Whithorn and York, c.1128-c.1250', *Innes Review* 42 (1991): 83-100.

Oram, Richard, 'Prayer, Property and Profit: Scottish Monasteries, c.1100-c.1300' in Sally Foster, Allan Macinnes and Ranald MacInnes (eds), *Scottish Power Centres: From Early Middle Ages to the Twentieth Century* (Glasgow, 1998), pp. 79-99.

Ormrod, Mark, *The Reign of Edward III: Crown and Political Society in England, 1327-77* (London, 1990).

Ozment, Stephen, *The Age of Reform, 1250-1550* (London, 1980).

Pacaut, Marcel, *Louis VII et les Élections Épiscopales dans le Royaume de France* (Paris, 1957).

Pantin, William, *The English Church in the Fourteenth Century* (Cambridge, 1955).

Pantin, William, 'Grosseteste's Relations with the Papacy and the Crown' in David Callus (ed.), *Robert Grosseteste* (Oxford, 1955), pp. 178-215.

Parisse, Michel, 'Une Élection Épiscopale Disputée à Metz en 1296-1297: de Bouchard d'Avesnes à Gérard de Réninge' in Wolfgang Haubrichs, Wolfgang Laufer and Reinhard Schneider (eds), *Zwischen Saar und Mosel: Festschrift für Hans-Walter Herrmann* (Saarbrucken, 1995), pp. 77-83.

Partner, Peter, *The Lands of St Peter* (London, 1972).

Paul, Jacques, 'Les Religieux Mendicants Évêques en France au XIIIe siècle', *Dal Pulpito alla Cattedra: i Vescovi degli Ordini Mendicanti nel '200 e nel Primo '300* (Spoleto, 2000), pp. 249-303.

Peltzer, Jörg, *Canon Law, Careers and Conquest: Episcopal Elections in Normandy and Greater Anjou, c. 1140-1230* (Cambridge, 2008).

Pennington, Kenneth, 'Henricus de Segusio (Hostiensis)' in Kenneth Pennington, *Popes, Canonists and Texts, 1150-1550* (Aldershot, 1993), XVI.

Pennington, Kenneth, *Pope and Bishops: A Study of Papal Monarchy in the Twelfth and Thirteenth Centuries* (Philadelphia, 1984).

Peterson, David, 'An Episcopal Election in Quattrocento Florence' in James Sweeney and Stanley Chodorow (eds), *Popes, Teachers and Canon Law in the Middle Ages* (Ithaca, 1989), pp. 300-325.

Petkov, Kiril, *The Kiss of Peace: Ritual, Self and Society in the High and Late Medieval West* (Turnhout, 2003).

Phillips, Seymour, *Edward II* (London, 2010).

Plöger, Karsten, *England and the Avignon Popes: The Practice of Diplomacy in Late Medieval Europe* (Oxford, 2005).

Plongeron, Bernard, *Le Diocese de Paris* (Paris, 1987)

Potter, David (ed.), *France in the Later Middle Ages* (Oxford, 2002).

Power, Daniel, 'The Norman Church and the Angevin and Capetian Kings', *Journal of Ecclesiastical History* 56 (2005): 205-34.

Powicke, Maurice, *King Henry III and the Lord Edward*, 2 vols (Oxford, 1947).

Powicke, Maurice, *Stephen Langton* (Oxford, 1928).

Prestwich, Michael, *Edward I* (London, 1997).

Prestwich, Michael, 'Gilbert de Middleton and the Attack on the Cardinals' in Timothy Reuter (ed.), *Warriors and Churchmen in the High Middle Ages: Essays Presented to Karl Leyser* (London, 1992), pp. 179-94.

Prestwich, Michael, *Plantagenet England, 1225-1360* (Oxford, 2005).

Prestwich, Michael, 'Royal Patronage under Edward I' in Peter Coss and Simon Lloyd (eds), *Thirteenth Century England I* (Woodbridge, 1986), pp. 41-52.

Queller, Donald, 'Thirteenth-Century Diplomatic Envoys: *Nuncio* and *Procuratores*', *Speculum* 35 (1960): 196-213.

Reuter, Timothy, 'Gifts and Simony' in Esther Cohen and Mayke de Jong (eds), *Medieval Transformations: Texts, Power and Gifts in Context* (Turnhout, 2001), pp. 157-68.

Reuter, Timothy, '*Velle Sibi Fieri in Forma Hac*: Symbolic Acts in the Becket Dispute' in Timothy Reuter, *Medieval Polities and Modern Mentalities*, ed. Janet Nelson (Cambridge, 2006), pp. 167-90.

Richardson, Henry, 'Clement V and the See of Canterbury', *English Historical Review* 56 (1941): 97-103.

Richardson, Henry and Sayles, George, *The Governance of Mediaeval England from the Conquest to Magna Carta* (Edinburgh, 1963).

Ridgeway, Huw, 'The Ecclesiastical Career of Aymer de Lusignan, Bishop-Elect of Winchester, 1250-60' in Brian Golding and John Blair (eds), *The Cloister and the World: Essays in Medieval History in Honour of Barbara Harvey* (Oxford, 1996), pp. 148-77.

Ridgeway, Huw, 'Foreign Favourites and Henry III's Problems of Patronage, 1247-58', *English Historical Review* 104 (1989): 590-610.

Roland, Em, *Les Chanoines et les Élections Épiscopales du XIe au XIVe siècle* (Aurillac, 1909).

Rosenthal, Joel, 'The Bishops of Worcester in the Fourteenth and Fifteenth Centuries: Easy Come, Easy Go', *Midland History* 37 (2012): 17-44.
Rosenthal, Joel, 'Even Money that Your Bishop Has Come and Gone: Episcopal Appointments and Translations in Fourteenth- and Fifteenth-Century England' in Linda Mitchell, Katherine French and Donald Biggs (eds), *The Ties That Bind: Essays in Medieval British History in Honour of Barbara Hanawalt* (Farnham, 2011), pp. 71-86.
Round, John, *The King's Serjeants and Officers of State* (London, 1911).
Sayers, Jane, *Innocent III: Leader of Europe, 1198-1216* (London, 1994).
Silano, Giulio, 'The Apostolic See and the Elections of the Bishops of Perugia in the Duecento and Trecento', *Medieval Studies* 50 (1988): 488-511.
Silano, Giulio, 'Episcopal Elections and the Apostolic See: The Case of Aquileia: 1251-1420', *Diritto e Potere Nella Storia Europea* (Florence, 1982): 163-94.
Sinclair, William, *Memorials of St Paul's Cathedral* (London, 1913).
Smith, Damian, *Innocent III and the Crown of Aragon* (Aldershot, 2004).
Smith, Reginald, 'The Place of Gundulf in the Anglo-Norman Church', *English Historical Review* 231 (1943): 257-72.
Smith, Waldo, *Episcopal Appointments and Patronage in the Reign of Edward II: A Study in the Relations of Church and State* (Chicago, 1938).
Southern, Richard, *Robert Grosseteste: The Growth of an English Mind in Medieval Europe* (Oxford, 1992).
Southern, Richard, *Saint Anselm: A Portrait in a Landscape* (Cambridge, 1990).
Southern, Richard, *Scholastic Humanism and the Unification of Europe: The Heroic Age* (Oxford, 2001).
Southern, Richard, *Western Society and the Church in the Middle Ages* (London, 1970).
Spencer, Andrew, 'Royal Patronage and the Earls in the Reign of Edward I', *Historical Research* 93 (2008): 20-46.
Stacey, Robert, *Politics, Policy and Finance under Henry III, 1216-1245* (Oxford, 1987).
Strayer, Joseph, *The Reign of Philip the Fair* (Princeton, 1980).
Stringer, Keith 'The Emergence of a Nation State, 1100-1300' in Jenny Wormald (ed.), *Scotland: A History* (Oxford, 2005), pp. 38-76.
Stringer, Keith, *The Reformed Church in Medieval Galloway and Cumbria: Contrasts, Connections and Continuities* (Whithorn, 2003).
Strocchia, Sharon, 'When the Bishop Married the Abbess: Masculinity and Power in Florentine Episcopal Entry Rites, 1300-1600', *Gender and History* 19 (2007): 346-68.
Stubbs, William, *The Constitutional History of England: In its Origin and Development*, 3 vols (Oxford, 1891-98).
Stubbs, William, *Registrum Sacrum Anglicanum* (2nd edn, Oxford, 1897).

Summerson, Henry, 'Fearing God, Honouring the King: The Episcopate of Robert de Chaury, Bishop of Carlisle, 1258-78' in Michael Prestwich, Robert Britnell and Robin Frame (eds), *Thirteenth Century England X* (Woodbridge, 2005), pp. 147-54.

Swanson, Robert, *Church and Society in Late Medieval England* (Oxford, 1989).

Swanson, Robert, 'Mendicant Bishops in the British Isles in the Thirteenth and Early Fourteenth Centuries' in *Dal Pulpito alla Cattedra: i Vescovi degli Ordini Mendicanti nel '200 e nel Primo '300* (Spoleto, 2000), pp. 306-47.

Sweet, Alfred, 'The Control of English Episcopal Elections in the Thirteenth Century', *Catholic Historical Review* 12 (1927): 573-82.

Tabbagh, Vincent and Bony, Pierre (eds), *Fasti Ecclesiae Gallicanae*, vol. 2: *Diocèse de Rouen* (Turnhout, 1998).

Taylor, Maria, 'The Election of Innocent III' in Diana Wood (ed.), *The Church and Sovereignty, c.590-1918* (Oxford, 1991), pp. 97-112.

Thomas, Sarah, 'The Diocese of Sodor between Nidaross and Avignon-Rome, 1266-1472', *Northern Studies* 41 (2009/10): 22-40.

Thomas, Sarah, 'Rival Bishops, Rival Cathedrals: The Election of Cormac, Archdeacon of Sodor, as Bishop in 1331', *Innes Review* 60 (2009): 145-63.

Turner, Ralph, 'Richard Lionheart and English Episcopal Elections', *Albion* 29 (1997): 1-13.

Twyman, Susan, 'Papal *Adventus* at Rome in the Twelfth Century', *Historical Research* 69 (1996): 233-53.

Tyler, Jeffery, *Lord of the Sacred City: The 'Episcopus Exclusus' in Late Medieval and Early Modern Germany* (Leiden, 1999).

Ullmann, Walter, 'The Disputed Election of Hugh Balsham, Bishop of Ely', *Cambridge Historical Journal* 9 (1949): 259-68.

Vale, Malcolm, *The Princely Court: Medieval Courts and Culture in North-West Europe* (Oxford, 2001).

Vaughan, Richard, 'The Chronicle of John of Wallingford', *English Historical Review* 73 (1958): 66-77.

Vaughan, Richard, *Matthew Paris* (Cambridge, 1958).Vilar, Herminia, 'Canons and Cities: Cathedral Chapters and their Social Composition in Medieval Portugal', *e-journal of Portuguese History* 5 (2007): 1-19.

Vincent, Nicholas 'The Election of Pandulph Verracclo as Bishop of Norwich (1215)', *Historical Research* 68 (1995): 143-63.

Vincent, Nicholas, 'Jocelin of Wells: The Making of a Bishop in the Reign of King John' in Robert Dunning (ed.), *Jocelin of Wells: Bishop, Builder, Courtier* (Woodbridge, 2010), pp. 9-33.

Vincent, Nicholas, 'Master Alexander of Stainsby, Bishop of Coventry and Lichfield, 1224–1238', *Journal of Ecclesiastical History* 46 (1995): 615-40.

Vincent, Nicholas, 'New Light on Master Alexander of Swerford (d.1246): The Career and Connections of an Oxfordshire Civil Servant', *Oxoniensia*, 61 (1996): 297-309.

Vincent, Nicholas, *Peter des Roches: An Alien in English Politics, 1205-1238* (Cambridge, 1996).

Vincent, Nicholas, 'The Politics of Church and State as Reflected in the Winchester Pipe Rolls, 1208-80' in Richard Britnell (ed.), *The Winchester Pipe Rolls and Medieval English Society* (Woodbridge, 2002), pp. 157-81.

Vincent, Nicholas, 'Stephen Langton, Archbishop of Canterbury' in Louis-Jacques Bataillon, Nicole Bériou, Gilbert Dahan and Riccardo Quinto (eds), Étienne Langton: Prédicateur, Bibliste, Théologien (Turnhout, 2010), pp. 51-123.

Vincent, Nicholas, 'The Thirteenth Century' in Peter Meadows (ed.), *Ely: Bishops and Diocese, 1109-2009* (Woodbridge, 2010), pp. 26-69.

Viollet, Paul, 'Guillaume de Mandagout, Canoniste' in *Histoire Littéraire de la France*, 43 vols (n.p., 1733-), xxxiv, pp. 1-61.

Waley, Daniel, *The Papal State in the Thirteenth Century* (London, 1961).

Warren, Wilfred L., *King John* (2nd edn, London, 1978).

Watt, John, *The Church in Medieval Ireland* (Dublin, 1972).

Watt, John, *The Church and the Two Nations in Medieval Ireland* (Cambridge, 1970).

Watt, John, *The Theory of Papal Monarchy in the Thirteenth Century* (New York, 1965).

Watt, D. E. R. and Shead, N. F. (eds), *The Heads of Religious Houses in Scotland from Twelfth to Sixteenth Centuries* (Edinburgh, 2001).

Watt, Donald and Murray, Athol (eds), *Fasti Ecclesiae Scoticanae Medii Aevi Ad Annum 1638* (rev. edn, Edinburgh, 2003).

Waugh, Scott, *England in the Reign of Edward III* (Cambridge, 1991).

Weiler, Anton, 'The Requirements of the Pastor Bonus in the Late Middle Ages', *Dutch Review of Church History* 83 (2003): 57-83.

Weiler, Bjorn, 'Symbolism and Politics in the Reign of Henry III' in Michael Prestwich, Richard Britnell and Robin Frame (eds), *Thirteenth Century England IX* (Woodbridge, 2003), pp. 15-41.

Williams, Glanmor, *The Welsh Church: From Conquest to Reformation* (rev. edn, Cardiff, 1976).

Wilks, Michael, *The Problem of Sovereignty in the Later Middle Ages* (Cambridge, 1963).

Wilshire, Leland, *Boniface of Savoy, Carthusian and Archbishop of Canterbury, 1207–1270*, Analecta Cartusiana, 31 (Salzburg, 1977).

Wood, Diana, *Clement VI: The Pontificate and Ideas of an Avignon Pope* (Cambridge, 1989).

Wood, Susan, *English Monasteries and their Patrons in the Thirteenth Century* (Oxford, 1955).
Worby, Samantha, 'The Influence of the Learned Laws on Common Law Kinship: An Introduction' in Helle Vogt and Mia Münster-Swendsen (eds), *Law and Learning in the Middle Ages: Proceedings of the Second Carlsberg Academy Conference on Medieval Legal History 2005* (Copenhagen, 2006), pp. 207-22.
Wormald, Jenny (ed.), *Scotland: A History* (Oxford, 2005).
Wright, John, *The Church and the English Crown, 1305-1334* (Toronto, 1980).
Yates, Nigel, 'Bishop Peter de Aquablanca (1240-1269): A Reconsideration', *Journal of Ecclesiastical History* 22 (1971): 303-17.
Young, Charles, *The Making of the Neville Family in England, 1166-1400* (Woodbridge, 1996).
Yunck, John, *The Lineage of Lady Meed: The Development of Medieval Venality Satire* (Notre Dame, 1963).
Zacour, Norman, 'The Cardinals' View of the Papacy, 1150-1300' in Christopher Ryan (ed.), *The Religious Roles of the Papacy: Ideals and Realities, 1150-1300* (Toronto, 1989), pp. 413-58.
Zutshi, Patrick, 'Proctors acting for English Petitioners in the Chancery of the Avignon Popes (1305-1378)', *Journal of Ecclesiastical History* 35 (1984): 15-29.

Unpublished Theses, etc.

Creamer, Joseph, 'In the Footsteps of Becket: Episcopal Sanctity in England, 1170-1270' (University of Washington, PhD thesis, 2011).
Evers, William, 'Disputes about Episcopal Elections in the Reign of Henry III, with Special Reference to some Unpublished Durham Documents' (University of Oxford, B.Litt. thesis, 1934).
Huscroft, Richard, 'The Career of Robert Burnell, Bishop of Bath and Wells and Chancellor of Edward I' (University of London, PhD thesis, 2001).
Lala, Etleva, 'Regnum Albaniae, the Papal Curia and the Western Visions of a Borderline Nobility' (Central European University at Budapest, DPhil thesis, 2008).
Marritt, Stephen, 'The Bishops of King Stephen's Reign' (University of Glasgow, PhD thesis, 2002).
Norton, Margaret, 'The Bishops of the Archdiocese of York, c.1200-c.1250' (Trinity College Dublin, PhD thesis, 2004).
Pico, Fernando, 'The Bishops of France in the Reign of Louis IX (1226-1270)' (Johns Hopkins University, PhD thesis, 1970).

Scotney, Phyllis, 'An Examination of the Theory and Practice of Appointments to Bishoprics during the Reigns of Henry III and Edward I … and of their Historical Significance' (University of London, MA thesis, 1925).
Williams, Daniel, 'Aspects of the Career of Archbishop Boniface of Savoy, 1241-70' (University of Wales, PhD thesis, 1970).

Online Resources

Henry III Fine Rolls Project: www.frh3.org.uk
Oxford Dictionary of National Biography: www.oxforddnb.com
The Paradox of Medieval Scotland: www.poms.ac.uk

Index

Bishops, Archbishops and other clerical persons are referenced both under their names and place of incumbency.

References to 'King' are to the King of England, unless otherwise indicated.

All references are to England, unless otherwise indicated.